SPIRITUAL LEADERS

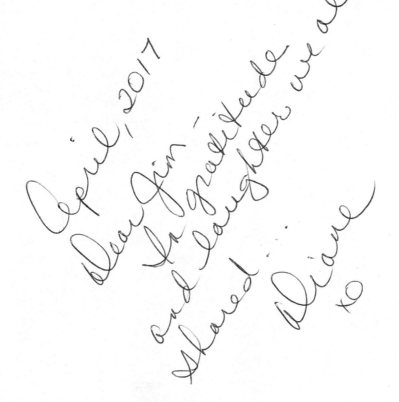

April, 2017
Dear Jim-
In gratitude
and laughter we all
shared...
Diane
xo

SPIRITUAL LEADERS

Visionary Insight Press
913 Beal Parkway NW Suite A #117
Fort Walton Beach, FL 32547

Visionary Insight Press, the Visionary Insight Press logo and its individual parts are trademarks of Visionary Insight Press.

Compiled by: Katina F Gillespie

Back cover photo credits: Duygu Ozen of Moments Photography Studio; Jase White; Kim Coffman; Charles Ferrell; Contempo Studio; Dan Skaramuca; Jeanette Dreyer; Stephanie Michelle Photography; Karen Shell; Paula Love Moore Photography; The Photography Room; Holladay's Photo Emporium; Roxyanne Young; Lorianne Giles; Richard Pickford; Hot Diggity Creatives; Michelle Smith; Kimberly Denham; Jennifer Armand; Lindsay Reiling; Heidi Phillips; Jill Ockhardt Blaufuss; Patrick Jones Studios; Sydney. Photographer Chris Walsh; Susan Chantal Photography; Russell Clarke; DoubleTake Visuals LLC; Geeta Studios; Aditi Mysore; Patricia Holdsworth Photography; Ashley Stivers Photography.

Table of Contents

❧ An Opening

Not all tunnels end in light. Set aside the searching for, and begin to create as well as generate with what is in every moment. To create one must cast off the fixed expectations of what "should be," which blinds us to seeing the possibilities that exist in the present and pregnant darkness. Choose the darkness. This is not acceptance, yet it is the end of resistance and simply learning to be with what is and being open to what exits therein. No more life as a waiting room. Pick up your life's pen, create and BE in the opening.

Charles Ferrell

HALINA KUROWSKA

HALINA KUROWSKA is an inspirational author, spiritual counsellor, licensed Heal Your Life® teacher and Life Coach.

Upon meeting her, many people remark on Halina's calm and peaceful demeanor, as well as her gentle approach to life and to others. Her serenity comes from having spent many years on the path of spiritual development, which led her to a total transformation and transcendence of her life.

A graduate of the University of Toronto, Halina holds an Honours Bachelor of Arts degree in Philosophy. During her years of study, she took courses in Buddhism and meditation, putting her on the path to discovering how the practice of meditation can change a person's life.

Impressed by the beauty, depth and practical application of Buddhist's teachings, Halina further pursued the practice. Now she is a long-time practitioner of meditation and has spent the last seven years attending retreats where she takes vows of silence for many days at a time. To date, Halina has spent close to 100 days in silent meditation.

Having experienced the enormous benefits of meditation first-hand, Halina has made it her life's work to help others to also realize the profound value of adding meditation to their daily lives.

She is the founder of *Living with AWE: Awareness, Wisdom, Empowerment,* where she lovingly empowers others in their transformation.

Halina teaches meditation classes and has created an online course on Mindfulness Meditation. This course offers a practical and theoretical foundation that prepares students to facilitate their own meditation classes. Students who complete this unique course will receive a Certified Practitioner Diploma.

To learn more about Halina, please visit:
www.livingwithawe.com
www.facebook.com/livingwithawe
www.visionaryinstitutecertifications.com

❧ Into the Woods

Reflections on Meditation

The day is just waking up with the first gentle rays of sun and I've already completed two hours of morning meditation and had breakfast. The morning is still somewhat cold and damp, and the path is covered with a fresh dusting of snow. It is very early spring in Canada after all.

At dawn, just a few minutes after seven o'clock, into the woods I go.

As I walk deeper into the forest, it becomes denser and darker. I stray slightly from the path as I approach the ravine to see the creek down below … that's where the animals are the easiest to spot. Beaver is gathering wood for his feat of engineering; a new dam is being build and the little creek is already wider than it was last year when I was here.

On the trail, I see the footprints of coyote on the pristine white snow, he was here just a moment ago, walking the same path. I look down towards the creek and I see him heading into his den. The night is over, time for the creatures of the dark to rest.

On my path, I meet another soul puttering around the forest and then another. I begin to realize that in a way, we are all in the forest — the forest of our own mind. Signing up for this meditation retreat is very much like entering the woods, not knowing what to expect, and being ready and willing to encounter whatever will present itself. And, very much like the forest, our mind is a peculiar place, quite often an unknown and uncharted territory.

We came here to this sacred place to have a deep look at our minds and to get to know it well … or at least better. To have a glimpse into the dense, at times dark, recesses of our minds.

Meditation is like walking in the woods of our own psyche, where we get in touch with our own thoughts and feelings: with our fears, our 'boogey-man', our perceived inadequacies, and our deeply rooted negativity. We meditate, observing all this without judgement, thus eventually freeing ourselves from the burdens we carry. At least that's the goal.

We go deep into the dark, scary, and not always pretty or pleasant places, and we are encouraged to face all this and just look and observe without judgement, without aversion, with compassion for ourselves and our own nature.

We are asked to look at our lives without aversion towards the unwanted things that did happen, and the wanted things that did not happen. We are asked to accept it all exactly as it is, to look at our lives with equanimity, and to treat ourselves and other beings with compassion.

However, this journey towards achieving a calm, equanimous, and compassion-filled mind takes us on a long, winding path infused with perils.

The meditation I practice is called Vipassana, which is the foundation of mindfulness meditation. Its first stage is Anapana; it is about observing one's breath: 'pure breath,' 'bare breath,' 'nothing but breath.' First the observation is about the deeper breaths and then, as one's mind gets more and more quiet and is able to discern the subtle breath, one is advised to observe the subtlest breath for prolonged period of time.

Although this might not be clear at the beginning, there is a purpose and a goal to observing our breath. Through this process, we achieve what's called the purification of our mind. Being aware, alert, attentive, and vigilant about observing our respiration, we achieve an alert and attentive mind. A sharp mind is able to focus on breathing which will eventually lead to awakening and transcendence.

If you are thinking, "oh, big deal, it is just observing the breath," I suggest you try it for a continuous period of time and you might find out how difficult this simple activity really is.

The first obstacle in this exercise is…can you guess?…my own mind. The moment I settle down on my meditation cushion, the mind starts working—and not in any coherent, sensible way. The thoughts that pop up are the strangest thoughts one can have. And they are jumpy! I look at them puzzled…where is the sense? Why this thought now? What does it even mean? No wonder Buddha called our untrained mind, the monkey mind, jumping from one branch to another. No offence to monkeys, they might be jumping with a purpose, but my mind does not.

I'm told to observe all this with compassion, and gently, lovingly direct my attention to my breath. Observe the breath.

And when I do that, I notice some awesome things I was not aware about that pertain to my breath, even though I've been breathing for over fifty years. Like, for example, there is a special spot where the air touches the nostrils when entering it; 'the touch of the breath'. It is quite an amazing feeling to discover this about yourself. But one has to get very quiet and very attentive to notice that.

That's why on this meditation course we observe what's called Noble Silence for ten days. This might seem excessive to some, yet there is a deep wisdom in it. When we get silent like that, for the first two or three days we still carry within us the conversations of the world we just left behind, but by the third day, they start fading away and silence embraces us all more and more.

As my mind gets more and more quiet, the noise and chatter of the world outside depart, the space opens up for beautiful lights dancing in my mind's eye.

Going deeper and deeper into my own being, with relaxed body, and calm and quiet mind, I reach what Buddha describes as the bangha state, the state of total dissolution. In this state the normal perception of the body as a solid matter is lost and there is no separation between my body and the outside world. I experience myself as a mass of tiny wavelets, bubbles—a mass of 'kalapas' as Buddha described the subatomic particles. Quantum physics describes the Universe as tiny vibrating strings of energy; Buddha came to the same conclusion 2600 years ago, stating that there is no solidity in this world, everything is waves and bubbles, arising and passing away with great rapidity. Everything is in a constant flux.

And now, on this meditation cushion, I'm experiencing this. I feel like I have melted, there is no boundary between my body and the world around me. If, for example, someone asked at that moment if my hands are touching, I would not know.

This very insight and awareness of no separation removes fear and expands LOVE. The consciousness expands as it's free from fear and free to love All.

Taking this experience with me into the world of everyday life allows me to have new understanding, love and compassion for all living beings. All is One. I Am One with everything.

So, we go to and through the woods, until the physical forest and the forest of our minds are bathed in the divine light. I stand in the forest elated by its beauty and I sit on the meditation cushion immersed in Oneness.

I lovingly dedicate this chapter to my beloved sons, Wit and Mateusz. I'm grateful for your love, kindness, support and for choosing to spend this lifetime with me. You are my greatest teachers of LOVE. Blessed be both of you.

I thank the Divine for holding my hand and guiding my steps on this wondrous journey of life. For leading me deeper and deeper through an awakening process, to knowing oneness and beyond.

A very special thank you to Izabela Jaroszynski, my lovely editor with impeccable editing skills, for fine-tuning my words.

A big thank you to Lisa Hardwick, an amazing publisher whose heartfelt inspiration and encouragement leads to fulfilment of my dreams.

Huge gratitude to Virginia and Bill Hamilton, founders of the Dhamma Torana — Ontario Vipassana Centre, where my path toward enlightenment began.

CAROLE CASSELL

CAROLE CASSELL is a licensed Heal Your Life® Coach, Workshop Leader, Law of Attraction Coach, Assertiveness Coach, author and speaker.

Carole spent many years questing to understand the deeper meaning in her life experiences. Along the way she acquired countless tools and techniques that allowed her to heal from her painful past, follow her dreams and design a life she loves.

Carole is passionate about sharing those tools of transformation to help others reconnect with their inner wisdom, find the gifts in their life experiences, heal from past wounds and design a life rich in love, happiness, inner peace, confidence and abundance.

Her greatest joy is spending time with her amazing sons, D.J. and Zach, and incredible husband, Roger. She also enjoys relaxing on the beach, hiking, traveling and spending time with her friends.

www.carolecassell.com

🌿 Weighted Down

"When are you due?" asked the smiling stranger standing behind me in the line at a public restroom. She glided her hand ever-so-gently over my extended tummy.

"I'm not sure," I replied, barely able to make eye contact. Luckily a stall became available and I didn't have to figure out what to say next. The previous occupant was narrowly out of the way before I dashed in, latched the lock, fell back against the cold metal door and wept.

You see, the thing is, I wasn't pregnant … I was overweight.

This event set in motion a battle with my weight that developed into a crippling experience that impacted my life for many years and in many ways.

I'd always been thin growing up. In fact, I'd been teased throughout school because of it. The other kids called me names like "Skinny Minnie," "Beanpole," and "String Bean." It never really bothered me. I was what I was and I was fine with that. Even after the birth of my two children, I quickly bounced back to my slender body. I ate what I wanted (within reason), exercised several times a week and that was pretty much the extent of my thoughts around weight. That is, until my early forties when I began taking steps towards my dream life.

When I met my husband, Roger, I was at my ideal weight. But during our first couple of years of dating, I gained 10 pounds. We joked it was my "happy weight" as my pre-Roger life was filled with stress, bouts of extreme depression and lots of anger. I'm not suggesting that upon marrying Roger those emotions vanished. Quite the opposite. They magnified.

However, there was something different about this relationship. I knew, deep down inside, this man showed up in my life to challenge all that I believed, to illuminate how I reacted to situations, and to support me in uncovering the true me — the "me" that lurked beneath the incredible pain and disappointment that had plagued me most of my life and was desperately longing to be free.

The same was true for him as well. We were the proverbial soulmates. Both incredibly supportive and encouraging of each other's growth. But even though we offered each other a safe place to heal, our journey of self-growth was not a smooth one. We endured a lot of pain and suffering in the name of growth. Everything we'd stuffed down and ignored over the years, floated to the surface for healing. And every bit of pain, insecurity and fear rose up and manifested in unexpected ways.

My deepest pain could be traced back to being told repeatedly by my father that I was a "worthless piece of shit" — despite successes I'd achieved in life that proved otherwise. And although I healed this deep-seated belief in the areas of relationships and my general health, as I began to step into the truth of who I was and serve others from my Higher Self, those old insecurities found a new way to stop me from shining. Crafty, little devils.

And what does this have to do with my weight?

Everything.

The Bully

Years ago, I received a call from the Divine to leave my corporate job as a controller and enter the world of the healing arts. I followed my calling to open a massage and bodywork practice and became successful very quickly. To compliment my business, I studied to be a life coach. I wanted to help people make peace with their pasts so they could be free to create a life they loved—just like I was doing. But it was also during this journey that I began to gain weight. Lots and lots of weight.

As I trained for the various licenses and certifications to assist clients in areas such as assertiveness, stress management, Law of Attraction and Louise Hay's *Heal Your Life*, more of my own "stuff" came up for healing. I'd work on one thing, and then another would surface. I'd heal that, and then another would come up.

Being an overachiever by nature, I welcomed the awareness and opportunities for growth. I enjoyed the challenge of learning something new and then figuring out how to apply it to become an even better version of myself. And over the last seven years I healed childhood abuse, the pain and guilt from multiple failed marriages and family drama among other issues. If it came up, I healed it and moved on. My life was finally becoming the life I'd envisioned.

Except for one little thing... well... maybe not so little.

With each step I took to becoming more in alignment with my true essence, the bigger my goals and dreams became. The bigger my goals and dreams became, the bigger my dress size became. And as my weight climbed, I reacted the way I'd been taught to react.

I dieted.

I tried everything, but my weight wouldn't budge. And when dieting failed, I consulted my doctor. I knew there had to be something amiss in my body. He agreed; knowing weight had never been an issue for me before. But he couldn't find anything wrong and said I needed to face the fact that I came from a family with weight issues and should make peace with it.

He asked me a question, however, that stuck with me all these years later. He asked if I'd rather be fat and happy, or go back to the way my life once was, but be thin. Without hesitation I said I'd rather be fat and happy. Yet I wondered: *Why couldn't I be happy AND thin?*

My doctor suggested I watch what I eat, exercise regularly and see what happens. So I hired a nutritionist and a personal trainer and worked diligently. I ate exactly what they told me to eat, exercised precisely for how long and how often my trainer prescribed, and I lost nothing.

Nada. Zip. Zilch. My weight remained unchanged.

After a few months, I felt defeated. I called it quits and decided to make friends with my weight. After all, my husband still looked at me like I was the most beautiful woman in the world (thank you, Honey). And my family and friends didn't care how much I weighed. So for the next couple of years, I did my best to accept that I was simply a bigger woman. And that's when things got worse. I became my own personal bully. Each time I saw myself in a full-length mirror, I'd say the most horrific things to myself like:

Disgusting!
Look at you, you're no good for anything.
You're a fat pig.
You're an embarrassment.
You're a worthless piece of shit!

Yep, you read that last one right. I used the exact line on myself that my Dad used to say to me. I picked up right where he left off. Every time I saw my reflection, I'd stop and verbally abuse myself, taking care to point out all of the things that were *wrong* with me. I'd call myself names, names that I'd never dream of calling anyone else who looked like me:

Fatty.
Loser.
Heifer.
Ugly.
Worthless.

I made fun of myself on a regular basis, joking about my size when I was around other people. No one else said a word to me about my weight. I was doing all of this to myself. I bullied myself into tears day after day. I became a skilled tormenter, inflicting verbal beatings, slowly ripping away at my soul and dimming my own light.

By the time my "making friends with my body" experiment came to a close, I'd been so ruthless that I once again felt the worthlessness I'd felt most of my early life. Although I didn't realize it at the time, I'd found another way to feel "less than" and to keep myself down. All of the lovely healing I'd done felt like it was for naught. I'd lost my shine and let my weight define me. I became a hermit. I declined social invitations and stopped going to things like festivals, concerts, or the beach—all things I loved. I quit everything that once brought me joy because I was so uncomfortable in my own skin. It was a living hell—but a hell of my own design.

The Gift

I begged the Universe to help me figure out the root cause of my experience. I cried, begged, and then cried some more. I couldn't figure out what I was doing wrong. I'd done everything society tells you to do to lose weight—but ended up heavier than ever. Then, during my meditations, I began receiving messages that my weight was a gift from my body.

A gift? Are you kidding me? Seriously?

Although my mind rejected this theory, my Spirit recognized the truth. And after months of meditation, more messages from Spirit and many conversations with people I loved and trusted, I began to see the truth too, and applied the healing modalities I'd been trained in, upon my own body. I changed my mindset, repaired my abusive relationship with myself and practiced self-acceptance and unconditional love for my body.

And what I came to realize was that because I still had an underlying belief (albeit deeply buried), that I was worthless; each time I stepped into my power, my body added a layer of fat —that is, protection—to keep me safe. Protection against the pain and disappointment I was certain would follow any good I allowed into my life.

Diet and exercise alone was like rolling a boulder uphill. Until I healed the deeper issue and changed the focus of my thoughts, I would continue to "fight" the battle of the bulge. But once I accepted my body, showed it appreciation and changed my focus to what I wanted to create (instead of what I didn't), everything began to change.

This was the missing piece to my painful puzzle. *This* was the key to ending my pain and suffering. And *this* would help me heal the damage I caused my Soul.

Once I truly accepted my body's gift of excess weight, I could get on with the business of healing. Once I truly realized that the transformation needed to come from the inside out, not the outside in, I could use the beautiful tools I'd been trained in to change my reality and create the body I wanted. And once I truly released what society told me about weight loss, and began to listen to the wisdom from within, I became empowered.

And that's when my body began to lovingly release the excess weight.

Unconditional Love

Sometimes we're too close to a problem to really see what's going on. Sometimes we're so used to reacting in the way we've been conditioned, that we ignore our inner guidance that's screaming there must be another way, a better way.

Because I was so focused on changing my outer world—spending my time and energy dieting, exercising or beating myself up—I wasn't in the space to hear what my soul actually needed—kindness, acceptance and unconditional love.

I have since apologized to myself—body, mind and Spirit.

I now accept myself just as I am and that acceptance has created an environment for my body to return to its natural state of wellbeing.

And *now* when I pass a mirror, I stop and tell myself things like:

I love you!
You're so beautiful!
You're an amazing woman!
You deserve to have it all!
You are worthy!

I spend time each day in gratitude for my body and the way it was trying to protect me. I thank it for showing up for me 100 percent while it carried around 80 extra pounds and suffered the negative effects of yo-yo dieting, punishing workouts and verbal abuse.

I spend time each day feeding my Spirit with positive self-talk—loving words that honor me and highlight my worth.

And I spend time each day meditating and visualizing my future self, deeply connecting with the feeling of once again having my ideal body and the freedom of no longer feeling weighted down.

I'm both happy and excited that my body is releasing its excess weight naturally. No more diets, no more brutal workouts, just simple, healthy eating and exercise I enjoy.

And of course … the power of the mind.

Dedicated to those of you for whom the battle of the bulge has taken its toll on your soul—may my story empower you to practice unconditional self-love and to remind you that you are beautiful, amazing and worthy—just the way you are!

A huge, heartfelt thanks to my family and friends for your unwavering support and unconditional love. And to my husband Roger—thank you for always looking at me the way you did on our wedding day.

Special thanks to Debby, Dawn and Christine—the greatest friends in the world. Thank you for picking me up when I was down, reminding me of my gifts and for letting me see myself through your eyes. My love for you is beyond measure.

TONIA BROWNE

TONIA BROWNE is a bestselling author, teacher and coach. She is a strong advocate of inviting fun into our lives and encouraging people to experience their world from a new perspective.

As a teacher, Tonia has worked in the United Kingdom and internationally for over 20 years and was an Assistant Head for seven. In addition to her mainstream training as a teacher, Tonia is a Heal Your Life® Workshop Leader, Coach and Business Trainer. She also has a Diploma in Life Coaching and Neuro-Linguistic Programming, along with a Certification in Counselling Skills and Spiritual Coaching.

Tonia's writing includes coaching strategies interspersed with spiritual insights, often sharing personal anecdotes. She takes a holistic approach to change and believes in liberating the inner child within us all.

Tonia has received support from amazing people during her life and enjoys returning the favour by assisting others in their development.

Her book *Spiritual Seas: Diving into Life* includes 12 strategies to help you ride the waves of life.

Connect with Tonia @ toniabrowne.com

✿ Planes and Trains

I am constantly amazed by the stories people share about the highs and lows of life. Each story is unique, often heart breaking, but also captivating and inspiring. Many stories involve chance encounters and synchronistic events. These stories indicate to me that we are all spiritual leaders. We either push each other's buttons or we share important insights. Both provide opportunities for reflection, action and healing. Both can result in significant change that brings lives back on track and lifts spirits to a better emotional plane.

Train of Thought

Sometimes our journey through life takes place in a first-class carriage. We know where we are going, it's exciting and we feel in control. We have plans and goals. We have friends and family. We are happy. We take action and we see results. Life feels good.

Then there are the times when every train seems to go by without us. If we do manage to jump on we sense we are being taken along the wrong track. These are the times when it feels as if life is passing us by and that we are merely looking out of the window as a passive observer. We look at our life and ask, 'Is this it?'

There are also times in our linear world when our journey along the tracks of life suddenly and unexpectedly changes. Our train gets derailed or uncoupled and we are brought to an abrupt standstill. Events such as death, divorce or betrayal, unemployment, financial or family concerns can leave us emotionally ransacked. At such times, we feel lost, vulnerable and confused, let down and alone or angry and afraid. We feel powerless and can remain stuck and indecisive, needing inspiration to know which train to travel on next in order to arrive at a better emotional plane.

Emotional Planes

Ups and downs are part of life. How resilient we are and how quickly we bounce back from a down and how long we remain on a high is influenced by our inner programme and our sense of self.

Emotions are our compass. If used well they help us make decisions that result in us feeling a little better. Our emotions can guide us up the vibrational ladder. If we are in tune with our emotions, they indicate when life is not in alignment with what we want. They therefore provide us with the opportunity to take action to ensure that we correct this before a drama results.

However, some people have consciously or unconsciously blocked this intuitive guidance system, often due to a series of life events. Instead of feeling empowered and alive they feel powerless and at the mercy of random events. This general malaise can lead to depression, a loss of direction, a lack of energy, fractious relationships and ill health. This means there is little appetite to take action when the train becomes derailed or uncoupled. Instead, at these times we can nose dive further into a challenging place.

The Journey

The good news is our emotional plane isn't permanent. It can change. We can change it by one thought, one decision and one action after another. Life changes, so does our energy and so does our perspective on life. We might need a nudge, a helping hand or some advice, but when we are ready to receive, that ticket to our next destination seems to arrive.

It wasn't until much later in my life that I became aware of the idea of an inner child and also the concept of choice. I had not appreciated that we had a choice about how we think and how we perceive ourselves. Change wasn't instant. It took information and time. It was like a muscle that needed practice in order to strengthen. But it was worth flexing. The result was an increase in self-esteem and an inner programme that was in alignment with who I really was, not who I thought I should be. When the inner world shifts, the outer changes are significant.

What I discovered during my exploration was that I was not in control of my inner programme. I had a very stubborn inner child who was putting the brakes on my life. I was not alone. We often find, if we do not acknowledge and take ownership of our inner programme, that we end up with the belief systems of others, as well as redundant aspects from our past influencing our present. This is often under the control of our inner child and why we can easily find ourselves stuck in life. We feel inertia. If we do manage to instigate change, we can find it doesn't lead us to the place that we thought it would. This is because we have opposing belief systems within us and why the manifestation process can get frustrating.

Sometimes, in our fast-moving society, the importance of our emotional plane is overlooked, with people focusing on external manifestations of success: what we do, what we have, what we look like and what we have achieved rather than how we feel. Shining the light into the darkness and becoming aware of our inner programme can shift our lives.

When we meet, acknowledge and form a new relationship with our inner child and the unconscious programme that influences our lives, we better understand our choices and their consequences. We are then more able to consciously change our usual responses until, slowly but surely, we reprogramme our subconscious so we can start living the life we want rather than the life we feel we should be living.

Dreams and a Better Feeling

We are all children of the universe with dreams that we came into this world to realise. For some, the dreams seem impossible to achieve and the beauty of life is lost for a while. When we understand our inner programme we can start to reclaim our power over it. We can quieten the inner voice that tells us we can't do things. We can replace such negative sentiments with more empowering ones such as 'We can try again!' There are tools and strategies that can help us shake off the cloak of negativity and choose another way. There is a path that we can travel where the gentle souls and dreamers come together to share their vision for a better world.

I have enjoyed learning about strategies and techniques I had previously never heard about. My perception of how I viewed my world was challenged as I acknowledged my part in how I saw it. The idea that we have something to learn in life and that this is usually the same thing we give to others is, in my experience, true. After more than a decade of learning and gaining certification in areas such as Heal Your Life Achieve Your Dreams, Spiritual Coaching and Counselling Skills and over two decades teaching children within the mainstream educational system I decided to merge the two. Many people, whether consciously or unconsciously, are striving to feel better about their lives and there are concepts, strategies and tools to help them do so. Paradigms are shifting. Many more people are aware of these ideas. However, there are still people who feel derailed and who are searching for help and direction. As a consequence I started writing in order to share my learning and experience. My aim is to support others in gaining ownership of their inner programme so they can feel a better external experience and a sense of peace.

Fast Tracking

Many of us are looking for quick ways to make shifts in our lives. We seem to be living in a world which hurtles along faster than ever. I enjoy sharing the idea of our inner programme with others as this had such a profound impact on my life, in the hope that it may help fast track your journey if desired.

I have contributed to a number of multi-author books sharing my journey and the strategies I have used to shift my life, and have recently written my own book. This book, Spiritual Seas: Diving into Life, was written in order to share my reflections whilst diving in turquoise seas and to offer strategies to support the personal development of the reader at a deeper level. It was written to encourage you to reflect on your internal world so that you can impact your external experience.

Dedicated to the inner child in all of us.

Thank you to my mum, dad and my sister for always being there, and to my friends and extended family for their loving hearts. A huge thank you to Lisa and her Visionary Insight Press team who have been a pleasure to work with, and to my fantastic husband, who gave me confidence and space to write. Special gratitude to Louise Hay and her Hay House Community for their enthusiastic endeavour to help hearts, souls and minds find love through their inspirational stories and practical advice. You have been my lighthouse.

MICKEY MACKABEN

Throughout her life, MICKEY MACKABEN has fulfilled many roles; professional hair stylist, mother, healer, teacher, student, mentor, business owner, but most recently "acrylic artist" and author. Her love of bright bold color, beautiful textures, and intricate details is prevalent in each of her paintings and a direct reflection of the woman herself.

Mickey has always felt this desire to express herself creatively, and has done so for the majority of her life as a professional hair dresser. She has always been known for her phenomenal color work and flawless haircuts. Her ability to transform a person's life through her work even earned her the nickname "the hair whisperer" amongst her clients.

In the winter of 2014, Mickey had a revelation, she wanted to paint, like REALLY paint. And so she did. It started with the pestering of her kids trying to plan her upcoming 50th birthday, which was 7/11/15. It was decided that she would create 11 paintings to show and reveal them in celebration of her 50th year. And so began the journey of an artist.

Find her on Facebook @mmmstudiosinc and follow her on Instagram @mmmstudios
www.visionaryinstitutecertifications.com
The Certified Visionary Therapeutic Painting Practitioner Course

Express Yourself, My Artistic Journey

> Painting: the practice of applying paint, pigment, color or other medium to a solid surface. Painting is a mode of expression.

I've tried to remember when the artist in me first emerged. I believe it was when I received a pair of white GoGo boots. I was around 4 or 5 at the time, and I vividly remember my bedroom. This room was small. As soon as you walked in the door, you walked into my twin-size bed with a brand new pink bedspread on it. So, I'm in my room where I was supposed to be taking a nap... still wearing my white GoGo boots, because I loved them, as I did all shoes. As I'm lying on my bed "taking a nap" I see this pretty box with pictures on it and I get curious. I get up, bring the box to bed with me and start opening it to see what's inside. There's paint, all this paint in these little tubs hooked together with numbers on the top, and these lids that you had to pop open, there were even paint brushes. Yep! I used the "Paint by Number" paint on my GoGo boots... and my new pink bedspread. It was so exciting! I just remember thinking, *"I'm gonna make these pretty!"* Suddenly my bedroom door opened and all hell broke loose. I was discovered! My mom was sooooo mad. I remember her grabbing me and tossing me into the hot bath, the whole time telling me I ruined the boots, I ruined the bed spread, I ruined the paint... and that was the moment I became an emerging artist.

As I opened this door to my memories, I began to have a revelation. I know as children we tend to make up stories in our mind, our take on what we thought happened or how the story went. We tend to exaggerate or piece memories together to make one memory, the story that fits, the one we want to tell. As I was dictating this story, because I suck at typing, I found myself conflicted about if the boots were GoGo boots or cowboy boots, so I decided to call my mom. First, they were definitely GoGo boots, thank goodness... way cooler than cowboy boots. Second, this turned into a very healing conversation and I soon realized the universe had intervened and I really just needed to talk to my mom. As we were sharing, I felt my heart open up to her. I've always had this block with my mom and felt that it was hard to love her with my whole heart, I always kind of held a piece back. I was stuck in my story and was holding onto a lot of anger about things that I wanted to happen in my childhood that I didn't think or feel had happened. As I was talking to her I could tell she enjoyed that memory and sharing that moment with me. We were able to connect. She proceeded to tell me that I ruined her paints and the new bedspread, and she made sure I knew the bedspread was pink. The paint that I thought was my sister's actually belonged to my mom (interesting). I had always felt invisible. I felt that my brother and sister always got to do things that I wanted and never got to do, this was the story I was always telling myself.

While I had her on the phone, I asked her about a dance experience I also had in my memory. My mom told me a lady by the name of June Riggs had started dance classes in our basement. All three of us kids took the class. Eventually June started a studio and my brother and I continued to take classes with her because we had liked it so much. While taking classes, I remember a guest teacher named Miss Toe, yeah, her name was Toe and she was dance teacher. Miss Toe was my favorite. She seemed so cool to me. She was shorter (like me) and her hair was light brown with a pixie cut. Her tights were pulled up to her mid-calf and she always had bare feet, she reminded me of a Modern dance teacher. I just remember feeling good around her. I think I secretly wanted to be like her … and I think I secretly wanted to be like my mom. I specifically remember us dancing around the room, following each other like a train and her pulling, no swinging me through her legs. Whooo! It was so fun! I share these memories, because I had this story in me that my creative spirit was not nurtured as a child, but it was. Could it be that I was looking for someone to blame for why I couldn't nurture the artist in myself as an adult? Maybe some of that story is true, but probably not as much as I think or choose to remember. I'm happy I was brave enough to ask, because I want to be fully engaged with love in my heart when it comes to my people and all people. I'm sure there are many clues and moments as to when the artist in me tried to emerge. Thanks mom! I definitely was an artist that day in my bed when I was "napping." Before I knew it, I was an adult, a mom, a wife, all these things … but not an artist. Or so I thought …

The Mothership

I always found it easier to gift my children and other peoples' children with artistic experiences. Every year at Christmas time, Santa would make sure to fill the stockings with art supplies. The visual and performing arts were something I felt important to foster in my children. All three of my children played an instrument. They all had an opportunity to act, sing, dance, and/or write. I would take them to art classes, summer art camp, theater camp, dance camp, and more. I spent a lot of time, energy, and money to ensure my children had the opportunity to express themselves creatively. I was so passionate about the arts, I started an after-school art program that allowed any child to participate for free. It began with the Reflections Arts program. PTA Reflections is a nationally acclaimed student recognition program to encourage artistic creativity in the classroom and at home. During one of the first PTA meetings of the school year, this program was on the list of items needing someone to take charge of. I was unsure about doing it because I had never done anything like it before, but said I would do it if someone could help me. Many people helped to make it happen. We had initially started out with a really small budget, but it became so successful and so many students participated that we soon had to make a bigger budget for the program. We even had a gallery showing for all the participants and personally invited every family to come celebrate their child's entries. I had so much fun doing this and it helped to start build my confidence in the art world. However, I found I was still searching for a way to express myself personally as an artist, a way for me to be the artist. I still didn't know how to step into that and give myself time to create and foster my own creativity. I felt unqualified, untrained and unworthy. I couldn't see that I was already pulling from within. I was so focused on being the mom, the nurturer and taking care of my people that I couldn't create space for my inner artist.

Turning Point

I bought my first home during this time. I bought this house sight unseen and the first day I stepped in it was the day we moved in. When I was looking for homes online with my realtor, this house showed up in our search and I thought, "hmmm, I could work with this." I made an offer, but I really low-balled from the original price. It was an extremely old home, it was actually one of the first to be built on that side of town. In the pictures, I could see it was outdated, like seriously outdated with the old wallpaper and everything but I could see the potential. I already knew I would want to make it my own. I knew I was going to "make it so pretty!"

I started with the walls. There was this big wall covered in wallpaper, eww! After I ripped that nasty wallpaper down, I realized this wall was going to need more than just paint. I went and bought a gallon jug of texturing and some trowels, and so began my love affair with texture. I fell in love with that textured wall, it made the paint show beautifully. The colors I chose were so fun, nothing plain about them. I loved it! We lived in that house for nine years and during those years I did so many projects I should have had my own DIY television show.

What I'm learning is that creativity shows up in unexpected ways. Whether it be with my finances, what I cook for supper, how to get everyone where they needed to be when the kids were little, or repainting an old house; it's all part of a creative process.

Soon, it was time to downsize. My two oldest children were getting ready to move on in their adult lives. I needed things to be simpler and less to take care of so I knew I had to sell. During this process, my realtor informed me that I needed to paint my current home more neutral—boring! I complied then bought a new home. This home was smaller, more fitting for this next chapter of my life, but also boring. Something told me to wait, maybe I wouldn't live here very long, so don't create all these projects and things to do. Just be. That's what I had asked for. I gave myself a year.

Before I knew it the year was up and it was time to paint and gut the basement. The drop ceiling had to go, along with a partial wall and the nasty paneling. Before I tore the paneling off though, I wanted to paint a picture on it. Alicia Keys' "As I Am" album was my painting fuel. I'd be down in that basement with my music blaring, my beer in one hand, giant paint brush in the other just going to town on that wall, belting out "I! AM! SUPER WOMAN! YES, I AM!" I was feeling sexy and attractive again and less like "martyr mom." Pretty soon I had painted a huge face of a woman. It was me! I really began to feel like I was reemerging and coming back to myself. I was taking my power back and sustaining my own happiness.

You see, when you're raising your children, everything you do becomes about them. You kind of forget how to nurture yourself. When my two oldest moved out, I started to feel this void. I started to feel like, "Wow, well what now? How do I sustain that now?" It was just me and my youngest and we had to learn a whole new way of being. It was a big transition. Our family dynamic had changed so much and it was challenging. Beginning that painting was the beginning of a new me. Superwoman, yes, I am!

I decided to practice painting body parts on the other walls next. Something I had no clue how to do. Tempest, my youngest, was a little confused, she asked me why I was painting naked bodies. Although she was pretty neutral about it, she would still put pieces of paper over them. She even put one over a butt and it said "lift here." Funny kid! I went on to completely remodel this house, finishing the basement and tearing down those paneled walls. But I missed my paintings. I had begun to see how creating is therapy. Painting had become my therapy.

Still not having actual canvases, I decided I didn't much care for the white painted cinderblock garage. Sound familiar? White GoGo boots? I painted another woman's face on one of the walls. Another, had a mermaid, some eyes, a Polynesian woman. I painted pretty things, but I also started to paint "ugly" things. I'm sure my children, along with my neighbors thought I was crazy painting all over my garage walls. This became how I journaled my emotions and journal emotions I did! Creatively. Soon, I had filled my garage walls and I knew it was time to paint on a canvas; but I was scared. I wasn't sure if I could paint so small or how to begin deciding what to paint. In my mind, I knew I could probably paint a tree, since I like trees it seemed like a good idea. My thought was to add texture to my canvas first, just like that wall in my old living room. The only thing I had was paint spackel, but I figured it would still work. I was right, it looked amazing and added all this awesome texture. I loved how it added dimension to my tree. I also realized that I COULD paint on a smaller area.

 It's not what you look like when you're doing what you're doing … it's what you look like you're doing when you're doing what you're doing. EXPRESS YOURSELF!

Once again, I found myself desiring to simplify and move. I sold my townhouse and became a renter. This meant no more remodels, no more painted walls, no more projects. And no more excuses. I was inspired and needed more canvases.

Hobby Lobby and I were about to become best friends. I needed paint, better brushes, texture tools, oh yeah and don't forget the gesso … liquid eraser. Oh yeah, and canvases.

My first project after stocking up with all my goodies was creating paintings for my new salon space. Guess what I painted? A tree. I am also a reiki practitioner and I had this vision in my mind of a Chakra tree, so that's what I did. Next I decided to paint the ocean, after all I am a mermaid. It only made sense, and once I began this too, evolved into a beautiful painting. I remember thinking, "Wow! I'm pretty good at this."

As my 50th birthday approached, I knew I didn't want to do the typical 50th birthday thing, but something epic was in order. There was this tickling in my brain...a whisper...and then a shout, "ART SHOW! YOU'RE GOING TO HAVE AN ART SHOW!"

The inner dialogue began. *Ugh! How do I this?* I knew I had to paint more than a tree. *Oh yeah, I need paintings. How many paintings do I paint? Where am I going to have this? I can't have this at my house. I wonder if anyone knows of a place for this art show?*

I called my friend who was experienced in this field because I knew she could help. She began by asking me all the questions I had asked myself. Then I asked her how many paintings I should have to have a good show, she said ten. I chose 11...one of my numbers. I just thought I would invite my family and closest friends, you know, so they could come and admire what I did, but her vision was much larger than mine. I was afraid to think that big. What if everybody thought it was terrible? It was exciting and scary all at once, but I did it anyway. I had no idea what I was painting, 11 paintings was a lot to come up with. I figured I better just start — maybe throw some paint on the canvas and see what appears. I knew I liked texture (remember that wall?) and bright colors, and before I knew it, BAM! I had a style all my own. This was how I did everything in life, I just went for it.

Doing my art show inspired me to continue to open and find more things I loved to paint. Mermaids! Duh! While painting mermaids something occurred that made me realize, yet again, that painting is my therapy. I had painted this sad looking mermaid. I was so pissed, I thought, "How did this happen?! Seriously?! What?! Mermaids are supposed to be happy! What the hell cookie?!" Oh, I had channeled my emotion into the painting. I could see in my art what I was feeling, I was communicating from my soul. I had confirmation of this, when a client asked me if I was an energy artist. It took me a moment to understand what they were asking me, then it hit me. Yes! I am an energy artist!

The colors that I chose to paint with, the size of my canvas, the way I approached my painting, all of it was telling a story. The story was about a little girl with white GoGo boots that wanted nothing more than to become an artist, create beautiful things, and express herself!

I dedicate this story to my mom, Jerilyn Jan Johnson MacKaben. A woman who unknowingly has been inspiring me my whole life.

Thank you to my children Britny, Kirk, and Tempest, my forever and always inspirations. Knowing you're there supporting me in all my adventures makes it easier to follow my heart and my path. You're always on board and push me to be brave and just go for it. And Brit, thanks for helping me organize all my giant sticky notes and being my grammar nazi. Panda.

RICK NICHOLS

RICK NICHOLS NICHOLS is on a life mission to inspire people the world over to higher levels of thinking about who they are, what they've got, and how to lead healthier, happier, more fulfilling lives. As a self-declared "teacher of love," Rick is an internationally recognized author, speaker, and trainer in the field of spiritual growth and personal development. He has authored and co-authored inspirational books such as, *Who Do You Think You Are? A Fairy Tale for All Ages*, *In the Flow of Life*, and the, *Pearls of Wisdom* compilations.

Through an exclusive worldwide license agreement with Hay House Inc. Rick together with his wife and business partner Dr. Patricia Crane, facilitates trainings worldwide, which prepare people to lead Heal Your Life® workshops and provide life coaching based on the philosophy of Louise Hay.

You may learn more about Rick Nichols at:
Rick-Nichols.com
HealYourLifeTraining.com
Rick@Rick-Nichols.com
Facebook.com/rick.nichols.9674

✿ Returning Home

> ✤ How can you get very far if you don't know who you are?
>
> How do you do what you ought if you don't know what you've got?
>
> And if you don't know which to do of all the things in front of you,
>
> Then what you'll have, when you are through
>
> is just a mess, without a clue
>
> of all the best that can come true if you
>
> knew what, and which, and who.
>
> ~WINNIE THE POOH (used by permission)

The poem above is excerpted from my book, *Who Do You Think You Are? A Fairytale for All Ages*. It is a book written in the genre of what I call "personal fiction." By that, I mean a story based on real life experience presented in the form of fiction. I found this process to be a wonderfully cleansing experience because it offered a way to safely process some of the pain and sadness of earlier life through the surrogates of fictional characters.

Briefly, the story follows the path of the little bird named, Eagerlet as his life unfolds from the womb to self-discovery. It seems a farmer's son discovers an egg in a nest high on the mountain and through an act of mischief or grace (we don't know his motivation) removes the egg from its nest and places it in a Turkey's pen on the farm. This, of course, results in a creature destined to fly high and wild, being born into a family of turkeys and confined to a small farm (sound familiar).

All the creatures of the farm, including Eagerlet himself, soon realize that something is terribly wrong, this fellow doesn't seem to fit in; he doesn't belong here. Eagerlet tries his best to measure up to expectations as he is passed from one bird family to another on the farm. His problem is that the turkeys want him to look and behave like a turkey, chickens want him to be like a chicken, ducks expect him to behave as ducks are expected to behave, and he doesn't seem to be able to comply with their wishes. Well, it doesn't take very long before Elder Duck informs Eagerlet that he had best leave the farm and seek for who he is and a place of belonging.

Who am I? Why am I? Do I have a purpose? What might that purpose be? What happens to me when **my** time here on earth is done? These haunting questions are very much like the riddles or koans of Zen masters. The answers simply cannot be found at the surface of the questions; one must "sit" with the question for a long while and *allow* the answer to bubble to the surface. The answer to any koan, including the ones listed above, can never be found by trying to figure it out, analyze it, or deductively reason your way to a solution (btw, there may be more than one solution).

Seekers on the Path

Most of us on a spiritual path consider ourselves to be seekers. We are on a mighty quest to discover something very important. Think about that for a moment, what is it that we might be seeking? What is at the end of this "spiritual pathway?" Are we doomed to be forever "seekers" or might we someday actually discover what we are looking for? And then there's the really big question, "What are we to do with ourselves once the seeking has been transformed to found?" Hummmmm

I believe what most of us are seeking is the answer to the above-listed question, "Who am I?" Once that question gets answered all the other questions simply fall into place. Some people are born clearly knowing who they are. Some discover it through a sudden revelation, a sort of blast of grace from "out of the blue." Most of us, however, must trudge, one step at a time, along some spiritual path or another for a very, very long time. These pathways are usually full of twists, turns, potholes, dark forests and dangerous poppy fields. And then, when we finally manage to reach the Emerald City of our dreams we get the startling revelation that it isn't at all what we expected it to be. We discover that this city is ruled by a fearful and angry dictator (our own ego), who informs us that we are not worthy, and orders us off onto yet another dangerous quest to prove our worthiness. The task we must ultimately accomplish on the final quest is none other than to slay or be slain by the terrifying shadow figure that represents our supposed sin and shame and guilt. OH, MY!!!

Fear not mighty warriors and seekers of the light, much help is on the way. As we trek along our spiritual pathway, we make rich discoveries. We discover that we really do have everything we need to lead a healthy happy and successful life, regardless of what we may have been told in the past. The pathway is long and arduous for a very good reason. It requires us to move slowly and carefully, which gives us the time we need to mend our broken hearts, discover our true wisdom, and to bolster our courage for the long journey home. And yes, dear travel companions, the sojourn along the spiritual path is indeed born out of our longing to go home.

Discovering the Holy Grail

When you think about it, you may realize, as I did, that our is quest is to discover and claim for ourselves the grandest prize of all, the Holy Grail. That of course, begs yet another question, what exactly is the Holy Grail. In truth, the Grail is a part of the grand mystery. It is something that is impossible to describe; it can only be *referred* to, as it is in myth and legend. It is something that can never be seen with the eyes. However, when you finally discover it, the heart will instantly recognize the awesome treasure of this blessing. The Holy Grail, beloved fellow travelers, is none other than the light of your own true self! It is more beautiful than anything you can imagine, discovering it will result in a sacred baptism by tears of joy and gratitude the moment it appears. It is a profound, permanent state of grace.

Once you have discovered and claimed the Grail for yourself, you can never again be a victim. You can never again experience even an ounce of shame, fear, or guilt. You will know with absolute certainty that you are safe in a universe that is beautiful, loving, and wholly perfect in every way. You will have finally arrived at that place of the *peace which passes all understanding.*

Sacred Map to the Holy Grail

Before we travel on, I must ask you a question — are you an orphan? The answer to this question is of the utmost importance because the seeker's pathway is, in fact, a Hero's Journey. In Joseph Campbell's model of, *The Hero's Journey*, he states that the primary prerequisite for the hero to "receive the call" is that he/she must be an orphan. Only orphans will receive the sacred call to the new earth. If we take a close look at the great stories, myths, fairy tales, and legends, we will find that the heroes are *always* orphans. Dorothy in the Wizard of Oz, Indiana Jones, Cinderella, Snow White, Luke Skywalker, and the list goes on. So, dear one, are you an orphan?

Regardless of how you may have answered that question, I am going to suggest that you are indeed an orphan and therefore qualified for the journey! Here's how that happens, in truth, precisely at the moment of the conception of your body, your true godparents, father/mother God/Goddess, placed you in the care of a pair of foster parents. Moreover, these foster parents are usually a couple of youngsters who haven't a clue of what to do with you — and from there the journey begins.

On this final leg of our sacred journey home, we will need to be well prepared. Be sure to pack your own true and faithful heart safely in your knapsack of courage, and don your hat of wisdom as we set out on this exciting quest for the Holy Grail.

We begin by identifying our major steppingstones to the Grail, 1. **Desire** - maintain a powerful desire, **2. Intention** - set a determined intention, **3. Allow** - focus on your desire and intention (this is the equivalent of "sitting" with a koan, it can take a long time and be painful), **4. Surrender** - this happens automatically, it is great a gift to allow ourselves to surrender to the will of the higher power because that power will in return open us to the Grail.

The Great Discovery

The conception or creation of your physical body is the outcome of your parent's act of *making Love.* As a result, three elements came into play, 1. A sperm cell, 2. An ovum or egg, 3. A spark of divine light, scientists call this phenomenon a "zinc flash," (search words, conception flash) I call it the light of your eternal soul incarnating into a human body, no spark, no conception. *Important Note: parents making Love.* What is the outcome of your effort to make something? When you make a cake, the outcome is cake. If you make a chair, the outcome is chair. When you make Love, the outcome is Love. If your parents were making love at the time of your conception, whether it was an act of love, lust, just having some fun, or whatever, the outcome was indisputably Love. Therefore **you are Love**. Love ignited by a spark of divine creative potential. Glory be!

Follow the Bird He Knows the Way

Let's catch up now with our fellow seeker, Eagerlet, as he completes his own journey of self-discovery. His road has been long and harrowing, including rejection, loneliness, dark night of the soul, and bullying. Finally, during a desperate leap of faith he received the blessing of a powerful epiphany which delivered him onto the wings of a couple of wise mentors, through which he finally discovered his wings and …swishhhhhhhhhhh, he caught the wind!!!

"…Eagerlet slowly regained the sense of his surroundings. Everything was exactly as before, except that his two newly found mentors were gone. Rather than the sense of abandonment and loneliness that he may have felt earlier, he now felt perfectly at ease, comfortable and safe as he sat there joyously full of aloneness in the fading light of the day. In the deep recesses of his mind, he heard what felt like haunting echoes of old Owl's voice as it questioned: 'Who? Who? Who Do You Think You Are?'

'I am, I am, I am a spark of divine creative potential, expressing uniquely as the One who is known as Eagerlet."

So finally — *how can you get very far* if you don't know WHO you are, WHAT you've got and WHICH to do? The answers are, even now, deep in your own heart, *allow* them to rise to your highest level of consciousness, and find yourself instantly at home, the searching is over.

Be Still and Know

I am a spark of divine creative potential expressing uniquely as the One who is known as

[your name here]

Welcome home dear Ones, welcome home. Peace be with you always.

Dedicated to all seekers of the light. May you soon arrive at the realization that what you seek is immediately at hand, closer than your own breath. Simply be still and touch your hand to your heart - breathe into the light you seek. Blessed be.

A note of gratitude: I am writing this on the morning of my 70th birthday. Looking back on my life I see many mentors; some seem to be blocking the light while others cast their light brightly that I may find my way. At this point I have learned that you were, each and all, a priceless gift, an important plank in the bridge suspended between then and now. There are far too many of you to mention by name, so I will now simply turn to the past, put hands together in prayer, bow deeply, and humbly offer gratitude, thank you, thank you each and all, namaste.

PATRICIA J. CRANE

PATRICIA J. CRANE, PH.D., is on a mission is to empower people worldwide with the inner resources and outer skills they need to achieve their dreams. Her company, Heart Inspired Presentations, LLC, provides workshops, training, and products to support this mission. With the authorization of Hay House, Inc., and approval of Louise Hay, she and husband Rick Nichols offer the Heal Your Life® programs, which train people worldwide to provide workshops and coaching in Louise's philosophy. In addition to the Heal Your Life® programs, Patricia has led hundreds of other workshops on increasing prosperity, creating powerful affirmations, Reiki healing, and success strategies for women.

Patricia is also an author and speaker. Her book, ***Ordering From the Cosmic Kitchen: The Essential Guide to Powerful, Nourishing Affirmations***, is an easy-to-read and entertaining book on how to clear the past and use affirmations and visualizations to cook up a delicious future!

www.heartinspired.com
www.drpatriciacrane.com
patricia@heartinspired.com
Facebook: Patricia Crane (San Diego)

❧ The Courage to Risk

As my mother tells it, dad paced the floor for two days threatening to disown me. He ranted he'd wasted money on my education. Why? Because I had made the shocking decision (to him) to quit the Master's Degree program in chemistry at the University of Southern California (where I had a teaching scholarship) to become a social worker in Watts, the low income black area of Los Angeles where there had been riots two years before. Mom said it took all her persuasive powers to calm him down and convince him that I had to try this. Ironically, it was the encouragement I'd received from my parents all my life that was a significant part of my being able to take the risk of quitting grad school. The other part was the intuitive guidance I didn't even realize I had at that time. That guidance had led me to Southern California, three thousand miles away from my family. In the late 60's, that was the place where my spiritual awakening could really begin.

What neither of my parents knew, nor anyone else prior to this, was a commitment I'd made during the summer of my 20th year that prompted the change. That summer I had an internship in a dental research lab at the University of Pennsylvania, and it turned out to be the most boring job I've ever had. There was plenty of time to read and think about my life and what was important to me.

It was a time of turmoil in the US, with the Vietnam war protests going on, marches for black rights, and women's lib. I began recalling experiences from my early years in Georgia, and my innate understanding that bigotry was wrong, and knowing all humans deserve respect. In that summer, my consciousness was re-awakened to the need for equal rights for everyone. Disillusioned with conventional religion because there was a lot of preaching about unconditional love but few people seemed to actually do it, I labeled myself an agnostic, and made a commitment that my life would be dedicated to service and helping others in any way that I could. Little did I realize that I had begun a spiritual journey, regardless of the label I gave myself.

While working in Watts did fulfill my decision to be of service, it was also very stressful. The stress began to affect my health and my emotions. Fortunately, a caring co-worker introduced me to the idea of meditation. Not wanting to continue the anti-anxiety medication my doctor had prescribed for me, I gave it a try. This was a turning point for me as I found my spiritual center, my connection with Divine Spirit, and the strength to take more risks in my life. Meditation enabled me to trust my inner guidance when I decided to separate from my husband, and later leave a lucrative internship with a humanistic psychologist to work with Louise Hay and start leading Heal Your Life® workshops and training. While I felt deeply that these changes would support my growth, the process was certainly difficult at times. Following your heart doesn't always mean an immediate path of rose petals. The divorce brought times of deep loneliness, and the change of career, financial stress. During meditation, I continued to receive messages of comfort and reassurance for the eventual positive outcomes. My mantra became: *I am safe, it's only change.* And then there was the risk to enter a relationship with a man who had no job and no money. I argued with God about that guidance and some friends had dire warnings for me! But in the ensuing twenty-one years together, our partnership in love, life, and business has provided the means to share the life-changing philosophy of Louise Hay worldwide and to be of service in ways meaningful to both of us.

When you listen to most people talk, you will often hear complaints about what isn't going right and what they want to change. And yet, aren't there people you've known a long time who talk about changing for years, and never go for it? It's more comfortable to complain about things than to change because change is a step into the unknown and the ego fears that! And yet, that inner discontent continues to grow. As the Anais Nin quote says,"*And the day came when the risk to remain tight in a bud was more painful than the risk it took to blossom.*"

Often the opportunity to blossom comes from some life crisis: loss of a relationship, a life-threatening diagnosis like cancer, loss of a job or finances. While these challenges do offer opportunities for life changes, many don't seize them, preferring instead to remain as victims to circumstances. Our society actually supports being a victim—just watch the news for a few minutes—so choosing a new path takes great courage. It requires acceptance of your responsibility for your life and forgiveness of self and others.

How do you build the inner skills to be a risk taker who is willing to make significant life changes? For me, meditation was the key to learning to trust my inner guidance and trust the Universe to support me when taking risks. Dropping into the quiet, peaceful place became a welcome refuge from my chattering mind. After several months of meditating regularly, I discovered I would think things and they would happen. I didn't realize I was doing affirmations until I was drawn to read *Seth Speaks*, a channeled book by Jane Roberts that explained how we create our reality with our thoughts and words. This revelation provided the ability to consciously begin shaping my future with affirmations. In my journal, I wrote pages of affirmations and started a daily practice of gratitude.

The foundation for Louise Hay was learning to love and accept herself exactly as she was. This may sound easy, but really loving yourself requires honesty with yourself, especially confronting the parts of yourself and your behavior you have judged. To accelerate the process of loving yourself, Louise recommends going to a mirror and saying to yourself: *I love you.* If you haven't ever done this, do it right now. That's right, put down this chapter and go do it. Tears may well up. Welcome them—you are touching a deeper part of yourself than usual. Be willing to practice this technique everyday with the willingness to really love yourself and you will experience amazing changes.

In my mind, there is an image of five pillars that support my growth: meditation, affirmations, loving myself, forgiveness, and gratitude. These bring additional gifts such as greater unconditional love for others when I love myself, a lightness in my mind and body, trusting my life path even when it is rocky, and knowing that there is a Power and Presence in my life that guides me.

When you are traveling a new path of spiritual growth and risking to follow your heart, you may find you no longer resonate with some of your friends and even family members. They don't understand your new attitudes, and some may even resent the joy for life you've found. They are puzzled by your decision to show up differently in the world. You no longer commiserate with them or play "ain't it awful." So, it's important to find your own tribe and get involved with like-minded people who can support you. There are so many ways to do that today: local meetup groups, meditation groups, Facebook groups and more. Affirm for the perfect ones to help strengthen your spiritual muscles.

Caution—if one day in meditation you get the message to quit your job next week, sell all your stuff and go to the Himalayas to meditate, take a breath and wait awhile to make sure this is your spiritual guidance and not just the desire to get away from the challenges happening in your life! If you decide that a healing center or a retreat in the woods is your way to offer a sacred space for people, start by working at one or volunteering at one so you know the joys and the pitfalls.

One of my favorite metaphors for stepping out in faith comes from a wonderful scene in the movie, *Indiana Jones and the Last Crusade*. Indiana is on a quest for the Holy Grail (the chalice Jesus drank from at the Last Supper). The quest becomes truly urgent when Indiana's father is shot, and only the water from the Grail will save him. Using a small book with ambiguous clues, Indiana passes two obstacles and arrives at the third, a huge crevice resembling the Grand Canyon. His only clue is to "leap from the lion's head." To do so appears to be falling to his death in the abyss. His inner struggle is apparent as the camera shows the close–up of his face. Does he trust the clue and leap or not? Suddenly, he leaps! Incredibly, there is a bridge he lands on that was invisible before.

Life is like this. Spirit always has a safety net waiting for us. In the midst of a challenge, it can be difficult to trust there is a solution already in Divine Mind. When this happens, breathe deeply many times, meditate, and ask for guidance. Focus on the result you want, not the challenge. Remember that what you resist persists. I once heard philosopher and futurist Jean Houston say, "Depression is not the medium of miracles." How true. The medium of miracles is trusting that there is some solution for the challenge you're facing, even when you have no idea how it will happen. When you focus on trusting that Spirit has a solution, the solution will appear.

What helps **you** shift from fear and anxiety to trust? Perhaps it's meditating, reading a spiritual text or listening to an inspirational tape, or dancing to your favorite music. Perhaps it's watching children at the park or taking a walk-in nature. Whatever it is, do it. And do it regularly, not just when you are in crisis. People tend to wait until crisis strikes to turn to our spiritual source. Why wait? The first step is to experience your spiritual center, and then all else will unfold in Divine Right Order. Get intimate with Spirit: feel the Power and Presence you are a part of now.

Dedicated to all those who are following their hearts and spiritual guidance, taking risks to change their lives and help others discover how to live meaningful and fulfilling lives, and especially to Verity Dawson, dear friend and loving teacher, whose entire life was focused on service.

Deepest gratitude to my primary mentor, Louise Hay, who has trusted Rick and myself to take her work forward. Twenty years ago, we never imagined how it would expand. And to all the Heal Your Life® teachers and coaches worldwide who share an uplifting message of love every day, thank you for your dedication to this work. To Christy Dickson, our amazing admin, who takes care of so many details and makes my life easier. To my family friends who have supported me on my journey, thank you for your love and support. To Lisa Hardwick, whose Visionary Insight Press offers a positive vision of life to so many people. And finally, to my amazing husband, Rick Nichols, whose sense of humor, love and support makes each day an adventure.

JANET BRENTZEL

JANET BRENTZEL is an author, life coach, and mother to three wonderful children. She has published several cookbooks including Dinner Party Diva and has embraced the world of Numerology and has shared her life experience, insight and expertise in an easy to follow online certification course.

She enjoys spending time on and near the water with her children on the Gulf Coast of Alabama. She applies life lessons and enjoys sharing experiences in fun, off beat ways to inspire and help others when they are struggling with life situations and lack of direction. She is rarely seen without a smile on her face and believes that positive thinking and confidence are always going to be the BEST best friends.

🌀 Revolution

Change...that word holds your mind captive at times. Often filling our minds with negative connotations and fear as we begin to realize that change is imminent. We have all faced periods in life where we feel life is moving faster than we are prepared for. Death, divorce, loss of employment, and moving are major life events in which the energy surrounding these occurrences urge us to take courageous, creative steps to living an excellent and prosperous future.

Often the feeling of change doesn't come with a life changing event attached to it. It's sensed deep inside and sometimes we cannot quite place what these feelings inside us are revealing. When we are feeling unsettled and restless in our lives, it is often because change is on the horizon and we are subconsciously allowing the negative vibrations to intermingle with our actions and not fully embracing what is being presented. The future is being unveiled and we are unsure of what it looks like so we allow fear to sabotage our growth and understanding. The universe is unveiling your future at this very moment and telling you that you are strong and ready for your destiny to be revealed! (yes, stop and take that in a moment! Exciting, right sister?) You have been given all the lessons, knowledge and skills from past experience to embrace and fulfill this newly dawning opportunity! It is TIME to move to the next level of your life's destiny, and let me tell you, put on your shades, it's a super bright future!

Now, let's explore other words for change.

SHIFT
TRANSITION
RECONSTRUCTION
DEVELOPMENT
TRANSFORMATION
GROWTH
REVOLUTION

REVOLUTION?!?!
YES!! REVOLUTION!!!

Begin to embrace and interpret change with the word revolution. Change the thoughts in your head from the negative to the exciting and positive! Revolution is defined as "A time of great change" Do you feel the positive energy you are emanating inside when you shift your thoughts from change to revolution? Revolution invokes feelings of unstoppable force, great rewards and passion. Take a moment and really embrace this, hold onto the feeling and allow it to encompass and exhilarate every cell in your body, breathe it in.

We choose the energy we allow inside our thoughts. If we continue to allow the negative connotations of change to under mind, doubt and outright battle with change we cannot thrive and feel joy. Shifting our thoughts to revolution and growth empowers us as our destiny is unveiled. We are giving ourselves the freedom to openly and lovingly embrace the opportunities that are being presented and we THRIVE!

Now that we have our minds and hearts willing to explore new possibilities, adventures and understanding we may be asking, "How do I see where my opportunities are being unveiled?" That my dear is the million-dollar question and the million-dollar answer is right at your fingertips, quite literally.

How do you express yourself? Words, art, music? All of them are standard forms of self-expression for creative and joyful living. We use images and words to convey the majority of our thoughts and feelings. Maybe we have given ourselves labels, artsy, unique, and unconventional. Expressing ourselves can feel challenging at times because if we are limiting ourselves to the verbal language we are not speaking the universal language of numbers. How can numbers speak you ask?

The mysteries and manifestations of numerology are far reaching in our lives and even when we have been unaware it has been occurring throughout our worldly existence. Numbers allow us to express and take in where words have proven to be barriers. Numerology is a universal language regardless of location, language or understanding.

Creative living can be challenging for many of us. How and where do we look for signs for our destiny? How do we choose which path to follow? There is not just one answer for these questions but a pattern is often easily discovered when we open our minds and hearts to the possibilities.

When I was experiencing a big revolution in my life, i began to be aware that I would see the number one over and over. Perhaps it was an address, the time on the clock, a new friend's birthday. No matter where I went for a period of eight months the number one was always in view, often in obscure and unexpected ways. I began to research and develop my affinity for this number and finally realized at this point on my path I was to follow where ONE led me.

I discovered that one was the number of new beginnings and change (revolution!) It beams life energy and the beginning of manifestation of light. In retrospect, it is very fitting for a recently divorced stay at home mom who was struggling to see what her future looked like. Fear and confusion had been the guiding force prior to this enlightenment. I began day by day, actually hour by hour to see where one unveiled itself and when it did I followed its path. I embraced the unknown with excitement to discover the path I was to follow. One is the alpha number and is only divisible by itself, independent of all other numbers. One is a complete number without the need of any others and is the number of new beginnings. I found everything about the number one to inspirational and empowering in my life journey.

Without fail, everywhere one appeared I would follow and consequently have been presented with the most amazing opportunities of my life, including the opportunity of sharing this with you. I have gone from change to revolution and have received the joy, growth and destiny can only attain from abandoning emotional confusion and fears and preparing for a new chapter with light and love in one's heart.

The driving force and the power of one that will help develop your new potential is upon you! When I say, it is upon you, I mean it is undeniably coming at you at full velocity! Allow me to share with you how I know this.

We have started a new nine-year cycle with 2017. To determine the year cycle, simply add the numbers until you a single digit sum.

$$2+0+1+7=10$$
$$1+0=1$$

We are all in this new cycle together and where you may look back on last year as confusing and emotional (the nine year, the end year in the previous cycle.) You can rest assured the past is over and the anchors that have tied you to it need to be released, it is time to embrace your exciting future and what lies ahead. The trials and tribulations you have previously experienced were necessary to give you the experience and understanding needed to fully be able to manifest what this new cycle will bring to you. Each and every bit of energy and opportunity presented to you has purpose. When you remind yourself of this you will more easily process change and understand the purpose behind hardships.

I am using the year cycle as an example but all of the principles for self-expression and self-actualization can be used when you feel revolution coming on. You should absorb this information and keep it close for the times you will need to pull from it. This is an exciting time but it is not an easy one! What one is working toward in revolution is freedom. In history freedom is something that needs to be fought for, you must work diligently towards your goals to be successful. The universe will only present your opportunities and pathways, it is your job to do the work required to make the most of what is presented.

ACTION
What You Can Do Right Now To Make The Most Of Your Journey

Self-Acceptance! Self-acceptance is critical to your best life path! As you move toward freedom you will start to be less dependent and less self-critical. You will not hide your fears but accept them as part of the process to work toward your goals. You will not have all the answers at once but you will gain the confidence to work through your feelings and turn the negative feelings into positive ones. Don't look at insecurities in a negative light! WE all have them but embracing them will give you the confidence to move throughout them so they do not stifle your growth. As you continue your study and awareness of numerology, you will begin to recognize patterns that will aid in guiding you to confidently embrace and discover the chosen path for your journey.

Begin new activities. The thing about change is it has a domino effect one will always lead to another. So, taking baby steps on living the life you want starts with ONE simple change. Maybe it's a dance class? want to play tennis? Take a painting class? Or how about an online class in numerology to guide help you guide you through the exciting year to come? Maybe you want to become a certified numerology practitioner and share this knowledge with others while starting a successful new business? Any of these are easy ways to start your revolution!

Start imagining yourself free of toxic relationships, negative thoughts, unhealthy activities. See how good that feels! Let it all go and work toward the bright light that is heading for you! This is a year of breaking free, not judging and holding tightly to the shifts that you have tried for so long to get to.

Are You Ready To Start Something New?

My most recent project, The Certified Numerology Practitioner Course featured at Visionary Insight Institution is a great way to catapult your revolution! The course can be completed quickly and will give you a basis to understand and start practicing numerology to help guide you in the future. Additionally, and included, a short exam follows the training course if you choose to take it and become a Certified Numerology Practitioner to share your skills and knowledge with others. Topics covered are numerology history, life path number and their meanings, detailed information on number meanings and how to interpret them, business checklist for those who choose to become a certified practitioner (included with the course) and want to share with others while starting an exciting and profitable new business. To get more information on how this course will meet your needs go to www.visionaryinstitutecertifications.com

The Certified Numerology Practitioner Course will help you discover a unique way to more clearly see your future path and make the most of your effort. As you study this easy to follow course, your new and increasing understanding of the universal language of Numerology will empower and motivate your year of Revolution! Seize your every opportunity today and build a lifetime of opportunity for tomorrow!

To my three amazing children, Chelsea, Tyler and Mackenzie, thank you for always believing in me and supporting me no matter what. To Lisa and her Visionary Insight press, thank you for seeing possibilities in me when I didn't see them myself and for supporting me along the way.

KATINA GILLESPIE

KATINA GILLESPIE is a bestselling author, Peace Love Wings® Mind Body Spirit Practitioner and Workshop Facilitator, Project Director with Visionary Insight Press, a Human Resources Training and Development professional, and an active volunteer with animal rescue and Women's Resource Centers.

Katina's calling has a focus on life balance and emotional awareness, to assist others in finding their light within and provide others with tools to succeed. She has found that most of people's issues and concerns are easily solved through self-awareness. Her desire is to transform others into confident, self-loving individuals that motivate and inspire those around them.

An outcome-oriented leader who builds cooperative, knowledgeable teams through planning, directing, and project coordination. She has a track record of collaborative, innovative, and effective delivery of training programs with full knowledge, commitment, and uncompromising devotion to value others and appreciate their contributions.

KatinaEHW@gmail.com
www.EmotionalHarmonyWellness.com
www.linkedin.com/in/emotional-harmony-wellness
www.visionaryinstitutecertifications.com

🌿 Asking and Accepting Assistance

'm not exactly sure when it happened, but at some point in my life, I started to believe 'help' was a bad word. Somewhere, I picked up the idea that asking for assistance was tantamount to admitting weakness, and ultimately failure. It is a sad irony that it is during times when we most need assistance that most people are reluctant in asking.

It was not until I had my own team to manage professionally that I realized that there is value in admitting the need of assistance. I had a few team members who were in their first jobs out of college and had a great deal to learn. I was very willing to provide training and valued information. I did not expect them to know everything. However, they seemed to think that I <u>did</u> expect them to know everything and, by consequence, that they should not ask questions. This frequently created stressful situations to say the least. They would work endless hours trying to figure out something on their own to prove that they could perform the task assigned. When all it did was to slow down the process and add unnecessary stress on themselves and the team and therefore, ultimately on me as their leader.

I have learned that asking for assistance is a delicate endeavor—but when done correctly, it will get the task done more quickly and most likely better. Plus, all those involved will gain knowledge and strengthen their base for future success. When you do not ask for assistance when you need it, you assume all a burden that might easily be shared. But you also deprive those who would love to assist you of the opportunity to do so. Whether it be looking for assistance with a work assignment or seeking treatment for a minor illness, asking for help is the first step towards positive outcomes. Life's many obstacles cannot be tackled alone—we simply do not live long enough to learn how to do everything on our own. We all have individual strengths, resources, insights, personalities and skill sets that are unique to our experience. The fact is that most people are genuinely delighted to do a favor and are flattered when someone is comfortable enough to reach out and request their assistance. You never know, the very thing you need help with may be something that your colleague just took a course in online and they would be delighted to share their newly expanded expertise. We can do much more together than we ever can do alone. Too often we 'tough it out' rather than reaching out for assistance when we need it most. Fear gets in the way while depriving others of the opportunity to show they care and share their knowledge.

It is important to risk the possibility of seeming needy, or even of being rejected, and to reach out to ask for help when we need it. We also must be willing to accept it when it is offered. Not only can it help us when times are tough and we are hard-pressed, but it also provides others the chance to make a difference while helping them feel more comfortable to ask for assistance themselves. In the end, collaboration provides opportunities for us to discover that we can be more successful ourselves when we support and enable those around us to be more successful. Everyone is better off when we share our gifts with others. I ask you to consider that by having the courage to ask for help you are not putting them out, you are pulling them up! It takes a village!

After spending time gauging my own reactions when my team and love ones approached me for assistance, or didn't, I have pulled out a few key suggestions to soften the anxiety of requesting assistance when I need help myself. The first step is to make certain that you need assistance. Explore all the possible solutions, including the obvious ones. It only takes one time for someone to ask, "Why didn't you try X?" to realize how much it pays to check the simple solutions first. So, before you try to knock down a door with your shoulder, try turning the handle first.

There is something to be said about attempting to resolve an issue yourself, however, torturing yourself for hours or days, before admitting you need assistance is almost NEVER productive. In the past I have been known to stay late on a project trying to resolve a specific issue, and although fatigue and frustration were clouding my mind, I still felt it necessary that everyone knew how hard I was working to solve the problem. I quickly learned that the long hours did not win me any points with anyone. While people appreciate dedication and diligence, they loathe inefficiency. The trick is knowing when to suck it up, swallow your pride and admit you are stuck. I suggest you to consider that if you can't figure something out after a minimum of three attempts on your own, it is time to admit you need a little inspiration from someone else.

When you know that you need to ask for assistance, do not just go knocking on someone's door to surrender. It is best to enter the conversation armed with a few potential solutions. This shows that you have thought it through on your own and you are not just asking for a handout. You are attempting to get the job done together! I've discovered that asking for assistance can be a powerful tool to collaborate with others. This is true in professional, personal, and unexpected situations. Keep this in mind next time you find yourself a little over your head and I guarantee your colleagues, loved ones, and strangers will not be complaining when you need their assistance! They will be delighted you asked and the task or concern will be completed with team work and you will develop long term relationships and future networking opportunity.

Another example of where I learned the importance of asking and accepting assistance was when I was out of a job and seeking employment immediately after I graduated from college. I was in a new city and knew very few people. I wanted to prove that I could secure employment with my impressive resume and tenacity! After a week without success, I was speaking with my new neighbor discussing my frustration and he said ... *"I work at a restaurant that is looking for management. I can put in a good word for you if you would like?"* The following day, I did that very thing and was interviewed immediately. Shortly after, I was hired for my first management position. I would have NEVER thought to ask my neighbor for assistance. He was practically a stranger. I felt that asking anyone for help would mean that I was inadequate. When in reality, it is just being resourceful. It taught me a very important lesson. The answer is always "no"; unless you ask. The worst thing that can happen is for them to say "*No*" or have nothing to offer. The result may be just what you are looking for and may create new opportunities. In this example, I truly believe that it was guidance from the Divine. I did not know where to go for assistance so the assistance came to me. It is important to trust the process and be open to answers as they naturally arise. When the Divine is invited in, it is always a majestic experience. Trusting that your project, goal or event is part of a Divine path helps you to keep the faith and stay the course.

I recall another time when I was in college, making a six-hour drive to visit my parents for a long weekend. I was extremely tired and struggling to stay awake. Suddenly I heard a loud noise that sounded like a gun-shot and my car quickly swerved out of control. I had no idea what happened but miraculously I was able to safely bring my car to a halt at the side of the road. I had blown a tire! I had no idea what to do. I knew how to change a tire but was frightened and frustrated. I should mention that this occurred before the comforts of cellphones and road-side assistance. As all the worst-case scenarios were scrolling through my mind, a blue pickup truck pulled up behind me and a man stepped out of the vehicle. I was shaking in fear. He first asked me if I was okay. I have no idea what I said but he clearly saw that I was scared and uncertain about what to do next. He offered to take me to a gas station down the road that sold tires. I was very reluctant but accepted his offer. I'm not certain of the exact details of the event but I believe that he helped me in paying for the tire as I did not have enough cash. He drove me back to my car and exchanged the tire for me. I attempted to get his name and address so I could send him money for helping me and he would not allow it. You see, he explained that he had a daughter my age and he only wished that someone would do the same for her if she was ever in a similar situation. He stepped in his truck and drove off. Never to be seen again. This did not create a lasting relationship but it certainly made an impact on both of us. He could feel good about doing a kind thing for a stranger and I could get home safely without any of those worst-case scenarios happening to me. God certainly sent an earth angel to help me on my path. You don't always have to ask for assistance, but you must be open to receive it! The energy flows both ways.

Many times, I have requested assistance from a colleague or a new acquaintance so that I could measure their knowledge and their ability to work as a team. As a leader and friend, this is a very useful tool. Accepting the assistance of others allows you to benefit, others to feel a sense of purpose, and a joint contribution will be more than what could ever be achieved alone. I focus on emotional awareness in my coaching practice and recently authored an online Spiritual Development Educator Certification program that can be used for personal development or professional practice. If I can help YOU, just ASK!

I dedicate this to the Divine for providing confidence, strength, and forgiveness. Every experience has given me more compassion and understanding of the world. To my angels for surrounding me with healing light, encouragement, and love. My heart is filled with gratitude for all my spiritual gifts.

Thank you to my unbelievably supportive immediate family and close friends for sticking by me through the countless phases where I have reinvented myself and for your unwavering confidence in me throughout this process.

A special appreciation to my husband, Charles! You've believed in me since the moment we met and have brought forth my courage to connect with my inner knowing and follow the wisdom of my wild heart. Your continuous faith in me, combined with your absolute love, drive us closer to live the life we both know is our destiny. I love you completely!

SUNNY DAWN JOHNSTON

SUNNY DAWN JOHNSTON is a world-renowned author, inspirational speaker, spiritual teacher and psychic medium. Over the last sixteen years, Sunny has performed thousands of private sessions, readings and workshops which have helped people **connect with their heart** and **release the things that hold them back** from being their greatest version of themselves. Combining the ***unconditional love*** of a mother and the ***tell-it-like-it-is honesty*** of a best friend, Sunny helps people move into a higher vibration of living... *and* a higher vibration of **Being**. Using her spiritual and intuitive gifts, she shines a light on the areas of lack, fear and insecurity. Sunny feels strongly that at the heart of these issues is a lack of ***Self-Love***. By reflecting the **true nature** of her clients back to them — **which IS Love** — they can experience, and then allow in that unconditional love, and begin to heal themselves.

In December 2003, Sunny founded Sunlight Alliance LLC, a spiritual teaching and healing center based in Glendale, Arizona. Following her intuitive guidance, Sunny created a place where people could get to know themselves, learn how to find and follow their personal spiritual path, recognize and own their natural intuitive gifts, and cultivate a spiritual connection with loved ones who have passed on. Sunny teaches her students that even in moments of adversity, we are not alone; our angels, guides, and loved ones are here to help us.

Sunny is the author of 16 books, including the best-selling books *Invoking the Archangels* and *The Love Never Ends*. She teaches all over the world on the subjects of **Intuition, Healing the Heart, Angels, and Self-Love**. Sunny has been featured internationally on television and radio shows and has appeared in the award-winning documentary *Sacred Journey of the Heart*. Her most recent television endeavor has been starring in *"A Séance with…"* on Lifetime Movie Network (LMN). Sunny's latest book and course, ***DETOX Your Life—A 44-Day Mind, Body, Spirit Detox*** was released in January 2016. For more information about Sunny, please go to www.sunnydawnjohnston.com

🌸 Don't Let Your Weight Determine Your Value

Have you ever had this experience? You wake up, ready for a great day. You have lots of To Do's and some fun plans with friends and you are ready to get going. You are all set for your day, but there's just one thing you must do first. You must get on the scale. You don't WANT to, you certainly don't NEED to, but... **YOU HAVE TO!!!**

So, you take your shoes off, all of your clothes off, and your jewelry. You go to the bathroom, get as much out as possible (so the weight is the lowest possible) and then you head to the scale... the dreaded scale. You look at the number, and you are **UP ONE POUND!!!!!!**

And it is the end of the world. Now, you know FOR SURE that it's going to be a bad day. The scale just told you so. And in a few precious moments, your To Do list and your friends are all pushed to the side as you berate and degrade yourself for "gaining" a pound or two". You have scale self-sabotage. Can you relate?

This was my life for about 15 years. I struggled with weight issues, body-shaming, body acceptance, self-worth, self-esteem. You name it. I've actually been on both sides of this struggle... the fat side and the skinny side and what I realized was neither side was easier. The thing that is interesting is that when I weighed over 170 pounds, I knew for sure that when I lost weight, I would never feel depressed, obsessed or down again. I knew that the scale would have no power over me because life would be GREAT. I wouldn't feel BAD about my body if I just weighed under 130. I was convinced of that. Several years later, when I weighed 110 pounds, I felt the same feeling about my body. I had the same negative self-talk. I just wanted to feel ok in my own skin. That was an experience I wasn't familiar with and one that I desperately wanted.

You know how it is, right? You have a moment in time or a picture that is locked into your memory, never to be released. Mine was at the age of 15 with my best friend, Shelly. Shelly was on the dance team—a cute, bubbly, thin, popular girl. By this time, spring of 1986, I had quit high-school, was working full time, was depressed and had thoughts of not wanting to be in my body. I wanted to be seen as a happy-go-lucky girl, but I was miserable inside... and out. I remember the day, and the picture that was taken that day. It is burned into my mind of how fat I really was. It wasn't a very flattering picture of either of us really. The shirts I picked out to cover up my fat made Shelly look big too, but I was ok with that. To be honest, it made me feel a little better about myself since she didn't look AS thin as she really was. What stands out to me when that picture appears in my mind, is how sad I was behind that big body and that fake smile. I hated pictures and there are only a handful of pictures I took as a teen. I simply refused to take them. I felt disgusting and was embarrassed of my body. Have you ever felt that way? The funny thing is, if you knew me now, you would know that I LOVE pictures. I love the fun and play and joy and happiness … a big change from so long ago. But back then …

I HATED my body … Actually, I hated myself too. I felt that if I could just lose weight, just be "normal", just fit in more, then people would like me and I would be happy … finally. The day, and that picture, that is forever etched in my mind was the day we were going to Shelly's Sadie Hawkins High School dance (the only one I ever went to because I was never invited to a dance, because I was fat, or so I thought). Although I smiled for the camera, I was really hiding. I was hiding that fact that I had starved myself all week in an effort to "look better and be accepted". I was hiding the fact that I was so uncomfortable in my own skin that I wanted to go home and hide in my room.

I remember that day as if it were yesterday and the feelings of worthlessness that ran through my mind as I went to the scale to check my weight. I had to see if I was "worthy" of going to the dance or even being seen. When I stepped on the scale, it said I had gained a pound. How could that be? I literally had starved myself by eating less than 800 calories a day for over a week, and I gained a pound? I got dressed for the dance and became more and more obsessed with my feelings of inadequacy and comparison. I remember this day so vividly, because when I saw the pictures, I was mortified. I felt as though I should not exist … that I didn't deserve to breathe the same air as everyone else. This feeling of self-hate and loathing had become my normal. I have hundreds of memories just like this one. Not all are etched in my mind like this one, but man do I have some stories. I literally was obsessed with these feelings … and they became a theme in my life, until I healed my self-love issues.

It Was A Long Journey
Fast forward 10 years … 1996

By this time, I had gotten a better grip on my weight, but the self-talk never changed. I realized 170 pounds or 140 pounds didn't make a difference. It wasn't about the weight. I didn't like me. By this time I had a great husband, an active life and a wild and busy 6-year-old son. And, I was always sick. I had gotten a parasite a couple years earlier in Mexico, that took me four years to heal. I lost 30 pounds in the first two weeks and struggled for the next four years to get healthy. I never gained the weight back. I was the thinnest I had ever been in my adult life … 108 pounds. By my previous standards, I should be the happiest person ever, because I am the thinnest … but that was not the case. It was during this time that I began to really realize that weight wasn't my issue, it was my lack of self-love.

Earlier that year, I had earned 4 trips on a Caribbean cruise — all expenses paid and a beautiful balcony suite — a huge room by cruise standards. I was the top supervisor with a party plan company, House of Lloyd. The trouble was, I struggled with feeling worthy of the FREE trips and the luxury of staying in one of the best rooms on the ship … and all of the attention too. Being the youngest and most successful supervisor in the company's history brought up feelings of inadequacy and judgment. I felt as if I needed to PROVE I was good enough to everyone else somehow.

I was doing pretty well, with my thoughts of deserving and appreciation... or so I thought. I really tried to prepare myself to take it all in, reminding myself that I deserved this trip and I needed to allow myself to enjoy it. The trip would be a special time for me and my husband. We had a great week of vacationing ahead of us. I was excited. We boarded the cruise ship, went into our cabin, and wow was it was BEAUTIFUL! Everything was great... I was relaxed and joyful, anticipating the coming events. That is, until I noticed that with this FABULOUS room... came a scale. **My greatest self-sabotage tool.** Right in my beautiful little cabin. The obsessive thoughts started.

I made an agreement with myself that I would not step on that scale the entire trip. I did NOT want to feel bad about myself and I "KNEW" how it would turn out. So, I put it in the bottom drawer... so as not to be tempted. Outta sight, outta mind I thought. But, it haunted me. I really wanted to just see "how I was doing". The judge and jury within me wanted to tell my confidence to take a hike, but I wouldn't let it. I distracted myself by going to dinner. At dinner, although I was happy, the thoughts of what I couldn't or shouldn't eat overshadowed the entire experience. I remember eating very little, not wanting it to "show" in my tight formal dress. My thoughts were completely focused on the food—really, on what I couldn't have—but I was also proud of myself for not eating too much. Whatever too much is for a 108 pound girl, right?

BUT... After dinner, with the "undeserving of good" feelings rolling around in my head and heart, I gave in. I gave in to that self-shaming, berating, mean voice that always spoke louder than my kind and supportive voice... and it won. I walked into my cabin and pulled the scale out of the drawer. They whole time thinking to myself, **"Don't do it Sunny."** The negative voice got the best of me though, and I got on that scale. I weighed two pounds more than the day we had left our house. I could literally feel myself shrink inside. Although I "knew" I was ONLY 110 pounds, and at 5'7 (almost) that was underweight, it didn't matter. My head kicked in.

I was bad, and wrong and worthless. I felt like that fat teenager that wanted to hide. I heard that berating critical voice in my head telling me I wasn't good enough That same voice that told me I didn't deserve good in my life and that I wasn't deserving of self-love or positive attention. As I looked in the mirror, at this 110-pound woman, I saw the tree trunk legs that my dad would "poke fun" at me about.

All I did was step on the scale and everything, in one swoop changed. Has that ever happened to you? One negative belittling thought and your whole day, week or life changes.

That night I got extremely sick—puking my guts out, diarrhea... for three days, until I was so dehydrated I had to go to the infirmary and get a shot to stop the vomiting and diarrhea. At that time I called it sea sickness. Now I know better. Now I know that I was rejecting all of the good in my life, literally pushing/puking it away because I didn't feel deserving of it. I literally made myself sick, unknowingly. It was my way, unconsciously, of sabotaging myself and getting what I really deserved ... nothing good. I was experiencing the contrast between my heart and who I knew that I truly was, and my head and who I thought I should be. It was an ugly reality. I laid in my beautiful cabin for three days of our 7-day vacation — isolated, sick, and stuck.

Stuck because for me, I gave my power away to the scale. This little device that measures if you are "good enough" today or not. That was what the scale had become in my world. I had based my life on what the "scale" said I was or wasn't. I made decisions based on what it said, almost daily. If the scale showed me down a pound or two, then I would go out and have fun. If it was up a pound or two, then I would stay home and hide. It was torture. My mind tortured me ... and I let it.

Fast Forward 20 years ... 2016

So, why am I sharing my story with you? What's the point? First of all, to let you know that if you relate to any of these stories ... I get it. I KNOW how you feel and what I want you to know is that you can release that feeling. It isn't about the weight and it never will be about the weight. It is about the energy/emotion within. It is possible to heal. It is possible to take your power back from the scale, the critical voices, the old patterns. **The mom or dad in your head. IT IS POSSIBLE!!!!!!!!! I am living, breathing, happy, loving, healthy proof.**

I won't bullsh*t you and tell you that it's easy. It wasn't. It took a lot of time, energy and **dedication to ME.** It took me sitting with the old stories and rewriting the messages, recreating the voices and reminding myself of my own innate value. I AM NOT THIS BODY. I love this body ... now, but I am NOT this body. I am **Spirit** within this body. We are a team and I am forever grateful for every experience that has brought me to today. To **THIS** exact moment.

Today, I love and embrace my body. It has been a sacred amazing vessel for my journey. It isn't perfect, but man, for what I have put it through it sure is perfect for me. It's still carrying me through this life in a beautiful way. I am beyond grateful. What I have learned as I have walked this journey is that as I began to have gratitude for my body, my body would respond. As I was kind, my body showed kindness by releasing pain and disease. As I was gentle, my body would allow me to experience more peace and less stress. As I was loving, my body would relax and release. It was amazing. My body and I have become friends. We are on the same team — and when you get on the same team as your body, when you get that Body, Mind, Spirit Connection ... it is a powerful force for change!

Most importantly, what I have learned is this: Everything that happens to the body is an effect of the mind and the emotions!!!!!!!! Therefore, when you get those into a healthy loving vibration, the body shifts ... it has to. Be kind and loving to yourself. Surround yourself with loving kindness, within as well as without. Your body is listening to everything you say. It was never about the body, the weight or the disease. It has always been about seeing the utterly beautiful amazing person you are. When you see, and know, and hear and feel that truth my friend ... When you LOVE that person, YOU, wholeheartedly ... When you honor your mind and spirit and treat your body as a friend ... You will have self-love. And then you will know that your value has always been because **you are you.** There is no way to measure the greatness within—no measuring device can do that. There is no need to compare yourself to anything or anyone. There simply is no comparison.

You are love and are loved my friend—always remember this truth!

This chapter is dedicated to you the reader. May your heart be blessed with insight, awareness and amazing aha's as you travel this journey of life ... by putting one foot in front of the other.

"One of the greatest journeys you will take in life is the journey from your head to your heart."

DIANE S. CHRISTIE

DIANE S. CHRISTIE, SCP, is delightfully retired from her Human Resources Manager career. She was a past recipient of the Governor's award for Leadership in Management; all now happy memories.

As an author, a licensed Heal Your Life® coach and workshop leader, her personal mission is to 'Inspire and conspire with others to claim our prosperity, in *all* forms.' She loves to partner with people worldwide to create abundant life results, one experience and one conversation at a time.

Diane currently lives in Olympia, Washington. She and husband, Bill, know and understand the Oneness of us all. New adventures and heart connections are their life's 'work'. As global citizens, they are out and about the world as much as possible being curious, sharing joy, living peacefully.

Contact Diane at dschristie8@gmail.com or through Facebook at Diane Sundt Christie.

❦ The Jetty

We honor our parents by carrying their best
forward and laying down the rest.

~BRUCE SPRINGSTEEN

A Story Of Deliberate Creation.

October, 2014. Here we were, in a suburb of the Toronto, Ontario metropolis, in a widely spread out cemetery. The cousins' group searched intensely for grave markers. We walked, in straight lines and in circles. We each took small sections of the cemetery and crisscrossed the other's paths, seeking landmarks and specific names. Finally, after close to two hours of inch by inch, foot by foot coverage of significant areas of grounds and mounds, the flat, horizontal gravestones were found. Tears of frustration were released in a choreographed shout of jubilation. Then homage.

Driving away from that experience, none of us could barely speak. Yet, we insisted we were ready to continue our journey. Through tense laughter, growling and agitation, we all gave a nod to 'tomorrow's another day'. Someone laughed, nervously. Words were uttered: 'What do we want? Surely, we have a guardian angel. We need Vision and focus. We need guidance.'

Twenty-four hours, one overnight stay and a couple of hundred westerly kilometers later, we arrived in the green, rolling hills and expansive farming area of Bruce County. The rental cottage was on a pebbly inlet shore of Lake Huron. We had come to stay and were on a mission. The way into town included a stop at the local visitor center for a map, and hopefully insights. Sharing our quest with the receptionist, we asked for help, took notes. We focused on finding information with grace and ease. With each success, we affirmed '*but, of course.*'

Back in the car, directions in hand, we drove off, headed for the Town of Walkerton Cemetery. Once there, Jim guided the car slowly along on the tree lined cement drive as we craned our necks and peered, left and right, at marble markers. The upright gravestones were of many shapes, sizes. Some stones were a soft reddish color, some an overcast gray, some light coffee color. Names and dates of birth and death were neatly engraved on each. Some stones had two names on them. Everything reflected a shine from late Fall afternoon sun.

Barely 200 yards along the cemetery road, we looked to our right, out the car window. There it was, at eye level, the one we were seeking. The car stopped and the three cousins, Pat, Jim, Bill, promptly got out of the car. They shivered in the chilly autumn air, took a few steps. They gathered together in a half circle in front of the almost burgundy colored, square, upright marble gravestone. The etched name was that of their Irish immigrant great-grandfather, standing amongst several graves with the same surname. I joined them in viewing, as a cousin spouse, as a witness.

A short distance away, off to the left, the groundskeeper was riding and deftly maneuvering the bright green and yellow John Deere lawnmower. I waved, walked over to chat with him and ask questions. He was Dave; he had been caring for the cemetery lawns and gardens for many years. After sharing with him who we were, why we were there, I asked about a certain gravestone in the family plot, the one with no 'end' date yet. Dave said that when her time came, the empty plot was for his aunt. Oh my, it clicked that Dave, the groundskeeper, was actually a cousin of sorts to Pat, Jim, and Bill!

Then off to the local library which was 'coincidentally' hosting an introductory genealogy discussion right when we arrived. We met many people. Doors opened. Information 'showed up.' Schedules fit perfectly. Appointments were arranged. The following few days were full of connections ... with librarians who searched County records; with historians who explained community settlement. At her farmhouse, we visited with a genealogist cousin, complete with family artifacts, and who completed the story of why their family left Ireland. That cousin arranged a meet-up with more cousins at another family farm. On a genealogy chart, some cousins were closer than others; cousins none the less. Everyone involved seemed excited about meeting each other and grateful for family facts that came to light. Amongst shared memories, some questions were answered; some were not, probably never would be. Happily, though, our cousins' vision of meaningful connections had come to pass. *But, of course.*

Witnessing Pat, Jim, and Bill's family search and 'roots' experience was personally exciting and impactful. During almost every month following, I thought of the Walkerton Cemetery, the family gravestones, discussions and findings about lineage. The cousins' descriptive words and phrases such as 'journey of family discovery', 'connected', 'meaningful coincidences', 'loving spirit', 'sense of history' imprinted themselves in my brain. One phrase in particular, 'my place in the Universe', profoundly stirred a curiosity gene.

Memories swirled. I thought more of my own history, my roots in Seattle. I fondly remembered Mom and Dad. They were married over 65 years. Dad was a CPA, and worked independently in his own accounting practice. For 32 years, Mom worked in Dad's office. She was the family glue; the all-around organizer, keeper of order and stories. They died in 2010, Mom 64 hours after Dad.

Through thought and deed, Dad and Mom each consistently conveyed many messages about successful living. Work hard, study and go to university, be kind to people, and opportunities abound. They themselves were children of immigrants. Take a look, within two generations we were living 'the American dream'.

I remembered visiting Mom and Dad one warm August evening, in the early 1990's. We sat outside, rocking on their backyard swing as Dad reminisced about his father, Odin. Although Grandpa Odin hadn't said much about his childhood, Dad did remember some stories about Grandpa's early life. Yes, it had been hard to leave his family behind in Norway, sail by himself at age 20, to a new land, to make a new life. Dad talked about his mother, Mary, and of the few stories she had told him about her childhood. It had been hard to leave her family behind in Sweden, sail by herself at age 16 to a new land, to make a new life.

I knew Grandma Mary better than Grandpa Odin. She and I spent a lot of time together, after school and on weekends. We shared many adventures: riding a city bus to downtown Seattle, shopping in big department stores, having restaurant lunches together. We frequently watched the rock and roll TV show, American Bandstand. She taught me to polka. It was fun to dance with each other around her living room. Grandpa Odin often was in the room with us, seated in his hard-backed, stuffed chair. He was minimally mobile and experiencing Parkinson's disease. Through tremors, he smiled at our joyful movements.

Another memory stuck. It was a story that Mom repeated. Apparently, at some point in time, Grandma Mary had been upset with and chided Grandpa Odin because he sent money home to Norway. Grandma thought he should keep his money at this home, for his American family. Over the years, that story morphed a bit, took on a different meaning. In my mind, Grandpa Odin became kind of a 'neglectful' man, a 'less than' provider for his family. My feelings for him reflected family lore.

 Making a movie in my mind about how I want to see my life.
I think I'll write it down ...

~MOVIE IN MY MIND, LUKAS NELSON, JIM BROWN

As time passed, an idea emerged: 'I want to do that same kind of trip; have my own experience.' This thought was occasionally intense, persistently present.

With these memories, that insistent poking whisper of an idea became a call to action. It was time to make a decision. I thought an updated visit to Grandma Mary's birthplace and roots was important on this journey of discovery. My second and most recent visit there was long ago, in 1984. A letter to my Swedish cousins asked if we could visit. They replied with a resounding 'Yes!' After Sweden, we would travel to and through Norway, to find Grandpa Odin's birthplace. In my mind, Mary and Odin together again was symbolic of 'my place in the Universe'.

February, 2016. With airline reservations made, detailed planning began in earnest. Time to sort through a box of memorabilia for clues. There was the Bible given to Grandpa Odin, by his father, when he left Norway in 1904. In my Dad's papers, there were a few postcards, a letter or two, photos of the family farm nestled on a serene inlet. Reading notes, asking questions and studying a map, I saw that Grandpa Odin's birthplace/farm was in the Afjord area, about 2.5 hours northwest of Trondheim. There were vintage

Polaroid photos, from 1967, of Dad with his cousin, Tor, standing in front of Odin's family home.

In this treasure trove of papers, I found receipts, in Odin's name. Yes, receipts for money sent to his father, in Norway. Apparently, the old family story was true.

My friend, Debbie, had a friend who translated the documents. Using Norwegian government public archives, Debbie researched Odin and produced his genealogy chart going back more than seven generations. Staring at that chart, tears welled up when I read his name. Suddenly, I saw Odin with new eyes. He had a grandpa too. At that moment, he became more than the chair ridden man with Parkinson's.

Google was a constant companion as scores of hours were spent in search of information. On the municipal website of Afjord, Norway, the Services directory listed a job title of Director of Culture and the employee's name. I wrote to that employee and asked for any assistance. The request was forwarded to a local community historian, Helge. That inquiry began a multi month correspondence as Helge researched records and provided more family data. He and I set a date to meet up in Afjord, in mid-September.

With more electronic sleuthing, there emerged a fisheries scientist with the last name Sundt. That is Grandpa Odin's surname, my middle name. Using the scientist's business email address, I wrote to her with essentially this query: 'My father visited Trondheim in 1967 and met up with his cousin Tor and wife, Nore. Are you and I related?' Seemed like a long shot, but unless I asked, how would I know? A week later, a return email, from a person named Catherine. Catherine said the scientist's secretary read my letter. The scientist and I were not related. *However,* the secretary's own next door neighbor was named Jan Sundt, *and* his parents were named Tor and Nore. Catherine was Jan's sister.

Thus, began email correspondence with Catherine. We became Facebook friends. We saw each other's pictures. We shared stories of our lives. On a genealogy chart, my friend Debbie demonstrated that Catherine and I were third cousins. In our exchanges, I shared with Catherine about the planned meeting with Helge, in Afjord. Surprisingly, *or not,* Catherine stated that she and her two brothers each had a cottage in the Afjord area. She offered us transportation to Afjord and an overnight stay at her cottage. We accepted. Even more, Catherine and Helge met up electronically, and in person, to plan for our September rendezvous. *But, of course.*

I believed purpose, preparation, inspiration, and lots of imagination were key to a fulfilling experience. Seeking ideas and support, in addition to googling, I reached out to many people from all times and aspects of my life. A childhood friend connected me with his cousins in Oslo. A church friend connected me with her daughter in Bergen. I shared my plans and ideas with anyone who would listen. I asked for support.

Because a focus of this trip was to learn more about and claim my Norwegian-ness, I read books about Scandinavian immigrants, their challenges, successes, and failures. I reminisced my way around and through Nordic Fest at a local university while eating lefse, meatballs and lingonberry jam. I attended a genealogy course, joined three Norway specific

Facebook groups, studied a Lonely Planet travel book, read a Rick Steves travel book, attended a local Sons of Norway meeting, and delved into whatever else seemed relevant.

One day while waiting outside a building here in my city, Olympia, Washington, I looked up and over to another window in the building. There was a sign for a travel agency, specialists in Scandinavian travel. The owner, Natalie, enthusiastically caught the Vision and became part of my 'team'. She had great suggestions and arranged transportation and accommodations for our exact wants and needs. It was happening, this making my own movie, with grace and ease.

❧ People don't take trips. Trips take people.

~SIGN IN HURTIGRUTEN LOBBY

August, 2016. My cousin, Stefan, and his wife, Lena, picked us up at our hotel in Kalmar, Sweden. We drove to their summer home, Grandma Mary's birthplace, on the island of Oland. What followed were four days of cousins' conversations, reunions with more cousins, parties, family chart sharing. At a local bicentennial celebration, we even were able to shout out a greeting to the king and queen of Sweden. We visited villages and sites where family once lived and worked, where some still live and work. And, of course, to the local Lutheran Church and cemetery where marble history stands in witness. As we left Grandma Mary's birthplace, I took a stone from the driveway.

We moved on and for 16 days, we travelled in Norway. We explored our way northward, experiencing much joy along the way. The public trains and various water transports were efficient, clean, and comfortable. We repeatedly gasped at the pristine fjord beauty. People were kind and helpful. There's nothing quite like the experience of standing on a street corner, turning and twisting a street map, turning and twisting our heads, desperate to understand where we were, locate where we wanted to be. Someone often approached with an offer of assistance, heartily welcomed. Our bodies and souls were filled with people, places, things; a cornucopia of culture and connection with past and present.

On a Saturday, our Hurtigruten ship docked in Trondheim. Imagine our nerves and excitement (they said theirs too!) leading up to the first meeting with Catherine and one of her brothers, Tor Erik. On that same day, in our hotel lobby, we all met and introduced ourselves. Then we hugged. I shed some tears, of pure joy, excitement, release of tension. We all walked to a historic, well-known local coffee shop. Within a few blocks, Catherine and I had linked arms, were laughing together, and conversing as best we could. The next day, we enjoyed dinner and met more family. Our cousin connection was becoming a bond.

On Monday, we three cousins, with Catherine's husband Torgeir, and my husband Bill, packed up the cousin's car and headed out for a grand and purposeful adventure. First there was the ferry ride across the aptly named Trondheimsfjorden. Then the road trip northwest for the rest of the 2.5 hours to their cottage, in the Afjord area. So many twists and turns in the windy road. We looked up to the cloudless sky and down on the scenic earth. The sheer, solid rock, dramatic beauty of coastal Norway is breathtaking. We laughed, ate lunch, explored beaches and communities, together.

That night at Catherine and Torgeir's cottage, we finally, happily met Helge. He and I had now corresponded for more than six months. A friendship had developed. For our meeting, Helge brought books he had authored. His books documented research about various area farms and family histories. As Helge and I studied my genealogy chart together, he referred to his Book 2. There in the family farm history, and subsequent documents, were statements about Odin's mother reclaiming her home. She somehow paid back taxes owed on the farm. *Could this be the same money that Grandma Mary questioned decades earlier?*

September 12, 2016, Tuesday. Six of us drove to Grandpa Odin's birthplace and farm. Just as Helge promised, the owners were there waiting to meet and greet us. Promptly, we three cousins, Catherine, Tor Erik, and I, gathered in front of Odin's house. We stood with arms linked, in the place where our fathers stood together in 1967. The house was now covered in chipped white paint and a rusting corrugated roof. The grass was a bright green, garden flowers a soft baby pink, barns a faded red, sky and water each a clear, cobalt blue. We all walked the land, put our hands in the dirt, rinsed our hands in the inlet water.

> Life shrinks or expands in proportion to one's courage.
>
> ~ANAIS NIN

On the collection of slate gray basalt rocks that built the small jetty, I stood in respectful silence. This was the very jetty on which Grandpa Odin stood, in 1904, Bible likely in hand. I could visualize him reading the inscription on the inside leaf of that book. It read, in part, " ... your hard days and the bad days to come. It doesn't make me happy that you are leaving. Your father wishes you everything good for your long journey. The Lord be with you and take care of you."

Imagine with me. What was Odin feeling? Were there others, if so who, at the jetty for his leave taking? What were they each thinking at the moment of departure? Did any or all embrace each other? Were there any tears or did stoicism reign supreme at the moment?

Odin stepped off that jetty, into a small boat. Someone in that small boat rowed him away from the inlet, to a larger boat, waiting out in the fjord. A still larger boat and other transport, took him and his father's sentiments, to the ocean liner, SS Southwark, to sail to Nord Amerika. I felt awe and admiration for this man, his courage.

And the rest of the story is ... I took a stone from the farm driveway. Back in Afjord town, we visited the local Lutheran Church where Grandpa Odin was christened. Helge introduced me to more cousins who live there still. I said many heartfelt goodbyes.

Back at home, I studied the international money transfer paperwork. All seventeen receipts documented transactions which occurred *before* Grandpa and Grandma were married. Did he send more money *after* he was married? Who knows? I no longer cared. I had learned new information and changed my mind about Grandpa Odin. I now believed

Grandpa had long contributed to keeping the struggling farm afloat. His contributions had somehow helped return the farm to his mother and into the family's name.

What I understood as a child was different now. The man I once thought was 'neglectful' was indeed something and someone else. Evidence indicates he fulfilled a sense of obligation to assist in his family's troubled times, even from a distance. I saw his beautiful, humble beginnings. I understood how he lived. For him to live fully, he had to leave. I know how he died. My circle of understanding had gone from half to full.

As the Hurtigruten sign promised, the trip 'took me'. Like a current day, Sherlock Holmes tale, this journey of discovery followed clues to people, circumstances, and life decisions… all contributors and building blocks to my life today. Similar to my understanding of the lives of Odin and Mary, I value autonomy, achievement, adventure, connection. In the name of charting my own course, I too have left familiar surroundings, moved to a new land, began a new life. Twice.

 Life is really very simple. What we give out, we get back.

~LOUISE HAY

People often ask 'Where did you get that idea? Why did you do that? How did you get what you wanted?' Provocative questions for sure. In reply, these questions are asked: What do you really want to do, be, experience? Do you know your own truth and live it? How do your actions align with your desires?

For those who express interest in learning another approach to living, the following information has been useful:

My personal creed is: Seek. Find. Claim.

Seek: Be curious and demonstrate it; actively engage my mind; be open to and fiercely search out new information and experiences. Some of my seeking activity is legendary. I 'go for it'.

Find: Know, in my body and mind, when something or someone makes sense, or not; determine when information, people or things are relevant; trust my gut and intuition.

Claim: Be present, every moment of my life. Know truth and Truth. Be around others who challenge me to grow. Apply life lessons, vigilantly. Integrate new information, people, experiences. To Claim may require a rewrite of 'my story' about something or someone, for the story that is more truthful, revealing, enriching.

 More than intelligence or persistence or connections, curiosity has allowed me to live the life I wanted.

~BRIAN GRAZER

Recently, the Unity Church of Olympia minister, Rev. Terry Murray, said "I wish ... " can be an expression of regret. Indeed. If I think or speak those words, it's a clue to be alert and urgently conscious in my own evolution. Life expresses like this: Idea becomes Vision, becomes Plan, becomes Action, becomes Results and Fulfillment. Interesting isn't it that *no* forward action also has its own result: life the same as always.

Each day, I stand on some sort of jetty, ready to Seek. Find. Claim. Then onward to make my movie a reality ... I know the Universe **always** has my back. And yours.

But, of course.

Dedicated to those who seek, ye shall find.

Debbie G. ... Odin's Spirit and I thank you for nurturing my curiosity. Look what happened.

Stefan and Lena ... Tak sa mycket for meaningful kindnesses and generous hospitality. Your beliefs and actions to restore, preserve and share family history is a profound legacy.

Catherine ... Tusen takk for your letter, your trust and grace. We are in The Circle of Life, together.

Tor Erik ... Tusen takk. We all rewrote a definition of family, didn't we? My man, Bill, and I love you too.

Torgeir ... Tusen takk. Cheerleader and organizer who kept us on task and schedule. We miss you, your joyous laughter. A glass of wine awaits you.

Helge ... Tusen takk. Your interest, knowledge, and curiosity were pillars of our success.

Odin and Mary ... In respect.

Mom and Dad ... In gratitude.

Bill ... As witness.

DAWN MICHELE JACKSON

DAWN MICHELE JACKSON is a registered nurse, grief specialist, writer and practitioner of multiple healing modalities.

Dawn resides in Portland, Oregon where she enjoys hiking and exploring the Pacific Northwest with her son, friends, and family. As well as working with Veterans in her nursing profession she also helps individuals recover from grief as a Certified Grief Recovery Specialist by teaching clients new tools and ways to work through loss.

Her own spiritual journey began over a decade ago after a painful divorce and the realization that she desired to find new ways to navigate life. While working on her own growth she became passionate about passing on the gifts and wisdom she learned along the way. Although she enjoys working one on one with clients, she's most passionate about writing. It's in writing that she gains clarity, insight, peace and rediscovers her true self.

tobelieveinyou@gmail.com
www.dawnmichelejackson.com

The Tree of Magic, Wisdom, and Love

Waking up she had the realization that in only a week it would be Christmas. Upon looking out the window, there was still evidence of the snowfall from earlier in the week that had all but paralyzed the city. The house was quiet except for the usual morning meowing from her faithful friend requesting breakfast. Her son was out on an adventure with friends for the weekend leaving much time to ponder her own thoughts and present life.

Walking downstairs she remembered her efforts the night before to save the Christmas tree. The needles had curled into each other becoming dry and brittle as if to say, "we're tired, we've had enough." Seeing that the tricks she had read about last night on the internet hadn't seemed to perk up the dying tree she let out a heavy sigh. The hot water with aspirin and sugar dissolved in it hadn't been absorbed by the new cuts deep in the trunk. Pine needles appeared scattered over the presents but the branches were still using whatever strength they had left to hold onto the ornaments which had been collected over the last four and a half decades.

The tree was much more than just decoration for the holidays this year; it was a representation of her life. It was easy to see how the ornaments represented people she loved, some no longer physically present on our earth. There were also ornaments that were bought on her travels around the world, those made by her son when he was little (which made them all the more precious) and those gifted to her by special people. But she knew there was much deeper meaning that this Christmas tree presently held.

The memories of ringing in the New Year 2016 held tight in her mind; there was so much hope for 2016 being an abundant year filled with much joy. But a week before Christmas looking at the tree she realized she was as tired as it appeared. Where did the year go?

She again remembered that there was much change this year and that Christmas would look a lot different without either of her parents present. Her Dad had suffered with cancer and passed away during the summer while her Mom had moved just a month prior. To add to the list, she was on call for the whole Christmas holiday making any plans she had to celebrate with those she loved uncertain at best. These things, along with stress in other areas of her life, made her wonder why a simple thing like keeping her Christmas tree alive until the holiday seemed so difficult. "Really? Can't this one thing be beautiful, and right?" The truth was that it was beautiful if she chose to see it.

Sitting on the couch snuggled in a blanket she gazed at the Christmas tree. By standing back and observing from a distance, all she saw was the beauty. She wasn't close enough to see the curled pine needles; instead she saw the beautiful, rich green color enhanced by the white lights. The angel on top reminded her that there are always angels above watching over us, even if we can't see them or feel their presence. Each ornament represented someone or something she loved in life. Without standing so close that she could put the tree under a microscope its beauty was revealed. It may have been a bit dried out and at the end of its life but it still represented beauty and love for those who wished to see it. What a realization that the Christmas tree this year had so much symbolism and meaning which reflected her own life.

She spent the day pondering many things. She reflected upon how it can be so easy, when things go unexpectedly in life and our dreams, hopes, and expectations are shattered, to only see what we perceive as "wrong." Putting our own lives under a microscope enlarges things for our view but if we focus on those pieces that are less than desirable we miss the beauty. Standing back and observing from a distance gives us perspective; it allows us to see the whole which is undoubtedly coupled with joy and sadness, peace, and struggle as well as many other opposites. We cannot have a full life without experiencing its entirety, which means In order to grow we are given opportunities which stretch us as well as times of peace and rest. The important thing to remember is that it's not one given moment that defines our life; it's the compilation of each experience, memory, and moment.

Looking at the Christmas tree brought back so many of those memories, moments, and experiences from the past. It might be easy to get stuck in "what was", but when we live in the past we rob ourselves of what lies in the present moment. Some may say the past was more joyful than the present which can be a valid point. The truth is that when we are stuck in the details, having our lives under a microscope, we miss what beauty the Universe is sending to us. It's completely possible to have our blinders on and not recognize what's trying to show up.

Remembering that everything which shows up in her life has a message to bring brought a smile to her face. Not only was an angel shining down on her from the top of the tree but a ceramic heart sat on a branch right below it symbolizing love. "I've lived a good life," she thought to herself. She realized that by standing back and seeing representations of different parts of her past it was easy to take any focus off what "isn't" present and relish in all that has been with the knowing that in another four decades she will have even twice the amount of experiences and memories to look back upon. She dug deep to open her heart to all the beauty before her, in her, and around her.

Reflecting back, she remembered what someone special had told her long ago and that was that every experience in life is a "gift." When those words had first touched her ears she wanted to scream because they came at a particularly painful time in her life. But over the years she came to see the truth in what was shared. Maybe it was easier to see the gifts in those magical, joyful, love filled moments but those aren't the only days which bring gifts. She reminded herself how over the years every struggle has been a gift in its own way because it led her to where she is today.

She remembered feeling a heaviness in her heart during past holidays but this year was different. Even though many changes had occurred during the year she welcomed the holidays, the love, the celebration. She looked forward to making new memories, sharing new traditions and spending time with those she loved. She realized that perhaps it is in change that we can see the true gifts presenting themselves in our lives. Just like in the movie "'It's a Wonderful Life" we can become so focused that we fail to see the absolute love and beauty before us.

Still sitting on the couch, looking at the beautifully decorated tree and hanging stockings above the fireplace, she knew how she wanted to live her life. She wanted to live it as the gift that it is in each and every moment. She wanted to cherish each moment, even those that feel less than perfect, because they are all part of the gift of life she was given. There was no doubt in her mind that with an open heart she could always see the beauty and love that surrounded her. And with that knowing she snuggled down into the blanket, with her kitty curled up on her chest, looking forward to the days ahead and spending time with those she loved.

Dedicated to my Dad, Wick, for when I look at my tree I see so much that reminds me of you. Thank you for giving me life and for watching on me from above; I know you are always there.

Thank you to my family, my friends and all those people who have touched my life over the past four and a half decades. For without all of you I would not be who I am today; I'm grateful for your presence, your love, your support, and the memories I've made with all of you.

MICHELLE MULLADY

MICHELLE MULLADY is a Spiritual Teacher, International Best-Selling Author, Master Energy Therapist, Angel Intuitive, and Transformational Healing Workshop Leader who specializes in helping adults and adolescents to create healthy and fulfilling lives through spiritual life coaching, energy therapy, intuitive direction, angel messenger readings, healing breathwork, simple guided meditation practices, affirmations, and prayer. By virtue of her individualized, holistic (body-mind-emotions-spirit) approach to life coaching, she can support you to enhance every area of your existence—relationships, health, finances, intimacy, career, and spiritual growth—all while living one day at a time in a busy world.

MichelleMullady.com

Unite With Serenity

> Wherever I go and whatever I do, I witness the obvious and
> subtle expressions of serenity. I allow serenity to guide every
> action. I allow serenity to pervade every thought. I allow serenity
> to soothe every word. I am a living expression of serenity.
>
> ~MICHELLE MULLADY

Ah, inner peace—what a pleasing contemplation! Feeling tranquil, satisfied and in harmony with yourself and your world. Merrily observing life from a place of calm and ease. But feeling peaceful inside—is it truthful? Can it really be achieved? The world around you are continually transforming. Through mass media and the internet, you are being exposed to how humanity, on all parts of the globe, is being challenged on a daily basis in a variety of forms. Many people believe that it is normal to feel constantly frazzled, restless, fed-up, afraid, unhappy, resentful towards everyone who's ever treated them badly, and generally fraught with surviving from one day to the next. Well, if that's what life feels like for you, then I have great news—life does not need to be that way. It was never *meant* to be. At this particular point, in history, your soul has chosen to manifest into human form during a unique and powerful time, because the world is having a spiritual awakening. Your individual journey is an important part of the growth process for the whole. There is a massive call for more enlightenment. Feeling inner peace *is* a realistic expectation, and it *is* attainable—for you, me and everybody. No matter how you feel about yourself and your life right now, you can begin to turn it around. Intuitively, multitudes find themselves on the spiritual path attempting to discover the support they need. Skeptics are filling meditation groups, yoga studios, and self-help workshops, and the call for "Peace on Earth" is growing stronger. It is your time to rise from within and bring forth more peace to the world by healing your own life. As each person awakens to the statement "let peace begin with me," larger masses will begin to vibrate with an energy that will heal the collective, releasing the need for the negativity and violence that corrodes us all.

Because of heightened conscious awareness, you, like many people, are undoubtedly on a quest for answers. I intend to guide you on the optimum path and help you to begin to free yourself from strife. I want to support you by offering you ways to clear your stress and fear quickly because having tools for creating fast shifts, that will lead you back to tranquility, is imperative in this day and age. I want to let you know that you can begin to restore your inner harmony and start experiencing life from a place of joy, contentment and happiness on a consistent basis, in the same way I have taught many individuals including myself to do. And it doesn't need to be difficult. It is as simple as learning to consciously choose to create daily present moments of peace.

Seven Soulful Methods for Achieving Serenity

 I stop for a moment, breathe into the stillness, and call silence to myself.

~MICHELLE MULLADY

People have various ways of seeking and finding serenity. What is exciting about the following techniques, I've chosen to share with you is that you can use them at any time to bring yourself back to a balanced center—even if you only have a few minutes to spare in what can so often feel like an overwhelming day.

1. Calming the Body with Breath and Thought

Let's begin with your breathing. Focus on your heart center and concentrate on your breath cycle for a few moments, quietly inhaling and exhaling through the heart. Using the simple rhythm of your breath, find the point of peace within, where all is calm and tranquil. Then, begin to repeat these words to yourself:

> *"Breathing in, I know I am breathing in. Breathing out, I know I am breathing out.*
> *Breathing in, my breath is deep and easy. Breathing out, my breath goes slowly.*
> *Aware of my body, I breathe in. Relaxing my body, I breathe out.*
> *Smiling to my body, I breathe in. Releasing any tension, I breathe out.*
> *Feeling joy, I breathe in. Feeling happy, I breathe out.*
> *Breathing in, I focus on the present moment.*
> *Breathing out, I know it is a beautiful moment."*
>   ~ Adapted from The Blooming of a Lotus by Thich Nhat Hanh

2. Simple prayers that will take your mind to that place of synchronization with your soul

Prayer is perhaps one of the best all-around tools used to raise your vibration, attract solutions, and calm the mind, body, emotions, and spirit. When used as a regular "back to basics" method for achieving serenity, it becomes daily food for the soul. The secret is to hold your prayers in your heart, and then release them to higher forces.

Here are three of my favorite prayers for manifesting tranquility:

Angel Prayer for Inner Peace

> *"Angels of Serenity, in the silence of this moment, I thank you for connecting me to the place within that is untouched by any form of turmoil or distress. Guide me to tune in to this inner reservoir of Divine Peace and allow serenity to soothe my soul as I rest in the fulfillment of God's love.*
>
> *May I listen to the quiet and feel the peaceful presence of God inside me. In these sacred moments of conscious communion with the Divine, lead me to understand that I can reconnect with this inner peace at any time throughout the day."*
>
> ~ Michelle Mullady

Serenity Prayer

> *"God grant me the serenity to accept the things I cannot change, the courage to change the things I can, and wisdom to know the difference."*
>
> ~ A Nondenominational Prayer

A Healing Prayer for Peace

> *"The light of God fills my mind;*
> *The life of God fills my body;*
> *The love of God fills my heart;*
> *The energy of God shines forth through me*
> *It cleanses, heals, purifies, renews, and revitalizes me now.*
> *I am at peace."*
>
> ~ Michelle Mullady

3. Mantras

Mantras—a powerful word, phrase, or sound vibration repeated to aid concentration while entering a deep state of meditation—are one way of returning to your center. Mantras when repeated in a state of relaxation touch and heal your mind, the sounds and thoughts align you with calmness.

Begin to investigate and value the words and prayers based in a spiritual practice that attracts you, the thoughts that work for you, that harmonize you with your joy-filled Divine Light. These will help you discover your connection with the universe, the flow of life, the certainty that all is well and pulsating at the highest vibrations when you seek to enter the silence. This is when you begin to see that you and your life are on track, that your birthright is to be a beacon of serenity. Now is the time to receive all the guidance and grace you need. The most widely known is the Sanskrit mantra "om" (or "aum"). Try chanting this word out loud to allow it to vibrate throughout your whole energy field. It will raise your vibration to a higher frequency.

You can also try silently saying the phrase "I am" on your in-breath and then the word "peace" on your out-breath. Other words such as "purity," "love" or "bliss" are also good choices. As you inhale with each "I am," imagine you're pulling in from the universe the spiritual power that follows. When you breathe out, feel the ascendency flooding your entire being.

4. Spend Time in Nature

By tuning into nature, you can access your true self and savor its vital contentment—allowing you to reach your full potential as a calm and energetic being. The idea that enjoying time in nature can make you feel better is intuitive. People who have been suffering from stress, tension, ill health, or a trauma can spend silent, contemplative moments in gardens, woods, community parks, the mountains, or near a body of water to heal. Nature is a source of beauty, which can give us a happiness that is inherently spiritual. Furthermore, nature's sights and sounds are often soothing, perhaps because they remind us of a heavenly alternative to the human world. Another reason for nature's value is that we ourselves are an innate part of it, though we often forget this. To bond with nature is to unite with the inner core of the self, where authentic relaxation dwells.

The uplifting qualities of tranquil natural environments have been praised in literature throughout the centuries. Become familiar with a pleasurable location near your home and make it a customary excursion destination: simply sit down for 20 minutes, letting your surroundings seep into your spirit; or go for a meditative walk alongside a river or the ocean. Embrace the setting with all of your senses—breathe in the smells, listen to the singing birds, taste the air, touch the soft earth, and observe the limitless array of splendid colors.

5. Schedule Downtime

Train yourself to let go and take regular breaks from our intense, fast-paced world by scheduling downtime. It is necessary to step away from the hustle and bustle of your busy life to create an opportunity to refresh yourself holistically. Doing nothing but relaxing, hanging out, and simple BEing in the present moment liberates you from fear and overwhelm, and reconnects you to the pace and peace of Universal flow. It will afford you the personal space you need to recharge your being on all levels.

6. Practice Meditation

Use this five-minute mini meditation anytime you desire to rejuvenate your being with the healing power of peace. Practice this exercise alone. Settle down in a tranquil place. Separate yourself from any possible distractions … cell phones, televisions, computers, people. Get comfortable. For example, create a cozy haven in your bed with soft pillows and blankets. My bliss is propping myself up in a comfy chair, warmed by the sun in my garden. Whatever you do, make it your own sacred space to rest in for a short while. Discover inner silence by getting quiet. Gradually relax your body as you slowly inhale, then exhale. For the duration of two minutes, solely focus on the air streaming into your nose and out via your mouth. Allow the circulation of your breath to bring you back to balance.

Begin to feel the energy held within. Place your hands over your solar plexus chakra and speak these words aloud:

> *"I now release anything that disturbs me. My body is still and centered. I expand my awareness to the earth and sea and sky, feeling my oneness with all that is. Spirit pours and shines through me, restoring peace to my soul and blessing the world. I am serene and in perfect harmony. I know that in Truth, all is well in my world, I am grateful."*
> ~ Empowering Prayers for Everyday Life

7. Aura Cleansing Baths

The harmful buildup of psychic pollution that comes from living in today's world can shadow your awareness and lower your energy. The idea that energy or vibrations can influence a person's reality is nothing new, so don't worry; it's neither invasive or damaging. Instead it is very beneficial as a regular part of energy body maintenance to take aura cleansing baths. Making time for this occasional practice will soothe your soul and assist you to increase your health and vitality, allowing you to return to flowing naturally in good vibes. My recipe for a peace-infused soak is to add one cup of Epsom salts along with ten drops of chamomile, 5 drops of lavender, and 3 drops of peppermint organic essential oils to a fully filled tub of hot water. Then, I light a few candles and play some relaxing music, effectively washing away the world for 20 to 30 minutes.

As you relax, you can pray for your healing angels to release all negativity and clear you of all energetic cords and attachments while you concentrate on filling your mind with positive affirmations.

Work with the rituals that help you believe that serenity is yours, rituals that connect you to the Divine in the universe. Invite peace to course through your days and nights.

My contribution to this book is dedicated to the everyday spiritual teachers who have walked this path throughout my lifetime. This includes my family, friends, colleagues, and global clients. The light and love I see in you is a reflection of my own inner truth.

A special thank you to my life partner, Mauricio Gonzalez, for his patience, commitment, and dedication to our relationship of love and healing. We have come so far together and I look forward to the many decades that lie ahead of us to enjoy your presence in my life. Te amo mi amor!

KIM RICHARDSON

KIM RICHARDSON is an author, teacher, motivational speaker, coach, mentor, ordained minister, and certified Mind Body Spirit Practitioner. Through sharing her own personal experiences, she empowers individuals to transform their lives.

She resides in Payson, Arizona, where she enjoys the warm weather and sunshine with her family. Her passion is helping people discover their true gifts and how to use them in the world. Kim facilitates workshops and coaches those looking to heal, forgive and expand.

kim@leadcoachinspire.com
www.leadcoachinspire.com

A Journey to Loving Yourself

Why is it so hard to love ourselves?

There may be various reasons for everyone as to why it is so hard to love ourselves. However, no matter the reasons, I often notice some very common themes. It all starts when we are very young. Did you feel loved growing up? Did a teacher, family or friends criticize you or tell you that you were not good enough? Were the relationships you built often one-sided and often hurtful? Has society given us a skewed view of what we are "supposed" to be? You see, over the years we have allowed all these outside influences to plant these little seeds in our minds. Then, unknowingly, we water that garden until it has grown in abundance. We become whatever it is we tell ourselves.

We take on the beliefs that others have given us; feelings of not being enough, skinny enough, and just not good enough. We start living our lives through the expectations of others and become fearful to show others and our self who we really are. Soon we are so lost and do not even know who we are anymore. This becomes our life cycle where sadness, depression, anger, and unhealthy relationships continue to flourish.

I grew up with a young single mother who did everything she could to ensure I felt loved and I knew that I made her proud. My father was extremely abusive to her. I'll never forget the day we left. I was three or four years old and my mother in her early twenties. Early that morning, my mother watched from the upstairs apartment window as my father drove away headed to work. The moment he was out of sight, she started moving with an urgency like I had never seen before. She grabbed large black garbage bags and started frantically throwing clothes in them. Leaving most everything behind, we ran down the stairs looking over our shoulders praying that he would not catch us. We both knew that if he did, he would kill her.

Fortunately, we could stay with her very close friends that offered us a new beginning. My mother worked hard to rebuild our lives and moved us as far away from my father as she could. Throughout the years, she had several unhealthy relationships while searching for someone to love her. Thus, I felt the void of not having a father figure and the examples of men that came in and out of my life were not examples of what loving relationships should be.

As a child, there were many occasions of men molesting me, none of which my mother could have had any control over. I was always in a supposed trusted situation and the attacks were usually when someone else was in the house. Most of the time it occurred during sleepovers at a friend's house; and involved their brothers, friends, fathers, or their mother's boyfriends. I learned that men wanted sex and if I wanted them to love me, I should have sex with them.

As a teenager, I would have sex with these boys and of course, that was all they wanted from me. When they would no longer showed any interest, I would start with the debilitating dialogue in my head; *What's wrong with me? Why am I not lovable? I must not be deserving.*

Throughout my adult years, I continued to have dysfunctional relationships with men, most of who had issues such as alcoholism, drug addiction and/or financial issues. Even worse, I felt it was my responsibility to take care of their problems. You see, these relationships gave me purpose. Taking care of them made me feel needed even if the relationship was abusive. I worked hard and made good money, only to give it away to everyone else. I have always been a go-getter. I have always been successful in whatever job I had. I have held high management positions and was a real leader. Yet, through all of this, I did not understand how much I really did not love myself.

Usually with great change in our lives we need a "rock bottom" moment to open our eyes. My "rock bottom" moment was when my boyfriend of five years committed suicide. I knew at that moment things needed to change in my life. I did not know what needed change. I did not know how. The only thing for certain was I could not live like this anymore.

 Pain doesn't just show up in our lives for a reason. It's a
sign that something in our lives needs to change

~MANDY HALE

Taking Responsibility

For change to take place in our lives we must first own our own shit! What I mean is, there is no longer room for blaming others for where you are at in your life. What if these things that happened in our lives were all are just part of the process? I believe these things, good or bad, are life lessons that occur to help teach us and shape us into who we are. Without the bad there would be no good. Maya Angelo said, "When you know better, you do better." I did not know better before. As I learn and grow I am starting to know better; therefore, I can make the conscious choice to do better. I choose not to blame anyone or my past and I forgive those that have hurt me.

There were many things in my life that happened that were not in my control. Those things are the past and simply that. There were even things that maybe I did have some control over but still allowed, and for that, I need to forgive myself. It no longer serves me to hold onto any of it. The truth is, I allowed many of the things in my life to happen because I did not feel deserving. I did not set boundaries. I did not put myself first. Now I know better so I am going to do better!

Self-love isn't always poetic; sometimes it's a nice big triple back flip kick in the ass. You've got to call yourself on your own nonsense; on the incredibly efficient way you can be self-destructive.

~STEVE MARABOLI

How do we love ourselves?

Understand there is no magic switch that will just miraculously change you overnight. Loving yourself is a journey and it takes time. I have been on this journey my whole life and I am still finding ways to improve in this area. Loving yourself is a DAILY practice. As with anything the more you practice, the better you get at it. Let's start practicing!

First, own it! This means you must identify the areas where you are not loving yourself. Without knowing what needs to change, how can you know where to start? After my boyfriend's suicide, I was having a conversation with my best friend telling her all the ways I had discovered that I was not loving myself. Her response was, "Are you kidding me? You are the most beautiful and confident person I know!" I explained to her that what she saw was the mask I had put on to survive in the world. What she saw was not truly who I was. I had realized that I had not been loving myself in so many ways. Such as settling, allowing myself to feeling undeserving, not setting boundaries or ever saying no, allowing others' judgements to become my truths while not standing in my truth and by being very critical of myself.

Next, it is time to weed your garden! Take those seeds of false beliefs planted by others and pull them! It is time to replace them with new seeds, seeds that are nurturing which will become your new beliefs. For example, if someone has always told you that you are not good enough, replace that thought with: *I am good enough, in fact I am more than good enough!* Take inventory of your bad seeds and replace them with new positive ones. We become what we tell ourselves. If we are using others' negative dialogue, that is what we will believe to be true. Why not change the dialogue? If we start telling ourselves that we are beautiful inside and out — that we are deserving and so on, then this will become our truth. Even if at the time, you truly do not believe that you are beautiful, do not stop telling yourself that. With repetition, it will become your truth.

Many times, the seeds come from ourselves and we may not even realize it. I found that I was more critical of myself than anyone else in the world. I believe you would agree that we can be our own worst judge and jury. Also, we tend to hang onto the negative more than the positive. Why do we do this? I discovered there were a lot more people saying wonderful things about me than negative things. Yet, all I could focus on was the one negative thing someone said in years past.

Let go of the fear of judgments from others. My favorite saying is, "Your opinion of me does not matter." Usually when people are living in the place of judgement, it is about them, not you. If I catch myself judging someone, I stop and look inward to see what is really going on with me. Why did I feel triggered? If you love yourself enough you will not need the validation from others, nor will their words tear you down.

 You alone are enough. You have nothing to prove to anybody.

~MAYA ANGELOU

Exercise

This exercise was life changing for me and I utilize it every day. It is a guided meditation that after you complete you should journal about your experience. You will be amazed at all the things that come up for you.

Imagine ... you have a child living in your heart space. Take the time to imagine the living space; What color are the walls? Are there any pictures? Is there furniture? What kind of floors does it have? What does it smell like? What does it feel like? What does the child look like? Get descriptive; What are they wearing? What does their hair look like? How do they feel? How old is the child? Now imagine you walk into this space and greet the child. What does the greeting look like? You are now sitting with this child having a conversation. What is the conversation?

This child represents your inner child. You will have some of your own discoveries around the conversation you have with the child. Jot down your conversation in your journal. Through my own conversation, I discovered that I was not nice to her at all. I said hurtful things to her and I did not protect her. I said things like; *You are so fat, you are a failure, you are not deserving, you are not good enough and you are so stupid.* Of course, I would NEVER say those things to my own children whom I love unconditionally. Why am I saying them to my inner child?

From that moment on, I vowed to love her unconditionally and to start protecting her as if she was my own child. I consciously watch my inner dialogue and try to lift her spirits every day. I now protect her as if I was protecting my own child. I set boundaries, surround her with people that lift her higher and say no. I am helping her to discover she is deserving of all great things in life. When she is tired, I let her rest. When she needs something, I tend to her needs. I am gentle, kind, forgiving and loving to her every day. We have become best friends and she has forgiven me for my lack of being there for her. We now have a great relationship.

It's all about falling in love with yourself and sharing that
love with someone who appreciates you, rather than
looking for love to compensate for a self-love deficit.

~EARTHA KITT

You've got this!

Imagine you are living the life of your dreams. What does that look like to you? Create a list of what your perfect life would look like. Then review that list and circle everything on your list that would change if you honored and loved yourself more. Loving yourself will change just about every aspect you feel is lacking in your life. If you are not happy in your life, love yourself more. If you continue to have failed relationships, learn to be your own best friend. You will then attract the better relationship. You see, we are a mirror for the world and whatever vibes we put out we will get in return. We also show people how to treat us by the way we treat ourselves.

I may not be completely there yet, I know I am a work in progress. With continued practice, every day it gets easier and loving myself comes more naturally. People may not like the new you, and that is okay. As we grow and shed our skin, we sometimes shed the people in our lives as well. Remember; people come in and out of our lives for a reason, a season, or a lifetime. The truth is, you have not changed. You are on a journey of getting back to where you came from . . . infinite love.

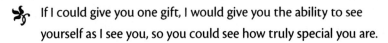 If I could give you one gift, I would give you the ability to see
yourself as I see you, so you could see how truly special you are.

~UNKNOWN

Dedicated to you, the reader on your journey of loving yourself. Sending you much love on your road to discovery.

To all my angel friends and family that show me how to except and give unconditional love, you are a beautiful mirror for me.

TONYA THOMAS DOKMAN

TONYA THOMAS DOKMAN, PsyD is a Habits & Relationship Coach, family therapist, Reiki Master/Teacher and author. She has a bachelor's degree in business and a master's degree in Marriage & Family Therapy, and a doctorate in Psychology.

She resides in central California and enjoys traveling to her home state spending time with her children, grandchildren, family and friends. She also enjoys sharing Reiki through both giving and training others. Her deepest passion is helping people by challenging their limiting beliefs towards finding the love within and empowering them to live their life to the fullest. Please visit her website for information regarding her life history, services provided, and upcoming classes at www.lotussoulawakening.com.

Facing the Unknown to Finding the Love Within

March 2011 — I sit here today watching the latest snowfall melting away, although it's late March and should be sunny and warm by now. It's beautiful sitting here watching mother earth being cleansed in preparation for a new journey, a new season promising to bring new life and joy. As I sit here enjoying the beauty, I too am being cleansed and prepared for my new journey, a new season promising to bring me new life and much joy. As I prepare to leave a 27-year career in a few months to follow my passion, both excitement and fear are stirring within. However, this is not the first time I've faced the unknown and I'm sure it won't be the last. I remember back to a time when I began a new journey, a time I was forced to embrace my fear of not knowing what lay ahead of me. I was very young at the age of 18 when I left the only life I knew.

It was late into the night as I lay in bed asleep when I was abruptly awakened by the burst of light and an angry voice screaming for me to get up. This voice was calling out horrible names such as, "*You bitch, you slut, you whore…I will kill him!*" The voice then came towards me, grabbing my arm to pull me from the bed and throwing me across the room. I could feel a most crushing fear that totally engulfed me, as I knew right then the man who had controlled my body, my mind, my life had come back to do exactly what he had promised if I ever shut him out. After throwing me across the room, he turned and moved down the hall towards my younger brother's room screaming, "*I'm going to kill him. I'm going to take him away from you*" as he went for a gun. He was going to kill the man I loved, my fiancé. At that moment, it all became a blur and I don't remember running to the living room, but when I got there my mother was screaming "*NO*" and was crying hysterically as she placed her body against the front door. I quickly ran to the kitchen in case I needed to escape when I saw my brother standing in the hallway showing me bullets in his hand, letting me know the gun was not loaded.

At that moment, I saw my chance to negotiate, in whatever way I needed, to bring calmness back to our family. I began talking to my step-father in a calm, soft and loving voice telling him how he could come back into my life and we could then be the family we once were. He started to cry as he let go of the gun and sank down onto the floor. As I stood there watching, I felt a deep sadness as my mother fell to the floor in exhaustion, and yet I could see the relief in her eyes when I told them we could be together as family again. I had seen her eyes so full of pain over the weeks before while he was in jail and listened to her continuous begging of me to forgive the one man she loved for hurting me all those years, so that she could be with him again and no longer feel alone. As I stood there looking at my mother, her sadness reminded me of the first time I saw her in pain, I was only 7 years old.

"We were very poor and had no beds to sleep on. Our beds were made of blankets laid out onto the hard wood floor. Food was scarce and my mother ate only after we had finished. Then one afternoon my mother was very sad. I watched as she carefully placed towels under the doors and had us lay down on the bed made of blankets. The sun was still shining and I wondered why we had to go to bed so early. Then I saw her turn on the gas stove and blow out the flames, allowing the fumes of gas to fill the air. I silently watched as my mother prepared for us and herself to die as she could no longer handle her sadness. She then picked up the phone while she cried and reached out for help. It was a day that I would forever remember and I knew I would always have to protect her. Little did I know what that meant until the day she met a man who soon became my step-father. I remember looking up at him as he smiled down at me. I did not like him, but my mother was happy."

The house that night became very quiet, a tranquility of peace as everyone went to bed, that is everyone but me. When morning came, I left and never returned.

I began a new journey that scared the hell out of me, and yet I was free from the life I once knew. I soon had my own apartment and although I felt a sense of freedom, I still felt fear. I feared that my step-father would follow through on all the promises made throughout my childhood years, promises of hurting anyone who took me away, or if I ran away how he would find me. This fear was so deeply etched in my body that if a light was left on at night or there was even a slight sound in the other room, I would know he was there. It was 20 years later I learned about *triggers of sexual abuse* and then realized why I was never able to sleep. I had to have total darkness and pure silence. Friends would laugh at me saying, *"That's silly, put a mask over your eyes."* However, it wasn't actually about seeing with my eyes, but the sense of my body knowing that he was awake and would be visiting me soon.

It didn't take long before Jeff, my fiancé moved in with me and became my full-time protector. He would stay with me every night, tucking me into bed and locking the door behind him as he left to return home. Jeff had taken on the role of my protector at 17, moving in with me just months before we married. But I still lived in fear even though he was with me. Fear that one day those promises would come true and I'd lose the man so dear to me...and my freedom. I was constantly trying to keep my balance and deal with my fears, and yet still not feeling like I belonged. I knew my step-father was always watching me no matter what I was doing or where I was. He would come into my work reminding me he was there watching and waiting. Then one day Jeff just happened to be standing behind me and escorted him outside. I never knew what was said, but he never came back.

Over the next few years my step-father continued to reach out to me through my mother. By this time Jeff and I had two children and I had learned to deflect the comments and constant requests to allow him back into my life. I was now strong enough to know that he was incapable of following through on all the promises he made. He no longer had any power over me. I always protected my children by never allowing him to see them and would visit my mother and siblings away from their home. Then one day I received a call from my mother begging me to allow my step-father back into my life. I could hear him in the background coaching her when she said to me, "*I know at such a young age you didn't start the abuse, but you were a part in keeping it going. You benefited from it. You got special privileges the others didn't.*" I remember standing there, Jeff watching as the warmth of my blood drained from my face and body. My only response was, "*Believe what you want. You are no longer my mother.*" and then I hung up the phone.

It was ten years before we spoke again at the hospital when my grandmother was dying. My grandmother, the only true love of my life until my children and grandchildren were born … and I'd now lost her. A few years later my step-father died from a long fight with cancer, and so did my marriage.

I remember the day so well. The day Jeff said he no longer loved me as he cried and turned away. It felt as if someone had just taken their fist, shoved it through my body, grabbed my heart and pulled it from my chest. I couldn't breathe. I couldn't think. All I could do was cry, as I curled up like a baby. I walked around in a daze as if I was a ghost and feeling like everyone could see right through me, as if I wasn't there. I was being launched into a new life, one I did not want. I was facing the unknown, again. My life had been built around my family, so I didn't have many friends. I felt so alone and sad. My heart was so broken. There was nothing but a deep hole left in my body. *WHY* … is all I could scream. *Why now*? I was just finishing my bachelor's degree. I was growing in my career and now my world just fell apart. As painful as it was, I again embraced the unknown and then I began to grow. It was the right decision for Jeff, as he had been my protector since 17 and no longer needed to fulfill that role. I needed to let him go so that he could find himself apart from my fears and pains that he so carefully and patiently protected. It was time to launch back out into the world so that I could experience life in a new way. And, what a ride it was!

The next five years I call "my crazy life". From 1996 through 1997 I partied as if I were in my 20's staying out most nights until 3 a.m. and then crawling into bed to get a few hours of sleep before going to work the next morning. I met new people who became good friends and others who quickly passed through. I was a walking zombie with little regret as to who I might hurt, while staying safely out of reach from anyone who might want a serious relationship with me. Coworkers lived vicariously through my adventures of travel and excursions saying, "*You have the life.*" Little did they know how much I cried myself to sleep and kept pushing to keep from feeling. Between 1997 and 2001 I met and married my second husband, helped him fight for full custody of his children, continued to battle the relationship between my children and his, dealing with his and my needs … and not lose me in the process. I had returned to school to get my degree and license as a Marriage and Family Therapist, and then I was divorced in 2001 for the second time. *STOP!!! Let me off this rollercoaster … NOW! I don't want to continue living like this.* So I started asking God, "*Who is this me I'm searching for? Why am I making these choices? Who am I? Why am I here? Please help me!!!!* Soon after I met a new friend who handed me a book called, "The Celestine Prophecy." I began reading and it led me to more reading and even more reading. I couldn't get enough. I started paying attention to my surroundings and sitting in silence, really listening this time for answers. I studied things that didn't make sense to me. My brain would hurt, my stomach would ache. I would toss and turn with each new level of learning about why I had experienced what I had.

I always felt a connection to God, but I had never related God to actually being a part of me and how I am connected as ONE with all. I had never thought about something higher or more powerful as this universe and how it all works together in synchronicity. How everything happens for a reason, there are no mistakes. I was blown away when I had a reading one day where the reader asked me what happened at such a young age that dramatically changed my life. It freaked me out how this person could know I had a life-altering change by merely looking at my charted course and his intuitive reading. He told me I chose the parents and the experiences to have before entering this world so that one day I could teach and help others to heal. Okay, now this is way beyond my Baptist upbringing, but why did I feel comfort in this knowledge? Is it possible what he was saying was true?

My world began to change more rapidly now. Doors began to open. I started meeting people who led me to what I needed to learn next and I continued having new experiences that brought me growth; some good and some not so good. If I needed money I'd pray and light a green candle, but always remembering to pray for others too, so as not to be selfish. I'd find money in my mailbox from refunds granted out of the blue, additional work would come my way, and when I was told I had to pay taxes one year I received a call that an entry had been missed and after being corrected, the IRS ended up giving me a refund instead. Now this got my attention in a big way! It woke me up to the flow of the universe … and my life. I was feeling pretty good.

In 2005 I began feeling restless and felt a need to make some major changes in my life. My children had left the home and I was on my own. So … I moved myself to California and returned to school to obtain my doctorate in Psychology.

I have experienced both pain and joy in my life by facing many challenges I call *gifts* that have provided me growth and launched me forward to who I am today. I've always been a survivor and never saw myself as a victim. I strongly believe it's up to each of us to find the healing within so that we may live our life to the fullest. I believe we are here to experience love and to help each other live the best life possible … and be happy! Throughout my life I have always felt guided and protected by something bigger, and once I learned about listening to the "God" that I was one with, I became more aware of when God was speaking to me. I began ***asking*** for direction, ***listening*** to my intuition and ***allowing*** my heart to forgive those who hurt me. I met and married my twin soul who previously resided in Istanbul Turkey, and are now co-creating our lives together. I love my life and I love helping others by challenging their limiting beliefs, guiding them to finding the love within, and then empowering them to live the life they desire.

I am truly happy and living my life to the fullest each and every day. I'm no longer just a survivor, I am a thriver!

I was once asked, "How does someone go from a 2.0 grade point average to becoming a Doctor of Psychology?"

I believe…

 Each of us is in truth an idea of the Great, an unlimited idea of Freedom. Everything that limits us, we have to put aside. Don't believe what your eyes are telling you. All they show is limitation. Look with your understanding, find out what you already know, and you'll see the way to fly.

~RICHARD BACH, JOHNATHON LIVINGSTON SEAGULL

"I am flying!"

Dedicated to my first love, my maternal grandmother Jessie Mae Hopkins — because of you, my heart always remains open to love.

Dedicated to my children and grandchildren—because of you, the light in my heart continues to shine.

I have much gratitude to all the heroes who provide a loving and safe space for healing and growth. I also want to thank the male partners of female childhood sexual abuse survivors for participating in my dissertation study and sharing their experience of conjoint therapy with the survivor. Thank you for opening your hearts and sharing your experience.

A special thanks to my dear friends, Colleen Williams, Jackie Kranz, Lucy Her—for your incredible friendship and unconditional love. I also want to thank all the teachers and mentors who have crossed my path and provided me with opportunities and support to learn and grow.

SANDRA J FILER

SANDRA J FILER, MBA, proprietress of The Happy Goddess, has an amazing zest for Life and infuses everything she does with this energy. "Happie G" is a vibrant artist, author, Goddess retreat creator/host, Empowerment Coach, and co-creator of the Self-emPOWERment PlayShop for Teens. She is also the United States East Coast Heal Your Life® Teacher-Trainer. You can reach Sandra via her website: www.thehappygoddess. com or email: diosafeliz@hotmail.com

Thomas the Teaching Tom Cat

On a quiet lantern lit street, in the big bustling city of Houston, a striped tom cat lives on a condo porch. He has been lovingly named Thomas. Why he has chosen *our* particular building, on a street full of condominiums and apartments with porches, I can only guess. The story that I make up about it is that somewhere underneath his fraying coat, he knew that he would receive love, which he does. In addition to receiving love, Thomas also gives love.

He has also been a great teacher. Just recently, he gave me the opportunity to really see my life purpose in action. This purpose is to be of loving service.

When I was a very small child, my mother would sit me down with a little plastic record player, turn it on for me, and I would sit by that record player listening to music for hours. One of my favorite stories of all was The Ugly Duckling. My mom shared that it always intrigued her that as such a small, small child, I would cry whenever I listened to that record. Her summation was that I was a very tender-hearted child. As it turns out, I am also a very tender-hearted adult and it is all a very special part of my life's purpose.

Thomas the tom cat is a cast away. I guess you might say that he was someone's ugly duckling. At one time, as the story goes, he was a beloved pet...and then he got left behind. I can relate to this. Maybe this is why I have a tender spot for Thomas and other animals tossed out by their owners to live on their own.

Over the years, Thomas and I have developed a special bond. Each morning I shuffle down my hallway with his bowl of food. When I reach the porch, he is either right there ready to greet me, or he is perched on my window ledge waiting for his meal. If it is the latter of the two, I only have to yell out his name and he comes running. Actually, it is sort of like a cat gallop.

On really special days, he gets a hand full of diced ham snagged from the salad bar at lunch. He loves that! Each day I refill his water bowl, check to make sure that his bedding is comfortable, and I make the time to pet him and let him know that he is loved.

This relationship is reciprocal. You see, each time that I pull up in front of our building, much like a dog, Thomas comes running off the porch, over the esplanade, and into the street to greet me as I open my car door. It fills my heart to be so loved.

Recently, Thomas developed an infection on his nose. Immediately, I took action. I began treating it with an ointment. I found myself completely consumed with wanting him to be well. I'd visit him on the porch 3-4 times a day. I'd take him treats. I'd put ointment on his nose each and every visit.

One night, I met a new resident in the hallway. She asked me if I was caring for "that cat on the patio." I assured her that I was and he was on the mend. She turned and looked at me and said, "That is so awesome. He is the reason that I chose to live here." This really intrigued me. She then proceeded to say, "When I saw Thomas on the porch the day I looked at my unit, I thought to myself, I want to live where people care for animals and allow them on the porch." Wow! This really touched me deeply. Not only because of the impact Thomas had made on this resident but also because I knew that I was the one caring for him, and until then, I had no idea that my caring had such an impact on someone else.

On another occasion, I was exiting my back door to cross paths with yet another resident. In my hand was a can of cat food. He looked at me and with a smile across his face asked, "Are you the one taking care of Thomas?" This was followed up with, "What is wrong with his nose?" My excited reply was something along the lines of, "Doesn't he look 90 percent better?" My neighbor then shared, "That is so wonderful. God is going to bless you even more for what you do." I closed the door. Again, wow! I had no idea that so many people were paying attention.

Yet, I was one of the only ones taking action. Something began to stir inside of me. As a result of all the dealings with Thomas, I began to really take a look at myself and my life. The question that surfaced for me is why am I the one who is taking action? Why am I the one that feels so passionate about helping an abandoned animal? After all, it isn't just Thomas that I feed. My patio seems to be a magnet for all of those furry castaways.

One awareness after another began to enter into my consciousness. I realized first of all that Thomas was on our building's porch because I was meant to learn from him. The first lesson that I learned was that one doesn't have to "do" anything to serve a purpose.

This was big for me. I have been the person who equates my worthiness or purpose with the amount of money I do or do not make. Whether or not I am truly serving my purpose has been measured by the number of participants in a workshop. Not necessarily "what" the participants got from the workshop. When I heard the neighbor share that having Thomas on the patio was her reason for choosing her residence, I had one of the "aha" moments. Thomas was simply being himself. Thomas was being a cat.

Taking this a step further, I had lunch with a friend. During the lunch, we were catching up on life. We've been friends for 13 years. Over the years, we have each done a lot of personal growth work. We shared stories after stories. She was embarking upon a transition with her job. As the conversation continued, she looked at me and said, "Diosa … You have no idea the impact you have had on my life." I leaned a little more forward as I listened.

She went on to say, "Remember the time that you said to me, Marie, you deserve a man with two legs of the same size and a head with hair." I sat sort of stunned. The memory did not surface for me. She elaborated, "The point was that I deserved someone "better," it really wasn't about the legs or the hair, it was about the man that he wasn't. I was playing with the turkeys instead of the eagles." Again, I sat there and listened. She said, "That feedback from you shifted my life." My eyes welled up with tears and again, I thought of Thomas. He just sits there on the porch and has an impact. I apparently just sat at that infamous lunch sharing from my tender-hearted self and made a difference.

It is amazing what happens in the Universe when one ponders such a thing as purpose. Life begins to bring example after example. This is because often times, we need to be given multiple examples for it to truly settle in. At yet another lunch, I sat next to sweet little Gabriella. She is five years old. As the conversation ensued, she said, "Tia you are my rainbow." Her rainbow? Again, the tears welled up in my eyes. What was happening here?

The power in *that* example is that not too long ago, I was literally in tears because I didn't feel like I was "enough." As usual, I was measuring my worthiness by the number of participants or the lack thereof. As I sat on my pity pot, I cried and said to my husband, "I might as well change my email signature to say, good friend." He consoled me in his own way and assured me that I was enough and that I was exactly where I needed to be. Of course, he was absolutely right. I was and I am exactly where I need to be.

Purpose seems to be something that so many of us are searching to find. For years, I earned title after title believing I was on purpose. Over time, I saw that I was reaching for one accomplishment after another believing I was living my purpose.

However, in caring for Thomas' nose on the front porch, it finally really became clear to me. Doting on him and mending his boo boos felt right. Sharing lunch with my friend and listening to her share our past and how it has affected her future felt right. Being Gabriella's rainbow felt right. It all felt really good at the level of the soul and I felt fulfilled, enriched, loved, and ultimately, filled with purpose.

Who knew that a striped tom cat living on a porch could be such a great teacher? I believe that Thomas' example is a testimonial to the fact that we are each here to be exactly who we are and *that* is our purpose. We are here to live fully. We are here to receive love and to give love.

I am grateful to have Thomas in my life. I am grateful to be given the opportunity to love him and receive love in return.

So often we make things far more difficult than they actually need to be. We search and search and look outside of ourselves. In reality we come fully equipped to live our purpose. All we need to do is open our eyes and hearts to the experience. It is a matter of embracing it!

Now I ask you, what is *your* purpose?

Did you hear it? If not, I invite you to allow the answer to come to you in the whisper of the wind. Or, maybe it will come when a stranger enters your path. All I know is that whether you believe it or not, you are someone's rainbow, too.

How could life be any more beautiful than that? What greater purpose than to be known as the one who "cares" or puts color into another's life.

Yes, my purpose is to be of service... Now, onto more rainbow moments.

This story is dedicated to everyone out there wondering if they are enough. You are.

I wish to especially say thank you to Thomas. I am infinitely grateful for all he has given me. Also for everyone (and anyone) that has stopped for a moment to pet him, provide water, and/ or rearrange his fleece blanket. I wish to express my extreme gratitude to the animal control employee that released Thomas to me this past summer when his "job" was to do otherwise. Without my sister sending antibiotics and my neighbor Eric's assistance, Thomas would not be here today... so, I thank both of them from the bottom of my heart! Finally, I thank my editor and fellow feline lover Dr. Denise Coleman for lovingly assisting with the end result of Thomas' story.

BRENDA FEDORCHUK

BRENDA FEDORCHUK, an Amazon #1 Published Author, a Licensed and Certified Heal Your Life® Coach and a Leadership and Engagement Consultant. Having spent over 30 years in Leadership and Management in a corporate arena, Brenda shifted her own life and created her company, Heart Centered Solutions, to create a safe and sacred space to support others seeking true personal growth and professional development.

Brenda is known for her gentle ability to create long lasting transformation, whether she is teaching a workshop, delivering training or coaching clients individually. Brenda uses a unique combination of proven "inner and outer' techniques that release limiting beliefs, overcome fears and supports people to claim their personal power and step fully into their life.

www.heartcenteredsolutions.ca
brenda@heartcenteredsolutions.ca
www.facebook.com/heartcenteredsolutions

🎋 Stillness For The Sensitive Soul

Who, me? A Sensitive Soul?

Head hung down, looking at the floor, tears welling up in my eyes, I sunk down into the smallest version of myself. Feeling embarrassed and betrayed once again by my sensitivity.

Oh Brenda, "you're just so sensitive".

Feeling the familiar burden of shame, I sat on the hard chair in the coffee shop, sipping my lukewarm coffee having yet again vividly shared my painful story with someone who was not able to fully hear it, and it dawned on me: she's right!

I was sensitive! I blush often. I am very shy. I cry easily, often having to hide my tears from my friends while watching a sad movie. I am deeply affected by things. I feel overwhelmed and often confused especially if I have a lot to do in a short period of time.

According to Dr. Elain Aron, author of the book "The Highly Sensitive Person" a highly sensitive person is someone who is found in only 15-20% of the population. Can you relate to the list of highly sensitive traits she uncovered in her research?

- ᴄᴏ Are you easily overwhelmed by such things as bright lights, strong smells, coarse fabrics, or sirens nearby?
- ᴄᴏ Do you get rattled when you have a lot to do in a short amount of time?
- ᴄᴏ Do you make a point of avoiding violent movies and TV shows?
- ᴄᴏ Do you need to withdraw during busy days, into bed or a darkened room or some other place where you can have privacy and relief from the situation?
- ᴄᴏ Do you make it a high priority to arrange your life to avoid upsetting or over-whelming situations?
- ᴄᴏ Do you notice or enjoy delicate or fine scents, tastes, sounds, or works of art?
- ᴄᴏ Do you have a rich and complex inner life?
- ᴄᴏ When you were a child, did your parents or teachers see you as sensitive or shy?

I wish I had read this book when I was growing up. I hated my sensitivity because I feared people would think that I was weak or fragile. I even tried to find solutions to cope with it and to my disappointment was offered prescription medication. I knew that medication was not a solution for me.

Why Bother?

Without wanting to, I found that being a highly sensitive person paved the road for me to easily give my power away to those who I thought knew better. I allowed others to have power over me when I believed that their opinions, thoughts, and ideas about me were more important than my own. Giving away my power left me feeling small and with little self-love or self-respect. If someone treated me badly, my first thought was that there must be something wrong with me. I lived very unconsciously during that period of my life. There seemed to be a long lazy river of never ending situations that left me feeling powerless and victimized.

Deep inside I knew, I was different. I felt things others did not feel. I saw things others did not see. When I witnessed an injustice in someone's treatment, I particularly felt moved to right that wrong. I shared my observations with those in power that I thought shared my same values and would want to change these situations but the reality was my observations were often met with disbelief and deep resistance to take action. I didn't feel heard. Life began to feel hopeless. What's the use? Why bother? No one listened. I remember feeling that I simply wanted people to get along, to have equality and peace for everyone. I started to spend more time by myself because I felt at peace alone, often spending time listening to music or reading.

How I Coped

My way of coping with the sensitivities of life was to do the one thing that I knew I was good at: to work hard! I worked hard at having a perfect life, trying to find the perfect paying job, having a perfectly clean house, and ensuring I always had a flawless appearance. It was all so stressful, to continually be pushing and striving to the next best thing, working harder and harder, hardly ever having down time for myself.

I now know that making sure everything was done perfectly on my TO DO list was fueled by my desire to hide my sensitivity, to fit it, to be accepted, to be loved, and to be finally seen as good enough.

The Gift of Giving Your Power Away

Overtime, living unconsciously and pushing myself too hard began to have an effect on me. Living with that constant stress and pressure eventually took me out. I experienced physical pain in my neck and shoulders and back that just would not go away. I had no energy. I was tired all the time and found myself with very little patience.

I was so outwardly focused that I did not even realize that I was burning out!

The Power of Stillness

I realized I needed a change. I started my journey of self-discovery when I first read Louise Hay's best-selling book *You Can Heal Your Life*. I learned about this concept of creating inner peace and change from within. I practiced using affirmations and began to see some personal transformation by taking personal responsibility and owning my personal power. Every moment of every day in my life, I know I have a CHOICE to get still and embrace my power or give it away! I've learned how easily I give up my power when I'm on that hamster wheel of pushing and striving and give meaning to other people's thoughts and opinions about me.

I Hire My Inner Coach to Guide Me

In *You Can Heal Your Life*, I read that all my answers were within. Something I had sensed all along. Dr. Elaine Aron discusses that highly sensitive people are actually coded to be the mentors, coaches, healers and creatives of the world. We think, feel, and listen more deeply than the other 80% of people. Imagine that! My sensitivity that I once thought was a burden is actually a very valuable gift.

So I decided to hire my own inner coach to guide me. The wise inner self that has always been there for me. Internal power comes from taking personal responsibility, staying awake, being aware, living in my truth, accepting my sensitivity, and knowing I am worthy just because I was born. I trust and believe that I am now co-creating my life with an energy that comes from the universe that is loving and compassionate.

Gary Zukav explains in the "Seat of the Soul" that the essence of a fulfilled life is when we align our thoughts, emotions, and actions with the highest part of ourselves we are then filled with enthusiasm, purpose, and meaning. When the personality comes fully to serve the energy of its soul — that is authentic empowerment. What this means to me is when I'm aligned with what my sensitive soul came to earth to do, there is NO ONE more powerful than me. I was born to be more and fully completely ME! Just me!

My Daily Practice

I have learned how to stay out of overwhelm and confusion consistently by managing my energy and truly own the power I have over my own intentions, my thoughts, beliefs, and actions. To remain in my power, it is very important that I have a consistent daily practice. Every day I stay on track by taking time to be still and listen. I connect into my inner wisdom for guidance. I choose the energy I wish to send before me for my day. I keep track of what I am grateful for. I trust the messages I receive from my gifts of intuition and deep listening.

My journey has led me to embrace and use all my gifts as a highly sensitive person. I now use these gifts that I once thought were burdens to teach other highly sensitive people how to own their own power and live an inspired peaceful life.

While I am still evolving into my role is as a highly sensitive person, I do not pretend to have all the answers, but what I know for sure is that real power is born out of alignment with your soul's calling. Each of us has a responsibility to figure out what that calling is. Once we connect with it, our burdens get lifted and the universe rises up to support us in our truest power and any transformation you can dream of can be yours.

I understand now that I'm not a mess but a deeply feeling person in a messy world. I explain that, now that when someone asks me why I cry so often, I say, 'For the same reason I laugh so often — because I'm paying attention.

~GLENNON DOYLE MELTON

I dedicate this to all the heart centered souls who are learning to embrace their gift of sensitivity!

I'm so grateful to my husband Pat for loving me unconditionally and believing in me no matter what. To my amazing children, Amanda and Jeremy, who inspire me every day to show up and do my part to create healing and peace on our planet.

A special Thank you to Lisa Hardwick and Katina Gillespie whose inspiration, dedication, talents and gifts make this amazing work possible.

CHERYL GUTTENBERG

CHERYL GUTTENBERG is a licensed Heal Your Life® Coach and workshop leader, healer, author and speaker. As a Human Resources executive for over 25 years, she has worked with many people to achieve their success and fulfillment in the corporate environment. Cheryl has also coached executives to achieve their success both at work and on a personal level. She works with people one-on-one through her workshops and coaching practice.

Cheryl lives in Southern California and enjoys traveling, spending time with her family, friends, and dancing as much as possible.

www.CherylGuttenberg.com
CherylGuttenberg@gmail.com

✿ My 6 Steps Back to Serenity

As I'm living my full life, working at a wonderful job with a fabulous family owned company, suddenly I'm thrown a curve ball. Last January, when I learned the company I was working for had been sold to a large publicly traded company, I knew I was in for a turbulent ride! As the Vice President of Human Resources, I was in charge of moving all the employees from the existing company to the new one. Dealing with the employee's fears, apprehension and their unknown future was a challenge, and at the same time, I was dealing with this on a personal level.

Eight weeks after the completion of the acquisition, I learned my position was going to be eliminated. Okay, now I really need some help!! Being laid off as a single woman, at my age brings up all kinds of mental and emotional upheaval. I'm not ready to retire on any level. How am I going to take care of myself without my full-time job? I'm heading into potential financial ruin.

As I worked through this season of my life, I had to come up with some coping skills, quickly! Here are the 6 practices that helped me and will continue to help me through this journey:

1. Trust—No, I really mean trust in God and the Universe to provide for me. This has become a daily ritual for me of thanking the Universe for meeting all my needs today. And tomorrow I thank again and the next day, and the next. Any time during the day when any fear or panic arises, I thank the Universe again. I am learning the true meaning of trust, while remaining peaceful inside. None of us know what will happen in a year, or even next month. What we all know is things NEVER remain the same. When life is going along smoothly, it's easy to trust. When things get tough, our faith is REALLY challenged.

2. Self-Care—What do I need to do to take of myself? Self-compassion needs to be first and foremost on our list when we are going through a challenging time. Wikipedia defines self-compassion as "extending compassion to one's self in instances of perceived inadequacy, failure, or general suffering." So often we treat others with more compassion than we extend to ourselves; I know I have. I'm learning to be more loving and gentle toward myself and ask myself during the day, "What do I need right now, how am I feeling?" When friends are going through a challenging time, I'll ask them, "What can I do for you?" Now I check in and ask myself this question, several times a day.

3. Forgiveness—I knew if I didn't work through and release my anger about losing my job, I would stay stuck and unable to move forward. I got my journal and wrote how angry I was at the company for eliminating my position and potentially placing

me in a financial vise. I also found it helpful to distance myself from the company quickly. I signed my exit paperwork, changed my benefit options, and limited my communication to only one employee who used to work with me. When I found myself talking about the situation, I could feel my entire body tense up. Quickly, I realized I wanted to let this go. The desire to discuss this situation dwindled as I shifted my attention to what was ahead of me and what I wanted to create, not what was left behind. Whenever I thought about my prior supervisor, I just sent her love.

4. Setting Intentions—Last Tuesday morning everything seemed to be going wrong. A box I had packed up to return to Amazon, leaked powder all over the inside of my car. Walking back to my car from Starbucks, I spilled water on myself and in my tote. I was feeling like I was starting to circle the drain. When I got back in my car and dried off, I affirmed aloud, "My day is going to turn around right now!" Before I started my car, I noticed I had a voicemail on my phone. It was from a former colleague I used to work with and she was asking me to call her to discuss a potential job opportunity. I called Ellen and told her I had recently been laid off. She said before she called me, she set an intention that I would be available for her potential opportunity. We planned future discussions, and we'll see what happens. Setting intentions really does work!!

5. Declutter—Cleaning out a closet, drawer, or cabinet has proven to provide me with numerous benefits. When I'm finished, I feel cleansed, refreshed, more organized and have energy to tackle the next project. It feels as good as a fabulous session with my therapist. I feel lighter with more energy to create my new abundant future. To date, I've decluttered almost my entire apartment including cupboards, closets, photos, books and paper files. I have two small areas left to complete. Before I started to declutter, I set an intention I was clearing out to allow space for my new life to come in.

6. Visualization—Mike Dooley teaches us the importance of visualization. He says we need to feel the "WOWs" of what we want, and not the "HOWs", that's the job of the Universe to attend to the details. That seems much more fun than trying to figure out every detail. I'm still in training on this one. Many times my type A personality wants to assume this job. A couple of times a day, I will review my list of what I want to create in my life and visualize in detail how I would feel if each item was already a reality in my life. What would it look like, who would be there, how elated I am with the results?

7. God Box—I read about this in Outrageous Openness by Tosha Silver. You simply write down your worry or concern and place it in your designated container. You can use a jar, box or whatever you choose. I have a beautiful box with a multi-colored peacock on the front. The idea is once we "turn it over" to God, we don't have to worry about it anymore. Once I've written and placed my concern or desire in my box, if I find myself worrying about it again, I remind myself I already submitted it to my God Box. It's like placing your order at a restaurant, we don't keep checking

with our server to make sure they have placed our order. We just wait for the results. Here is another area to incorporate step 1, Trust.

I have started sharing these steps with my coaching clients and friends and they find them very helpful.

Life is full of constant change and sometimes we are faced with challenges that are not easy. My hope is that you will use these steps when you find yourself in that position. They have worked for me and I will continue to use them. Please let me know how they work for you, I'd love to hear from you.

Namaste.

To my Mom, Lorraine Fuhrmann ~

Thank you, Mom, for being my biggest cheerleader throughout my life and always believing in me and teaching me that I can accomplish whatever I want. Happy 93rd Birthday!

I am grateful for my entire tribe who surrounds me with love and support. You all know who you are… I am blessed to have you in my life. I love and adore all of you.

BARBARA SIMPSON

BARBARA SIMPSON grew up in South Australia and often felt that she was different than others and experienced things that were spiritually fascinating and intriguing, as well as things that were destructive and traumatizing. Going into adulthood she had a sick and unhealthy body which she believes developed from the traumas experienced as a child and teenager. In her early 20s a Doctor said to her, "If you don't change something in your life you are not going to be here for long." This shocked her but also had her thinking, "Do I actually want to be here?" and "What is my purpose here?" It was an Aha! moment.

This began her journey of self-discovery and personal growth to overcome the emotional, physical and spiritual issues of the past. To move to a life without the "baggage" and be free to choose what she wanted in her life and not let someone else choose for her. Through this process, she finally found love in her heart, peace and calmness in her soul, courage and wisdom to grow and happiness and joy to be alive.

She decided to share these gifts and has been doing so for many years, assisting others to heal the past and inspire happiness into their lives.

Barbara@thehealingcoach.com.au
www.thehealingcoach.com.au

🦋 Inner Rainbow

Eleven-year-old Amelia lives with her Mum and Dad in a small country town with her cat, Bailey, who has green eyes and golden fur. On this particular Saturday morning, Amelia awoke to the sound of birds singing outside her bedroom window. It had been a long, cold winter and the last of the snow had melted and now she was so excited to be able to go outside and play. She jumped out of bed, got dressed and while she waited for her Mum and Dad to wake up, she thought she would play with her teddy bears. She placed them all in a circle, turned on her favourite music and sang at the top of her lungs. This soon woke Bailey, who had been curled up asleep on the bed, and he came over to Amelia and rubbed up against her, telling her it was now time for breakfast.

"Pancakes!" squealed Amelia, she loved pancakes. After they all had breakfast, her Dad explained that he had received a promotion at work and they would be moving to the city. Amelia felt sad and scared at the thought of moving away from her friends. It was planned that she would stay with her Auntie Amanda near the city for a few days while movers came. That made her feel better as she adored her Auntie and loved to play in her beautiful garden. Still, when it came time for Amelia's parents to leave her and Bailey at Auntie Amanda's house, she was very upset. She felt like her whole world was changing, she had no home, no parents, no friends so she felt very sad. Auntie Amanda tried to cheer up Amelia by making a chocolate cake together. Amelia did start to calm down, especially after she got to lick the icing off the large mixing spoon which she shared with Bailey. Once the cake was finished Amelia took a slice into the garden to eat. The sun was high in the clear blue sky, flowers were blooming, bees buzzing and everything looked vibrant and colourful. In the corner of the garden was an enormous oak tree with a wooden bench beneath it. Amelia thought that would be a nice place to sit and enjoy her cake. She could hear the birds singing in the tree above and she laughed watching Bailey chase some butterflies. When she had finished eating her cake, she felt tired so she laid down on the bench and Bailey curled up next to her.

When Bailey woke Amelia by licking her face, she thought that she must have been asleep for quite a while as she felt cold. She sat up and cleared the sleep from her eyes and immediately realized that she was no longer in the garden. Instead, there were lots of tall pine trees all around her. She thought she was dreaming, but was excited about exploring this new place. As she was walking through the pine trees, she felt very much alone, but comforted by Bailey being with her. The sounds coming from the trees and birds were so different than she had ever heard before. Out of the corner of her eye she saw some mushrooms covered in bright red dots, at the base of a tree. As she walked closer she realized the red dots were moving. They were ladybugs, flying, in and around the mushrooms. Amelia smiled and went over to them and said, "Hello, my name is Amelia, what are you doing?"

At that moment, Amelia heard rustling in the tree above and a large brown owl swooped down onto a branch nearby. The owl said, "I'm Olbert, they are busy eating before their long journey to the Golden Temple." Amelia asked, "Why are they going to a temple?"

"They wish to ask for rain, the forest has been without rain for a long time and there is very little food left for them here. Anyway, what is a little girl doing in our forest, with a cat?" "Meow, my name is Bailey, I'm hungry and I want to go home to my favourite chair for a nap." Amelia was amazed that Bailey could talk, she cuddled him and said, "I was asleep in my Auntie's garden and when I woke up I found myself here. Can you help me get back to my family?" "I can show you the way once we have reached the Golden Temple." When the ladybugs finished eating they flew into the air with Olbert, and Amelia and Bailey followed them walking through the forest.

Olbert realized that Amelia might be feeling lonely and frightened without her family. He knew the journey ahead could be challenging and so he wanted to support and prepare her by teaching her about energy centres that exist in the body. The 1st energy is located at the base of the spine. It relates to the foundation of your life, family, comfort, safety and security. Imagine seeing the colour ruby RED filling this area of the body.

As they came down the hill Amelia's legs were tired, so they stopped and rested for a while and watched the most amazing vivid orange sunset. Later as they reached the village, all the streets were glowing with candlelight. Olbert flew into a tree in front of a quaint little house and Amelia bravely walked up the path and knocked on the door. The door slowly opened and a lady stood there, "Hello, I'm Amelia, Olbert and the ladybugs brought me here, can we please stay with you tonight?" The lady said, "Any friend of Olbert is welcome here. My name is Mary, and who do we have here, a cat, we don't see many cats around here." "Meow, I'm Bailey and I'm hungry," brushing his body up against Mary. "Of course, come in, you must be famished, you can stay and keep me company." Bailey was excited to have some food and found a nice warm place in front of the stove to curl up and have a snooze.

As they ate dinner Mary spoke about the village and how it was controlled by a powerful Governor and why she felt so restricted—everyone had to be inside before it got dark, permission was required to leave the village and all the money earned went back to the Governor—and so she had no money to leave. Olbert had been very kind to Mary, often bringing her oranges from the next village as a treat. Amelia shared how she was moving home and how scared she was about that.

The next morning the ladybugs were buzzing in Amelia's ears, trying to get her attention. She got out of bed, followed the ladybugs out of the house and down the street where she found Bailey tied up in front of a house. He was crying out, "Help, help, Amelia, please untie me." As she got closer a man sitting on the porch asked, "Is he yours?" Amelia said "Yes, but why is he tied up?" "He ate one of my fish," the man said, pointing to a pond in his garden. "I had 8 goldfish and now I only have 7." "Hmm, how do you know he ate your fish?" asked Amelia. "Last night there were 8 fish and I came out this morning and caught him by the pond, so it had to be him."

Bailey exclaimed, "I went to the pond, as I was thirsty, and the next thing I was grabbed, a rope put around my neck and I was tied up here." Amelia left Bailey and ran back to Mary's house and explained what had happened. Mary was quite worried, "Oh no, that is where the Governor lives, we must find a way for Bailey to escape."

Amelia couldn't hold back her tears any longer, she was so upset, "I want my Mum and Dad, if we weren't moving to a new house, none of this would have happened, I want to wake up from this horrible dream." Mary hugged her and reassured her that everything would be okay. Amelia took some long deep breathes to calm herself. While Mary placed a blanket and some food in a satchel, Olbert flew into a tree nearby to watch and wait for the Governor to leave his house so he could help Bailey escape. The ladybugs quietly flew to Bailey and slowly chewed through the rope. Then as soon as Olbert gave the signal, Bailey ran back to Mary's house and Amelia placed him into the satchel and covered him with the blanket.

Mary quickly showed them a way out of the village, so they wouldn't be seen by anyone, and told Amelia that she could trust Olbert to guide her to the Golden Temple where the Rainbow Circle would take her home. Mary hugged Amelia, wishing her the best and Amelia thanked Mary for her kindness.

Amelia had learnt a lot about emotions and how it felt good to release them from her body. She also learnt about power and control. The 2nd energy is located just below the belly button and relates to emotions, i.e. blame, guilt, anger, fear, power, control, love, happiness, gratitude and joy. See bright ORANGE in this area of the body.

Once they had left the village there were wide open fields ahead with no trees to hide them and Amelia started to worry that they would be seen, because they weren't out of danger yet. The ladybugs knew the directions to take through the fields, so Olbert flew high in the sky to watch behind, leaving Amelia, Bailey and the ladybugs to go ahead. Soon the trail changed into a field of vibrant yellow sunflowers towering above them and Amelia felt calm and safe again. When she let Bailey out of the satchel, he was thrilled to be out of harm's way with her and stayed close by. After a few hours, Amelia's stomach started aching and groaning, the morning had been very upsetting, so she decided to stop for a while and have something to eat. Bailey sat in the sun and his golden fur glowed in the sunlight, he was appreciative of being saved and so proud of Amelia for being brave.

Amelia overcame her fear of the situation and by trusting, they were now safe. By experiencing so much emotion her stomach was reacting to her feelings. The 3rd energy is located just below the rib cage. Information within us and from the outside world is stored here and relates to trust, fear, beliefs, self esteem and confidence. See vibrant YELLOW in this area.

Everyone felt reenergized to continue on the journey. At the edge of the field of sunflowers there appeared a mountain. Olbert remarked, "Wise old Bob lives at the top, we can stay with him tonight." So, they made their way up the steep trail towards the top of the mountain. Bailey got tired so Amelia placed him back into her satchel. The ladybugs were having a lovely time along the path stopping every now and again to eat. As they got higher and higher up the mountain Amelia became short of breath and her shoulder was beginning to hurt from carrying Bailey, but she pushed on.

As they reached the top of the mountain, they saw Bob's little wooden hut with smoke billowing from the chimney. Since they were up so high, there were clouds all around them. In front of the hut was the old man with his long white beard and brilliant blue eyes. Bob gave them all a welcoming smile. He had been tending his vegetable patch where he grew zucchinis, peas and spinach. By the time Amelia had told Bob her story it was becoming dark, so he insisted that they stay. Amelia was very grateful and Bailey brushed against the old man to thank him. Bob explained that he had lived there for 20 years and grew all of his own food. Just below his house was a waterfall and he loved to go there to sit and meditate, as he found it very calming and peaceful. Amelia could see love and happiness in his eyes.

As Amelia and Bob sat outside talking, the clouds cleared and they looked up into the night sky at the millions of stars, and Amelia said, "I feel so small when I look up into the sky." Bob said, "You are just as important and powerful as every star in the sky. Shine brightly and this will create love in your heart and others will sense the power of your love. The heart hears your thoughts before your brain. If love lives in your heart it will attune to love, if fear, sadness or anger lives there, the heart will experience negativity." Amelia thought a lot about what Bob had told her and the fact that her parents and Auntie must be wondering where she was. In her mind, she imagined them with her, giving them each a hug and telling them she was okay.

Amelia was learning that love and happiness start from within and that what we think and feel can change our experiences. The 4th energy is located in the heart area, it relates to self love, love for others, compassion, hope, grief, hate, connection with yourself and others, with the earth and the spiritual world. See emerald GREEN in this area.

The next morning the sun was shining through the clouds, there was a gentle breeze and Amelia felt calm and peaceful. Bob gave her a bag of supplies and walked with them down to the waterfall. Amelia could hear the roar of the rushing water before they arrived. There in front of them was a magnificent gushing cascade falling into a pool below. There were blue lotus lilies in the crystal-clear water and trees and flowers were flourishing all around the edges. Bailey found some red dragonflies to chase.

Amelia loved it there and didn't want to leave. After a rest the old man collected some water, and said, "You have two options for your journey ahead, you can go through the waterfall or climb up the side next to it." Amelia quietly thought and decided, "We will go through the waterfall. Sorry Bailey, I know you don't like water, but it feels like the correct choice." When Bob gave Amelia a hug goodbye, she felt a surge of energy well up inside of her and go through her whole body. Olbert said, "The ladybugs and I will fly ahead and meet with you later."

Amelia felt proud about making a decision on her own, she was learning to listen to her inner wisdom. The 5th energy is located in the throat area and relates to speaking your truth, expression, strength of will, choices and judgement. See sky BLUE in this area.

Amelia placed Bailey into her satchel, took off her shoes and walked into the water carrying the satchel above her head. As she got closer to the waterfall she saw steps, so she followed them until they came into a huge opening behind the waterfall. In this cave, it felt cool and damp and there were deep blue pools of water. Amelia looked inside the bag that Bob had given her and found a candle, some matches and a sandwich. Bailey was hungry, but Amelia decided that they would not eat until they caught up with the others again. Suddenly Bailey called out, "Amelia, there's a tunnel here." Amelia felt that must be the way, so she lit the candle and off they cautiously went into the tunnel. It was very dark and there were indigo coloured bats flying around them. Bailey was frightened of them as they kept flying at him, but luckily, they didn't like the candlelight so they stayed away from Amelia.

Amelia was now becoming more aware of her senses and ideas from others. The 6th energy is located in the centre of the forehead — it relates to the senses, being open to others, new ideas and insights. See INDIGO in this area.

Auntie Amanda had taught Amelia how to say affirmations out loud. Doing this might help her nervousness so Amelia stood still and said, "I am safe, I am loved, I am happy and all is well," saying it over and over again until she started to relax. With the candlelight shining on the walls of the tunnel, they sparkled with amethyst crystals. Suddenly all of the crystals in the tunnel lit up and there was violet light all around them. Amelia was much calmer and soon she could see the end of the tunnel. As she reached the opening, Olbert and the ladybugs were waiting for them and they were so pleased to see they had made it through. Olbert said, "now onto the Golden Temple."

Amelia was nearly ready to go home, she had grown so much emotionally in her journey. The 7th energy is located at the top of the head, it relates to the connection with the spiritual world, courage, values, oneness, inner guidance, forgiveness and inspiration. See the colour VIOLET here.

Knowing they were getting closer to the temple gave everyone renewed energy and enthusiasm. After traveling awhile Olbert said, "I can see it, I can see it, we are nearly there." Amelia was so looking forward to seeing her family again. As they reached the Golden Temple Amelia marveled at its beauty and magnificence. It was a gigantic golden bell-shaped structure supported by massive pillars. There were many people and animals coming and going, and occasionally the bell would ring with the sound vibrating through the ground under their feet. Amelia said goodbye to the ladybugs who were going straight to the temple to ask for rain. Olbert took Amelia and Bailey on a tour of the paintings and statues in the great hall attached to the temple. Later, as they entered the temple, it started to rain outside, Amelia was so excited, "It's a miracle, the ladybugs will be overjoyed!"

Amelia was learning if you have a strong desire for something, intentionally think about it and ask the universe, it can be created. Olbert knew his teachings were almost complete and Amelia's energy centres would be clear enough to make the trip home.

Within the temple, everywhere Amelia looked everything was covered in gold. There were hundreds of glowing candles and it felt very serene. Olbert pointed to a garden next to the temple where a tremendous ring had been carved out of rock in the ground. Amelia asked, "Is that the Rainbow Circle Mary told me about? How can that take us home?" Olbert said, "Wait until the rain has stopped and I will show you."

Amelia sat down against a pillar and opened the bag that Bob had given her, he had placed a note in there which said, *"Imagine, Believe and it will Be"*—Amelia liked that. Bailey shared the sandwich, then curled up and had a sleep. As soon as the rain stopped Olbert flew over to get them, "Amelia, quick, place Bailey into your satchel and come to the circle." As she got near, a beautiful vibrant rainbow appeared above it. "Stand in the centre, Amelia, close your eyes and imagine in your mind seeing each colour of the rainbow forming a sphere around you." Amelia stood in the centre, closed her eyes and thought of all of the colours of the rainbow and what Olbert had taught her on the journey—red, orange, yellow, green, blue, indigo and violet, and realised that each colour could connect with each energy centre in her body to make a complete circle.

Now she understood what Bob said, *"Imagine, Believe and it will Be,"* so she believed it was possible to see the rainbow become a full circle through her, as she did, her whole body started to fade into the rainbow energy and she was gone. In her mind, she saw white light all around her and as she slowly opened her eyes, she was sitting back on the bench with Bailey by her side in her Auntie's garden. It was like time stood still while she had an amazing magical, healing journey.

She thought a lot about the power of the rainbow and how, by focussing on her inner wisdom, it allowed her to be one with the universe. She had discovered many things about herself including how the energy in the body is affected by different emotions and the importance of clearing and releasing negative emotions to enjoy a happy and healthy life.

In memory of my godmother, Joan, who shared her inner sparkle with everyone she met.

Much love and thanks to Michael for being the special soul that you are!

Thank you to every person who has entrusted me with their story to enable us to work together to release the past and start living in the now.

I am very grateful to Lisa Hardwick for allowing this opportunity to come into my life and to Katina Gillespie and Chelle Thompson for assisting in the process.

CHARMAINE VAUTOUR

CHARMAINE VAUTOUR is known by her friends and family as a funny, caring and compassionate person. Her extreme transparency and authentic personality paves the way for others to do the same. Charmaine's ability to wholeheartedly share both her triumphs and challenges continues to inspire many. Charmaine's dedication over the last eleven years working hands on with Dual Diagnosed adults has served as a reminder of her higher purpose. Spending much of her time writing, she created a blog where she shares stories of both her successes and challenges showing others how to seek the silver lining within. A network marketing entrepreneur and advocate for Young Living Essential oils, she passionately educates others on how to live a chemical and toxin free lifestyle. Charmaine's resiliency in overcoming her childhood traumas has uniquely positioned her as a trusted and respected Spiritual Leader.

🌿 Silver Linings

I was once asked how I could be so positive, how could everything be so amazing for me? My response, "It's not. It's a CHOICE." One of the biggest gifts my journey brought me was being able to find the silver lining; to look at each experience as a personal teaching tool and find the thing about it that was amazing. If you look hard enough you will always find it. Don't get me wrong, I have sat in the midst of some of the most troublesome circumstances, been that girl who was hanging on by a frayed rope but from all of that I grew. I learned and most of all I remained grateful. This is my story and how it began!

My name is Charmaine, I'm the youngest sibling of four and I have always secretly been grateful for that. Being the youngest allowed me to watch my older sibling's milestones but also their mistakes and choose whether or not I would travel the same paths. I grew up in a fatherless house and while there were times I found myself wondering who my father was, or what he was like, I mostly sat in gratitude for at least having my mom, who by the way is amazing. Besides, I had two older brothers who gave me all the male influence I needed. I have been through lots of drastic changes in my life, each one teaching me something different. The biggest and most self-morphing was about eight years ago when my coworker and soul sister (as I like to refer to her), gave me a book called "The Secret". She encouraged me to read it and see how I felt. Perhaps she knew I was ready, or maybe it was on a whim? Regardless of her reasons, I love her for all of it.

I could have never imagined the journey her gift would take me on. For months I brought that book everywhere with me. Sometimes, I would even just randomly open it up without calculation like shaking a magic eight ball after asking it a question and eagerly anticipate its answer. To my surprise its random page would miraculously be what I needed. The sentence was always something that resonated deeply with what I was supposed to know in that moment. I spent months after that trusting the Universe and its energy to lead me in perfect unwaveringly timing to the next place in my journey. I made vision boards, set daily intentions, recited gratitude lists, repeated daily mantras to myself like...I continue to grow in self-love and awareness. I am inspired and yes even "money comes easily and effortlessly to me". I then sat in gratitude open minded to the promise that it would show up. I began appreciating conversations about abundance, inspiration, mental expansion and vibrational energy. Anyone who wanted to converse about enlightenment, purpose, earth energy or the mind body connection, I was all ears for. It seemed the more I learned the more I wanted to learn. I literally could not get enough.

I began finding myself forgoing shopping (a favorite past time) to spend my time at our local bookstore looking for the next book to be inspired by. There I would be, standing in the spiritual section allowing myself to be drawn to the book that picked me. Holding my hands over the spine of each book until one magnetically drew me in and I'd just have to own it. I trusted that the universe would work its magic that the book I'd chosen and its contents would give to me more than I could hope for. Too eager to wait until I got home to open them, I'd sit right there on the carpeted floor beneath the tower of books above me and around me, reading the beginning pages. Every book I chose and devoured, I would find another that would lift me to the next level of consciousness. Taking my mind in a million and new adventurous places, reaching mental awareness I hadn't thought possible. Inspired and expanding, it was not long after I started to notice the synchronicity in why I had chosen those books. It seemed to be divine orchestration of the Universe. The experiences that would follow seemed less likely now to hurt or hinder me but rather provide me with a situation to master my new skills. Manifestation became a new way of life. Every uncomfortable situation thereafter somehow seemed a lot less scary as I brought with me my new awareness. I knew that I was able to choose what I thought about, how I responded and observe from an experience stand point and then proceed to my silver lining within it. Each book opened me up wider, shattering all my preconceived perceptions. I learned that the biggest part of this process was releasing my ego brain and servicing myself from my soul space where unconditional love resides. I realized that circumstance was merely an experience with which to grow. The problem could actually be the opportunity, pain the platform. I had become so moved by my personal revelations and authentic self that I would quickly go to social media writing post after post. I began sharing my experiences and more importantly my strategies for working through them, in hopes of teaching and inspiring others the same way.

My life was rapidly changing. I was glued to its winding path as if on some thrill-seeking roller coaster anticipating every new experience, good or bad using each resource as a means to grow and learn. I did not realize way back then that those experiences were preparing me for one of the biggest challenges in my life. An opportunity was about to present and I would be tested on how I was going to show up!

Two years ago, my eldest sibling got sick. His illness was sudden and took us all by surprise. He was the strongest person I knew both mentally and physically. While we were not always close growing up being that he was eleven years older and had moved out of our home long before I could remember; I still loved him dearly.

It was a Friday night when I drove my eldest brother to the hospital and within days his condition went from bad to worse. Slipping into unconsciousness and requiring intubation, the doctors took no time to diagnose him with end stage liver failure. Devastated and in shock I offered without hesitation to give him my liver. In fact, I insisted. I quickly got to work filling out the sixteen-page questionnaire and completing my blood work which would eventually prove we were a match. There was not a person or doctor who could share enough facts about this lengthy surgery or its potential risks that could deter me in my quest to save his life. Believe me, they tried. I knew the lists of risks, how long the recovery process would be (for both of us) as well as the uncertain guarantee that his body would even accept my donation. Yet still my decision remained the same.

One afternoon as mom and I were standing at my brother's bedside in the ICU crying and uncertain, the transplant team of doctors walked in. There must have been eight or nine of them in white coats shaking our hands one after the other when one of them introduced themselves He was a very tall and thin doctor with a full head of silver streaked curly hair and kind blue eyes. As he explained their game plan heading into the weekend I can still remember the excitement and hope he passed along as he spoke. His plan to bring my brother out of unconsciousness and prepare him for his transplant surgery brought all hope. I could feel the color restore in my cheeks as his promising words ignited my desperate and saddened heart. I mean, this was the first glimmer of something positive I was hearing since he first fell ill. He went on to explain that the transplant team would be meeting with me on Monday to go over the details of our surgeries when I noticed one of the doctors standing at the foot of my brother's bed abruptly walk out. I assumed that perhaps one of the many pages that went out over the intercom system were for him. Moments later he returned just as he'd left and announced "The transplant is off the table!" Surprised and in shock, I asked him to repeat. Again, he replied, "The transplant is off the table!" Crying and scared I asked him why? He explained that my brother had a massive cancerous tumor in the main vein of his liver and transplanting was no longer an option. How could this be? How could all the cards land so perfectly in our laps at a second chance at life? I mean, I was willing to give him my liver. I was right there healthy and happy to do so, no hesitations. Willing to accept all risks and in a moments time have that completely striped with just one word, Cancer. Those words hit me like a ton of bricks; each breath thereafter took extreme effort. It felt like I was drowning and the only tool to save me was a boat with no bottom. I hadn't left my brothers side in eleven days, remaining faithful in my promise to stay with him. I spent all my waking hours pouring my love and prayers onto him. Slept restlessly in a metal chair so that I was close by should he have miraculously woken up and needed me. I spent endless hours laying my head next to his, careful not to touch any of the multiple life sustaining tubes and wires coming from his body. Wondering what his subconscious mind was thinking, if at all. Hoping he could hear my endless pleas for him to fight harder.

It would be seven days later that my brother would take his final breath. I was still there holding his hands as I had all the days before, whispering my farewells to his spirit. Pleading for his return from the afterlife to guide me. I pressed my forehead over his, watching as my tears meticulously left my eyes and rhythmically slide down his cheeks. Why this outcome had to be I'm not sure but what I was about to learn is that this situation and its devastation could either break me or elevate me and it was going to be up to me to choose.

I have never been so close to death, to give love and comfort to someone who is crossing over. While this experience was one that was hard and tested me, I chose to seek the silver lining. I quickly found I began to feel extremely fortunate. Blessed if you will, to have been that pillar of strength for him and my family. To have my faith and strength tested; stretched far past my mental capacities so that all of who I was could unravel and be reborn. I feel honored that in his last days he gave me such a gift, that he trusted and chose me to see him through his journey onward. There's something to be said about how you get through these tough life changing situations. Something to be learned about ourselves and those we're caring for. Something about the resilience of the human mind when you put it into its best practice. My brothers passing transformed me. I CHOSE to let this journey elevate me rather than sit in the devastation of it. To see the gift within. Leaning fully into it rather than resisting it so that I could honor both him and myself. Allowing all we had both just gone through to launch me forward onto the path I believe I was meant to walk.

This experience of life and death broke barriers for me, stripped away the foundation for which I once stood and catapulted me forward into the next phase of my journey. It taught me the value of time, how we choose to utilize it, what mark we want to leave and more importantly whom we may impact along the way.

We ALWAYS have a choice when faced with life's most challenging situations. We, get to decide how we want to write our endings. I'm not saying you can change the circumstance you're in but you can certainly change how you let it define you. That does not negate from acknowledging the pain of our experiences there is growth in that too. Just don't let it be your final resting place. When you seek to find the lesson in all your experiences, good and bad, you set yourself free from the bondage of fear which holds you back. I could have certainly let this painful experience and all others before it, be an excuse to sit in discernment or depression. Questioning God, of my mere existence as we sometimes do but where would that have gotten me? What purpose would that have served and to whom would that have ultimately hurt or hindered? Choosing to allow myself to grow past the pain, ultimately allowed me to heal and help those long after me who suffer the same. That was never more evident as it would only be six months later that I would be beaconed to do it all over again with my uncle who too was journeying onward. I can't say I was prepared or even that I had fully processed through the pain yet of losing my brother but I allowed this to be validation of an early job, well done.

We cannot prevent life's hardships but we can allow them to teach us. What we gain from them is up to us. I learned a very valuable life lesson in which I will carry with me all the places I travel next. Being able to seek the silver lining is empowering. Knowing that whatever life is throwing at you can be used to your advantage. Allow it to guide you to walk a transparent path, of understanding and growth. Strengthening you for all that lay ahead.

If I leave you here with anything let it be this. Seeking the silver lining does not mean that you maneuver through your situation finding bliss immediately on the other side. Sometimes the silver in your circumstances are hard realizations. A truth you were unwilling to previously negotiate. Let me explain it this way. Have you ever felt like you were constantly challenged by the same things over and over again? Struggling with the same emotions time and time again, only to walk away feeling endlessly defeated. This continues to happen because we are not growing from the lessons the universe is providing.

Be present in the moment. Commit to processing through the pain rather than avoiding it as this is where true transformation exists.

Seeking to see the silver lining can be an eye opening experience when it reveals the disservice we do to ourselves. Remember this, YOU are not your circumstances but rather a product of how you allow them to teach and define you. Be fearless in the pursuit of your growth, fearless on the pursuit of your path. For YOU and I were perfectly chosen to walk it.

Namaste

I dedicate this chapter to my Soul sister, Anna Young, whose leadership skills saw to it that I was ready to walk this path. Your continued guidance and sister ship will be something I will forever hold gratitude for. To my brother, Roy, whose gift of choosing me brought lessons I could have never foreseen and from them allowed me to shed layers and be reborn. I dedicate this chapter to my family who proudly allows me to be everything authentic. Your continuous encouragement fuels me to lead by example and be all that I have envisioned for myself and for you. I dedicate this chapter to every teacher and tribe sister who has risen up for me growing and guiding me on this path of spiritual awakening. Lastly, to everyone I've not yet met but who are being divinely orchestrated to my path in perfect universal timing so that we may continue to elevate and inspire the Spiritual leaders in others along our paths.

VICKY MITCHELL

VICKY MITCHELL — Health is a process and a journey. So far, my journey has included eczema, psoriasis, allergies, difficult periods, learning uniqueness, infertility issues, weight fluctuations, candida overgrowth and cataracts. I have studied with many mentors and teachers to understand and overcome these conditions. This training has resulted in earning certifications from The Institute for the Psychology of Eating and the Institute Of Integrative Nutrition. With food, attitude and energy as medicine, I have developed a passion for self-improvement and health. I would be honored to coach you to help you reach your wellness goals.

I am a healing coach who empowers you to improve your health and joy by reducing stress the easy way.

vicky@vickymitchell.com
vickymitchell.com

A Battle For Accountability

I recently found myself in a battlefield with truth.

When I am happy and voice what others desire to hear, the verbal cannons of my audience are filled with love, acceptance and other forms of positive feedback. Yet, when I speak of things they do not want to hear, I am bombarded with bullets, belittlement, hate, resentment and fear. If my words are music to their ears, we are allies; accepting of the boundaries and requirements of one another while working together to accomplish mutual results. The battle ignites when I hold others accountable for their committed actions to follow agreed upon requirements.

These battles are more than disagreements. Rather, they become forms of emotional bullying. I have been the victim of bullying both in my personal life and my real estate investments.

The objective of my real estate business is to offer homes for rent that I myself would enjoy occupying. I purchase houses, renovate them and practice proper and timely maintenance to provide my tenants with a comfortable place to call home. I have been blessed to have tenants who understood and appreciated my philosophy of comfort and care to help make their lives better.

A recent experience with one of my tenants proved to be an exception. I employ a property management team to conduct quarterly walk-through inspections of my properties, oversee routine preventive maintenance, and address any issues that may arise.

The tenants in this story told the property management company that they were planning on building a house of their own and agreed to sign a 12-month lease to live in one of my properties. One of the terms of the lease was that they agreed to take financial responsibility for any repairs required as a result of any damage caused by their two cats, which I allowed under the terms of the lease.

Sixty days before the expiration of the lease, the tenants informed us that they were experiencing building delays and requested a month-to-month lease. This came as a surprise because each time my management team completed a quarterly inspection the tenants reported that their move-out schedule was still on track to vacate the property at the end of the lease term. I made an exception to my 12-month rule and offered them a 7-month lease. They declined my offer and confirmed they would vacate the property on the originally agreed upon date. And at this point the dynamics of our relationship changed.

I met with my real estate agent to discuss the timing of selling the house. I gave the tenants more than the required 24-hour notice that my agent and I would be conducting an inspection of the premises in preparation of selling the property.

When we arrived, the male tenant opened the door and invited us in. Immediately upon entering the house, my agent and I were overwhelmed by the smell of cat urine and noticed spots of cat urine on the carpet, which I had not been informed of by the property management company.

I explained to the tenants that we were there to evaluate whether or not to place the house on the market while they were still living there, and decide if we should update the pictures for the new listing. Even though the lease stated I was allowed to market the house while they were still living there, the male tenant proceeded to fire off a round of verbal ammunition, listing all the things that I could not photograph. I immediately reacted to his attack by turning to him and firmly stating that, "I will be contacting my lawyer to determine everyone's legal rights."

So the battle had begun. I could feel my fight or flight response awakening by my quickening heart rate. I then told him that we came on friendly terms. He laughed condescendingly and disagreed. My response was to be aware, listen and act based on how my intuition was guiding me at that moment. I then turned to my agent and said, "We're not getting anywhere with this. Let's do the walk-through." I asked the man if he would like to join us and he snarled, "Yes, I don't want you touching any of my stuff." I told him that it wasn't in my best interest to touch his belongings.

I then asked if they had my contact information and the man's wife replied that it was in a letter they had received from the property management company. I asked to see the letter because I had not received a copy of it. I read the letter and noticed that the management company stated the tenants owed an additional month's rent after their lease ended. I told the tenants that the management company made a mistake and that they would send out a corrected letter. The man then chose to cease fire.

All three of us then proceeded to tour the house. Upon completion of the inspection I thanked him and told him that we had not yet decided if we were going to list the house at this time, and if we would need to take additional photos. My agent gave him her business card and told him she would call him when we made the decision. She also assured him that if he or his wife were not home during a showing she would be there to ensure the cats remained in the house. Once we decided to list the house we informed the tenant, even though we legally did not have to inform him we were selling the property.

To our surprise, a second confrontation with the tenant took place after my agent left him a voicemail 48 hours prior to the first scheduled showing. This was well before the required 24-hour notice as stated in the lease, and well within our legal rights. Twenty-four hours later the man returned her call and demanded to speak with the property management company or the property owner. He said he was not given the required 24-hour notice and would not "talk to the likes of a real estate agent."

My real estate agent and I discussed his demands and worked with him to reschedule the showing, and I agreed to personally inform him of all the viewings. The tenant and I were cooperating. Another cease fire had begun.

There were many potential buyers, all of whom expressed that the house was well maintained, but that the cat odor was overwhelming. One cat owner said that, "I like the house but the odor is too strong and would drive my cat nuts."

After the tenants moved out my agent and I conducted our final walk-through and were pleasantly surprised that the cat odor seemed to be gone. But the smell began to return during the following week. Upon further inspection, we discovered stains on the living room carpet, and the padding and flooring underneath the carpet. My team of professionals repaired the floor and installed new padding and carpet throughout the house.

The following morning during my daily spiritual routine of gratitude, prayer and protection, I decided to hold the tenant accountable for damages to the house. My intuition told me he would not be pleased. I sent him a text telling him that I appreciated the condition in which he left the house, but I would be returning only a third of his security deposit to cover the damage made by the cats. I was relieved that I spoke my truth, but fearful of his reaction.

While I was driving the tenant called and I answered my cell phone using my hands-free option. He demanded in a defensive tone of voice that we discuss the partial return of the security deposit. And so began the next in a series of battles.

He proceeded to use his verbal artillery of hate, telling me that his wife "hated my guts and my house" and that, "you are a horrible landlord". He was glad I decided to sell the house, "so no one else would have to put up with me". He threatened that he wanted to "sue the pants off me", but that his pregnant wife did not want to deal with it. During a pause where he reloaded his verbal gun I calmly stated, "I am overnighting your check today." He conceded slightly and told me that as long as he received the check within five days he would not sue me. I then calmly reiterated that I would overnight the check even though I legally had 30 days to return the security deposit, and ended the call.

I felt shell-shocked and was shaking. I pulled into a parking lot, took some deep cleansing breaths and tried to process what had just happened. A friend called and I explained the situation to her. As the conversation turned to other things, I was able to push my feelings down. After the call ended I went to the post office and sent the check by overnight mail, clearly indicating that the package could be delivered only if signed for by the recipient.

I tracked the package online the following day and learned that the first delivery attempt had been made. The tenant took several days to pick up the package from the post office. I was surprised and felt nervous until five days later when I confirmed that he had deposited the check. I was relieved this battle had ended, but still felt dazed and confused as to why this man's verbal bullets continued to ricochet through my mind.

I thought about why the attack still mattered to me, because I had been within my legal rights with respect to the damage done to the house. I knew his comments to be untrue. The question now was how to be proud of myself for keeping calm while in the line of fire, and for not reacting to the war he waged with his words.

To begin healing, I asked my heavenly team to remove the tenant's negative energy from me. I journaled about the experience and transmuted this energy by burning the paper which contained my thoughts. I focused on nourishing myself by doing things that brought me joy so I could replace the void this battle had caused with love. But my wounds were not healing, so to feel heard and to seek validation from others I trust, I discussed the situation with my husband and sales agent.

I then visualized severing the cord that was still binding me to my former tenants. I assigned a color to the battle and pictured taking back my energy from them and returning theirs. I also imagined myself in a washing machine removing their essence. I forgave both the tenants and myself by journaling what I had learned from the battle.

Even after using several tools, I did not understand why I felt that I was still in the battle. I kept replaying the events over and over again in my head. Then I spoke to one of my spiritual teachers who explained that even though I did not react in words or deeds, I had absorbed the man's negative energy. I had not realized that observing is an important part of not reacting. I had left out an important piece of amour which resulted in me absorbing his anger and frustration. By understanding this, I was able to release the trauma from my mind.

I now recognize that a better approach on that day would have been to park my car before I spoke to the man. In addition, I could have taken a deep breath and asked my heavenly team for additional support. My hands would have been free to put over my heart, which helps me listen by being fully present, so I could send my tenant love and compassion.

I am human and know that I may not always be able to accomplish this, but I learned an important lesson: that part of not reacting is to avoid absorbing the negative energy of others. My peace was restored after I let go of the situation and my perceived expectations of what *should* have occurred.

I have come a long way in my journey to voice my truth and boundaries. I recounted this story to show that humans are continually learning. This lesson is about finding the courage to increase self-care and self-love by slowing down and being present in a situation. In my healing coaching business, I empower others to do the same.

May we all learn from interactions, whether it is a battlefield, a celebration, or anything between.

I wish you love, light and laughter on your journey called life.

I dedicate this chapter to everyone who has ever experienced bullying. May you find the courage to stand strong as you maintain your boundaries.

I would like to acknowledge and thank my heavenly team, family, friends, mentors and editors for encouraging and guiding me to have the power to speak my truth.

MISTY PROFFITT-THOMPSON

MISTY PROFFITT-THOMPSON is a best-selling author, psychic medium, intuitive teacher, a Certified Angel Card Reader, Mind, Body, and Spirit Practitioner, business owner, and speaker.

She resides in Thatcher, Arizona, where she enjoys spending time with her husband, four children, and her four grandchildren. In her work, she assists clients on their spiritual path through connection with angels, passed loved ones, and the use of her intuitive abilities.

contact@mistymthompson.com
www.mistymthompson.com

✭ Turning Judgments Into Light

We live in a world filled with judgments, but I no longer accept that way of living. I once let my ego lead me on that journey, as I am sure many others do. We are spiritual beings and that aspect of our nature, rather than the judgmental, self-focused ego, requires nurturing so that our inner light will shine bright.

Making decisions from the mind and not the heart can produce an unfavorable outcome. No matter the path you take, you will ultimately encounter and receive the life lessons you are here to learn. With free will, we each make decisions about our life and if you decide on the path created with your mind, those lessons will be difficult and more challenging. Traveling another path, of living from both the mind and heart, with a mental and spiritual compass, will result in the perfect destination. Living in a place that is suitable for both your mind and your heart will ensure a balanced perspective; you will learn your life lessons with less hardship. With your mind and heart in harmony, you will live without judgments. This connection brings about true joy and happiness, which we all truly deserve. Your heart is represented by the light you emit to the world, while judgment comes from your ego, or the mind. In judgment, your ego is guiding your decisions and the leadings of your heart are neglected. In this dynamic, your connection with others is also disrupted. You are giving your ego permission to make decisions that affect your relationships with others, and that does not lead to an acceptable outcome.

When our power is given over to our egos, chaos and drama will follow. When this occurs, judgment of yourself and others will come. This will create low self-esteem and a lack of self-confidence. When judging others, you are really judging yourself, as it is only a deceptive reflection; those flaws that you see in yourself will be the flaws you see in others. Conversely, seeing the positive in yourself will guarantee that you see in others those positive attributes.

 When you judge another, you do not define them, you define yourself.

~WAYNE DYER

I am working through judgments myself and I am hopeful that the insight I have found in that process, shared in this chapter, also helps you to see the challenges you face in a more positive light.

Feeling judged is an awkward, uncomfortable, and daunting experience. Being honest about who I am, where I fit in, and seeking the approval of others is difficult. My entire working career was fraught with judgments. I now realize that when I felt that others were judging me, I was replaying the feelings I had about myself. What you give out, you receive, and since I was giving out judgment, that is what I was receiving.

That was and continues to be one of my biggest life lessons, even now. When employed at a federal prison, I realized the environment there was different from outside the prison. We had to act in a prescribed manner when present with the inmates. I also worked in the prison business office for much of my career, and I learned not only about the job but the people. Not many women worked in our institution and for a while it was as though we all banded together. With a new generation coming in, the judgments started. The women became more cliquish and I wondered why I was being left out of the group. Deep down I was glad, as those women were great on a one-on-one basis, but when together they were mean and bullies, and I did not want to take part in that destructive behavior.

But those judgments started filtering into my ego. "Why wasn't I included?" I would ask myself. "I must not be good enough. They hate me. I am different." These phrases haunted me. I understand now that this experience was one of my greatest teachers because my ego was crushed and my heart began to seek what truly matters.

We have all been in similar situations. Again, the outcome depends on how you respond. If you are utilizing your ego, those lessons will most likely be painful. Or, we can choose to act in kindness and love, respond from the heart, and those same responses will come back to us. We cannot avoid the experiences that touch our lives, with darkness but as the lesson is revealed, we can transform that darkness into light.

I consider judgment one of the dark emotions. Making assessments, whether based on what others say to you, or what you say about yourself, will only produce a gloomy outlook. I picture this darkness as a layer of black dust that can attach to my heart. This magnetic dust will affect how you respond to yourself and to others. As we now know, the darkness that we display to others is really the darkness we use against ourselves.

I consider joy, happiness, true friendship, kindness or any other uplifting emotion as light. When these emotions fill our heart, we display that light to others. Strangely, we then start aligning ourselves with those who also emit this light of love.

Learn How to Shift

We can learn to shift our thinking when it comes to judgment. As discussed previously, those who judge us aren't really directing those feelings toward us. They are instead appraising themselves. It is still hurtful but each time we recognize this truth, the blow becomes softer. When reflecting back on the people I worked with at the prison who tried to intimidate or bully me, I realize how hard they were on themselves. I take pity on them and recognize that it wasn't about me at all. Any resentment I had towards them is gone and only forgiveness remains. If I were to see them, I would thank them, as they have taught me so much about myself. I only wish that they could forgive themselves of the heartaches they must suffer from. I only wish them well. Does this mean that I would be willing to spend time with them should they contact me? Most definitely not. My life is fine without them. Bringing peace to the world must start with each of us, and I do not want to put my peace in jeopardy. But I also hope that they can find that place of peace.

Besides finding peace by looking within, you can also make a shift by writing out your perception of how you were treated when you felt judged. Describe how you feel, what happened, and what was taken from you. Anything and everything is fair game. Get it out of your head, from your ego and your heart, to rid your spirit of these painful memories. The following negative outcomes can result if you don't release it from your body:

1. It will be trapped inside your soul and pushed further and further down until it is buried so deep that you will become numb and desensitized to the world around you. You will start treating people the way you are feeling inside and you will only see the darkness in others. Not a healthy choice. Or,
2. It will end up festering, growing more toxic until it explodes and becomes extremely destructive. Either way, it is much more damaging to you than you realize.

Writing those feelings down that are trapped inside you is the healthiest outlet. Depending on how long you have had those feelings, this exercise may take some time, as it is a continuing process. Be patient with yourself and return to this as many times as needed. Writing out those feelings and getting them out of your mind and heart will cleanse your soul. The energy of describing those feelings will move the pain and darkness out of your body. Once you have finished this practice, tear up the paper, ensuring that you are destroying those feelings to let the positive ones in. I have learned that burning the paper puts that energy out into the universe for God to handle. I think of it as putting it into God's in-basket. You are no longer carting that negative energy around inside.

 A shift in energy is always followed by a change in reality.

~PANACHE DESAI

Focus on Your Outcome

While these negative and judgmental emotions that you once felt are literally being burned and lifted into the universe, think about what you would like to have fill the space where those negative emotions once lived. It is necessary to fill in that open spot with something positive and loving that will nurture and support your soul. This is where you can create your heart's desire. Exciting, but also a bit daunting as well, with this action you can do or be anything, and the best part is that there are no limits. Maybe your experiences can help someone else and you'll write about it, as I am. This is a journey, as we are a work in progress, and once we complete a cycle of understanding and learning, we can move forward. Journal about the outcome you would like to achieve. If you are unsure what to write just start transcribing any word or image that comes to mind and do not stop.

Picture the ending you are seeking in your mind. Answer specific questions about all that is going on around you during this visualization. Notice not only the emotions you are feeling and displaying, but also the visible components. Exactly what does your house look like, your office, your car, or wherever your vision takes you. The more specific the better; this means if you are in your dream car, get the make and model of the car you are driving, the color, and even the year. What does your house look like; better yet, what do you want your house to look like? What pictures are on the wall? The key is that you must own this like you already have it. Do not be concerned with the how. God, the Angels, and your Spirit Guides will take care of that. What emotions do you want to feel? Instead of judgment, how about feeling only love, acceptance, and excitement. What would your heart feel like then? I would imagine it would be full and overflowing with joy. That is the goal we are all working towards.

Embrace Your Shift

Continuing to do work on yourself calls for celebration. This is a reminder that now, since you have completed the healing of your heart and mind, you can discard your damaging feelings. Focus only on the outcome you are seeking, and the shift you have accomplished can now be fully embraced. It is almost unbelievable how the negative people that you once had in your life will drift away and new, more positive people will come into your life, as if by magic. Because you have made that change within and are no longer in a place of judgment, the mirror image you project will be that of love, peace, acceptance, and understanding. What you send out, you receive, and as a result, the people in your life will begin to reflect what you are feeling inside.

This is only the beginning, as you will continue to do the work needed to embrace that shift you have made. The process will start over with other emotions you are ready to face. I understand that life is busy and we have many responsibilities and obligations. Start with only 10 minutes in your day to at least read something inspirational, to journal, to mediate, or whatever it is that brings you one step closer to self-fulfillment and ultimate joy. That will make the light you have inside shine a little brighter.

 Don't use your energy to worry, use your energy to believe.

~UNKNOWN

Dedicated to those who have taught me about judgments.

I must acknowledge my family. You all have been my teachers and I know you always will be.

WENDY KITTS

At 42, WENDY KITTS went from a nine-to-five cubicle-gray existence in accounting to living in Technicolor as a writer—without ever having written anything before.

Seventeen years later, Wendy has published over 200 articles for publications such as *More, Reader's Digest,* and the *Globe & Mail.* She's the author of *Sable Island: The Wandering Sandbar* (Nimbus, 2011), a non-fiction children's book for seven to nine-year-olds; the author-illustrator of the upcoming picture book, *I Spy a Lighthouse*; and the co-author of several anthologies including *The Empowerment Manual* (Visionary Insight Press, 2015), and *When Heaven Touches Earth: A Little Book of Miracles, Marvels & Wonders* (Hierophant, 2016) featuring James Van Praagh.

She's also an editor and book coach, as well as a popular writing workshop facilitator. She's always open to sharing whatever she knows whether about freelance writing through her *My Life in Pajamas* classes; writing from the soul through her *Accessing the Writer Within* workshops; or removing limiting beliefs and engaging the power of the Universe through her *Infinite Possibilities for Writers* program (based on Mike Dooley's *New York Times* bestselling book *Infinite Possibilities: The Art of Living Your Dreams*) as an Infinite Possibilities certified trainer.

Wendy's following her own dreams of living and writing at the beach year-round, splitting her time between Caissie Cape, New Brunswick (Canada), and San Diego, California. But most importantly, Wendy is passionate about helping fledgling writers find and share their voices, thereby transforming themselves, their lives, and, by extension, the world.

For more information on how you can follow your writing whispers within, or to get your free copy of *Write for Profit & Bliss: Get Paid for Your Writing Now!* go to www.wendykitts.ca.

My Something Better

🌺 Just Do It.

~NIKE...AND MY COUSIN, DEBBIE

*S*ometimes *I lie in bed at night and try to connect the dots. The dots of how I got here. How I created this magical, authentic life as a writer living at the beach practically year-round.*

Did the magic start when I uprooted my tired life on the east coast of Canada and moved 3500 miles away? Or was it a year earlier, when my friend Helaine asked me to help with a cross-border book drive for a school in Los Angeles? Or maybe I needed to go back even further... when I first met her at a literary festival not long after I decided to finally follow the whispers within and fulfil my desire for a more creative life, a life of writing and art.

Or perhaps a few years before that, when I first connected with another friend through A Course in Miracles online group—the start of a seventeen-year friendship that was the catalyst for so much growth in my life and included a desire to go to Los Angeles to meet him.

Was Wes the first dot...was he my ground zero?

Wes who took me to San Diego for the first time because I'd always felt an inexplicable pull to the oceanside city. Where I stood next to him on Mission Beach, six-foot waves crashing in front of us, feeling like I'd finally found "home."

Was that where the journey to my authentic life began? When I proclaimed with a deep and ancient knowing, "I'm going to live here."

Or maybe, just maybe, the magic began the day I was born, a gift from my real home to accompany me on my physical adventure. Is it possible the Universe lovingly scattered its breadcrumbs beckoning me to follow even back then? Even though my eyes were closed to its magic? Even though I was already lost in the dream of my life?

A few weeks after my life-altering trip to California, my cousin Debbie asked me on Facebook about my visit to the "land of purple trees" as I called it. I told her I fell in love with San Diego and its jacaranda-lined streets and wanted to move there, but just couldn't figure out how. Debbie answered with three simple words: "Just do it."

Just do it? Was she nuts? I raged inwardly. How could I just do it? Sure, as a Canadian I'm allowed to live in the US without a visa for roughly six months a year. And even though my life as a freelancer is a portable one, what would I do with all of my stuff? And what about my apartment?

I'd scoured the Internet for weeks looking for options—storage rentals, home exchanges, sublets. Nothing felt right. And where would the money come from, since I'm not allowed to work in the US? Even the woman from San Diego who I was introduced to via email by a stranger who "randomly" contacted me for writing advice, turned out to be a dead-end.

No matter which way I turned, I hit walls. My dream came to a screeching halt. San Diego suddenly felt very far off.

Just do it, indeed. Angry, I shut my laptop and went to bed.

And then I got it. Like one of those Hollywood movie moments when a person sits straight up in bed roused from a deep sleep with an "aha" moment, *Yes*, I thought, *just do it*.

If my goal was to ultimately live in the place that felt like "home," why would I hold onto my life in Canada? Maybe I was sending the wrong message to the Universe. Maybe I needed to let go of my old life first, in anticipation of the new life.

I thought about a quote by author Joseph Campbell that I'd scrawled on a sticky note and stuck to my fridge years ago: *"We must be willing to get rid of the life we've planned, so as to have the life that is waiting for us. The old skin has to be shed before the new one can come."*

As long as I was focused on the "cursed hows," as author Mike Dooley calls them, I'd never see the path to my desires.

Yes. I had to ante up. Take the first step toward my dreams. Show the Universe I'm serious. State my intention, and then just stand back and let it work its magic.

The next morning I gave my notice on my apartment and started getting rid of decades' worth of stuff. I trusted the Universe would fill in the blanks and take me the rest of the way.

Nothing had changed. I still had no plan. No place to live. No way to earn money. But I never once wasted a thought on it. I just kept doing what someone would do if they were moving to another country.

And I never wobbled.

Not even when offered a lucrative three-month writing contract because it required me to be in Canada during the time I planned on being in California.

I had to act as if I were going. I had to take a leap of faith, *before* I knew the outcome.

And that's when the real magic happened.

That's when as Campbell also predicted, doors would appear where there were once only walls—doors just for me. And the spaces made empty from the shedding of my old, tired life, would be filled with something better. Something better than what I gave up. Something better than I could have imagined.

It was only when I stopped "trying" to find a way to move to San Diego that a way appeared. It was only when I trusted it would happen, that the ground rushed out to meet my bold, sure steps.

That's when that same woman, the one that I'd hit a dead-end with only weeks before, contacted me to say she suddenly and serendipitously had an opening for a roommate.

That's when a company, who I'd sent a résumé to months previously, offered me a monthly writing contract that I could do from anywhere in the world.

So, with everything in place, I booked my flight to the land of endless summer for the next six months.

But the magic didn't stop when I landed in San Diego.

In fact, the opposite happened.

Things fell spectacularly apart.

The roommate situation was not a fit. Plus, the house was inland—way inland. It took five hours to get to the beach and back by transit.

I scoured *Craig's List* and put down a deposit on a room. A dump, but it was just a block from beautiful, man-made Mission Bay. But mere days before I was to move in, the landlord changed her mind. She worked from home and wasn't keen on having someone else around all day. Disappointment flowed through my veins.

But Wes was adamant. He said something better was out there for me. I whined to him on the phone. Something better? What could be better than living next to a sandy bay framed in palm trees?

"It's not your place," he simply said.

And then, one early Sunday morning, just two weeks after arriving in San Diego, it was clear the roommate situation was a bust, and I checked into a Best Western.

I tried not to panic, despite being alone in a city where I knew no one. I held onto Wes' words that something better was coming. Surely the Universe didn't bring me all this way just to pull my dreams out from under me like a carpet?

I decided to trust that it was all part of the plan—that everything that had happened so far was just a stepping stone towards my something better. I gave myself a week for a new living situation to show up, and if it didn't, I'd go back to Canada and consider my time in California a respite from the brutal winter raging back home.

So instead of throwing a pity party for one, I consciously made the choice to enjoy my time. After all, it was January. Normally I'd be shivering and buried under snow, but instead I was at a nice hotel with a pool—an empty pool. No one but Canadians, I learned, swim in San Diego in January.

I spent my days floating on my back focused on the majestic palms swaying against the bluest sky I had ever seen in my life.

And by Tuesday, I had a place to live—a vacation rental in Mission Beach, rented sight unseen on *Craig's List*.

The woman from the rental agency had just returned from the East Coast where she had been visiting her daughter. She told me that she had gone to the Eric Carle museum. As a recently-signed children's book author, I took it as a sign.

The next day Wes drove down from LA and took me to my new place. Our jaws dropped as we pulled into the driveway of my new home. It was practically on the beach. The patio of my tiny studio cottage overlooked the patio of the sprawling beachfront house in front of me providing a clear ocean view. And since it was off-season, the rent was not much more than I'd paid inland.

And that place, that place that I just had to have, was on the far side of the bay just two blocks behind me.

Two blocks behind me.

When I stood on that bay a week earlier, I had no idea Mission Beach was just beyond the palm-rimmed bay. No idea that everything I dreamed of—the wild and glittering Pacific—was just beyond the palms.

I was ready to settle for a man-made beach. Ready to settle for something less than what I wanted—ready to settle for a dump—but the Universe wouldn't let me.

And even more unbelievable, my new place was not far from the spot where I had stood with Wes just three months earlier when I'd said I would live there one day.

This time, the magic was not lost on me.

The Universe had a plan all along.

The Universe always has a plan, but how many of us give up before the dots are connected, the magic engaged? How many of us settle for bays when what we really want is ocean? How many of us give up, when if we would just continue to trust, something better would show up?

And now.

Not years from now. Life's magic is engaged immediately.

But first, we must do our part. We must pry our sweaty, tired hands off the controls of our lives, and let go. Take a running leap: free fall with unwavering trust into the open arms of a loving Universe that's conspiring *for us*—not against us.

That's when the real magic happens. That's when the Universe rushes in to fill the now empty spaces with something better than what we let go of. Something better than we could even have imagined.

But we've got to continuously let go of what's not working. We need to be open and trust that everything that happens to us is a stepping-stone along our journey.

It was only a couple of weeks after moving into my magical cottage-by-the-sea that I realized the curriculum writing contract was too tech-heavy for me. I was spending my days with the blinds closed, shutting out the beauty around me in an effort to understand something that did not come easily, that would never come easily.

But by then, I was well-versed in the ways of the Universe. I knew I hadn't come all that way to be holed up inside. I could do that back in Canada. I recognized that, like the roommate that didn't pan out, that maybe the promise of financial security was just a way to get me there—like a carrot in front of a horse—to help me trust the magic.

And maybe, like those relationships you think you can never live without, I had to accept that some situations aren't necessarily forever, but simply another connected dot to help propel me to greater growth, to where I most needed to be.

So, I let the contract go willingly and continued to follow the signs. I spent my days browsing art stores and taking writing classes which took me even further down the path of my creative dreams. And I never looked back.

But it was up to me to take that initial step.

And yes, it was scary. I'm not going to lie. But just at first.

The fear was all in the first step.

So, go ahead—jump. Dare to have your "something better." Dare to live the life you've been too afraid to imagine because you thought it out of reach—the life that whispers to you conspiratorially in unguarded moments—like when you first open your eyes in the morning, when anything and everything is possible.

Because it is.

It's all there waiting for you. Just behind the proverbial palms.

Dedicated to my long-time friend, Wesley Doherty, who helped me connect so many dots in my life and believe in my "something better"; my soul-sister, Helaine Becker, who had a hand in many of my dreams coming true without even knowing it; and my cousin, Debbie O'Reilly, for pointing the way.

Thanks to Lisa Hardwick, Katina Gillespie and the Visionary Insight Press team for making this book possible. I'm honoured to be included in this anthology with all these amazing authors.

ANGELA ANDERSON

ANGELA ANDERSON is an essential oil loving mama of 2 currently based in Sherwood Park, Alberta. She is an Independent Platinum distributor with Young Living Essential Oils and has fully embraced the network marketing profession, especially the sense of purpose and accomplishment it brings, as well as the ability to help others achieve their goals. She is admittedly a work in progress, but strives daily to grow into the woman the universe intends her to be.

You can learn more on her website or contact her via the address below.
www.dropsofdestiny.ca
dropsofdestiny@yahoo.com

What? I Can Just Be Myself?

When I first started my business, I remember feeling completely overwhelmed. I looked at the women succeeding in my field and they were all uber religious homeschooling moms of eight. Their social media feeds showed them baking bread and making their own shampoo, all without a hair out of place in their perfect little homes with darling children in matching pinafores. Or at least that's how I interpreted it. (Disclosure: I have since met many of these women and they are absolutely lovely.) Me? I swear like a trucker and love a cold beer. My kids generally go to school with the remnants of breakfast still on their cheeks and my house often looks like it is one dirty dish away from being a hazmat site. See? One of these things is not like the other.

For a (very short) bit I tried to fit into the mold because that's what I thought it took to succeed. I attempted to DIY my own beauty products. I failed miserably. Most of what I made I couldn't post because it didn't turn out or it looked like one of my kids had packaged it. Truthfully my kids probably could have done a better job than I did. More importantly, I hated it.

I quickly realized I was not capable of pretending I was something I wasn't. I didn't want to succeed if it meant lying about who I was. I made the decision to do it on my terms, regardless of the result. I knew I might fail miserably, but at least I would be authentic. I took a deep breath and decided to be real (gulp!).

My first leap was posting on Facebook so that everyone could see what my "home office" really looked like. It was a picture of my laptop on my kitchen island with note-books, papers, reference guides and goodness knows what else spread from one end to the other. In the background you could see dirty dishes on the counter and pots and pans still sitting on the stove. It was scary, it was humbling, and it was real. You know what? People loved it. The feedback was mind blowing. It was like I had shown people what was behind the emerald curtain and at the same time had given them the opportunity to admit their lives weren't perfect either. Crazily enough, it actually gave me and my business more credibility instead of less. Who knew?

I was expecting people to react with disgust and judgement, but it didn't happen. Instead I was met with a resounding "me too" or "amen" or "thank goodness, someone is finally showing us what it really looks like". The perfection police paid me no notice. They just scrolled right past and if they rolled their eyes, shook their heads or clucked their tongues, they at least had the grace to do it in the privacy of their own homes.

In that moment I realized there was far more power in speaking to my tribe, those moms who were trying their best to make it through the day with their sanity still intact, the ones who desperately needed something they could call their own and achieve some success with, than there was in trying to appeal to the masses. I realized my words had far more impact if I allowed myself to speak my truth and let people see the real me, warts and all, instead of a watered down or fluffed up version of me. Suddenly I felt free to show people the cupcakes that were baked from a box and looked like they had been iced by a 3-year-old (sometimes they actually were, because she did a better job than I could). I let people see how disorganized I sometimes was and that I procrastinated just as much as everyone else. I admitted my kids sometimes got way too much screen time because I was busy working on a presentation. It was freeing, it was glorious, and it was transformational.

It's not always easy. We have corporate events where I stand out like a sore thumb. Other leaders are getting all gussied up in ball gowns and attending galas while I'm in blue jeans with my team at a dive bar, drinking beer and listening to live music. Sometimes that brings judgement from others. I can take it. I've accepted the fact that I'm probably never going to be the poster child for my company. I don't need to be. I've found success on my own terms and that far outweighs other people's opinions.

It became even trickier when my marriage ended. I worried about how my team would react. I was terrified about how my colleagues would judge me. I didn't know how to tell people. My solution was to face it head on and to tell my truth from the stage instead of hiding it away. I shared my journey, my struggles and the end of my marriage, but the moral of the story was how my business had been my salvation. I was able to take over the mortgage and stay in the same house. I was able to continue to stay at home with my kids instead of having to find a different job outside of the house. I was still able to have the flexibility to make skating lessons, art classes and dance recitals, all because of this outside the box business that I had worked so hard on. I focused on the positives instead of making it a "poor me" story.

I was once again shocked by people's reactions. Almost everyone was super positive and supportive. More importantly, many were inspired by my honesty and candor and I suddenly realized the impact I could have on other people. Sure, there were those who felt the need to tell me how sorry they were and let me know they were going to pray for me, but I chose to believe they were coming from a place of love instead of judgement. Again, focusing on the positive instead of dwelling on the negative.

As my journey continued I slowly morphed into a much hippier dippier version of my previous self and I struggled with knowing how much to share. How would people react to crystals, energy work and all that other woo hoo? In the end, I decided to just be honest. I shared my skepticism. I shared the baby steps. I shared my disbelief and wonderment at the person I had transformed into. Once again, it was met with nothing but support and love. I started attracting a whole new tribe, while enlightening and empowering some of my existing tribe along the way. It was pretty cool.

Even scarier was admitting to people I was working on myself. Some posts were far from pretty. Not everybody is comfortable with hearing about sorting through baggage, processing triggers or clearing old patterns, especially if it rings true to them. Some don't want to look too closely at themselves and realize how much work they have to do. Again,

I chose to focus on those I could reach and push out of their comfort zones, those I could inspire to be more authentic instead of worrying about offending those who weren't open to the notion of working on themselves.

I know that my journey is far from over. I know that I will continue to transform and evolve. I know that I will make some people uncomfortable and possibly alienate others as I muddle my way through. I also know that I will be supported with love and understanding every single step of the way.

All I can do is continue to live each day according to my purpose. "I am a woman of integrity, inspiring others to leave authentic lives."

Dedicated to my children. May you both always feel the freedom to be yourselves in all things, in all ways, always. You are perfect exactly as you are. I love you.

Thanks to NS for offering me this opportunity. Thanks to KN for reaching out to a stranger and starting me on this journey. Thanks to my friends and rock stars, JB and J9, for telling me to get out of my head, shut up and just do it. Thank you to LG for kicking my butt, reminding me not to limit myself and challenging me to do better. I have no idea where this journey will take us, but I do know I will always be thankful for everything we have taught each other.

DONNA TOBEY

DONNA TOBEY is passionate about living limitless possibilities out loud while teaching others how to do the same! She is a personal coach, mentor, workshop teacher, writer, and speaker. She is trained, certified, and licensed as a Heal Your Life® Workshop Teacher and Coach, based on the philosophies of Louise L. Hay.

Donna lives in New Hampshire, with her son, Ian and her lovely Maine Coon cat, Athena. She is founder of *You've Got Power, Baby!* inspiring everyone to find their answers WITHIN. Learn more at ugotpowerbaby.com.

Mostly, she is a student of Life who allows Divine Intelligence to be her teacher!

Ask And You Shall Receive

"Hurry! We're running behind, I don't want to miss this train to Paris!" I said as my friend Judy pulled into the crowded parking lot to return our rental car. We had luggage upon luggage, piled deep and high. It was my first trip out of the United States, abroad. Speed walking, we made it inside the small train station in Marseilles. Now what? In our best fake French, we communicated where we wanted to go and *voila*, tickets were in hand.

We made it through the first entrance only to hear the conductor shouting what must have been, "All aboard!" Three hours and we would be in Paris! We were meeting friends in the City of Lights and had reservations for a dinner cruise on the Seine River. We can do this, I thought. Bogged down in a mountain of luggage, I was moving slowly. Judy was way ahead of me and very near the conductor. In my head, I screamed, yes, screamed, "Where is my help?" In that instant, a gentleman who was sitting on a bench jumped up and asked me if I needed help. I graciously smiled and said *"Oui!"* He grabbed my luggage and ran to the conductor. Some words were exchanged. Some stronger words exchanged and just like that, the train left the platform--without us.

There we stood with looks of bewilderment about what had just happened. Our new friend, Vincent, spoke English well enough to tell us that we were too late to board and the conductors were sticklers with their timetables. He brought us back to the ticket counter, and explained what had happened to the clerk. A refund was issued for the exchange of tickets. We ended up with new tickets and with money back, too. What a fortunate turn of events! Not only did we have new tickets and extra spending money, we were still going to make our dinner reservations. To top it all off, we were on the same train as Vincent.

We had some time before boarding so Vincent kept us company with his quick wit and delightful personality. We decided that we liked each other enough to sit together for the train trip into Paris. What a blessing to have someone from the local culture riding with us sharing stories of France, stories of his life, hopes and dreams. Vincent even wanted to learn as much about us as we did about him.

In no time, it seemed, we were approaching the Paris train station. Vincent was giving us directions on how to navigate through the very busy terminal so we could connect with a taxi to the hotel. Before we knew it, Vincent had decided to stay with us and our mountain of luggage as we trudged through the crowds of people. He safely deposited us in the correct taxi line, knowing that he would need to take off in a run to make his next connection. We exchanged contact information, hugged and kissed goodbye. His parting words were for us to contact him if we needed translation help while in France, still willing to be of service to two strangers from America. To this day, we remain friends.

We refer to each other as angels. He was ours as much as we were his in that moment. A most memorable experience, one I hold deeply in my heart, transpired from my willingness to ask God for help.

Closer To The Heart

Many years ago, one of my teachers planted the seed within me to allow "the Energy" to teach me. She taught that if you asked "the Energy" to teach you and worked closely with that Energy, it would teach you in just the way you needed to learn. As a student of life and a "finder" rather than "seeker," I have discovered this to be true. Though one would think that it should be an obvious observation, it is only recently that I have come to understand that "the Energy" is in fact, the Holy Spirit. And this Holy Spirit is invisible, living and *alive*.

Foster that silent partnership with the Creator by spending quiet time every day to connect to your heart. Be still and listen to that gentle voice that knows everything and has all the answers about you and your life. There is a world beyond our natural world. It is more expansive than that which we can hear, see, feel, taste and touch. Even more than that, actively ask those questions that you want answered. Your Higher Self is connected to the Creator with those answers and the solutions. But I've found that you do need to *ask*.

Some would call it supernatural; super, including all that is natural and then some. For me, it is quiet answers that appear during meditation. I hear the communication as loving guidance, words, but not words spoken out loud. It's more of a vibrational frequency of inner peace and knowing. What a difference it can make in your life if you decide to go beyond the merely "natural"! You can communicate with a living God who has the answers to every obstacle that you encounter. Right then and there, you can choose to ask, "Higher Self, please show me the solution to this situation. One that is win/win for everyone involved. Open my heart to bring more light into this challenge so I can see that which I have been unable to see in the past."

You were born with free will, which means that you have a choice. God in His magnificence is always present, always wanting to give more life to your life. More life meaning, more blessings in the way of more goodness aligned with your heartfelt desires. The more you receive, the more you are able to share with others to bring even more goodness into the world. The Holy Spirit works in, around and through you. You are the instrument that God uses to help others.

What good does God want to bring into the world through you? What piece of the puzzle is yours? Are others waiting for your piece to be in place before they can add their piece? Many times life does seem like a puzzle with pieces that just don't seem to fit. You start your life headed in a direction that feels certain and true, then unexpectedly there is a turn of events. What you thought was your life path has had a correction. By opening your heart, you will find the piece of the puzzle that miraculously appears and fits just right! Ask those questions and you will receive your answers.

Same Old Song And Dance

Living life experiences has taught me that each encounter ignites soul growth. Challenged to go beyond our comfort zones, these experiences push us to practice what God is teaching us at a deeper level. We discover new connections in a world of synchronistic meetings with people, even strangers. Like a falling stack of dominoes, each encounter means something to the other, and leads each of us to still other people. Each of us may never know what that one seemingly random connection meant to the other. And yet, we know they are meaningful and purposeful.

What if we decided to take a leap of faith, knowing that there is a divine plan in place? Have you ever tried that? Have you ever just trusted and rambled where you were being led? When my son Ian was younger, about eight years old, we took a road trip with no ultimate destination in mind. We wanted to be spontaneous so we packed a suitcase and headed out. I allowed Ian to lead the way by giving me directions on which way to go. We drove toward the White Mountains on some familiar roads and every so often, Ian would have me take a turn. We honestly had no idea where we were or where we would end up. We saw the most beautiful scenery, taking in each breathtaking new vista. Rounding one corner we suddenly came upon the most extraordinary resort nestled sweetly in amongst the trees and mountains. We pulled into the road leading to the resort, but instead of going right in, Ian wanted to drive more. He told me to take a turn down this one-lane dirt road. It was becoming dusk. You know that feeling you get in the pit of your stomach, that pain actually? Well, I had it and began to feel anxious about our decision to follow this path. Where was it leading? There was nothing but forest on both sides of this narrow road and very soon it would be pitch dark. My overactive mind conjured up all sorts of dangers trying to get me to abort this mission. My heart, though, said, "Just a little longer."

Silently, I asked Spirit what we were doing here. Immediately from the side of the road two adorable black bear cubs emerged, just beyond the greenery! I knew right away we had just seen what we were meant to see. We were both delighted…and no mama bear in sight! After enjoying this delightful peek into the wild, I turned the car around and headed back to the magnificent castle nestled in the mountainside. The Mount Washington Resort in Bretton Woods has become one of our most favorite places to visit and stay. I learned a most valuable lesson, as I trusted the directions of an innocent child. Yes, there can be some scary moments and yes, it may feel like you are lost. But every time I find the courage to trust, some wonderful life experience is lived.

The same old song and dance creates a life of looping similar experiences over and over again. While there is some comfort in doing what you know and are comfortable experiencing, it holds you back from *living*. A prosperous and adventurous life is waiting just outside your comfort zone. But the experience is different for each one of us. For some, life outside of the "same old" means extreme feats of physical endurance. For others, it may be joining a group of strangers with the same interest, hoping to meet a companion to share your experiences with. And still yet, it can be that collaboration with Holy Spirit into the unknown, beyond the natural into the supernatural, where all life connects as One.

I'm A Believer

There really isn't anyone outside of you who can tell you about your life and your purpose in life. Many people try. I have sought those answers myself. As I reflect back on predictions and prophecies that have been made, I recognize that I was not in right relationship with my own heart. Not in right relationship with God. I was searching for love in all the wrong places.

It is only through my personal, heartfelt communication with God, that I have received answers that have led me to bear succulent fruit in my life. It's an ongoing relationship of questions and answers, and receiving guidance. A receivership of light in just the right way for me to understand my life and what God intends for my life out in the world. There have been countless examples and stories in my life of divine right order. Many would call them miracles.

When you nurture this living and loving relationship with God, you will come to understand that you are safe and secure. You also understand that the Holy Spirit is your friend and it is through the grace of God that all things come together divinely. After all, the One who created you and all that is living is walking right with you, knows your needs and how to provide, and will keep you safe. Just ask, and you shall receive.

Dedicated to my loving son, Ian Daniel Tobey who continues to teach me and believes in me each and every day. You were brought into this world as a gift from God and for this I am eternally grateful. Know that whatever you decide you want to do in this world, you are never alone. Ever.

In deep humility, I give thanks to God for the love, the laughter and the many blessings that I have received in my lifetime. I am grateful for the reconnection with my Italian family especially my mother's only sister, Nancy Natale who is 94 years young! I appreciate the chance to learn about my mom, who she was as a young woman growing up, where she lived in the North End of Boston and what she loved in life. This special connection to family stories and relatives has been a gift beyond measure! Special hugs to my cousins, Desiree, Teresa and Mary Ann...we grew up as children and now are growing up as adults... I love you!

ANTOINETTE COLEMAN-KELLY

Antoinette Coleman-Kelly from Southern Ireland is a Holistic Communicator, Life Coach and Counsellor, Licensed Heal Your Life® Facilitator, Coach and Teacher, International Speaker and an Independent Wedding Celebrant.

Antoinette is dedicated to inspiring and empowering people to discover change, achieve their dreams and reach their highest and best potential.

She is a world travelling enthusiast and relishes the constant adventure of each new day.

www.lifehealing.ie
acolemankelly@gmail.com

🍂 Remember YOU Are A Limited Edition

K nowledge comes from books and wisdom comes from your life. I have always truly believed that as we negotiate life, it's always about our attitude, action, respect, experience and love.

> 🍂 Our deepest fear is not that we are inadequate
> Our deepest fear is that we are powerful beyond measure.
>
> ~MARIANNE WILLIAMSON

Do you truly know how amazing you are? You are one of a kind and it's time to celebrate you. There has never been another you. Being awesomely authentically YOU. You are a once in a lifetime event.

The amazing human brain weighs about two and a half to three pounds and is made up of about thirty billion cells called neurons. Each neuron is capable of handling approximately one million bits of information.

Your amazing body has approximately 62,000 miles of capillaries; millions of electrical warning signals, a fabulous conveyer system and five wonderful senses — sight, hearing, taste, touch and smell.

Your amazing instincts have been received from the vast number of your ancestors who were fast, smart, strong and courageous to survive many natural challenges. Often when you might think you are merely "average", you actually are the latest version of your human success story, all your hidden strengths are only just emerging.

As age is only a number, you are never ever too old to set a new goal. It is always reassuring to know there is always a bigger picture, no matter what is happening for us. Moving beyond your comfort zone can be challenging, for example, a new job, new house, new area of study or a new hobby. Always allow the best version of you moving forward.

Now here is a question I often ask people. "How do you rate yourself? Yes, you as a person? This is just for you today.

Are you

- Important
- Very Important
- Average
- Above average

౿ Ordinary

౿ Extraordinary

Your answer is perfect for you today remembering you always have choice to change.

> ❧ If we all did the things we are capable of doing
> We would literally astound ourselves.

~THOMAS EDISON

I have been gifted in my life with many great teachers, some of them, I believe are quite possibly saints. Being inspired helps us to make sense of the world, displaying qualities we admire and aspire to, including courage and using our ability with strength. I am inspired by many people and it all began with my Mum and Dad and my sisters and brothers and as my world widened, Santa was the magical genius who could make everything bigger, better and brighter.

As each decade passes there are new people who genuinely inspire me. It's not always about great deeds, and it's always all about the love, kindness and compassion. I always believe that our hero must inspire us into action and not just admiration.

> ❧ Every production of genius
> Must be a production
> Of enthusiasm.

~BENJAMIN DISRAELI

For example, Louise L Hay has devoted her life to assisting others in discovering and using their full creative potential power, therefore totally changing their lives for the better. Louise teaches by example and lives what she teaches. I am also inspired by my Sons-Gerard and John, Oprah Winfrey, Nelson Mandela's life and Richard Branson, and so many others, which allow me the curiosity to know and be more.

Who inspires you on your journey? And who do you inspire?

> ❧ Believe in yourself as you are an amazing limited edition.

Creating the experience, concentrating in a specific way helps register and deepen the experience in a most special way. I tend to focus on the beautiful, awe-inspiring experiences, capable of making me grateful for the opportunity to appreciate, learn and grow.

For example, recently I was travelling in India, actually to be precise, travelling deep in the Himalayas, the last glimmer of summer twilight produced the most magnificent stunning sunset I have ever seen. I scanned the panorama, the mountains, the clouds, the valleys and the colours. What an unbelievable sight. I remember thinking, I will never ever forget this experience.

> Look deep into nature
> And then you will understand everything better.
>
> ~ALBERT EINSTEIN

It's not just mountains and sunsets that create the most awesome feeling. Vivid learning experiences can occur in the humblest of places and are equally as amazing. Remember to lock it to your memory. Take the seasons, the fall is majestically colourful, the magnificence of the brilliant colour autumn foliage is forever breath-taking. The long summer sunshine and the flowers in spring leave the cold, snow and frost a distant memory.

> Make the most of to-day,
> Get interested in something
> Shake yourself awake
> Let the winds of enthusiasm
> Sweep through you
> Live today with gusto.
>
> ~DALE CARNEGIE

Gratitude plays a pivotal role in my life. I regularly ask everyone at my workshops to share the best thing that has happened to them that day. Once the awkwardness is surpassed, the good tidings flow.

Gratitude is another word for thankfulness and always implies a readiness to show appreciation for kindness received. I always suggest to clients to treat themselves and purchase a gorgeous notebook and write a minimum of four things you are grateful for each day and remember it's not rocket science as being grateful for your health, your eyesight, hearing, and ability to walk are massively important.

Celebrate those who have helped you to where you are to-day. The people who have made a difference always deserve a thank you.

If the only prayer you ever say in your whole life is
Thank you ... that will suffice.

~MEISTER ECKHART

Being kind even with a smile is wonderful. On any given day, without even realizing it, you may be the answer to someone's prayer. Remember that your thoughtfulness, touch and love can work miracles in the lives of others.

 The secret of genius is to carry the spirit of the child into old age,
Which means never losing your enthusiasm.

~ALDOUS HUXLEY

Being optimistic is being hopeful and confident about the future. Being positive is always seeing the bright side and both optimism and positivity are delivered from our awareness.

- To look at life's sunny side
- Thinking only of the best
- Try being the best
- Expect only the best
- Being supportive with yourself and others.

The dictionary tells us that optimism is a feeling of hopefulness about the future.

 Positive thinking is a form of thought
Which habitually looks
For the best results.

~NORMAN VINCENT PEALE

Most optimists have the opinion that people and life are inherently good and no matter what the situation one can always find a positive response.

An optimistic person normally takes control of their lives including their thinking, beliefs, values, goals, confidence, success, gratitude and health. They see the world as a benevolent place, enjoying their own freedom and being true to themselves.

Optimism has been proven to lower the risk of cardiovascular disease.

The optimist sees the glass half full with a sense of opportunity. Would you agree with the following thoughts?

- An optimist is always thinking about all the exciting things happening today, tomorrow, next week and further on.
- An optimist notices all the good and great things happening as well as the not so good.

 Some men see things as they are
And say *Why?*
I dream things that never were
And say *Why Not?*

~GEORGE BERNARD SHAW

This is your life, your one and only life and you can decide how it's going to be. How about deciding to make your life more amazing, productive and satisfying. What changes could you make, what possibilities are there for you?

- What do you really want to do?
- What do you really want to have?
- What do you really want to be?
- Where would you really like to visit?

People often say they don't have enough time. You have exactly the same number of hours per day that were given to Helen Keller, Michelangelo, Saint Teresa, Louis Pasteur, Leonardo Da Vinci, Albert Einstein and everyone else.

In five years… 260 weeks… 1820 days… 2,620.800 minutes. What can you do, what could you do within five years?

You have brains in your head and feet in your shoes
You can steer yourself in any direction you choose
You're on your own and you know what you know
And you are the one who'll decide where to go.

~DR SEUSS

I have a daily practice where I set two alarms on my phone (11am and 8pm) and when they alarm, I ask myself, what am I creating? What am I doing? What am I saying? This is shining a light on my awareness and if I need to change something, I can set it in motion.

The way to the sky … is within
So flutter your wings … of love.

~MEWLANA RUMI

Meditation has many forms and mindfulness is all about living in the present.

- Be mindful as you do everyday things
- Slow down
- Take notice of the world around you
- Be grateful for what you have
- Enjoy the little things
- Stop and breathe

Peace is always possible and with meditation it is similar to the anchor that keeps life's storms from blowing us off course. With practice, we can develop a sense of calmness in the world. Approach meditation with an open heart.

 Learn to get in touch
With the silence within yourself
And know that everything in this life
Has a purpose.

~ELIZABETH KUBLER-ROSS

There is no perfect way to practice, various approaches suit different individuals. It all begins with reclaiming your attention and focus on your breathing. When we become still we hear the answers.

Laughter is great for our health and being well. While it relaxes us, it also boosts the immune system along with many other benefits. Allow yourself to be around fun people, go to a comedy show, watch a funny movie or TV show, and find someone with an intoxicating laugh. Your greatest super powers!

Forever loving
Always courageous
MAGICALLY joyful
FANTASTICALLY friendly and kind
COURAGEOUSLY tolerant and patient
TOTALLY humble and respectful
AMAZINGLY graceful and positive
UNCONDITIONALLY enthusiastic.

~ANTOINETTE COLEMAN-KELLY

Life is a gift. Live it. Enjoy and celebrate it...as wisdom comes from life, be courageous and develop the ability to see magic in the ordinary and the extraordinary.

Your Personal label says

 Made in Heaven
Because you are an Angel
Only hand wash because you are fragile
Cold iron, don't want to burn your wings
And handle with care
Because
You are truly an Amazing Limited Edition

~UNKNOWN

Total Gratitude to my family and friends
For their continuous unconditional love, encouragement and support.

In Memory
Of my Most Amazing Mum and Dad.
Thank You

DEBBIE LEDFORD

DEBBIE LEDFORD is an author, hypnotherapist, and a Heal Your Life® coach and workshop leader as well as a passionate advocate for families who are struggling with mental illness.

Some of Debbie's recent accomplishments are bringing guided meditation and the *Heal Your Life* principals into the workplace. She enjoys helping employees bring balance into their lives.

Debbie and her husband reside in Grass Valley, California. She enjoys spending time with her children and their families.

Sharing the *Heal Your Life* work and using hypnosis techniques to help clients embark on their own healing journey is truly her passion. Debbie believes that we have everything we need, right inside of us to live the most incredible life we can imagine. If you would like more information regarding Debbie's services, please contact her by email or phone.

debbieledford@rocketmail.com
www.debbieledford.wordpress.com
530-320-3717

🌿 The Sacred Journey of Healing

The journey of going from hopelessness and despair, to a place of surrender and renewed hope, is a sacred journey. And a journey I'd like to share with you.

I've always thought of myself as a spiritual person, but not religious, even though I was raised in a very religious home. In my heart, I have a connection to God. Though I can't explain it, I've always known God was part of everything. Even in my darkest hours, I always felt He was there, regardless of whether I understood His plan.

Growing up, however, I felt my religious background contributed to me feeling controlled by shame and guilt. This defined who I was for many years and fed into my tendency to hold onto things far longer than was good for me.

At the age of twenty-five, I found myself in one of those places, where I'd hung on way too long. I was married to a man six years older than I was. We were eight years into our marriage and had been blessed with three beautiful children to nurture, guide and love. I never knew a heart could love in such a way until I had children. They were definitely the gift of this marriage.

However, my husband did not share the joy I felt. He was resentful of the children and the sacrifices we had to make to give them what they truly deserved. Because of this, he looked outside the marriage for his comfort and fulfillment.

My youngest son had already experienced many difficulties in his short life. He had what the doctors called "failure to thrive." At two-and-a-half years-old, he weighed fifteen pounds and was losing weight steadily. The doctors were baffled and didn't know how to help him. As he got older, he had horrific tantrums and was destructive and abusive. He seemed so angry.

Eventually, he was diagnosed with Tourette's syndrome and obsessive compulsive disorder. Tourette's is a neurological disorder that involves tics, bad language and impulse control issues. Children diagnosed with this, will do exactly what they know they shouldn't do.

I loved my son with all my heart, but I had no solutions for him. I lacked the tools and resources needed to take his pain away and facilitate his healing. I couldn't imagine what he was feeling. I felt helpless.

During this time, I started having difficulty moving my body. I'd wake up in so much pain, I could barely get myself out of bed. I had to call my two older children to help me. They were only seven and eight years-old. They helped me get out of bed and to the kitchen where together we'd prepare breakfast and make school lunches.

Eventually, I was diagnosed with rheumatoid arthritis. My doctor said he didn't have a crystal ball and he couldn't tell me what the future would hold for me. Rheumatoid arthritis is a debilitating auto-immune disease where your body mistakenly attacks its own tissues causing inflammation which is very painful and destructive to the body.

Before long my hands were bent and twisted. I had no strength in my hands. I could barely lift a glass of water or open a bottle of Tylenol. My feet were deformed and painful. Birkenstocks were the only shoes I could wear comfortably and they were way too expensive for my budget.

I couldn't work and I could barely take care of my children. My husband became even more resentful and more detached from what was happening in our home. I allowed myself to become filled with guilt and shame because I was unable to be the wife or mother I needed to be.

I was not only crippled physically, but emotionally as well. And the more stressed, fatigued, angry, hurt and sad I felt, the worse my disease became. At that time, I was unaware of the mind-body connection. I had no idea that my negative emotions were making me sicker.

As time went by, my life became more and more out of control. At thirty-five, the emotional pain I felt had grown and I struggled with the idea of leaving the marriage. Because of my religious upbringing, I believed it was morally wrong to get a divorce. I thought if I just tried a little harder, prayed a bit more, things would improve. I cried and begged God to please make my husband a nice person—not knowing that God wanted so much more for me.

My children were struggling, too. My youngest son's condition escalated when he went through puberty. He needed more help than I could give him. He became violent and beat me. I remember my husband standing at the kitchen sink eating a peanut butter and jelly sandwich, watching him attack me. Not once did he try to stop him or help me.

My oldest son was now seventeen. He was desperately trying to learn how to be a man, but with no male role model to look up to, he struggled. He was angry with his father for not protecting me from his brother. And my daughter was sixteen and pregnant. My family's life was completely out of control and our whole family was in intense therapy.

I was advised to leave the marriage, but my disease had become much worse. My doctor said that he'd done everything he could for me and that if I didn't make some changes in my life, I would more than likely die from the arthritis. I had no job skills, which didn't matter as I was physically unable to work. The bottom line was that I had no money of my own. Although I couldn't see a way out, I knew something had to change.

I made the most difficult decision of my life to put my youngest son in a group home, a place where he'd be supervised by therapists and counselors 24-hours a day. This would allow me to focus on my other children, my grandchild and my health.

I'll never forget the day I sat across the table from him and told him that he could no longer live with the family. The look of betrayal in his eyes is forever imprinted upon my heart. This is where I lost my hope. I felt that I'd failed at everything that was important to me. It would truly take a miracle to rebuild my family. Yet, it was at that moment, I realized if I could set a limit with the child I loved so dearly, I could do it with the man who had emotionally left me so many years before. I'd finally gotten to a place of real surrender. There was no turning back.

At the time, I had no idea that this place of surrender was the perfect place to be. My life felt so tragic. The shame and guilt I felt—reminiscent of the shame and guilt I grew up with—was enormous. My heart was shattered into a million pieces. I had no idea, however, that I'd just experienced the greatest gift of my life. The wellbeing of my family was out of my hands and I was finally ready to let God do his work.

The Healing Begins

At this point, my prayers changed. I admitted to God and myself that I didn't have the answer. I asked Him to guide me and keep my mind open.

Around the same time, I went to a workshop about breaking the cycle of dysfunctional parenting. I realized I'd been raised in a very dysfunctional home. I learned to connect with my inner child, that little girl inside of me who was in desperate need of healing. I started going to Co-Dependents Anonymous (CODA). As a group, we supported each other as we worked the program's 12 steps.

The next stepping stone on my path was a women's group where I was educated about the mind-body connection. This group was run by a hypnotherapist and I had no idea what it was, but I'd told God I'd be open to everything.

I quickly learned hypnosis is a wonderful tool to clear trauma from the body. In my very first session, I learned that I stayed in my marriage, not only because of shame and guilt, but because I also had abandonment issues stemming from a move when I was six. My family moved away from my grandparents and I felt so lost without my grandfather. In a hypnosis session, I was able to re-experience this move with both the feelings of my child within as well as with the wisdom and maturity of an adult. I realized my grandfather didn't abandon me, but that my parents took me away from him. And that even though I was miles away from him, my grandfather still cherished me. My grandfather was an important male role model in my life and I now realized that I deserved a husband that would love and honor me as my grandfather had.

I was also introduced to the work of Louise Hay whose work is based on affirmations—positive, nurturing words we can say to ourselves instead of words of shame and guilt. Louise teaches that all "dis-ease" comes from our emotional wounds. When I read the emotional cause of rheumatoid arthritis in her book, *You Can Heal Your Life* (Hay House, 1984), I was speechless. Everything started to make sense. The root causes of this disease were feeling victimized, a lack of love, chronic bitterness and resentment. These emotions had been the foundation of my adult life. Louise's work, along with hypnotherapy, gave me hope that I could heal my disease. I quickly purchased one of her affirmation CDs. I'd lie in bed each night and listen to Louise's sweet voice saying the affirmations and I'd repeat them until I fell asleep. Finally, my hope was being restored. These tools were so powerful in making change in my life that I became a hypnotherapist and a *Heal Your Life* workshop leader and coach. I was now equipped to help others with their own sacred journey of healing.

My life changed directions as this work became my passion. I was able to focus on what was right and good. And as we know, where thought goes, energy follows—and without thinking about it, my body was getting better. I felt hopeful again. I looked forward to the future. And as I healed, I was able to open my heart to love again. I met a man with a kind and loving heart. We'd stay up all night laughing and talking. He embraced my family and shared the joy I felt in my heart for them, and before long, we got married.

I never expected my new husband to be a father to my children. But before I knew it, they had all formed their own relationships with him. It was such a blessing to sit back and watch those relationships grow especially as I desperately wanted to facilitate my children's healing. However, they had their own sacred journeys and the only way I could assist in their healing process, was by prayer, support and being an example. The more I healed my own life, the more they healed their lives.

Today, my children are their own unique, beautiful selves. My oldest son is a truly gifted artist and compassionate father. He demonstrates to his own son every day how a man navigates life. My daughter is a beautiful, strong, independent woman. She's a school psychologist and gives hope to other families in some of their darkest moments. What she experienced with her younger brother, has given her heartfelt empathy for the families she serves. She's a loving role model to her two precious daughters. And my youngest son, who taught me the gift of surrender, makes me proud every day. He works hard to be the best man he can, despite his disability. He's a single dad raising two boys of his own and doing a terrific job at it.

Lessons Learned

My life taught me that if we can move forward in faith and trust, the next step will be revealed to us. Surrendering is not giving up—it's releasing fear and the need to control. It's allowing a power greater than ourselves to guide us and take us further than we've ever dreamed possible. It's an act of courage and faith and opens ourselves up to amazing possibilities. When we surrender, we allow our hearts to heal and receive the love God intended us to receive. Surrendering teaches us to forgive others, and most importantly, to forgive ourselves.

If you feel like you've lost hope, I ask that you let my story speak to your soul. I invite you to dig deep and find insight. Affirmations create new neuro-pathways in our brains and help us make behavioral changes. One of my favorite affirmations of Louise's is "All is well in my world." These words are so comforting to me and bring peace to my spirit. Find affirmations that speak to your soul. Write them down and meditate on them. Record yourself saying the affirmations, and listen to them while you sleep. Imagine the life you desire and create your new story. Talk about it as if you are already living it. Our minds are so powerful they will create the life we imagine.

And most of all, please remember there is always hope. God is always listening and guiding us—we just have to be still long enough to listen. Don't be afraid to seek out help. When you are ready—your teacher will appear. Believe in miracles.

Thank you for reading my story. May it inspire you to start your own sacred journey of healing. And remember…

> Our job is not to deny the story, but to defy the ending — to rise strong, recognize our story, and rumble with the truth until we get to a place where we think, yes. This is what happened. This is my truth. And I will choose how this story ends.
>
> ~BRENÉ BROWN

May you choose a courageous, strong and delightful ending for your story.

Dedicated to my husband Mike Ledford: I am grateful for your love and support. I can't imagine this journey without you.

I would like to acknowledge my children Shawn, Michelle and Matt who have been my greatest teachers. I will be forever grateful for the lessons I have learned as we traveled this path together. I feel immense gratitude that God chose me to be their mother. I also feel so blessed that my husband, Mike, chose to join our family and share this wonderful adventure with us.

CAROLAN DICKINSON

CAROLAN DICKINSON is a psychic medium, angel intuitive, reiki master teacher and author of the book, *Walking with the Archangels* (Amazon, 2016).

Carolan can help you realize your own gifts and talents, connect with loved ones in the spiritual realm, heal and transcend grief, and establish a relationship with the archangels — all of which will enhance the quality of your life. She believes the decisions you make in the present, absolutely create your future. She can help you see things from a new perspective and with fresh eyes.

Based in Phoenix, Arizona, Carolan spends as much time as possible outdoors or with her yoga community. When she's not writing, or teaching a class, she devotes her time doing psychic readings or walking and talking with the archangels.

carolan903@gmail.com
www.carolandickinson.com
Walking with the Archangels (Amazon, 2016)
https://www.udemy.com/walking-with-the-archangels/learn/v4/overview

🌀 The Magic of Healing With the Archangels

There isn't a situation or experience in life that you've gone through that God and the archangels don't know about. There's no way that you can shock or surprise them, or earn their disappointment. More importantly, there isn't any situation or experience in life that cannot be healed with their help.

You may look at a particular experience, trauma, or wound in your life and feel that it is unhealable. Yet, *these* are the places and experiences that call for healing the most. It is *exactly* these wounds, that create the biggest impact on our soul; that skew our life in a way that has us repeating the same choices, behaviors, and beliefs that shape our lives.

When I realized this, my life changed. I now know that there is no such thing as "unhealable." And that like beauty, healing is in the eye of the beholder.

Fumbling in the Dark

My own experiences that I once thought unhealable include childhood abuse and molestation; sexual trauma; domestic violence; and military sexual trauma. Looking back, I can clearly see the path that led from childhood, to my experiences as an adult. It reads like a road map.

Often in the wake of trauma, we develop negative thoughts or beliefs about ourselves. And unless we do something to change them; we'll only get more of the same, leading us to the same negative life choices. For most of us, that's the last thing in the world we want. How many of us would like to remarry our exes? But that's exactly what we're doing when we allow our wounds, even unknowingly, to dictate our choices.

You may feel like you're making different and better choices; you may even tell yourself that you're not going to make that mistake again. Yet, until healing occurs you will continue to attract exactly what you don't want. For me, that resulted in me marrying the same type of man over and over. Four times, to be exact. Each time I thought I was making a better choice. But all I did was change bodies.

Why?

Because at my core I didn't believe I deserved better. My belief was that because of my past traumas, I was damaged goods. My unhealed wounds tainted my opinion of myself, and were reflected in every aspect of my life. On some level, I didn't believe that I deserved to be treated with love, dignity and kindness, so I attracted the opposite of that.

It is these negative emotions and beliefs that stem from our unhealed wounds that keep us stuck. We are left fumbling in the dark. We feel separate, alone and unworthy—which are the biggest wounds of all.

But when we allow Spirit to enter these places, healing *must* happen. Why? Because darkness is simply the absence of light and it's impossible for darkness and light to exist in the same place at the same time.

Try it for yourself. Go into a completely dark room and turn on the light. What happens? The room is flooded, illuminated. You can see clearly.

Allowing healing to take place has the same effect on our souls. No more stuff muddying up our sight, intention or clarity. And no more stuff blocking the outward expression of our authentic self.

Be Open to the Possibility of Healing

When trauma of any kind happens and you have little or no tools to deal with it, a belief forms about *why* it happened. When that occurs, it's easy to get caught up in blaming ourselves. An entire cycle of shame, blame and self-flogging follows along with a whole bunch of "what if's?"

Wouldn't you rather heal than be trapped in this washing machine of negative emotions?

The first step is to think of your wounds, not as a foe to be battled and conquered, but as a part of you that needs support and understanding, much like a confused child.

Then the more you can separate yourself from your experience — the trauma — the easier it will be to shift your perception and consequently heal; to allow it to become an experience you *had*, rather than a part of your identity and spirit. And the easier it will be to transform a wound into a gift.

For some of us, the desire to heal comes in small doses as we realize that we need to make changes. With others, something happens that brings us to our knees, and is the catalyst for bigger change.

No matter how it happens for you, simply the awareness for change will propel you forward into a better way of existing in the world.

Be daring, be courageous, and be open to the possibility of healing the seemingly unhealable. You can transcend any wound or experience and adopt new beliefs, choices and behaviors that will uplift and enhance the quality of your life.

Ask yourself, "What do I believe is possible?" A smidge worth of faith is all you need.

Healing with the Archangels

Healing is grace personified. Nothing is more gracious, subtle and gentle than asking the archangels to help you heal. And it's so simple. All you need is the desire to heal and you will be spiritually guided to the right person, place, or thing that will allow healing to take place.

This feels like magic to me, how we can be so graciously led to the exact thing we need at exactly the right time and right place merely by asking?

The archangels want to help us, to heal us, and to assist us so we may lead happier, healthier, and more joyous lives. Their hope is that we'll share that elevated life with others — because we are all connected.

Each one of us is like a pebble dropped into the water creating a ripple effect that touches everyone and the world around us. Most of us will never comprehend the impact our healing has on the world around us. We become an example to others. Our change inspires others to change. And it all starts with asking the archangels for help.

They can't wait to help us. We are like precious jewels to the archangels and Spirit. We are loved beyond measure and they're waiting for us to make the first move.

When I started asking the archangels for help, I'd been trying to do my own healing for a while and was stuck. I was floored that anyone (code for "even me") could connect and communicate with them. I was shocked that I didn't have to be a religious leader, or an ancient holy man or woman to speak to them. And I was even more amazed that the archangels would listen, answer and help me, simply by my asking.

It happened very naturally and was surprisingly easy to do. I got to know them, what they do and how I sensed and felt them. I spent time with them in meditation as well as walking and talking with them. I got to know them just like I would a new friend; and over time, our relationship grew and deepened. I'm still in awe that it's so simple. The archangels exist to be helpers, and their help is so readily, willingly, and lovingly available to everyone.

Each archangel has a color and gemstone associated with them. For example, Archangel Michael's color is cobalt blue and his gemstone is lapis. If you want to feel closer to a specific archangel, you can wear clothing of the color, or jewelry with the gemstone, associated with that particular archangel. However, simply envisioning the color of an archangel's energy will help you sense and feel them.

Here are some easy steps you can take to invoke the loving, healing energy of the archangels:

1. Ask Archangel Michael to surround you with his powerful blue light so you will be guarded, guided and protected against any negative energies or entities, both seen or unseen, known or unknown.

2. Ask Archangel Michael to send white or clear energy from your crown chakra flowing over you, and through you, to the soles of your feet to dissolve all etheric cords. Visualize the dissolving of any etheric cords — the visual representation of attachment or emotional imbalances that connects us to people, places and experiences — as the energy moves through you. Ask for these rope-like cords to be cleared from both this lifetime, and others.

3. Ask Archangel Raphael to fill you with his emerald green energy to heal all places, both known or unknown, from this lifetime or others. Allow his healing energy to fill all the places that need healing in mind, body, and spirit.

4. Ask Archangel Chamuel to fill you completely with her rose-pink energy to heal all emotional wounds and grief with her unconditional love.

Welcome the cleansing tears if they come. Initially, your tears may seem like a tidal wave, but trust me, it will get easier. You are without a doubt in great hands. There are many excellent counselors that can help you, both traditionally and spiritually-based, so anytime you feel overwhelmed and need support, ask the archangels to lead you to the right person.

The Power of Forgiveness

Forgiveness is an essential piece of the healing process. Lack of forgiveness keeps us stuck in the emotion of the wound or trauma. Forgiveness changes the energy to one that will invite healing and allow any negativity associated with the trauma to release.

The archangels also play a role here as well. They let me know when forgiveness needs to happen. For example, the face of the person I need to forgive appears to me over and over again in my mind's eye or memories and feelings of an incident from the past that I've not healed keep coming up. These are spiritual nudges; the archangels are letting me know what to work on next.

Because of the nature of some traumas, it might not be healthy or even possible for you to have in person contact with the person you want to forgive or ask forgiveness from. And it's not necessary. It's the intention in this exercise that creates the change or shift. One of my first spiritual teachers, LaVeta Dilman of Palm Springs, California, taught me this simple and easy forgiveness exercise which even works with someone who's no longer in a physical body:

1. Envision the person or situation you want to forgive and say: "From my heart to yours, I forgive you for anything real or perceived you may or may not have done to hurt me."
2. Repeat three times.
3. Then reverse it and say: "From my heart to yours, I ask your forgiveness for anything real or perceived that I may or may not have done to hurt you."
4. Repeat three times.
5. Repeat steps 1-4 as needed by tuning into any spiritual nudges you may get.

You may be wondering why you would need to ask forgiveness if you were the person wronged. I know from my own experience that the aftermath of traumatic events often leaves us feeling guilt, shame and even humiliation. When asking for forgiveness you are actually forgiving yourself. Even if it doesn't make sense, energetically it works. The very action of asking for forgiveness allows the energy to change, to lighten and release and it will help clear and release those "what if's?"

And remember, when you forgive, you aren't absolving anyone of bad behavior. You are simply changing the energy of the situation to one that can be healed and released.

Finding the Magic

The magic in healing with the archangels is in the gracious, loving way their help is both available and delivered.

At each step of healing you will find the gift of each experience. Under all the layers of a wound—when healed—lies a gift. You may experience these gifts in the form of wisdom, forgiveness, self-love, strength, spiritual connection, or a multitude of artistic, creative, and spiritual gifts.

Choose healing, and you can make room for what you *do* want. Allow Spirit and the archangels to lead you into a life in harmony with your life's purpose, heart's desire and joy. It will be better than you ever imagined.

Dedicated to my wonderful sisters Gina, Dawn, and Lynn; my friends; and my yoga communities. Without every one of you, life would not be as wonderful as it is today. And special thanks to Mozart, my fur baby companion of 19 years.

I am so very grateful to Spirit and the archangels that heal, inspire, motivate and love everyone unconditionally. A special thank you to my editor Wendy Kitts, my co-authors, and publishing project director, Lisa Hardwick, from Visionary Insight Press, for breathing life into this book.

JACKIE RODGERS

Dr. JACKIE RODGERS is a Psychologist currently studying for a Masters in Psychology in London. She was born in the UK where she resides with her family in a house on a clifftop on the South-Coast. She is a member of the Complementary Medicines Association (CMA), International Association for Holistic Therapy (IAHT) and the IANPL (International Association for Neurolinguistic Programming)

Following her diagnosis, she started an online CBT & Mindfulness therapy practise to provide easily accessible therapy to those who need it, where-ever they are, to fit with their day. Her practise can be found at www.online4therapy.com

Jackie takes an active interest in holistic therapies and the power of positive attitude in dealing with life changing illness and problems which can occur as we follow life's path. Being mindful and focusing on the present rather than worrying about the past and future helped her get through a very stressful time, and she hopes that 'A mindful journey' will inspire others to do the same.

info@online4therapy.com
Facebook.com/Online4therapy-Mind and Body

🦋 A Mindful Journey

It presented as reflux.

For a couple of months, I had a problem swallowing and small quantities of food would come up in a frothy blob of salivary secretions. I was losing weight due to lack of eating which prompted me to make an appointment at a walk-in clinic in London.

One bright afternoon in October, I took the plunge and went to see the Doctor, thinking I could squeeze a consultation into my working day. I explained to him my symptoms and how long they had been ongoing. He thought it was probably Gastroesophageal reflux and started me on 20 mg Omeprazole, a standard first line therapy. I left confident that my symptoms would go, but they didn't, in fact they got worse!

A week later, I went back to see the same Doctor. Since I had already lost a stone in weight within a month, he decided to refer me to a Consultant Gastroenterologist.

I was given an appointment for that weekend, and asked to attend a clinic on Harley Street.

As I made my way out of the Doctor's office, I felt anxiety rear its ugly head and wondered why I was feeling so negative when I had no diagnosis yet.

I said nothing to my family as I didn't want to worry anyone until I knew what I was dealing with. They thought I was going to London for work that weekend and I let that ride.

On Saturday, I presented myself at the Gastroenterologist's office.

I remember a man in his mid-forties with a big grin and shiny white teeth. He invited me to have a seat and then asked a series of questions associated with my history and symptoms. An abdominal examination followed, which was unremarkable, he then concluded that an endoscopy needed to be done together with some general blood screening.

An appointment was made to undergo an endoscopy in three days' time. Blood would be taken routinely prior to the procedure. My head was a whirl. Things were happening so quickly! The endoscopy was done without sedation, just some cold banana spray to numb the back of the throat. Biopsies of my esophagus, stomach and jejunum were taken and I was told that the Consultant would call me with the results when he returned from holiday in 2 weeks.

I was not expecting the news I got when his email came two weeks later.

Dear Dr Rodgers,

I have your biopsy results back and they are all normal, however your blood shows that your inflammatory markers are raised and I do not know why. I think I need to refer you for a CT scan as a matter of urgency. Please can you let me know your availability?

I looked at the email in two minds; part of me relieved because no abnormalities were seen in my esophagus and stomach but concerned that my blood showed an abnormality.

I was no further forward in knowing what was wrong. I felt myself getting angry and frustrated but then realised these thoughts would do me no good. I needed to be patient and take this all step by step. I looked at my calendar; Saturday was a good day for me to have the CT scan done. It wouldn't affect work and my family would think I was working again.

Once at the clinic, I changed into a robe and then was led into a large cool room with the CT scanner in the centre. I was given an IV injection of contrast to show up in my blood vessels which left a metallic taste in my mouth and gave me the sensation of wanting to go pee. The scan took about thirty minutes and I was told the results would be back with my Consultant on Monday. After feeling anxious about the CT scan, I decided to go to London's Chinatown for a full body massage to relax. It was heavenly and for a couple of hours I could forget the whole experience.

I kept myself busy over the weekend so that I would not think too much about the scan. Monday came and so did an email from my Consultant.

Dear Dr. Rodgers,

I have the results of your CT scan which I would like to discuss with you. When would be a convenient time and what number can you be reached at?

It had just turned 8am so I knew that the Consultant had just started work and fired off this mail urgently. I would not want to hear the news. 'Be brave' I said to myself as my fingers tripped over the keyboard of my laptop.

I replied that I would be available from 6pm that evening and gave my mobile number. I did not want any bad news before starting my working day and thought it prudent to leave the call until the evening. Also, nobody else would be in the house when I took the call.

All day, the upcoming call with the Consultant played in my mind. I tried to keep myself busy but I could still feel the thoughts in my head racing around and giving me a headache. It was almost a relief when 6pm came, and within minutes of the hour mark, my mobile rang.

"Hello," I said into the receiver.

"Hello, Jackie?" said a male voice at the other end. I immediately recognised the voice of my Consultant.

"I am calling about the CT scan results which I have here in front of me."

I closed my eyes and pictured him sitting in his Harley Street office, behind his walnut desk, which smelt of beeswax, looking at the white printed paper containing my results. My life was in his hands.

"I am sorry to tell you that there is something which has come up that warrants further investigation."

"What do you mean?" I asked suddenly alert.

"I am reading directly from the report that the radiographer has sent me; a bulky mass has been seen on the scan and we need to do a biopsy of it to determine what it is."

"Bulky mass?" I repeated as if the words were a foreign language

"Yes. I have already contacted a colleague of mine who can fit you into his clinic on Wednesday evening as a matter of urgency. He is very good and highly recommended."

"Highly recommended in what?" I asked sounding dumb.

"Respiratory medicine."

"Why respiratory medicine?" I asked sounding both confused and dumb.

"Because of the location of the mass. It's in your chest."

It was as if I had been doused in ice cold water. I suddenly felt chilled to the bone. *"In my chest?"* I said totally confused. *"But, I have stomach symptoms"*

"Yes, well we don't know quite what we are dealing with here right now and its imperative that we find out as soon as possible so we can get you onto the right course of treatment."

The rest of the conversation was a blur and I felt that I was answering his questions automatically. I confirmed that I would attend the emergency appointment and the biopsy which had been arranged for the following day and then put the phone down.

I looked at the phone in my hand for what seemed like the longest time but it must have only been a minute or two. I was in shock. The thoughts in my head started racing again. There is a mass in my chest, it must be lung cancer! Just as quickly another thought took its place. It could be TB or something benign! I decided to look the 'highly recommended' specialist up on the internet. Within seconds of entering his name on Google, the picture of a pleasant looking man in his early forties appeared.

I scanned the summary of his specialty and found that he not only dealt with lung cancer but also emphysema, TB and other lung abnormalities. My mind grasped the word TB. We had an epidemic in the UK, and TB can cause large granulomatous masses which would raise inflammatory markers. Suddenly there was a flash of hope. It might not be lung cancer. The feeling of dread I had before was suddenly lifting, and although TB itself was an unpleasant disease to have, at least it wasn't cancer! Then I thought a bit more. What if it was cancer? I would need to be prepared.

It's almost a transcendental, 'out of body' experience when you start to look at all the possibilities of a serious situation affecting you. In my mind, I could see myself in the doctor's office, receiving the news that it was TB and then another receiving the news that it was cancer. I researched the different types of cancer that could make their appearance in the chest. It wasn't only Lung cancer. Esophageal cancer popped up along with Breast cancer and both Hodgkin's and non-Hodgkin's lymphoma. I started looking at survival rates and treatment for each. By the end of my research session, I felt more empowered, more in control. At least when I attended my appointment the next day, I would have some idea of what to expect and I had some questions I wanted to ask.

Wednesday evening, when it came, was a cold and rainy December night in London. I had just left Regent's Park tube station on my way to Harley Street, a five-minute walk away. It was so cold I could see my breath hanging in the air in front of me as I walked slowly, my legs heavy. At last, I came to the Physicians clinic, took a deep breath and mounted the three marble steps to the main door. Once inside, I registered with the receptionist and made my way upstairs to the Doctor's office.

I knocked on the door and shook hands with the specialist whose face was familiar from his webpage photograph. I followed his outstretched arm directing me towards one of two chairs located in front of his desk and took one. My heart rate was going up, so I concentrated on my breathing in an effort to calm myself down.

He sat and showed me an image of my CT scan and the bulky mass off to the right side which was opaque and large.

"It's big!" I said without looking away from the screen.

"Yes, it is. It's been identified as Hodgkin's lymphoma."

"Oh thank goodness!" I exclaimed visibly relaxing in my seat.

Now it was the Consultant's turn to be shocked. He was clearly dumbfounded by my response. I went on to explain the research I had read on possible outcomes and I knew from my work in hospitals that Hodgkin's was one of the better cancers to get with an 85% survival rate. It was coming up to Christmas and I had decided that I didn't want to tell my family anything until after the New Year. My Christmas present to them would be one more normal Christmas.

"There is one more thing," said the Doctor fumbling with the report. *"There is a slight opacity in your thyroid which we need to investigate and fortunately for you, we have one of the leading doctors on the thyroid here tonight. I have taken the liberty of calling his clinic to see if they can fit you in for a quick ultrasound to see what they make of this small opaque nodule."*

"You mean that the Hodgkin's may have spread?" I asked feeling the blood drain from my face.

"No. not at all. It's likely to be nothing, maybe a small goiter, but I think it's prudent that it be investigated before we start treatment for your Hodgkin's."

I nodded my agreement.

"Okay," he said. *"The appointment is now, so you will need to go down to the basement where medical imaging is situated. The team will see you straight away. With regards to your Hodgkin's, I am a Consultant in respiratory medicine not blood, so I will be referring you to one of the Consultant Hematologists here in Harley Street. You will need to see him as soon as possible, hopefully by the end of the week."* I nodded again and then hurried to attend my imaging appointment downstairs. It felt like I was on a conveyer being shunted from one doctor and department to another, a strange feeling when I had not been to a doctor for years!

They were waiting for me when I got downstairs and I was shown into the ultrasound room quickly. Within seconds the doctor had located the opaque nodule in my thyroid.

"Right," he said pointing to the screen. *"You can see here a round nodule. It's not a cyst and I am pretty sure that it's going to be a papillary cancer,"* he said outlining the small round tumor.

"What?" I asked again as if I hadn't heard him properly. *"I've literally just been told I have Hodgkin's."*

"Yes, I know," said the Doctor. *"I am very sorry, but the good news is that this is an indolent slow growing cancer, rarely invasive and it does not look like it has gone beyond the Thyroid itself. I need to do a fine needle aspirate to confirm it is cancer. It's literally a very fine needle which is inserted into your thyroid. You won't feel a thing, and I will aspirate off a little bit of the tissue from within, stain it and then look at it under the microscope. We can then confirm diagnosis in the next few minutes."*

I nodded my consent and lay back on the bed. I tried not to think about anything. My mind was screaming with the news that I might have two cancers. I concentrated on my breathing again to calm myself. I felt the tiniest of pin pricks as the doctor inserted the needle. The whole process took about thirty seconds and was over. Moments later he was looking down the microscope at my tissue.

"That's confirmed," he said nodding his head. *"A papillary carcinoma."*

"What's the treatment?" I asked in a daze.

"Oh, it's quite simple," he said putting my slide in a box and going to wash his hands.

"You will probably need a thyroidectomy where they remove your thyroid, and that's usually it. No chemotherapy. No radiotherapy. Quite straight forward when it comes to treating cancers."

The real question was which cancer to treat first? I had to grab a cup of coffee!

Now eight months later, I am sitting nursing another cup of coffee in a London café, my treatment all finished. Due to the position of the mass in my chest, it was decided to treat the Hodgkin's first as my breathing would be at risk for any surgical procedure. Apparently, there is not much room in your chest, and the bulky mass would almost certainly have an effect, which explained my constant tiredness at the time.

I had three months of chemotherapy followed by three weeks of radiotherapy. I lost 20% of my body weight due to acute sickness and an achalasia which developed, and I needed a feeding tube inserted into my stomach. Since I was at risk of refeeding syndrome, which was first recognised in malnourished prisoner of war victims, I had to be carefully monitored once I started taking nutrients in again. I am forever thankful to my incredibly supportive dietician who was with me each step of the way, and helped me in my quest to get a feeding tube put in, and the charming gastroenterologist who fitted it. Without them, things may well have had a very different outcome.

I also lost my hair.

Once my Hodgkin's was shown to be metabolically in remission via a PET scan, my doctor then arranged for me to see the Thyroid surgeons to have my Thyroid removed. I am now on 125 micrograms of Thyroxine for life.

A complete life style change but I am all the better for it. I have been on quite a big learning curve and found out things that I didn't know before. So, what have I learned? I have learned that we are extraordinarily strong when the chips seem to be down. Even with a diagnosis of two different cancers on the same day, my mind was set on beating the odds and surviving them both. To do this, I had to focus on what I wanted, and I set myself both short and long term goals. The short-term goal was never to miss a treatment even though chemotherapy left me on my knees with my head in the toilet, feeling awful.

My longer-term goal was to be well enough to see my eldest daughter graduate as a Doctor of Medicine from St George's school of Medicine London. She had worked so hard to get there. I was not going to miss it for the world. The antics of my granddaughter also kept me going when I didn't think I had the strength, and her mother, my youngest daughter, who despite being a busy mum, was always there to support me just like her sister who was up to her eyeballs in medical exams.

I also learnt that it was not just all about me. My family, when I did tell them at New Year, also hurt. They were naturally very upset with the news, but because I had done my research, when I did finally break the news, I was able to start with a positive. *"It's one of the good ones. 85% survival rate!"* Admittedly, I didn't blurt out that I also had thyroid cancer, I let that news come a little later, because sometimes news like that needs to be broken down into smaller pieces so that people can handle it better.

Now I am a stronger person. I will never be the same again. My old wardrobe has gone and I have had to buy new clothes several sizes smaller because my body has changed so much. I am much more mindful of the fact that family is extremely important when times like this come and that they do what they can, when they can, and that is enough.

I also learned that I have a very nice shaped head, and even though it took a while for my hair to grow back, when it came, it came back strong, healthy and curly!

There is no doubt in my mind that to get better, you need to keep a positive attitude not only for yourself but also for those around you, and that the practise of mindfulness, focusing on the present and not what might be and worrying about it, can help you get through it all.

I am living proof.

To my family, especially my children Lauren and Brooke, my grand-daughter Isla, Connor, Tom, Lesley and Brian, Robin, Paul and all in Teddington; my brothers Jamie, David and James; and Dad, I couldn't have done this without you. Thank you so much for all your help and support. I am truly thankful. Also, to Dawn for your inspiration to write this. Namaste! I am also extremely grateful to all the hospital and clinic staff that treated me and got me better. You are very special people! Thank you!

MEERA IYENGAR

MEERA IYENGAR is a Reiki Master/Teacher and a Heal Your Life® Coach and Workshop Facilitator. She has been a student of both Reiki and Louise Hay's Heal Your Life® philosophy for over ten years. Meera offers Reiki healing, Heal Your Life® workshops and one-on-one coaching sessions. She loves to meditate, is very happy to go on long walks and loves to spend time with her family.

www.meeraiyengar.com.au

❧ Act of Faith

A definition of Faith from the Oxford Dictionary is "complete trust or confidence in someone or something." Faith can mean a lot of things — it can mean faith in God, faith in one's own ability, faith in a system or religion, faith in another, etc. Looking back in my life, I can see that I have always believed in God, in a way that I was taught to believe as I grew up. I can also see times when faith was complete and when it was not. During both of these times, lessons have been learnt, for which I am grateful. I feel that lessons were learnt easily when faith was complete. A few years ago, I came across what Louise Hay says about God, *"Our concept of God has to be one for us."* This thought has made me see God in a new way — one where I know that I am God's child and where I am perfect just the way I am.

I would like to share with you a meditation where visualisation, affirmations and the concept of being God's child are all used. I believe this meditation makes me feel loved and fearless.

Sit in a comfortable position, with your hands open, palm side facing up. Close your eyes. Take a deep breath and as you exhale thank God for this meditation. Take a second deep breath, as you exhale thank the angels and your teachers for their guidance. Take another deep breath, and as you exhale thank yourself for this meditation.

Visualise God within your heart chakra. Take a few moments to continue visualising this. As you start becoming comfortable, visualise yourself praying to God and asking to help you meditate. Imagine yourself returning to your seated meditation position. Affirm "I am happy, healthy, strong and safe." If you are comfortable using chants, you could do so. I use "Om", the bija mantra for Third Eye Chakra as a chant.

With each affirmation or chant, visualise God becoming bigger, bigger than you; bigger than everything that you can see. Now imagine you are within God's heart centre, in a white-light-filled bubble. Visualise you are meditating within this bubble. Continue meditating in this way for some time. Give God all your fears, guilt, anger, frustration, shame and any other unwanted thought pattern that you are willing to release. Visualise God taking these thoughts away from you and filling you with Light and Love.

Visualise giving God all your happiness, love and joy. Visualise God enhancing these thought patterns by filling you with Light and Love.

Now, imagine doing things that you love — working in your garden, laughing at a joke, singing, dancing, at your workplace, sharing a lovely meal with your family and friends. Visualise everything that you would like to see happening in the future. For example, you may be seeking a new job and you can visualise being in a new workplace where your talents are recognised, and where you earn a good income for your services.

As you continue this visualisation, know that you are safe, you are in God's heart. Affirm "I am God's child and I am safe."

When you have completed the visualisations, return to your meditative position, still within the light-filled bubble in God's heart centre. As you continue chanting, visualise God returning into your heart. Visualise yourself filled with Light and Love. Stay in this state for a few moments, knowing you can always go back to God's heart centre at any point in time.

Take a deep breath and as you exhale thank God for this meditation. Take a second deep breath, as you exhale thank the angels and your teachers for their guidance. Take a third deep breath, and as you exhale thank yourself for this meditation.

Take this feeling of oneness with God, as you continue through your day. Affirm "Within me, there is God, there is Love, there is Light."

To me, this meditation is an act of surrender to God, an act of faith in something that is bigger than anything I can think of. An act of giving both negative and positive thought patterns and returning with Light and Love, knowing that God is working on manifesting all the positive thought patterns for us. We are God's children and God wants us to be safe and happy.

I would like to dedicate this chapter to God. Thank you for being with me always.

I would like to acknowledge all my teachers starting with my parents Vasantha and Rangaswamy, all my grandparents, my Reiki teacher, Maithili Varadarajan and my Heal Your Life® teacher, Susie Mulholland. Thank you all for your teachings, your love and support. I would like to thank my husband Seshadri, my daughter Aditi, my brother Manu and my mother-in-law Suguna Sampath for their encouragement and belief in me. Their support has made sharing my thoughts with you easy.

JENNY HOGG ASHWELL

JENNY HOGG ASHWELL is a gifted spiritual mentor and guide passionate about awakening Love and higher consciousness in the world by helping us remember that Love is all there is, we are Love, and spiritual guidance is always available. Offering a unique balance between the intellect and spiritual mystic, Jenny assists clients to open to Love and their unique soul purpose. She first studied business administration at the University of California, Berkeley, and then law at Northwestern University. In 1996 Jenny was working as a lawyer when she received a wake-up call from her soul that began her spiritual and personal growth journey. Through Divine grace and enormous trust, Jenny travelled a path from lawyer to student of spirituality and mother of three, to spiritual counselor and intuitive, to learn of her soul's essence as a star child and her gift as a bridge to the spiritual realm. Most recently, in fulfillment of her soul assignment Jenny took a courageous step to scribe the book, *Love's Curriculum: Messages of Enlightenment*, for the High Council.

The High Council includes Jesus, the archangels, and other teachers who have gathered in the spiritual realm to help awaken the world to the Divine Love that connects all. Not only an inspiring guidebook for lightworkers everywhere, Love's Curriculum is also a movement to awaken Love and higher consciousness. Fueled by her own transcendent experiences and strong inner knowing, her training and work in transpersonal counseling psychology, and a decade volunteering as an assistant at personal development workshops, Jenny has become known as a wise and skilled spiritual mentor and guide. She spreads Love's Curriculum worldwide through the book, speaking engagements, private mentoring sessions, group circles, and workshops. Explore ways to shine and awaken with Jenny and Love's Curriculum at www.lovescurriculum.com.

❧ SHINE! Your Light Matters in the World

Three years ago, I discovered my soul assignment to scribe the book *Love's Curriculum: Messages of Enlightenment* for the High Council. The High Council includes Jesus, the archangels, and other spiritual teachers who have gathered in the spiritual realm to help awaken the memory of Divine Love in the world. While they seem to appear outside of us as teachers, they are clear in communicating that in reality they and we are one, and they represent the enlightened part of the group consciousness. I now realize that *Love's Curriculum* is not just a book: it is a movement to awaken Love and higher consciousness that is needed now in our world.

I wasn't always able to state my soul's purpose with such clarity and openness. My relationship with my self and my purpose today is not what it was three years ago, or ten years ago, or twenty years ago. Reaching a place where I am able to state publicly and unequivocally that I am a conduit for the High Council's messages has been an incredible journey of trust and surrender that required stepping through fears and doubts . . . and the journey continues.

My hope is that by sharing what I have learned from my experience and by bridging you to the spiritual guidance available, I can help enlighten your path to shining your unique soul purpose in the world, for I know deep in my heart that you are called to important work. There is a star in you that shines bright and is uniquely *you*. This star light wants to be expressed. As the High Council states in *Love's Curriculum*: "[You] were placed and assigned to this time in order to ignite your heart light and center and begin shining that in the world" (p. 18).

Heeding the Call

I first felt the pull of my own star light when my inner intuitive guidance prompted me to leave my career as a lawyer because it was not my soul's calling. I continued to follow this inner star light through twists and turns, growth and realignments. This star light called to me through visions, dreams, and the voice of intuition and Spirit, all nudging me in new directions and through personal and spiritual growth. This journey included reading books, taking classes, counseling, and participating in healing workshops. My star light led me to an in-depth, three-year training program in transpersonal counseling psychology. It was there that I first identified my soul's purpose as a bridge to the spiritual realm. It guided me to a course aimed at heightening intuition and learning to connect with spirit guides. Soon, what was before only a dim view of my soul's essence and purpose became a more defined knowing. I experienced my soul's essence and higher self as an indigo, light-being quality in me—a star child. At the same time as this experience of my soul essence grew, intuition guided me to begin writing a book about how Spirit had guided my life.

As I worked on my life story, I experienced an even deepening awareness of my soul's essence and my soul's desire to share a message with the world. It was calling to me. So, I closed my eyes, tuned into that part of me, and typed the following:

> *I feel the presence of something that wants to write this book. It is love. It is fiery. It is burning to have all remember their innocence—that they are love, that we are one—and for me to express my unique purpose here. Tears stream down my face. I know many of you reading this can identify. In the worlds of Wayne Dyer, it is my highest self.*

This was the start of an ongoing inquiry with my highest self, my soul essence, my star light, which led to learning of my assignment to scribe *Love's Curriculum* for the High Council.

Believing in Your Star Light

You, too, are a star with your own unique light that wishes to shine in the world. From my highest self and star light to yours, I share this message:

> *You are great and small all at once—a star that is bright and grand and at the same time small, a pinpoint. You see, up close a star is huge, and yet from earth it is small and one of many lights that light the way and the path. So, you are one of many lights. Be glad that you are here with other star lights.*

Take a moment to let those words land within you now. You are a star that wishes to shine bright. Your heart desires to express in the world in the unique way that is meant for you. And you are not alone. Whether you are aware of it yet or not, you belong here with other lightworkers, and helpers in the spiritual realm guide you. Together we join to create peace on earth, a new age of unity and understanding:

> *As each light source, each person, begins to shine and spread Love out from [his or her] heart centers, the world will be enveloped in a pinkish-white light of Love. And it will filter out to the others who are not living there yet, and to the structures of the world . . . (Love's Curriculum, p. 18)*

What does this star light within you say to you? Have you heard the call? Have you taken steps toward your dream? We are all at different parts of the awakening journey to open to Love and shine our unique light.

We're all just walking each other home.

~RAM DASS

Barriers to Love

Deep within you, there is a star that has come here to shine. Maybe you have just glimpses of your soul's purpose and heart's desire at this point, or maybe you have stepped clearly on the path to realizing your vision. Wherever you find yourself, you may have realized by now that this journey of birthing your dream and shining your light is not easy! It takes stretching through fear and doubt, changing limiting beliefs, and healing the past. It is a process of removing the barriers to Love to reveal your authentic self, and it takes a whole lot of trust and surrender.

Why do these barriers, this confusion, these fears and doubts, arise in something as Spirit-driven as shining your unique star light? If you are following Spirit (God, Goddess, Creator, the Divine), shouldn't the path be effortless? Instead, my experience has been that when we step onto a Spirit-guided path, there are times of synchronicity, expansion, ease and grace, but these times are combined with periods of fear, doubt, contraction, and blocks that need to be addressed and moved through with love, support, prayer, trust, surrender, and faith.

In particular for me, the experience of owning my gift to channel felt like "coming out of the closet." I had to move past current fears of not belonging, as well as old, ancient fears, like the fear of being burned at the stake for possessing intuitive gifts. What I have discovered is that as you open to Love and expand to shine your light, the *ego* sets out to stop your expansion and to keep you thinking you are separate and small. The ego is the thought system within your mind and the collective mind that believes you are separate from others and from God (Spirit, Goddess, Source, Creator). The ego part of the mind also believes that you are guilty and flawed. It is the mistaken thought that you are separate from God, guilty, and going to be punished. The ego, then, has as its goal to keep you from shining your light; it thinks it must keep you hidden and safe from God and Love. It does this with fear, control, defense strategies, masks, roles, and judgments of others and self. New thought leader, speaker, and author Wayne Dyer accurately described ego as standing for *Edge God Out*.

It is important to understand that as you step forward to shine your light, the ego gets activated.

 Whenever fear intrudes anywhere along the road to peace,
it is because the ego has attempted to join the journey with
us and cannot do so. Sensing defeat and angered by it, the
ego regards itself as rejected and becomes retaliative.

~A COURSE IN MIRACLES, T-8.V.5:5-6

I call this an ego attack or ego backlash: you take a big, guided step on your path, you stretch and take a chance, and then you face a stream of fear, doubt, and inner criticism. When working on *Love's Curriculum* the ego judged me as arrogant, special, not worthy, and crazy. It warned me of partnering and getting support, and spoke to me of doubt. Part of the journey of awakening is to recognize the ego and its attacks, and to make a choice to listen to Love and not the ego.

Bringing the Ego Home to Love

As you step forward on your path to shine your star light in Love and purpose, the ego shows itself as judgment of self and other, comparison, self-consciousness, feeling that you are not worthy or that there is not enough, and the fear of humiliation, embarrassment, and ridicule. It is the inner critic as well, telling you all the reasons you are not safe or not good enough, and it screams louder as you take big steps toward shining your light.

Ultimately, the goal is to bring the ego home to Love, too:

> Let the Love shatter your old identification. Let it shatter, and let the ego self dissolve. Then you stand anew, still in your form but now shining with the Light of God, no longer hidden behind the mask of the ego and its roles and fear. Allow the ego, too, to be dissolved in Love and brought to Love . . .
>
> ~LOVE'S CURRICULUM, P. 73

Over the years, I have learned and discovered tools that help in choosing Love over the ego as you stretch and expand to shine your light.

Sharing with another what the ego voice is saying within your mind is one such powerful tool for quieting the ego so that Love and purpose can be heard and followed. As soon as you speak out loud to a trusted other what the ego is saying within you, it is much easier to see the ego for what it is, and its hold over you lessens. Sharing with a trusted other helps you to see that the ego is an illusion keeping you from the truth of who you are. Reach out to friends or a partner who understands the ego and its traps, or a professional therapist or coach. If no one is available, writing in a journal may be therapeutic, or writing to your angels, your highest self, the Divine higher power, for guidance and clarity.

Another powerful tool for managing the ego and its attacks is meditation. Meditation helps train the mind to recognize the difference between the ego fear messages and the messages of your higher self and Love. Meditation helps make it easier to decipher and know when the ego is attacking. It can also provide peace in the middle of an ego attack and a way back to the experience of Love and Oneness. Meditation generally prepares your mind and heart to better hear the guidance of Spirit.

Also helpful for moving past the ego attack is asking for and then surrendering to help from a higher power—Spirit, Creator, God, Goddess, whatever your name for the Divine. It is about asking for light in the darkness and to be reminded of a higher perspective when you feel mired in the swamps of the ego. You may communicate with Divine helpers like angels and spirit guides through your thoughts, spiritual card decks, journaling, or with the help of an intuitive. You may ask that these Divine beings or a trusted spiritual teacher draw near and help you. Prayer and setting intentions work well, and then surrendering and trusting that the guidance and shift will be there. Reading spiritually uplifting and inspiring words or about other peoples' journeys can be invaluable ways to connect and surrender to Spirit as well. Music that connects you and uplifts you is also a powerful tool.

This brings me to a final note about the importance of surrender. Along your journey to shining your star light in the world, you must surrender your limited human understanding to the unknown, to go where you have not gone before, to trust in Spirit's guidance and plan for you.

> ❧ We must be willing to let go of the life we planned
> so as to have the life that is waiting for us.
>
> ~JOSEPH CAMPBELL

You Can Do It

Shining your star light in the world is a journey: a continuing process of opening to Divine Love, removing the barriers to Love and your authentic self, surrendering, and learning to navigate the ego attacks. It is a journey you are prepared to take, and it is important that you take it. The world needs your light now more than ever. Should you feel called that I assist you on your path, I would be honored.

Dedicated with love to Kaylie, Kari, and Alex. May I be a shining example for you, inspiring you to live your own unique purpose and shine your light. I love you.

Thank you to my husband, Dave, and my children, Kaylie, Kari, and Alex, for believing in me and supporting me on my own unique path. Thank you to my parents, Will and Gerda, for joining me on this exciting journey of spiritual and self-discovery. Thank you to the High Council and all my mentors and teachers, both in spiritual form and physical form, who have guided me and continue to guide me on my journey. And thank you to my dear friends who support me to explore and grow, love myself, and laugh. Shining my light would not be possible without all of you. My heart is full with gratitude and joy.

SCOTT FERREIRA

DR. SCOTT FERREIRA is a licensed Chiropractic Physician, a fellow in Acupuncture, a workshop leader, an Ordained Minister, and a certified life and wellness coach serving the Seacoast of New England for the past 18 years. His passion is to help individuals achieve optimal health within the Wellness model and help guide them to living the life that they desire most. By lecturing, teaching, and practically using the Sacred Heart Trinity, Dr. Scott helps people find peace, purpose, and joy in their life.

He is the co-owner of Natural Care Wellness Center with his wife Dr. Jody Ferreira in Eliot, Maine. They have four amazing children and travel the country challenging themselves in running, biking, and obstacle races.

Together they use a "whole person" wellness approach to healing in order to help accelerate and maintain your journey to great health. This approach to wellness means looking for underlying causes of physical, emotional, nutritional, chemical, environmental, and spiritual disturbances leading to illness and dis-ease.

Drscott99@gmail.com
www.naturalcarewellness.com

THE SACRED HEART TRINITY

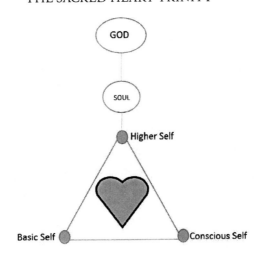

❧ Discerning From Your Sacred Heart

Have you ever wondered how you make decisions? Are they ego driven or heart centered? Are you receiving intuitive and divine messages? Discernment is your answer!

Discernment is a process we use every single day whether we are or are not consciously aware. Every time we are faced with a decision, discernment becomes a factor. Sometimes, our conscious minds will weigh out the options to help us decide if it's something that we want or something we should do. Other times, it will present as a feeling from our heart or deep within our soul. It is a calling, guiding us towards an experience. We can receive that call even if we cannot consciously recognize it as something we are interested in or had ever wanted to do. This call is from a deep intuitive level. Discernment can be defined as:

- The act or process of exhibiting keen insight and good judgment
- Perception of that which is obscure and the ability to judge well
- The trait of evaluating wisely and objectively
- The ability to decide between truth and error, right and wrong
- The process of making careful distinctions in our thinking of truth
- The interior search for an answer for a direction in ones' life
- A calling on the divine to lead or give direction

The art of discernment is a valuable tool in your "tool box". Our mind presents us with thousands of thoughts every single day, filled with opportunities. Yet, not every thought you have or opportunity that is presented is one that is meant for you and your life purpose. Some of these thoughts are distractions or "busy work" that your mind is creating. These thoughts are actually keeping you from ever discovering or unfolding what your truth actually may be.

As creators of our lives, it is imperative to get an understanding of just how important our thoughts really are and how they really do create our life experiences. Every event in your life begins and ends with a thought. These thoughts can either create a life with many positive or negative experiences.

A thought is an affirmation that is set in motion into the Universe; all thoughts. This is fabulous news and very powerful! In order to change a thought that you may previously had, all you need to do is have another more positive thought. It is very simple to make changes in your life if that is something you desire to do.

Our ego/logical minds have us seeking answers that are outside of ourselves. This at times makes us feel uncertain about who we are and want we want in life. We have all done this in searching for our life direction. We need to reteach ourselves how to go within so we can clearly hear and discern the thoughts and messages that your own soul is bringing.

Intuition is something that is deep within our soul and is a gift and talent that we all have within us. Sometimes it needs some cultivating, yet it is there within each of us. Many people have constantly repeated this phrase, "Everything you want to know about yourself and your life purpose lies within you." And it truly does. No one knows you better than you.

Let's face it, we all deal with fears and low self-esteem in our lives. These feelings block and separate us from our true desires. Unfortunately, our minds and life in general, constantly feed us that never ending "to do" list to keep us busy. Another obstacle is the repetitive negative self-talk that wants us to believe that we are less than, not worthy, and not deserving. When "the head" voice becomes involved in decision making, the negative self-talk can take over and your true heart's desires are buried. Fear, anxiety, not feeling good enough, and low self-confidence block what may truly be in our sacred hearts.

Living from our heart, our true sacred heart's desire is something we all must strive for. It is what God intended us to do in this lifetime. Some of us live in our heads and we find comfort there. Our intellect is where we live most of our waking moments. Our brain tells us what to think, how to act, and what we should or should not do. This is sometimes based on what others think. Other times, it is based on earlier life experiences. We may choose not to listen to our feelings because we may not trust them. This creates disconnect from our head to our heart that we may later regret.

For others, the opposite is true. They are primarily led by their emotions. How they feel about someone or something becomes their overriding thoughts. These individuals become focused on how their actions or feelings effect those around them. Now they wonder where their intellect went, when the decision made does not seem wise, well thought out and they're left feeling empty.

As a human, we need to have a balance between our head and our heart. We need to start to listen to that reassuring voice that resides deep within us called intuition. God has blessed us with this, and when used properly, we become very powerful individuals living in our heart's desire.

Feeling secure is paramount in listening to your intuition and stepping into your personal power. You can never make a giant step forward in your evolution if your basic self (inner child/emotional self) feels that it is not being heard and/or taken care of. When this happens, lower emotions of fear and self-doubt become personal prisons to our basic self. We start to box ourselves in to create security from these emotions. As we do this, we block our intuition and divine guidance. We begin to lose the ability to make positive life and fulfilling decisions.

Becoming in right relationship with ones' self is necessary to bring unity with your head and heart. There are three parts of who we are: your basic self, mentioned above, your conscious self (thinking brain/ego), and your higher self (spirit). Your higher self is what is connected to your soul. This is your creative co-partner and what connects you to the divine, to grace, to the Holy Spirit, and to God. These three parts form a triangle called your **Sacred Heart Trinity**. (See diagram in autobiography)

When these three parts of ourselves are not working in unison, your brain and emotions cannot be synchronized. Your basic self and conscious self, start to be independently controlled by the ego. I view ego as an acronym for "Edging God Out". When we do this, we start to make decisions that are self-serving and not for our greatest or highest good. Our negative emotions start to control us. We stop listening to our heart's desire and begin blocking positive life experiences. The basic self places us into a virtual box that makes you feel safe, however, it also confines our personal growth. This wall needs to be expanded and/or knocked down for us to be able to receive more of divine grace. This box, which is our vessel, can be expanded and grown. We just need to learn to trust the divine guidance and intuition we all receive in our sacred hearts. When we trust this, then our basic self lets down its' guard and begins to come in unison with the conscious and higher self.

The more we allow God to give us wisdom, our vessel grows. How expansive your box is, is in direct relation to how you let God fill you with divine light. You will not receive more than you can handle. You just need to prepare for this expansion. Be willing to grow and expand to manifest from your heart's desire. Within this limiting box, we can't live by the Universal Laws of more life, more freedom, and more joy. We feel suppressed and blocked in our lives with no hope for change. When our **Sacred Heart Trinity** is in sync, then all three parts of yourself come together. This creates a heart centered individual who is one unified being of divine force!

There is a Universal Law that states "As Above, So Below"; "As Within, So Without". Countless people know this saying. They have their own perceptions on what it means and how to utilize it in their lives. Over the years with teaching this law, I have realized that many still do not grasp the full depth of these simple words.

My experience is that when you consciously choose, using your own free will, to carve out time in your day, you go into receivership with the source of life. For some, that looks like quiet time in meditation and prayer to start their day. For others, it's a walk-in nature, or deep physical exercise; such as running and biking. There is no right or wrong, it is whatever works for you. It is the decision to desire a one-on-one holy time with your conscious and basic self, which is connected to your higher self and soul at all times.

That connection to your soul brings the ideas, inspiration, and creativity to your **Sacred Heart Trinity**. From here, you can discern using your intuition, if what is inspiring you is the right fit or if it needs to percolate a little more. In order for an idea to be a good fit, it needs to bring more positive expression into your life. That is more life, more freedom, and more joy. Sometimes, we are given an idea to sit with until we are ready to ask for the next right step. Often, it's a simple tweaking or slight change in what you are already doing that brings you joy. In other times, it looks like the Extreme Makeover! Your soul knows what you need and desire better than your ego ever could.

You were born with a divine blueprint waiting to express itself into the world. This expression is your unique gifts, talents, and personality. *Who are you and what do you desire?* When you begin to take the steps to answer these questions and make the decision to follow your own inner guidance, you become a magnet of miracles! That inner divine love has no choice but to manifest into your outer world. That is your "as within so without." God loves you and wants to give you everything your heart desires.

Choosing the above or a spiritual path is the catalyst that brings forth the below. When you recognize that you are a spiritual being having a human experience in the physical, you will observe your life transforming into an amazing and joyful one. It becomes one divine connection after another, aligning you to your sacred heart's desires. When you choose to act on this Universal Law, the below, begins to unfold perfectly. The below is your physical human experience that we are currently living out.

When we make that 18-inch journey from our head to our heart, magnificent things unfold. When you live from your sacred heart's desire, your life grows and expands with love, joy, and happiness. When we trust ourselves and God, we create balance in body, mind, and spirit. Using your mind to connect with spirit, to work with your body, develops an intimate and sacred relationship with all parts of yourself working as one; the **Sacred Heart Trinity**.

Many people wonder about the meaning of free will versus the meaning of fate. As you are aligning to your divine blueprint, it can seem like you have no choice. We always have a choice in everything that is presented in our sacred heart. The wise person recognizes that in choosing to align to your soul's purpose and divine blueprint, you are using the power of your free will. That decision to act upon the "above" spiritual wisdom, placed in motion your soul's plan and your divine purpose. Your soul is connected to a divine creative force that flows through you. God desires to guide you back to being a unified being of divine force with love.

Such is the connection of your sacred heart with God. The art of discernment is learning key principals when working with your **Sacred Heart Trinity** and placing discernment into action. Discernment in action is:

- Thinking and acting spontaneously, rather than with fears based on past life experiences and belief systems
- The ability to find joy in each and every moment while being present
- Loss of criticism, condemnation, and judgment of others and of yourself
- Loss of interest in conflict or drama and an increase in compassion
- Loss of interest in interpreting the actions of others, simply accepting they have a reason and beyond that, God's will be done
- Frequent episodes of smiling because you "Let go and let God". You trust that you are given the right next step
- An increased ability to accept love extended by others and being centered
  - in your heart with unconditional love for all

- ☞ "Doing the right thing", no matter what others may think or feel about
  - your actions. Having patience
- ☞ Being willing to receive answers to your questions that may surprise you
  - and may make no logical sense. Being in the flow with faith
- ☞ Asking if what is before you is for your greatest or highest good and
  - the greatest or highest good for all humanity with clarity and direction
- ☞ Divine guidance received is always with loving principles in a calm and caring way
- ☞ Divine guidance is consistently supporting and encouraging, not fearful or frantic
- ☞ This guidance can feel like:
  - When your gut matches the guidance given to you
  - Worry being replaced by a sense of peace and trust
  - You have an "aha" moment
  - Feelings of positive things to come that gives you a sense of passion
- ☞ Ask for signs to "prove" your guidance is true. Get three confirmations from GOD
- ☞ Will the guidance you receive limit or expand you?
- ☞ Does it give you: more life, more freedom, and more joy with divine creations?

Start to write down and meditate on the possibilities within your sacred heart. Ask for help. Take classes in personal development and spirituality. Put into practice the steps of discernment listed here. Use examples such as Christ, Buddha, and Moses who came to earth as an example of a way, a path to learn how man or woman can experience the divine.

Trust and discern that God and your soul desire great things for you. Begin by listening to what your sacred heart wishes. What makes it leap out of your chest when you receive an idea? Decide you will act on the message you received, even if your head decides to tell you otherwise. You are not alone; you are completely supported in all you do. Everything happens for a reason. There are no accidents, there are no coincidences, and no randomness to life. There is a divine blueprint in action connecting to your **Sacred Heart Trinity**.

Sweetly whisper to your mind that you have decided to listen to your sacred heart. Ask your mind to jump on board for the adventure as it unfolds, full of majesty and miracles. There is power in trusting your sacred heart's desire. Give yourself the chance to see, feel, and know the divine passion of what positive life experiences can bring! Life is an adventure! Enjoy the ride! Blessings!!!

I dedicate this chapter to God for gracing me with a beautiful life and for the wisdom of intuition and discernment. Secondly to my loving wife, Jody, and my four children, Jared, Evan, Logan, and Ella: I am blessed beyond measure to share this life and journey with you.

A special thank you to my Mom, Deb Nazario; my Dad, Bill Ferreira; my Sister, Lisa Ferreira; and mother in law, Jeannine Trenholme. You have always believed in me and supported all my new adventures. To my friends, Marcia and Gano Adair, for your unconditional support and heartfelt laughter. To my friend, Donna Tobey for your life encouragements, especially in writing. Lastly to my church family and work family, thank you for being part of this adventuresome ride.

KELLY VICARIO

KELLY VICARIO, (Victoria Kay), was born in Philadelphia, Pennsylvania in 1966. She grew up in a happy middle class home, with her sister and brother. She now resides in southern New Jersey, with her husband and two children.

Kelly and her husband have run a successful pre-school since 2001, and are now assisted by their daughter. Kelly also continues to work as a Mind, Body, Spirit practitioner and as a medium. She also facilitates spiritual workshops. Her first book, *A Cursed Blessing: My Empathic Journey*, chronicles her extraordinary life, dealing with anxiety and discovering her empathic abilities, which help her to heal others through mediumship.

Her website is: www.intuhealing.com

✿ MY BLESSING

In life, we may feel that we are less than our fellow man. Maybe we are not as "pretty as her", or as "smart as him", or maybe we feel that we are a "little inferior to others", or "a little damaged" in some way. We tend to accept that other people may expect very little from us, without even thinking that maybe, just maybe, there is something different and special about us. We begin to accept and believe that we have great limitations, and live our lives accordingly.

As a child, I was blessed with a wonderful life. I had great parents, siblings and friends. But it wouldn't be long before the tables would turn on me, and I would find myself pleading with God, to stop me from self-destruction. During my first pregnancy, I found myself in a debilitating depression. I could not understand why I was in such a depression, with a planned pregnancy, a wonderful husband, and a nice home. Maybe my life wasn't perfect, but it was certainly very good. Blaming my hormones, I struggled with insomnia, loss of appetite, and the inability to be happy about anything. I knew that I just needed to get through this pregnancy, and then everything would go back to normal.

Over the next eighteen years, I found myself in this same dark hole, with several bouts of depression, and I had no understanding of how I got there. Doctors diagnosed me with an anxiety disorder, and treated me with medication, but I knew that there was more involved than just that. I had a beautiful life and these episodes seemed to come from nowhere, and completely out of the blue.

This is how I led my life, until I could no longer accept it in my heart. My soul had a purpose, and this purpose had to emerge. I began the battle for my life.

"God, I do not want to live anymore! Is this what you want me to say? I hate what I am doing to my family! They do not deserve this roller coaster ride! How much more can they take? How much more can I take? Please Lord, help me! I beg You Lord, please help me!" The screaming pleas were loud and my voice was beginning to crack.

I remained on my knees and closed my eyes. And in my mind's eye, I could see and feel God standing on my right side. But I could also see and feel the presence of dark and evil energy on my left. The evil presence on my left was trying to overtake me and "console" me and I felt as if he wanted to help me. He wanted to take my pain from me. I could feel myself moving toward him because he was going to make me feel better. The evil was fighting with God to claim my soul, and maybe I should give in to him. I was feeling numb and hopeless, and the thought of taking my life was becoming real. I began to think that this was how it was supposed to end for me. In this moment, I felt in my heart that everyone's life would be better if I were not part of it. Why would I want to live like this anyway? The anger, depression, guilt and loneliness had finally won. My spirit had been broken and my faith was gone. My soul was going to belong to the evil entity that I could feel and see to my left.

Just then, as if to catch him by accident, I could see the face of evil look up at God with a smirk and laugh. It was as if he were telling God that he had won the prize of my soul, and how dumb of me to fall for his tricks. I felt no love or caring from this energy anymore! All I could feel or see was pain and suffering. Before I would let him take me, I managed to scream, "Oh God I need You now. Please save me!!"

At that point, I felt enraged. My eyes opened wide, "How dare you play with my life as if it is a game! You are playing with not only my life but the lives of my children and my family." I became so angry and defensive. I was trying to protect my soul like a parent protects his or her child. I knew that this was God's help that I was receiving to fight off the evil. God had given me the strength to wipe away the tears from my cheeks and fight.

I turned to look at the bed where I had spent so many days and nights. It was my private tomb. I had spent hours staring at a blank television screen and hours crying to the point of exhaustion. I hated that bed, but I knew that I would return to it immediately, if that was what God had planned for me. If I was going to leave this life, it would not be from my own hand! I would not allow myself to bring the pain that I had been suffering for fifteen years to the people who loved me. I would not give this evil energy the satisfaction of distorting my children by having me take my own life. I crawled back into bed with a renewed light and with the decision to stay and fight.

That night, I ventured down the path to recovery for the final time. Days grew into weeks and weeks grew into months. I continued with my therapy and medication again, and I started to return to normal. When I became well again, I took time to do research. I was looking for answers. I wanted to find out why my life had led me down the road of depression and anxiety, and what lesson that I was supposed to learn from it. I poured over many books on empowerment, life after death, and Heaven, all for a better understanding. This was when the next part of my magical journey began.

God led me to discover that I had strong empathic abilities, meaning that I can acutely feel the emotions of other people. I learned that I can unknowingly think that those emotions are my own, which I believe led me to a great deal of confusion and distress, and into several deep depressions.

It wasn't too long ago that I believed that I was cursed to be able to feel the emotions of other people. Not understanding your ability as an empath can become very challenging, and in some cases, as in mine, very destructive.

I began to research this subject and to take classes in meditation, which led me to realize that I also had the ability to communicate with the spirits of those who have crossed over. I then began my journey into mediumship. I found that I can often help people heal from the loss of a loved one.

I was blessed by God's grace to be able to emerge from the other side, with the ability to heal. I may never have known about these gifts, if I had not been blessed with my struggles, pain and heartache. I want to share my story so that you may know that we all can emerge bigger and brighter than we ever could have imagined. I have learned that we only need to ask God for his strength, and to have faith that it will be delivered.

A Reading

I would like to share one of my readings with you:

I was just starting my journey into mediumship. After I had taken several classes, I decided that it would be best for me to start practicing by giving readings to people. My sister had a friend named Claire. They had been friends for quite a while. They were co-workers. I had been introduced to her at one time, but I knew nothing of her past or of her family. Claire agreed to have a reading with me.

At this time, seeing spirits was starting to become routine for me, as I would frequently see them appear in my thoughts and dreams. At times, I even saw them standing at my bedside. They always had messages for me to give to their loved ones and friends. So, it was not a surprise to me, when a few nights before I was to meet with Claire at my sister's house, I had a vision. I had gotten into bed and closed my eyes. In a flash, I saw Claire's face and an older man. I assumed that this was Claire's Dad. He was wearing a mechanic's uniform. I heard, very distinctly, the words, "stroke" and "tattoo on forearm". The next day, I called my sister. After she spoke to Claire, she told me that Claire had confirmed that what I had heard was meaningful.

On the night of Claire's reading, I was expecting her Dad to come through. But to my surprise, her brother came through instead. When her brother came through, he was shining and happy. He was showing me things that he liked to do when he was here on earth. He let me see him playing basketball and working in his garage. He also led me into the woods. I could see his boots walking, and crushing leaves and twigs. I could smell the aroma of the forest and feel the warmth of the sun on my skin. This was the area where he had been shot. He brought me there for his sister's validation, so there would be no doubt about the messages that he needed to share with her. He did not want her to dwell on the circumstances of this event, or of his death. He wanted her to let go of the past, and to move forward, and to be happy. He wanted her to understand that he is in Heaven and is at peace, and that the rest is unimportant.

Just before the reading ended, her Dad came in. After my original contact with her father, Claire had asked for validation from him. Before she met with me, she asked him to confirm the image of his tattoo, and to show it to me. Her father did just that. Claire's father showed me the tattoo that was on his forearm. This was important to her, because it was unique. The tattoo was of the family Crest, a depiction of their family's heritage. Claire shared with me that before our reading began, she also prayed for her brother. I always have my clients say a prayer when we begin, so that they can ask their loved ones to come through to us. Claire often thanks me for the closure that she received from that reading. I was very happy that I could give her the healing that she needed from her loved ones.

It is my wish that I may bring hope and peace to other people who may believe that they too may have empathic abilities. Please know that you are not alone, and that there is always a light at the end of the dark tunnel. The stronger our challenges become, the stronger our blessings will become. You need to believe this and have faith. To read more about my journey, please pick up my book, *A Cursed Blessing: My Empathic Journey*, or visit www.intuhealing.com.

Dedicated to my husband and children.

I would like to acknowledge the tremendous support from my family and friends. Because of their love and understanding, I am now able to live my soul's purpose by bringing peace and healing to others.

KELLY ANN VASS

A little girl named KELLY ANN desired to be a student and teacher of love. She was told by many that she couldn't. She was born worthy as we all are. She was told she wasn't. As she grew, she worked at exceeding other's expectations and pleasing anyone who entered her life. She gave away her voice and her power. She started to believe that she was not good enough or lovable. She slipped further away from her Divine self.

One day Louise Hay's book *You Can Heal Your Life* found Kelly. Kelly read; she studied; Kelly practiced; she loved; Kelly forgave; she healed; Kelly Ann discovered authenticity. She began recovery from human perfectionism and people-pleasing. Becoming a mother, Kelly experienced joy and received two more reasons to love herself. She learned to release the past, let go of futuristic worries, and create her life in the now. She asked for help from her life coach Shawna Campbell. She treated books and their authors as mentors. She started saying yes to her life by creating kind and loving boundaries. She learned to trust the Divine Power and Divine Self.

At a reading with angelic medium, Jessica Tyson Salkeld, Kelly received a very important message from spirit: **Your life purpose Kelly is to teach people to create loving and kind boundaries for themselves and you will do this by just being you!**

She was trained and licensed as a Heal Your Life Teacher® and Life Coach. In 2016, her written story was published in *Manifesting Modern Miracles*. Kelly is presently a student of the Quantum Success Coaching Academy™ Certification Program. Kelly's workshop facilitating and spiritual life coaching business, In The Now, is located in Sherwood Park, Alberta, Canada. Kelly Ann Vass is filled with grace and gratitude for living her purpose!

inthenowkellyvass@shaw.ca
www.inthenowkellyvass.com
www.facebook.com/inthenowkellyvass

 Magic

> You have to believe we are magic
> Nothing can stand in our way
> You have to believe we are magic
> Don't let your aim ever stray
> And if all your hopes survive
> Destiny will arrive
> I'll bring all your dreams alive
> For you
>
> ~"MAGIC" (FARRAR, 1980, TRACK 1).

My Uncle Ken is a magician from Montana. When I was in elementary school, Uncle Ken visited his Canadian family members every few years. When he visited, my Mom arranged for him to do a magic show in the school gym for all the students. Each show, boosted my sister's and my popularity for a day.

Many people witness a rabbit pulled out of a hat but my Uncle's variation feels more magical and miraculous to me. My Uncle Ken sets a frying pan on fire; he places the lid on top to put out the blaze and says the magic spell abracadabra while waving his magic wand; he taps the wand on the lid and then pulls off the lid. Voila! A very cute and live baby bunny is in the frying pan. There are gasps of delight, then applause, and the murmurs of how did he do that! More of an exclamation, than a question because most people desire it to be magical.

My Uncle Ken entertains in a very unassuming way, which makes the magic even more surprising. It is almost as though he is thinking, if I can do this so can you. He says thank you after every laugh and every applause. His great smile and unique sense of humour creates a lean in reaction from the audiences.

My sister and I received the bonus of keeping the bunny as a pet after each magic show. These bunnies were indeed magical. My Dad thought that the pen was Houdini proof but the bunnies often managed to escape and then reappear days later pretending they never left.

What if we all are Magicians?

What if I am the magician creating my life? What if this starts with creating my day? What if this starts with being present and creating this now moment? What if in this now moment my thoughts and words are magic spells? What if the magic wand is The Divine One? What if these magic spells direct the magic wand to respond impersonally to create the result that the spell has requested? What if I am directing my magical outcome? What if my judgement of this outcome is what makes it good or bad, positive or negative? What if the wand itself is not good or bad? What if the wand is impersonally responding to the will of each magician's spell? What if the magic is in alignment with the magician? For example, if I believe in a positive outcome then I receive a positive outcome. If I doubt a positive outcome, I do not receive a positive outcome.

In law of attraction terms, the magician first states the spell with the desire in mind; the magician asks. Second, the magic wand answers the desire. Third, the magic is given and received in a magical way. The applause of gratitude is celebrated and the magician feels great. Then the magician continues to co-create from the stage of joy by releasing another spell...

To co-create, I give myself permission to be present. I choose to breathe and be in the now. Knowing that I create my future from this present moment, it is necessary to be clear on what I desire. To discover this, I choose to create space to hear my voice and my truth. It is a choice that leads me to my Divine Self (my highest self).

I often tell my clients that the thinking mind hollers and the heart whispers. My thinking mind or ego is often loud: KELLY, WHY ARE YOU DOING THAT? HOW IS THAT GOING TO WORK? My Divine Self whispers: Kelly Ann, dear one, you know your truth and you have all your answers. Everything is always working out for you. My past patterns consist of listening to the loudest and angriest voice as it paralyzes me into a state of freeze or propels me into over-pleasing. It is a newer practice to listen to the softest and kindest voice of intuition and to follow its knowing.

When listening to my intuition, it is important to ask how I feel. My emotions are a guidance system that informs. It is my point of attraction and my point of listening. If I am feeling good, I will hear my heart and intuitively act. When I am connected to my Divine Self, I can ask what I desire. The first, immediate answer that comes through is the whisper of my heart. It takes my ego 30-45 seconds to catch up to my Divine Self; my ego often arrives blaring, armed with doubt and fear. At times, it is hard for me to know who is running the show. I am born worthy as we all are. To discern between Divine Self and ego I ask myself three questions: Am I whole? Am I perfect? Am I complete? If the answer is yes to all three questions and I feel good, then I am ready to converse with my Divine Self and trust the answers that are gifted in my own voice or thoughts. In this moment, I can speak my voice, stand in my power, and rise as my true self.

Process for Connecting to my Divine Self

When the answer to any of the three questions is no or if I do not feel good, the following process assists me in connecting to my Divine Self. I know that it is all in my intentions and the exact wording is not important. I can trust The Divine One with the how. I take myself to a quiet space where I am alone. It can work when I am in a crowd but it may require more patience and breathing. I sit down or stand with my feet on the ground. I bring awareness to my breath. I will usually close my eyes. I breathe in love and I breathe out fear. I continue to breathe deeply and slowly, in and out. While I continue to breathe, I rub the insides of my hands, palm to palm, to activate my own energy and to welcome my Divine Self. I pull my hands apart and place them palms up to receive or I place my hands over my heart. With eyes closed I continue to breathe deeply. I ask a question and I receive my answer. I may also ask for my next small action step before ego catches up and tries to take over. I receive and trust my answers. I pray for spirit to stay with me and help me to send love to my ego. I pray for ego to partner with me. I think about how it will feel to take this small action step towards my desire. I envision the celebration when it is completed. I affirm that I am safe in the now. This process demonstrates that all the answers are within me; I believe this is the true for each spirit living a human experience. All answers are within. If this process is hard, I acknowledge the struggle or thank the struggle; this disempowers it. I might choose to participate in a calming activity and then repeat the process. Some of my calming activities are listening to music, meditating, writing, walking in nature, and playing with my children.

What is my Absolute Yes?

This practice of checking in and connecting with my Divine Self assists me in hearing my absolute yes when it calls me. I have also learned a strategy that assists me in listening to my absolute yes even when the busy has taken over. It is manual muscle checking that I can use on myself to receive the answer to my yes or no questions. It is for yes or no answers to questions that directly affect my will, not the will of others. A few years ago, I saw Louise Hay demonstrate this in a Hay House interview with Robert Holden; they were in conversation about Louise's "inner ding", her inner knowing.

Using my left hand, I pinch my index and middle finger to my thumb. This makes an oval shape. I pinch the thumb and index finger from the right hand around the pinch from the left hand creating a link. I ask what is my yes while continuing to pinch yet pulling both hands outward in opposing directions. I then ask what is my no while repeating this. For me, my yes does not pull apart; it is a solid link. My no causes the right-hand link to break through the left-hand link. The muscle check result may be reversed for someone else. I invite those who desire to test it, to ask a question with an already known, definitive yes answer.

Another process is to flip a coin and when the coin lands I receive a feeling of either joy or disappointment with the side I chose and how the coin reveals. This points me to my yes. Always follow the yes, not the coin toss result. My husband Scott taught me this.

In the book, *Life Loves You* (2015), Louise Hay tells Robert Holden: "Your Yes will always find you, wherever you are" (p.85). When I listen to my yes it feels great; when I ignore my yes, the feeling is regret. I do agree that my absolute yes finds me even when I previously ignore it. I find comfort in this.

When I wash dishes, I listen to Hay House Summit interviews. It is what makes washing dishes feel great to me. One of my favourite interviewers is Robert Holden. He asks every interviewee to tell him about their Daily Spiritual Practice. When someone like Robert Holden asks the same question repetitively I pay attention. I started looking at my Daily Spiritual Practice and I named it my Kelly Feeling Great Practice. When I act in alignment with what is best for my Divine Self and the body that houses it, I feel great. Feeling great creates great thoughts. Great thoughts encourage my belief that everything is working out for me. Then, everything does work out for me. This is evidence of the magic!

Creating a Feeling Great Practice

There is an invitation from my Divine Self to live each moment feeling great and feeling joyous. Practice repeated, creates habit. When I am in the practice of doing habits that feel great, life begins to flow with grace, ease, and joy in conversation with my Divine Self. I personally add the words, for at least one minute, to each desired practice: I wake up in the morning and I thank The Divine One for at least one minute. I meditate for at least one minute. I take a nature walk for at least one minute. I sip and hydrate with lime or lemon water for at least one minute. I write for at least one minute. I connect with my family for at least one minute. I pray for at least one minute. I say positive affirmations (magic spells) for at least one minute. For at least one minute, I look in the mirror and tell myself: I love and appreciate myself! I am more than enough! I am lovable! I celebrate my successes for at least one minute.

I achieve success when I manage my expectations. When I first created my practice, it was an all or nothing type of practice which defeated even calling it a practice. If I did not meditate for the full 40 minutes, the negative ego talk would flood in and I would require a long visit with myself in the mirror repairing the damages.

Magic Mirror

Mirror work is one of the processes that Louise Hay teaches to assist us in loving ourselves. It takes little time but much commitment. It consists of going to a mirror, looking deeply into my eyes while telling myself: Kelly, I truly love and appreciate you! If this is difficult I say, Kelly, I am willing to love and appreciate you! If I do this at least one minute each day, I feel great. It is a feeling great practice to say my magic spells to myself in the mirror and notice the magic! I often write these magic spells on sticky notes and place them on the mirrors around the house; every visit to a mirror turns into mirror work. I love catching my son reading the sticky notes on the mirrors.; he says them to himself with expression and so much love! It now is starting to feel like mirror play. I often catch myself winking at myself when I pass mirrors. My daughter loves the fun of doing mirror work together in public places like doctor's offices; we both get giddy with giggles!

Magic and Miracles

In the now, I intend to trust more than I worry. I choose to focus more on the magic and miracles than the potholes and detours. I even choose to see the magic and miracles in the potholes and detours. In the now, I truly intend to tame my ego mind, listen to my heart's whispers, trust this truth, and love myself into positive action so that I may serve in love. I choose to believe that we are all worthy of magic and miracles; that is how much life loves us all! We perform our magic in the best way that we know how. It is my deepest desire that what I am learning and sharing in this lifetime serves others in a positive way. Let there be grace, gratitude, magic, and celebrations in the now!

Magic Wand Treatment or Prayer

I created this treatment based on the teachings from *The Science of Mind* book by Ernest Holmes. The magic wand in this treatment represents The One Divine Power.

The magic wand, The One Divine Power, is the authority and creativity beyond my mind and my mind uses it. The magic wand, The One Divine Power, is responsive impersonally to all spells which are my thoughts and my words. The more, I, as magician, recognizes oneness with the wand, the more magic and miracles appear. It is co-creative. Therefore, I choose to open my heart, thoughts, words, and deeds in positive affirmative motion in each now moment. It is my knowing that choosing peace, love, and joy, I am freedom. I am thankful for freedom. All magic and miracles are received and appreciated. It is with grace and gratitude that I trust the law of The One Divine Power and I allow my open-heart to receive. I release this with a magical: And so it is!

Dedicated to the strong ones who open their hearts, listen to their whispers, and act in love! Dedicated to Scott, Matt, and Abby for your love, support, and strength as we create peace and space for our life!

Gratitude to the teachers who appeared and continue to appear when this student is ready. "When the student is ready, the teacher appears" (Hay, 1991, p.75). Appreciation to my mentors and coaches; thanks to Shawna Campbell for showing me my value! I thank Christa McAuley, Jody Gotell, Jessica Tyson Salkeld, and Melanie Thiessen for your authentic belief in me. Applause to Ken Avison for inspiring a little girl to grow up believing in magic! Thanks to Dorothy Sutton, Darrel Sutton, and Roberta MacGillivray for being my first teachers and for loving me. I love and appreciate my friends and family!

TINA PALMER

TINA PALMER is an entrepreneur, influencer and leader from the Seattle, WA area. Tina graduated from Washington State University and received her Bachelor of Arts degree in Sociology. During a time of transition in her life, Tina decided to sign up with the top direct sales cosmetics company, Younique, and now runs her very own successful international makeup and skin care company. Tina is a Top Level Black Status Leader in the company and has received awards for her mentorship. With the opportunity to uplift thousands of women in her job, Tina decided she wanted to learn from the best so she could share more wisdom and powerful inspiration with her team. The past two years, Tina has traveled to learn from some of her favorite authors and speakers such as, Panache Desai, Deepak Chopra, Elizabeth Gilbert, Tony Robbins, and Gabby Bernstein. Tina is a stay-at-home mom to her two beautiful children Jack and Kate and wife to her fabulous husband Ryan. While not working on her business you can find Tina relaxing with coffee in hand, wearing yoga pants and coming up with new ways to shine her light. Tina's interests are photography, the outdoors, yoga, and sharing her love for writing with the world.

For more information, please contact Tina at:
tina@tinapalmer.com
www.tinapalmer.com
Or connect with her on Facebook or Instagram.

My Past Does Not Define Me

I am a survivor of childhood sexual abuse. I know I am not alone as the statistics are as alarming as they are disgusting. One out of four women will be sexually abused before age 18. I am one of those four, and I kept it quiet and silently suffered for years until I was ready to let go of my past and no longer allow myself to be a prisoner.

Our past is a combination of experiences and stories. Sometimes our past is full of smiles, sunshine, and happiness and sometimes our past is full of despair and pain. More often than not, it is a combination of the two. There may also be things we have experienced in life that we would never have chosen for ourselves. Things that haunt us and leave us feeling powerless to create change for ourselves. It wasn't until I became more self aware that I learned that my past pain could empower me, and help illustrate the lessons I have learned to tell a story of strength.

Growing up, I lived a life of shame, blame, and pain. I lived a life hating myself for experiences that happened in my early childhood. The kind of experiences that can leave a tremendous impact on one's life. For most of my young and adult life, I was a prisoner constantly reliving my past. I felt stuck and unable to move forward. I did a good job hiding the pain. I covered it up and walked around town with a smile. In high school I was nominated Class Clown but inside it was a completely different story — one of depression, pain, and low self esteem. I feared commitment and being dependent on anyone or anything. I felt inadequate. I felt that if anyone discovered the "real me" it would only lead to rejection. I built up barriers to protect myself from others and my own insecurities. My relationships were a compromise between partial trust and partial testing. The abuse I suffered as a child devalued my sexuality, telling me it was meaningless and worthless and instead forced upon me the self concept of being less than everyone else. I was torturing myself over experiences from my past that I had no control over and that I could no longer change. The truth is that I didn't know how to make that change because felt like I was fundamentally flawed.

A dramatic shift in the way I perceived myself happened the summer of 2015. In July, I attended the very first Haven Retreat, a retreat in the mountains of Utah for women who had been sexually abused as children. The Haven Retreat is a four day "paid for" retreat that is funded by The Younique Foundation. Due to the generosity of donors and the founders of The Younique Foundation, Derek and Shelaine Maxfield, survivors are able to attend The Haven Retreat free of charge. As a participant, the only responsibility I had was to pay for my own travel to Salt Lake City, Utah and the rest was taken care of. I felt like a Queen for those four days. Lodging was in a gorgeous home with incredibly peaceful mountain views. I dined on 5-star food prepared by a private Chef. My belly was never empty! During the day, I focused on activities that helped me heal and find joy in my life again. I spent time learning how the brain responds to trauma and the impact it had on my development growing up. I experienced daily group therapy where I was given the opportunity to open up and share how I was feeling. Activities like yoga, mindfulness, art, and journaling helped me to ground and center myself. I was surrounded by 11 other women just like me, and we formed an instant bond. The trained staff that I met had the most tremendous hearts. They provided a safe atmosphere and helped me feel uplifted, validated, and empowered. Nobody was asking me to talk about the details about my past or even to forget my past. Instead I learned tools on how to focus on the present and live mindfully.

Healing from my shame and pain was not an overnight fix, but I was committed to my healing. I was tired of living in the perpetual emotional jail I had been living in. I prayed for healing and understanding. I read books from some of my favorite authors like Brene Brown, Marianne Williamson, Panache Desai and Gabby Bernstein. I also surrounded myself with friends who were positive, inspirational, and motivational, and I knew they would be there to empower me as well as support me during the times I felt weak. I came to peace with the fact that I am a work in progress and I am okay with that. I accepted what happened to me was not okay, and I did not deserve to be treated so horribly but also that it did not have to define me.

Over time, I started to forgive the people who hurt me and who let me down. Most importantly, I learned to forgive myself. I accepted that there was nothing I could have done to prevent the harm done. Eventually, I let go of the resentment, the anger and the blame. I started to allow more grace into my life. I learned that I AM NORMAL. I learned that I AM OKAY. I started to give myself permission to change. To grow. To evolve. To let go of the past. To release. To move forward. I have learned that our past is in the past, it's already happened, it's already taken place. We put so much energy into worrying about what happened when the past can not be changed. What can be changed is this present moment and our future. So if we keep holding on and gripping tightly to our past and all the things we wish we could change, what we're doing is preventing ourselves from growing. This is why we feel stuck and don't feel like we are moving forward.

Accepting that my past was a part of who I am and consciously moving forward in spite of it, was one of the best decisions of my life. Finally, I realized I could use my past to become a stronger individual, instead of acting as if it didn't exist. I let my mind rest and allowed myself to make peace with the things that went so terribly wrong. I started to use my own scars as fuel to catapult myself toward a better life. Who I was yesterday is not who I am today. Things in life happen and things in life shift and so do we. We shift. We learn. We grow. By holding onto the past, I was preventing myself from evolving into my true self. Think about it: are you really that same person you were five, ten, or fifteen years ago? You are different today than you were then. If you hold onto your past and hold onto the feelings of anger, regret and shame, what you are doing is preventing yourself from moving beyond. Give yourself permission to move forward. Give yourself permission to change. Aim for that evolution because evolution is a beautiful thing and it will help you get closer to your true self. Find the lessons that these situations have bestowed on you. Learn from them, release the past, forgive yourself and others, and move forward. You deserve that for yourself. No one can do this work for you; only you can. The longer you hold onto your past, the less likely you are to move forward and grow. Your past does not dictate your future and your past does not define who you are. What part of your crazy past do you need to let go of? What are you holding onto and allowing to suffocate your emotional freedom? Free yourself from your past as soon as you can. You can find healing and you may be surprised as how good it feels to let it all go!

Pain and scars are a part of the human experience. These scars can tears us down or build us up. They can make us feel scared and weak or give us strength and courage. Our scars can make us withdraw and isolate ourselves or they can deepen our connections with one another and expand our hearts to offer compassion to those in need. Wear your scars with pride. A scar doesn't mean you are broken or damaged. Scars mean you are real. You are human. Scars mean you are outrageously beautiful. If you experienced abuse in your past, it says nothing about your value today; simply that it is part of your story. Sometimes we have to revisit the pain, to collect the emotional tools we need to soar!

If you are a survivor of childhood sexual abuse, I want you to know this about you ...

YOU ARE WORTHY!
YOU ARE INCREDIBLE!
YOU ARE STRONG!
YOU ARE AMAZING!
YOU ARE COURAGEOUS!
YOU ARE LOVED!

You are not what you have been told. There is absolutely nothing wrong with you. Believe that! Read that again and soak that in. You, my dear, are worth it. You must believe you are worthy of experiencing the life you were meant to live. If you are an adult female survivor of childhood sexual abuse, please consider attending The Haven Retreat. All the information you need can be found at this website under Our Services, The Haven Retreat. www.youniquefoundation.org

I dedicate this chapter to all survivors of childhood abuse who are trying to find their way. Begin to love the person you see in the mirror. Give voice to your deepest fears. You are stronger than the pain. You can survive and you will thrive again. I believe in you!

I would like to acknowledge and thank all the men and women who represent The Younique Foundation. Thank you for being a beacon of light to survivors around the world. Shelaine Maxfield, you may have started with one match but you have made an explosion. You are changing the world! I also wish to acknowledge and thank my husband Ryan who has been my rock throughout this process. Your support has touched me more than you will know. Finally, I would like to acknowledge all my friends and family who have uplifted, empowered and validated me through this journey.

LINDSLEY SILAGI

LINDSLEY SILAGI, is an educator and professional coach with a private coaching practice, Step By Step Results!, located in Santa Teresa, New Mexico where she lives happily with her husband, Lon. She loves to hold healing and motivational retreats in the enchanting state she calls home. Lindsley loves dance, art, music, nature, little kids, hot springs, gardening, books, striking up a friendship, photography, and travel.

www.stepbystepresults.net

✿ Personal Essential Practices (PEP)

I am a practitioner on the path, a leader along the way. I am both learner and leader. Having awareness of each of these stances is important for me as it keeps me grounded. I believe it is important for all of us. And what is it that we are called to be and do in this life?

I believe that we are love, and that we are born to love. How we love, how we become this person who expresses love of life, and for one another is our uniqueness. How we give to life is our own way of expressing what is within. Within all of us, is a divine spark. And recognizing this is one of the many steps along the way.

Along the way

It has taken many years along this way for me to arrive at my point on this path. And it has also taken just one moment, one "aha" and it seems like I have arrived at a destination where everything seems new, and really it is just a heightened consciousness. I have experienced this sense of both on the journeying and arriving many times. And after a pause at some plateau I may bask in the wonder and joy of it before moving on, before taking another step.

Over the years, I have discovered what I call my Personal Essential Practices (PEP) that help me to stay on the path, or which put "PEP into my Step". They are practices which I have learned from reading great works and working with a variety spiritual teachings.

As you read through these practices you will find many familiar to you. It is my hope that you will find your own strength, or reinforcement for your own personal essential practices. Or perhaps my words will inspire you to define a set of practices that work for you.

Awaken Early and In Gratitude

I first heard about this practice from a talk given by Louise Hay. I loved the idea and decided to implement in my own life. For me starting the day in gratitude involves bringing yourself consciously to the present. I take a breath. I breathe in and then say thank you for the dawn of a new day. I may say thank you for my environment, the bed on which I am supported, the room in which I find my rest, the light coming through the window. Perhaps the call of a songbird, or a dog barking. For these I say thank you. Perhaps other familiar sounds in the neighborhood informing me that it is morning. It may be a distant crowing of a rooster. I may then move to gratitude for my cup of tea or coffee, my journal and a time to write. These simple actions help to create in me a deep appreciation for what it is each day, and it is a lovely way to begin and set the tone for a new day.

Meditation

Meditation is the most essential of all the practices. Learning to follow my breathing has been so useful for quieting my mind. I can now sit in silence and welcome more of it. Years ago this was not true for me. But today meditation is the foundation for me. I feel who-it-is -that-I-am and I get in touch with what I love and love itself. It is a daily practice and at times one I return to multiple times a day.

Journal Writing

The practice of writing in my journal has helped me in so many ways. It has helped me to find my voice and to express what is inside. My journals have quotes of famous authors, pictures, my poetry, songs, and reflections on the day's events. They have notes for new projects and are written in ink of every shade of the rainbow. Some entries are dated, others not. Sometimes I will journal on my computer and then put select writings from it into my latest bound journal. My journaling is a record of the journey and a treasure.

Connecting with Others

There are so many ways to connect with others: in person, on social media, in a video chat, on the phone, through writing. Each method of connecting may be beneficial, depending on how we approach it. Connecting with others is vital for us. It is our very life force in action. I am intentional in creating my connections and I value them. I invite people in. I think that is important and I get wonderful results.

Asking Opening Questions

I have been learning about how to ask great questions for a long time as a part of my early years of teaching and going to conferences and workshops on how to enhance my instructional practice. I then honed my practice even more when I became certified in professional coaching. Asking great questions is at the heart of coaching. And it is at the heart of self-inquiry as well.

Here are some of the ones I use to motivate, inspire, encourage myself on the path.

- What do I really want to do/know/have?
- Who could help?
- Who might I help today?
- What belief might be holding me back from…?
- What might I do if I let go of this (activity/belief)?
- Who might I reach if I were to focus on (a specific topic)?
- What if I were to wake up earlier? What might this open up within me?
- What if I went to bed earlier? What might this open up for me?
- How might this activity help me reach a new success?
- What possibilities are available to me right now?
- If not now, when is a good time to start?

Giving and Receiving

I love to give and I love to receive. It is wonderful to be within the gifting process no matter whether I am giving or receiving as really I am in the process of both no matter what. Thinking of what I will give myself to (a cause) or thinking about a gift to give another put me in a positive flow state. Taking action on it is what matters though. I also make it a practice to give to places that feed me spiritually and this has done great things within me and changed me for the better. It is a joy to give and it is a joy to receive.

Affirming, Affirming

Discipline the mind the great masters tell us. It is necessary to think constructive thoughts on a regular basis. It does great things for our brain and is one of the most important things to be successful in life. Affirmation is important for finding peace and giving yourself the love and encouragement you need to keep going even when the going gets rough. One of my favorite affirmations is one I wrote many years ago. I created a statement at an Insight Seminar workshop that I still use today to remind myself who I am and what I am about. I invite you to create one for yourself. The process is simple. Select 3 or 4 adjectives that resonate with you and that you want to bring into your life. Then think of one or two actions that you want to do to help others. Then put it together:

> I am (insert your name), a adjective one, adjective two, adjective three person (verb1) and (verb 2) others. That's it. Then use it daily and repeat it until you own it. May it be as powerful for you as mine has been for me.

Setting Intentions

I consciously choose to set intention by asking simply: What is the one most important thing I am to do today? What is the next important one? And the next? Then I work to keep those at the front and center of my attention to their completion. Another approach I use is a success quote from Louise Hay. I framed it and hung it in my office where I see and read it daily. It helps to focus my attention on success and set the intention for success in all my actions.

 I now establish a new awareness of success. I know I can be as successful as I make my mind up to be. I move into the Winning Circle. Golden opportunities are everywhere for me. Prosperity of every kind is drawn to me.

~LOUISE HAY

Using the Power of Imagination

I love the power of the imagination and I consciously work to access mine. This comes to me through some type of play, some type of down time. In the garden, doing an interpretive dance, or while reading I build up the images and ideas that feed my imagination.

Practicing Forgiveness for Self and Others

This is a powerful energy release process and a necessary practice for me. I find it freeing to forgive. I have used Catherine Ponder's treatments most effectively in my own practice and though I use others, I find I return time and time again to Catherine Ponder's work.

I will include one of Catherine Ponder's Treatments here for you to read and apply right now.

> All that has offended me I forgive.
> Within and without I forgive.
> Things past, things present things future, I forgive.
> I forgive positively everything and everyone who could possibly need forgiveness of the past or present.
> I forgive positively everyone. I am free and they are free too.
> All things are cleared up between us now and forever.

Making Room for Laughter

The practices I use daily or if not daily at least on a regular basis provide me with room within me. I no longer take myself so seriously and opt to find humor in the everyday experiences much more easily, much more readily. This is a wonderful thing and I am very grateful for it. I love to laugh at myself now.

I hope that as you define and work with spiritual practices you will find an ease within you, a space within you. May these practices help you to actualize more in your life for the benefit of countless others. May you create more peace, more harmony, more love. Be love in action, be kindness in action. The world will be better for it.

May you define your own Personal Essential Practices and put "PEP in your STEP!"

To Lon, my husband and my best friend,
who makes me smile every day of the week.

Thank you to all who have touched my life. You do know who you are. And because of you I know myself more fully.

JULIE GALE

JULIE GALE is a Colorado-based eco-therapist, intuitive healer, and co-caretaker of Joelie Farms. She resides with her life partner, Joel, along with their cats, cows, bunnies and chickens. She studies Shamanism through Paula Gerardi, is a Certified Mind, Body, and Spirit Practitioner with Sunny Dawn Johnston and studies Transpersonal Psychology at Sofia University. After the death of her mother, Julie was introduced to a spirit world and a way of life she had no idea existed, but had often yearned for her entire life. Her mother made sure she was not alone after she passed and doors quickly opened with helpful people to introduce Julie to the spirit world. These new-found connections helped her to communicate with her deceased mother and to show her that the truth lies within each of us. Currently, Julie is studying to achieve a Master's Degree in Transpersonal Psychology, working full-time at a software-services company and creating handmade items to promote healing. Julie continues to uplift those around her and guide them to awaken their own spiritual truth.

To connect with Julie:
julieannegale@julieannegale.com
www.julieannegale.com
Or connect with her on Facebook.

Gifts from the Afterlife

As a young child, I spent a lot of time asking myself questions about life and death. What happens when we die? Why are we here if it is so temporary and we have to leave our loved ones behind or be left behind by a beloved? Is there really a higher power or something greater than what we see in our physical world? What is my purpose? Many questions would float around in my head, perhaps because of my grandparents passing away before I was twelve years old. After my grandfather passed away, I would 'talk' to him as I did not get to say good-bye to him in person before he passed. He had been hit by a semi driver who had fallen asleep at the wheel. It felt like my natural instinct was to sit and talk to him after he had passed away and that he was still able to hear me, so I could still say good-bye. Throughout the years, I would sometimes drift back to my questions from time to time, but I did not receive any answers.

After my mother passed away, I began to receive the answers I had been looking for and I began my spiritual journey. When I was a child, I often thought about how awful it would be to lose my mother. The thought would leave me catching my breath with a feeling of readiness, as if to 'brace myself' for the impact. Well, just a few years ago the day did arrive. It hit me like a tidal wave. I couldn't wrap my head around how to go on with my life without her. Nothing would ever be the same. My heart felt completely empty, yet filled with absolute pain.

About a month after my mother had passed, my partner, Joel, told me his grandmother had suggested that I visit her 'shaman.' Joel explained how his grandmother had visited with this shaman in Denver who had communicated with her deceased husband and it had proven to be very helpful for his grandma's healing process. In the past, I had been skeptical of psychics and I didn't really know if I would trust what they said, but I wanted to give it a chance. Nonetheless, I figured I had nothing to lose and I found myself excited to visit with the shaman. I remember my first visit with the shaman very vividly. She introduced herself and told me to get comfortable, so I took my shoes off and sat cross-legged on her couch. She started the session by asking me, "Why are you here?" All I had to say was, "Well, my mother …" The shaman's eyes got real big as she looked to my left side and she said, "Oh! She's here." The shaman used clairvoyance, a form of telepathic communication, to 'speak' with my mother and then she would 'translate' for me. If you are unfamiliar with the different ways psychics and intuitive people can communicate with spirit, you may want to look up The Clairs. These are psychic terms used to describe any or all types of psychic sensitivity corresponding to the senses: seeing, hearing, feeling, smelling, tasting, and touching. During the session, I could feel my mother's presence in the room. With the words the medium used and the way she talked, it felt exactly like I was talking to my mother. She had me laughing and crying, sometimes both at the same time. My mother told me, through the shaman, I will feel closer to her if I put a picture of her next to my bed on my night stand and I should wear the ring she gave me. The medium told me many, many things that only my mother would know and only my mother would know to tell me to comfort me. I slowly began to realize...she isn't really gone! She is always with me!

Almost simultaneously, I learned from a co-worker that someone I worked with was also a medium. Someone I wouldn't have ever guessed. I set up an appointment to meet with her and the same thing happened. My mother came through and told me many of the same things I was told from the shaman and also a few other new things came up, such as to listen to the oldies station because, according to my mother, it is the only real kind of music there is. That is definitely something my mother would say. She continued and explained, while I listen to the music, my mother will be there singing and dancing with me. The spirit medium also told me to look for signs in my dreams and to look at the sun and smile. My mother wanted me to stop hurting and be happy again. Oh, but what a difficult task that seemed. After we had finished our conversation between my mother, the psychic medium and myself, I began to pay more attention and became more aware of my surroundings. When I would work on projects around the house, I would listen to the Oldies and could feel that deep connection with my mother, as I would dance and sing and know she was right there with me. I would also pay close attention to the lyrics to see if there was a message in there from my mom. I did receive a few messages and could tell because I would get goosebumps all over my arms.

Now that I had readings with two different psychics, I wasn't sure what to do next, so I booked another appointment with the shaman. When I went to visit with her again, it was much different. She asked me the same question, "Why are you here?" This time, though, my response was, "I'm not sure. I thought I would just keep coming to you." The shaman responded by saying, "For any questions you have, the wisdom and the answers are within you." I thought to myself, "What does that mean? I don't feel like I have all of the answers within myself." She went on to explain that I am very open and aware. She said my mother will come to me in dreams and other ways, I just need to remain open to receive the messages. After our session, she talked about a class that she teaches called Shaman Star. She said it is a class that meets once a month and teaches shamanism, a path to our own inner truth and bliss. This sounded very interesting to me, so I signed up immediately.

Again, almost simultaneously my medium friend asked if I would like to attend a class with her in Arizona, with Sunny Dawn Johnston as the teacher. It was a week-long intensive where we would study with Sunny and journey towards becoming a Mind, Body, Spirit Practitioner. The intensive was short and intense, but I learned so many things that would come to me months later that I would recognize as an, 'Aha' moment. Those times when something Sunny had said would just 'click' in my mind and I would think, "Oh! That is what she meant by that." Some of the concepts I was just figuring out were setting boundaries with our loved ones and many of the relationships we have are a reflection of ourselves and how we see ourselves. I felt very new to the spiritual world, but I knew I was just beginning. Both of these classes came to me at a time when I was open to receiving the messages and helped to give me the strength to heal from not only my mother's death, but to heal from every wound I had ever faced in this life and in my past lives. My mother gave me such wonderful gifts which helped me to deal with her not being in this physical world with me any longer, but to still be able to communicate with her while she is in the spirit world. The answers I was seeking were really within me the entire time, just as the shaman had said. I just needed some guidance to help me find them.

Now, you may still be skeptical of psychics or mediums, but want to connect with your own deceased loved ones. There are many ways you can communicate with your deceased loved one(s) on your own and I would like to share some of those ways with you. Typically, you will notice most of these when you are alone and aware of your surroundings and within the first few days or months after your deceased loved one has transitioned into the spirit world, but you may notice these ways of communication for years to come. Below are twelve ways you can continue to connect with your deceased loved ones, whether they are human or animal, on your own.

12 Signs a Deceased Loved One is Nearby

1. **Sensing**—This form of communication involves all of your senses and your entire being. The signs that your loved one is present may not be extremely obvious. You may learn different ways to sense when your loved one is nearby. Just sensing your deceased loved one can feel very comforting. Maybe you are feeling watched while you are in the middle of a task and no one is around. If you are alone on a walk, you may have the feeling of someone walking right next to you.

2. **Touch**—You may be able to feel their touch on your back, holding your hand or sweeping a piece of your hair. Your deceased loved one may move an object that either belonged to them or they find entertaining to move to a different location. My mother would move things around my sister's apartment after she passed away, as she knew my sister would notice any object not in place. I was more of someone that my mother would sit with and I could feel her presence very strongly at times when I would be sitting outside.

3. **Smell**—Your grandmother's perfume, your grandfather's tobacco, or your father's cologne are signs your deceased loved one is paying you a visit from the spirit world. If you pick up on a certain perfume and there is no one in your household that just sprayed a plume of rose and gardenia perfume around, and your great-grandmother always smelled of rose and gardenias, then this is most likely her paying you a visit just to say hello.

4. **Dreams**—Your deceased loved ones may come to visit you in the dream world. Sometimes they would like to give you a message, but usually it is a visit to let you know they are okay. My mother came to me in my dreams with a soft, white light

around her. She looked very angelic and she was smiling. I remember her coming into my room and looking over me, other times she would accompany me on my dream adventures. Her voice and her presence felt very surreal to me.

5. **Hearing** — Sometimes we can hear our deceased loved ones. This ability to hear your deceased loved one externally, as though they are speaking to you in human form or internally, in your mind, are common ways of connecting with your deceased loved one. Usually the voice you hear is internal, as though they are giving you a message about the current moment. For example, it seemed as though my mother talked to me quite a bit after her transition into the spirit world. I would hear her 'key phrases' and old sayings she liked to use running through my head when I would be doing something that she would have made that comment about. I especially notice these now when I am caring for a child. I know she would very much like it if I had a child and it would be just as though she were here with me, helping me along to care for them.

6. **Electrical activity** — Many of us have seen scary movies with lights turning on and off, televisions changing channels, and objects flying across the room. It is quite common for those in spirit to do these things to get our attention because we are all made of energy. My partner often has street lights go out after he has a sudden idea or an emotional thought as he drives past them. Phone calls from our deceased loved ones after their transition are common, as well. Computer issues can also be known to occur when there is a high amount of energy around electrical devices.

7. **Symbolic signs, gifts and messages** — There are many ways your deceased loved ones can let you know that they are with you but sometimes it can be difficult to perceive. Having a calm mind and being alone, makes it easier for us to sense another's presence, as we have fewer distractions. Spirits may leave us small objects, such as coins or stones along our path to get our attention. For example, one night after leaving a venue I found a unique coin on the sidewalk and I knew it was from my uncle. He collected coins and I was given most of his collection as a keepsake.

   Flowers — Flowers may bloom out of season in your yard or perhaps you receive an unexpected bouquet at your desk. Perhaps your mother loved lilies and you did not plant a bulb, but one pops up in your yard.

   People — This is one of the greatest gifts my mother has given me in the spirit world. Those in the spirit world can send meaningful people in your direction such as mentors, life partners, motherly figures, fatherly figures, and new best friends. Our deceased loved ones can and will use people to give us messages and the person delivering the message is typically unaware they are being used as the messenger.

8. **Music** — Your deceased loved one may want to share a message with you through a song. It could be a meaningful song that you both shared. An example would be if you are driving around town in your car and the radio DJ announces a song dedicated to Laura (which happens to be your name) and it is Whitney Houston's *I Will Always Love You* and every song after that is just songs calling to you, telling you that you are loved. Maybe you are going to an important track meet and you are

really nervous, when suddenly, Bette Midler's *Wind Beneath my Wings* starts playing in your head. Another example is your deceased loved one may be trying to give you a warning to get your attention, as well. Perhaps you are taking a road trip and the songs that keep coming on seem to be trying to get your attention, such as *Warning* by Incubus and then *Slow Ride* by Foghat and you slow down a little and move into the slow lane. Suddenly, a drunk driver flies by you, swerving back and forth in the lane you were just in.

9. **Animals** — Birds, butterflies, dragonflies, deer, our living pets, such as cats or dogs... spirit can use their energy to be with us through the animal world for a short burst of time. I had a friend do a reading for me right after I placed a few hummingbird feeders around and flowers the hummingbirds would be attracted to. She told me my mother could come and visit me through the hummingbirds. I had not told my friend that the hummingbird feeders were in my yard and she lived in a different state then me, so she had no idea these were around my house. I paid extra close attention the next time one came up to get a drink and stare at me through the window. That year, the hummingbirds visited every day. Our own pets can also let us know when we have an unseen visitor. Their hearing is far superior, as well as their vision, as they can see more into the red spectrum. After my cat transitioned into the spirit world, I felt his presence very strongly in the backyard. I even saw him walk by our patio door, just like he used to. If your dog is barking and becoming very excited, the same way he did when the deceased loved one was around, this may be a sign you are both receiving a visitor.

10. **Coincidences and Synchronicities** — These are signs that you may pick up throughout the day that seem to come together for you in a meaningful way. Synchronicities can be a sign of confirmation. Sometimes I ask for these, such as, "Spirit, please give me a message today which helps me to heal." I will then be given an idea which seems to come to me out of the blue which my entire being finds comforting.

11. **Numbers and Numerology** — Number patterns, such as a favorite number, anniversaries, birth dates, or ages are a common way spirit uses for loved ones to communicate. Repeating numbers is another way the spirit world uses to communicate. Perhaps every time you look at a clock, the time is 7:11 and this continues for a few days or more, you may want to pay closer attention to a message someone is trying to send you from the spirit world.

12. **Photos** — It is most uncommon to see an apparition of your deceased loved one with your waking mind, but you may see something that is of significance to you in a photo. Through orbs and flame images, I have seen signs from my deceased cat in the days that followed his transition into the spirit world. He was like a child to me and we were very close. He came to me in the image of a blue orb that dances around the picture, while everything else remains stagnant. There is the shape of a cat with his paw in the air, like he is waving, in another photo I took of flames dancing in the fireplace. When you lose a loved one, it may be very difficult to get yourself away

from the tidal wave of emotions, but when you have a calm moment, this is when your deceased loved one will bring you signs of healing and love.

These are all of the ways we can communicate with our lost loved ones that I know of, but I still may have missed a few. Although I communicate with my mother and other deceased loved ones a different way than I did before, often silently, I know they are with me sending love, always and forever.

I dedicate this chapter to all of those who have been on a spiritual journey to seek truth and guidance and to all of those who have lost a loved one and did not know where to turn to next.

I would like to acknowledge and thank my mother, Sharon Gale, with deepest gratitude and appreciation. I would like to give my sincere thanks and acknowledge my life partner, Joel Comstock. You have witnessed and stood by my side throughout this entire journey. Deepest gratitude to the Divine. Deepest gratitude to The Shaman, Paula Gerardi. You have taught me so much and I am so grateful for you in my life. Sincere thank you to my spiritual mentors, Kristen Marchus-Hemstad and Sunny Dawn Johnston. Thank you too all of my soul sisters and brothers. You have all changed my life.

JENNIFER ROSS

JENNIFER ROSS is a Certified & Licensed Heal Your Life® Teacher, Life Coach and Teen Facilitator who provides you with the tools and techniques for you to create the life you'll love.

Jennifer's life in recent years before being empowered by Louise Hay's philosophies was a struggle. She was struggling with major health issues with Emphysema and Multiple Chemical Sensitivity. She was angry at her poor health and angry at herself to the point she'd really had enough. Jennifer felt lifeless, low and wanted to blame and get angry at anyone who wouldn't help her cope through it. During this difficult time, Jennifer was also grieving from the loss of her beautiful mother to dementia.

Jennifer's sister, Melinda gave a precious gift of Louise Hay cards to help Jennifer cope through these hard times. These cards provided the small stepping stones she needed to put life back in her soul. Jennifer was now on the road to recovery with self-love in mind, body, and soul. A month later Jennifer bought the best-selling book by Louise L Hay *You Can Heal Your Life* which really started the transformation to a beautiful life.

Jennifer is now on a beautiful journey of self-love and beautiful affirmations that creates the life of her dreams. Jennifer will inspire and empower you to create the life you want with Louise L Hay's positive philosophies and healing techniques.

Inspire your beautiful life with coaching, workshops, and events!

Please contact Jennifer at:
jennifer@heartsoflove.com.au
www.heartsoflove.com.au
Facebook — *@hylheartsoflove*
Instagram *healyourlife_hearts_of_love*

❦ Freedom
___

F reedom is such beauty. Freedom can be experienced in many ways. Some of us do not realise that we already have the freedom we yearn for. We have the power; our freedom exists within us. Join me on this journey on freedom of self-expression within this chapter. I'll describe some ways for you to embrace and enjoy your own freedom. Definition of *Freedom* per the Oxford Dictionary — *The power or right to act, speak or think as one wants.*

Affirmations can be a beautiful way to express your freedom. I choose freedom in many forms, I am free to express the affirmation; *I am beautiful.*

Meditations provide you with all the freedom you want to explore. You can go anywhere and not be limited by anything or anybody. Your freedom is within your imagination. Go to wherever it is you want to be in your meditations. Breathe it, feel it, express it!

Let's take a moment to visit the natural emotion *anger* as it can make you feel uncomfortable and even out of control. It is important to remember we have the freedom to control our anger. By managing anger, you will certainly improve your health and wellbeing. We have many safe ways to express this natural emotion. Some of those ways include exercise, journaling and listening or playing music.

Throughout my training as a Heal Your Life® Life Coach, I experienced and learnt how self-expression through coaching brings about thoughts and memories about yourself that perhaps you didn't even realise or had forgotten. After careful exploration of my beautiful transformation, I was able to lead a more expressive and passionate lifestyle. This chapter is based on my personal experiences of self-expression of *effective communication* and *positive affirmations* alongside my *freedom.* These have revealed a pathway to superior, optimistic surroundings.

I begin with a beautiful meditation *"Oceans of Love"*. I was inspired to write this from my beautiful divine love for the ocean.

Oceans of Love — creative meditation

Prepare for a 5-10-minute creative meditation by removing any possible interruptions. Play some meditation music if desired, if possible some gentle soft sounds of the ocean but not necessary and proceed to gently close your eyes.

Imagine yourself laying in the water's edge of the ocean. Your body underneath is gently being splashed by the gentle waves gliding upon the ocean shore. Relax your mind and let your thoughts flow in and out just like the waves. When one thought comes in, let it flow out with the next gentle refreshing wave. Do not be discouraged by any thoughts, just let them flow in and flow out. Now let go of any fears and just be you, experience the freedom to be just you. Your whole body begins to feel weightless as the ocean drifts you into deeper water. Embrace the drifting sensation as you float amongst the calming waves and ocean treasures and know that you are safe. Place your arms out to the sides and embrace the freedom of the ocean of love as you float and drift whilst love is filling your heart and soul. Rest and relax and embrace all that love you so deserve. When you're ready, allow your body to float and drift back to the ocean shore. Take as much time as you need. Gently open your eyes when you're ready.

Part 1 — Effective Communication

Effective communication is vitally important for experiencing successful relationships with others, whether that be your partner, family members, friends, co-workers and even strangers. Taking responsibility for your reactions will ultimately guide you to having more success in your career and personal life. This involves being direct and honest in expressing your thoughts and feelings but also having respect for the other person involved. Consider these areas whilst using effective communication:

- Actively listening to others (not just waiting for them to finish to have your say)
- Taking responsibility for your reactions
- Believe in your personal rights

Begin by using "*I*" statements, for example; "*I would like some more support from you*" instead of saying "*You are just not supporting me*". By using the "*I*" statement, this demonstrates respect to the other person along with requesting your personal rights.

The idea of "*personal rights*" involves beliefs about valuing your own feelings and decisions. These can include:

- I have the right to express my feelings and opinions
- I have the right to disagree with someone
- I have the right to say no
- I have the right to make mistakes
- I have the right to change my mind
- I have the right to make a request

There are three main areas of effective communication: verbal responses, body language, and effective thinking.

Verbal behaviour — Effective verbal behaviour is honest and direct in respecting yourself and others. You state exactly what you want with words that are not demanding. There is no hinting either in the hope they will know what you're talking about. This doesn't necessarily mean you will get what you want but you have empowered yourself to make your needs and wants known.

Non-verbal behaviours — These behaviours reveal a large percentage of your message, in fact, 50% and over. These include eye contact, your posture, facial expressions, tone of voice and of course, your gestures. This makes it critical for you to be aware of your non-verbal behaviour when communicating. Practice communication in a mirror and record yourself if possible and see exactly what non-verbal behaviours you reveal to yourself.

If you were to ask your boss for a raise but show non-verbals signs of hesitation with poor posture and looking at the ground, do you think you will get the raise you want? The request was largely weakened due to the non-verbal behaviours. This is just one example in one area of your life. This can be applied to many areas of your life. Practice, practice, practice!

Effective thinking — Any negative thoughts can prevent you from communicating effectively. Psychologist Albert Ellis identifies some main "irrational" thoughts that get in the way of effectively expressing needs and wants. This one thought usually creates frustration and anger, "*People and situations SHOULD be the way I want them to be, and when they aren't, I can't stand it!*" A positive replacement thought can be changed to "*It is great when everything works out exactly the way I want it, but when it doesn't, I can handle it.*"

Some beliefs for promoting effective thinking include:

- Don't need to take it personally
- Everything is exactly as it should be
- It takes two to have a conflict
- We are only human

Part 2 — Affirmations

Your thoughts create your reality, if you change your thoughts, you can transform your life. Here's a few of my favourite short affirmations: *I am beautiful, I love life, I am divine*.

An affirmation is anything we say or think. It can be negative or a positive affirmation. When we are thinking negative thoughts, this brings us down in many ways, we don't realise the damage being created in our own minds. We need to bring ourselves back up by replacing the negative affirmation to a positive affirmation. An example from the divine book, *Experience Your Good Now* by author Louise L Hay is, "*If I get angry, I'll lose control.*" A positive affirmation to replace this is "*I express my anger in appropriate places and ways.*"

Creating and living positive and happy thoughts provide a happier life. Practice and be persistent with your positive affirmations even if they feel untrue, as soon it will begin to feel true for you. If you're unable to state an affirmation, for example, "*I forgive all past hurts,*" replace it with "*I am willing to forgive all past hurts.*" By using the word *willing* in your affirmation, this provides you with some strength within to begin the process to forgive. Believe in your positive thoughts. Turn the seemingly "*impossible*" into "*I'm possible.*"

Part 3 — Treatment

 In the infinity of life where I am, all is perfect, whole and complete, and yet life everchanging. There is no beginning and no end, only a constant cycling and recycling substance and experiences. Life is never stuck or static or stale, for each moment is ever new and fresh. I am one with the very Power that created me, and this Power has given me the power to create my own circumstances. I rejoice in the knowledge that I have the power of my own mind to use in any way I choose. Every moment of life is a new beginning for me right here and right now. All is well in my world.

~LOUISE L HAY

Dedicated to my beautiful mum Doreen Cleave. Mum was the mummiest of all mums. I'm so very proud of mum for my upbringing and guiding me to a beautiful life. I lost track after losing my beautiful mum to dementia, Louise Hay's philosophy guided me back to my beautiful life.

Acknowledgement, appreciation and warm thanks to my extraordinary son David Ross. David is my unique angel, always striving to do what he can to help and guide me. His love and devotion will be forever imprinted into my soul and heart. He continues to support me in every way possible and has always been there for me in the good times and the bad times. David is such a beautiful being who in life is extraordinary along with leading an extraordinary life. David, you are so beautiful, thank you and I love you. Love mom.

TARA MARIE JACK

TARA MARIE JACK is a renowned Jewelry Designer and Artist. Her designs include the highly popular Archangel Line for Internationally Acclaimed Author, Speaker, Sunny Dawn Johnston which recently reached Best-Seller on Daily Om. Her designs hit National Television on Life Time Movie Network's, Seance with Sunny Dawn Johnston. Her designs were most recently a proud sponsor of the LaFemme Film Festival in Beverly Hills honoring women of Film.

Tara Marie infuses the guidance from Spirit and her love for Creative Flow together to create jewelry that is not only beautiful to the eye but Spiritually vibrational. She allows her love for nature, color and her trendy chic style inspire her.

Tara Marie was guided to this work after many years of finding who she was and healing her past. She stumbled upon this path in 2006 while reading Sonia Choquette's "Trust Your Vibes" and looking for new ways to tap into her intuition. She found that her channels to Spirit are wide open when she is creating.

Tara Marie Jack is a certified Mind, Body & Spirit Practitioner and her goal in life is to help others through her designs and passion for Art. She teaches regularly, helping others see the profound difference creativity can make in one's life.

Each piece that is created has a story and she shares that story with all her designs and art. Tara Marie loves to combine the brilliance of Swarovski Crystal and high vibrationally charged gemstones to create the most magical of pieces to enhance one's life.

Email: taramariejack11@gmail.com
Website: www.TaraMarieJack.com
Social Media: www.facebook.com/taramariejack

❧ I Fit In

When I was eight years old, in the back seat of my parents 1978 sky blue Lincoln Town car, my mother turned to me and said "you are so pretty, one day you could be Miss America." My step father turned to my mother and said "Don't tell her that, she can NEVER be Miss America. What are you kidding me? Look at her big ugly lips!" I remember feeling awkward and sad.

My mother left my real father when I was the age of two years old. She was looking for love to fill herself up. After several years of up and downs, drugs, alcohol and abuse, she met Don. I remember being sick and her zipping up my blue winter ski jacket, telling me, "We are going to go live with Don. He has a daughter a year older for you to play with. Her name is Heidi." Intuitively at the age of 7 years old, I knew I was about to enter into something that was going to be life changing. We entered into a space where I gained three step sisters who had lost their mother very suddenly six months' prior at the tender age of 36 years old to a brain aneurism. They hated us. Two of them were Debbie, 11 & Terry, 12 years older than me and the one, Heidi was a year older than me. They were sad and angry. Terry was already out of the house and Debbie was an older teenager, already working long hours at a diner. Her and my mother fought constantly. Heidi was a brut to me. She loved to beat me up and I would get called a pansy ass and punished by Don if I told on her.

Don's way of making me tough was to hold wrestling matches in our living room where Heidi would beat me up until I was crying. Don would be laughing his ass off and my mother wouldn't stop it for she was too afraid to lose the love she had found.

My real father remarried a woman named Pat and they had a daughter together, Melissa. By the time I was seven years old, I had gained three step sisters and one half sister. I had two fathers and two mothers and yet I felt so alone.

Guardian Angel

When I was five years old, I was visiting with my father on a weekend visit. I was in the bathroom washing my hands. I felt a hand on my shoulder. The hand was strong but loving. I looked up in the mirror to see who it was and there was no reflection there. I turned around and there was a beautiful man, the most beautiful man I had ever seen standing before me. He had big wings that were the color of white and gold. He didn't speak a word. I heard him say inside of me; I will always be with you. I will protect you. You will always be safe. I was scared and ran inside crying to tell my father what had happened. I realize now I wasn't scared of the angel, I was scared of what he was going to protect me from.

Cinderella

The years to follow were one from the fairy tale Cinderella. My step sister Debbie despised me and my mother. They fought constantly. She would take Heidi to Six Flags, the beach and shopping, excluding me. I would have to stay home doing chores while Heidi would be out. I can remember crying so hard. I would ask, why I couldn't go. "Because you can't, shut up and finish your chores" was the answer I received.

My father's wife wasn't much better to me. I wasn't really welcomed there. She didn't like me because I was my mother's daughter. She treated me like an outsider and at the age of eight years old I intuitively knew that my presence threatened her. Her and my father would have explosive arguments over me being there. It was always very uncomfortable for me but I knew my father loved me dearly. I knew that but I also knew he felt trapped. During some of the weekends I was visiting with my father, we would go up to see his mother, my grandmother and her husband. On those weekends, at night, my step grandfather would sexually molest me while everyone slept. This went on for several years. On the last night, this would happen, I was eight years old and remember I was sleeping. I was dreaming that I was on a merry go round. It felt good to me in the dream. The dream started to get more vivid and more vivid when I awoke I found my step grandfather's head under my nightgown. When I realized what was going on, I began to throw up violently. Panicked because I was making so much noise and everyone was being awakened by the noise I was making. He started making up a story that I was eating candy all night and ate so much to the point that I was now throwing up. Everyone started yelling at me that I woke them up and that I was a bad girl. I remember feeling so bad about myself, gross, dirty and scared that night that after everyone went back to bed I just cried and cried silently so I wouldn't wake anyone up the rest of the night. I don't think I slept one minute the rest of that night. That was the last time I ever was alone with my step grandfather again. When I got home to my mother, I told her. Back then, people didn't go to authorities about situations like this. This gave my mother a reason to fight with my father which only made me feel worse.

Chaos

The years rolled along, and things progressed negatively on both sides of my life. Heidi and my mother fought more and more. Don and I fought more and more. By the time I was in my early teens, I was looking for love outside of my home and found solace with friends that had dysfunctional home lives as well. I began hanging with the wrong crowd to fit in somewhere. One day, Heidi and my mother had gotten into a very escalated argument and Heidi grabbed a large knife out of the drawer and charged at my mother. I tried to stop her and my finger got sliced almost completely off. Heidi was sent to group home for unruly teens and I was sent to my fathers to live. After about three months of living with my father and step mother who constantly complained and argued with my father that there was not enough room for me to live there. I left. I stayed with my friend and her family for a week and asked my mother to meet me at my friend's house to talk.

When she got there, I got in her car and I asked if I could come back home. She turned to me and said "Don doesn't want you to come back, honey. I'm sorry." It felt like a knife had stabbed me in the heart. I don't think I had ever felt so alone, rejected and unloved as I did in that moment. Then my mother gave me $500 to find a place to live. At sixteen, I had dropped out of high school with no job and nowhere to live. I was lost. I got out of my mother's car and went back into my friend's house, devastated inside but tough outside. "Well I have to find a place to live" I said to my friend. This was probably one of the most hurtful things that ever happened to me in my life. The woman I loved most in my life, my mother, had rejected me. I have worked many years on forgiveness but even now, as I type these words, my heart aches for that little girl in that car that day.

Paul

In the weeks to follow, I stayed from friend's house to friend's house. Then I met a man. His name was Paul. Paul was six years older than me. I was in love. He loved me so much that he moved me in with him. I quickly bonded with his family and friends. We were a family. I belonged. I fit in. Paul drank a lot and wasn't the nicest of people but he loved me. He was very possessive of me, but that meant he loved me. He began to beat me. And beat me. And beat me. I wore black eyes like women wear jewelry. It was my accessory. Oh the stories, I made up to people, "a pot fell out of the cabinet and hit me in the eye" or "I was playing softball and a bat hit me in the eye." As the years rolled by, I tried to leave but he would find me and beat me harder. One time I left, my mother set me up in an apartment. I was starting a new life. He had found out from a mutual friend where I lived, kicked the door down, dragged me kicking in screaming and threw me in the car. He pounded on my face the whole way to his house. When we got to his house, he dragged me in by my hair and duct tape me naked beating me until the police came. Luckily, for me, I had been on the phone with my mother at the time he kicked in the door and my mother had called the police. I finally left this man after almost seven years of this abuse when I ended up in the hospital, my face so disfigured, my mouth stitched from one side to the other and the doctor telling me that if I hadn't been drinking the night before I would have been dead from shock. Alcohol had saved my life. Paul went to jail for a year and a half after that and I walked away … NEVER LOOKING BACK.

I later realized through a dream I had that I had a soul contract with this man. He was one of my biggest teachers in life. Our souls had a contract. He taught me how to be strong. He taught me how to survive.

Guardian Angel

Shortly after I left Paul, I can remember it being a warm summer day. I had went to the beach to clear my head. I can still feel the sand running through my toes. I can still hear the waves crashing on the beach and the seagulls squawking in the sky above. I can still hear the wind in my ears say "I will always be by your side. I will always protect you". I looked around for the man with the wings again but he was not there to be seen, he was there to be felt. I felt him that day. I knew who it was. I remembered him from when I was a little girl. I knew I had a guardian angel. He had been with me and still is. I can still feel his presence.

New Beginning

It was not shortly after that warm summer day that I decided I needed a new path. I moved myself to Queens, New York and found a great job cocktail waitressing in Manhattan. I started making a lot of money, worked out three hours a day, partied. I went to college and earned a degree in Business Marketing. I was having the time of my life. But something was missing. I never forgot that angel. I always felt things. I had vivid dreams. On one of my trips out to Long Island to visit my mother and step father, I was leaving to get back on the train and needed some reading material. Since Don had lost his first wife so suddenly, he was very intrigued with life after death and had a ton of books in his library. That day, I was drawn to *Embraced by the Light* by Betty Eadie. I read that book cover to cover in twenty four hours. Yes. This is what I know to be true. Thereafter, I read as many books as I could find about anything spiritual and in the nineties, there wasn't many.

Love

I met my husband, David, when I was twenty-nine years old shortly after having my heart broken by another guy. I was jaded by this time in my life with men. After partying one night, David, at the time was upset about it and we had gotten in a heated argument that night. The next morning he drove me to work. It was an icy January morning, David had gotten out of the car when we got in the parking lot. He got down on his knees on the icy pavement, he took my hands, I looked down at him and he had tears streaming down his face. He said to me "You don't know what you're worth." Those words vibrated through my whole body, my essence. I knew in that moment I would marry this man. A year later, we were married. My life felt complete. David is my soul mate, my rock, my supporter, my number one fan and the love of my life. There was something so Universally Divine that brought us together and I am forever grateful.

Spiritual Path

I continued with my studies. Now there were books to read everywhere. Many Lives, Many Masters by Brian L. Weiss, Conversations with God, by Neale Donald Walsh, Ask and It is Given by Abraham Hicks. I couldn't get enough. Shortly after we got married my in laws moved out to Arizona. To get out of the cold winter we would visit for warm vacations. After our second vacation, and a trip up to Sedona I decided that I wanted to live here to expand my spiritual awareness. When we moved to Arizona, for the first eight months, I didn't work. I spent my days in meditation, reading and living on the money that I had taken out of my 401k. I searched for a teacher, a mentor, and found Sunny Dawn Johnston. I took as many classes as I could with her. Every class she offered, I took. I wanted to expand my intuitive gifts and share it with the world. I wanted to share with the world the knowledge I was learning. I was going to be a world-renowned psychic. It didn't show up for me like that. Shortly after I finished my Mind Body & Spirit Practitioner Program with Sunny, I discovered I hadn't healed the inner child inside of me.

Healing Through Creativity

I started creative endeavors when I read Trust Your Vibes by Sonia Choquette, one of the chapters is called *Get Out Your Crayons*; in this chapter, it explains how you can easily tap into your higher self by getting out of your head and tapping in. Me, never thinking I had a creative bone in my body set out to the local Michaels craft store and found a bracelet kit. I was hooked. Through the power of creativity I have learned how to tap into Source, God. I learned I could receive messages through creativity. I couldn't get enough. I still can't.

It didn't stop there, creativity has been life changing for me. I shared my past with you because my life story has been one of self-worth and self-love. Through my jewelry, it has given me a way to feel like I fit in. It has become a space in my life to feel safe. When I create jewelry, I can see its beauty. For so many years in my childhood I had been taught I was bad and ugly and not worth anything. When we create something, it is coming not from our head, it is a nudge from your inner most part of our souls. We take that nudge, that inspiration and create a tangible item which is a form of magic. When I create these master pieces, every time, it reminds of the beauty that is inside of me. It reminds me that there is something beautiful about myself. It reminds me of the light that is inside of myself and every other living being. We all have this gift. I can't tell you how many times I have taught a class and the student has said "I don't have a creative bone in my body". I tell them, we ALL have a creative child inside, it just needs a little love, and patience to play with him/her.

I later learned the power of Art Journaling, a mixture of Mixed Media art and expression. Art Journaling gave me the power to heal and forgive. It provided the power of healing my inner child, that little girl that was hurt. Through layers of writing it out on the paper the pain, painting over it with color and prayer. I would call in my Spirit Guides and my Guardian Angel, asking them to guide me. There is something so therapeutic to this process that I don't have words to express the feeling. The best word I can give to it is Freedom. When you can take your pains, and forgive them through art and look at it through an eye of a masterpiece, you can see your life as the same. Everyone has their pains, their lessons, their journey. I encourage anyone that is looking for transformative way to heal to explore the power of art journaling. There are many resources, books, and videos on this technique. This was my most popular teachings I could offer. I would have sold out sessions and the same students would show up repeatedly. It is a very empowering technique that I encourage anyone looking to discover a new tool to try. It is easy, fun and forgiving. There is no perfection to art journaling. You do not have to be an artist to use this technique and this is your book, your story and your healing that is for you to see.

Creativity literally saved my life. It gives me connection to my inner self. It provides me connection with Source. It provided me with a gift of healing. It provided me the gift of getting out of my own way. It releases tension, stress and worry. It is a vibe raiser. It is a gift. It is a space in my journey where I belong. Now get out those crayons and create your own magic. It may just change your life like it did mine.

Chapter is dedicated to my rock and soul mate David Daryl Jack. Also, dedicated to all the souls that are healing their inner child on their journey.

I would like to say thank you to my Mentor, Colleague and Soul Sister, Sunny Dawn Johnston. You have been a great rock in my life. You have given me so many tools, strength and guidance over the years that I am forever grateful for you

CATHERINE MADEIRA

CATHERINE MADEIRA is a freelance writer and artist. She has been receiving ethereal information for years and is now sharing it in the hope of helping others in their life's journeys.

Catherine is from the Reno/Tahoe area and has two children, Jason, who has always demanded an intellectual approach to life, and daughter, Kendal, who was born a very old soul. Catherine has been documenting her experiences for years. Subsequently, she has been able to receive, evaluate, and compile the information to pass to others.

umbriel03@gmail.com

Memory From Another Time and Place

I t is of primary importance that whomever reads the following, does so with the understanding that it should be viewed not as a fantasy or fictional telling, but that I relay it to you with full belief in the truth of the occurrence and the truth of its purpose, necessity and value of the result. An additional reason to give serious thought to the reality of this memory. To understand that this series of events, their purpose, are a thing I had never before heard of, a process that I couldn't have possibly imagined but stemmed from total logic throughout.

The time frame of the memory is unknown to me, it was either countless ages ago or eons in the future. The location is also unknown to me other than, it was a lush clean wonderful place, my mind equated it to South America or it could have been an entirely different place, or planet.

The Dream opens. I am looking down at my bare feet, there's a band around my left ankle made of a white substance, possibly shells and a brown leather tie. I was wearing a brown leather tong around my waist which was covering my genitals. At no time, did I see a reflection of myself so I don't know what I looked like. I do know that I was a young man approximately 16 years old, as were the other young men I saw in this place.

The ground I was walking on was short green and grassy, alive with growth. The air was wonderfully warm not as humid as a rain forest but with similar components in the type of foliage of a rain forest. I was walking between two buildings made of light gray granite like stone. These structures were large. One structure was 5 feet to my right and the other was 12 feet to my left. I did not gaze up at them (I had been seeing them all my life) but my feeling is that they jutted off at a stair step angle, much like the pyramids here. I walked about 30 yards clearing the corners of the buildings. I came to a larger path, 30 feet across. Looking to my right I saw that I was near the edge of the village, the forest began just beyond the building to my right.

I then noticed what seemed to be the chief, or an elder. He had long black straight hair. On his head was a simple unadorned head dress, he had a dangling necklace that looked similar to the anklet I wore and brown leather loin cloth, bare feet and reddish colored cape, in his hand a tall wooden staff. I thought he looked wise and enviably noble. His face was unwrinkled, and seemed to be confident in every thought, move, word, or direction. I believe he was a man I would like to know and emulate. He did not command respect, he just had it. He appeared relaxed, while waiting for me and the six additional young men who would also participate, one of which was my best friend. His straight thick brown hair was neat and clean. My friend had a choker also of the white shells or beads. He had brown eyes. I knew we had experienced many boyhood adventures together and we knew each other well. When I saw the other young men, I assumed I must look similar. We were small, 5 feet tall. The chief was taller 5/5 or 5/6. We were all lean and muscled. We were handsome with clear complexions, darkened skin, and white teeth. We could have been Mayan, but I am not sure. We were seemingly healthy and pleasant. Everyone was quiet at this moment but not intimidated or nervous about our meeting.

I don't know how large the village was but as I turned to walk towards the elder, behind me to my left was the rest of the village. The other granite buildings were far apart, in amongst trees and various foliage. I didn't see anyone else in the village.

It was early in the morning but the temperature was very pleasant. There were not clouds, no dew dripping off the leaves, the foliage was fairly thick. My feeling is that we were high in altitude because I didn't see any mountains.

My friend, the 5 others and I joined the elder. I don't remember any of us speaking. We formed a line, the elder turned and proceeded to follow a path into the forest. The plants varied widely. Some were much like ferns, others were plants I've never seen, with large green leaves. Occasionally on the side of the path there would be a granite-like boulder or rock. My instincts were that we walked in a southerly direction. We walked for a long time. Probably 3 or 4 hours. Other than the sounds of the birds in the trees, we encountered no other wildlife. Eventually we angled upward at a gentle slope.

As we reached the top of the hill, the living forest opened up into a clearing. In the clearing at the top of the hill was a building. The granite rectangular building was very plain with no decoration. Near the right end of the building there was an opening or doorway. It was squared off and the size of a normal door. The roof was flat. The sky above was indescribably clear blue.

We walked to the door. The elder stopped and stood to the left of the door. We all filed past him and into the building. Directly across from the door was a span to the opposing wall. In that wall was a highly set rectangular window, it appeared to be 5 feet long by 3 feet high. By the door and window, I could tell that the walls were about 8 inches thick. Through the window, I could see some big leaves and the blue sky. The only light in the building was provided by this window and the entrance. The inside of the building was not like the outside. The inside floor, walls, and ceiling, were a dark red and dark gray swirling clay. The inside was damp with moisture as was the air, and was noticeably cooler than outside. The purpose for the offset door revealed itself after entering the structure. Directly in the center of the building was a wall. It separated the interior in half. The wall was made of the red and grey clay and was also very thick, "8 inches". It went from floor to ceiling and wall to wall cutting off access to the other side. In the wall there were Octagonal holes (same size and shape as our stop signs). They were 7 evenly spaced openings across that center wall, they were 3 high from floor to ceiling, so 21 total openings in the wall. Through those cut outs I could see the other room on the other side of the structure. The 7 Octagons across the center of the wall were (head high) and were all filled with the soft, red, grey, wet clay, packed tightly, filling in the entire 8-inch-thick space.

The elder followed us into the room, no one spoke. We instinctively knew what we had to do next. The nature of this ceremony did not require works between us, but silence was not ordered or requested in any way. We were not a people living under the hand of dominance of any individual or group. The quiet nature welled from profound respect for the purpose for the ceremony, and we were humbled in that we had been chosen to partake in this unknown ascension. The entire ceremony was quite uncomplicated in view of the extreme importance of its purpose.

We stood in line. The first young man facing the first clay filled hole in the wall. I was the last person in line. My best friend stood just in front of me. The first young man stepped to the clay filled Octagon. He raised his hands up next to his face, his fingers spread wide. He then gently pressed his hands and face into the clay filled space. The soft material accepted the imprint of his hands and face, as he stepped back from the wall the clay presented to perfect portrait of him. He took one side step and in a natural unison he stepped forward in time with the second participant. He embedded his form into the second mold as the no.2 man erased the reflection of his predecessor and replaced it with the imprint of his own hands and face. Again the 2 men stepped back and man no. 3 added himself to the movement, in unison 3 men now stepped up. The first introducing his reflection to the 3rd mold, man no. 2 erasing the 2nd imprint of man no. 1 and man no. 3 temporarily dominating the first hole with his figure. On it went one man adding himself to the smooth quiet movement, step forward, immersion, step back, and step side. No. 5, on to no. 6 and on to me, no. 7.

My hands raised next to my face, fingers spread. Looking straight ahead, now we all step forward to meet the 7 windows of vision. As I moved those final inches towards the replica of my dear friends facial imprint, I could smell the wet clay. I closed my eyes, the clay was pleasantly cool to my hands and face, I felt myself enveloped as I immersed my imprint over the reflection of my friends image. I found that I was not erasing the face of my friend, I was absorbing it. I would have been stunned and confused by the instantaneous effects of what followed, but with the unexpected walked the all-knowing.

I came to this place barring the knowledge of only my life's experience. At the instant I touched the clay I first realized that I held the memory of (me) looking at me from a different place. It took only a millisecond to understand that I was seeing me through my friends' eyes. Recalling a memory we both had, as at that time we were together. But seeing it now from two perspectives. Now all at once I realized that in every aspect conceivable I had inherited not only his memories, thoughts and feelings, but also of the others. More over the joining with the clay bestowed to me the entire memory, knowledge and life experience of all who preceded me to this place and did this thing (sharing their souls) back to our peoples beginning.

I should have fallen, stunned to a catatonic state at the onset of the enormous, instant, inundation of information into my being, but just the opposite was the case. Along with the collision of awareness came the understanding of its origin, purpose and necessity. Vaulting from age 16 to an age unknown, and able to receive and utilize the information just as those who experienced and shared before me. 3 seconds ago this was new and mysterious, 3 seconds hence I had undertaken the absorption countless times. Suddenly the noble mysterious elder was an old friend. One who I took the ritual with when he was a young man so many years ago.

In unison with my companions I pulled my head and hands from the clay, stepped back, stepped side, I imprinted myself in the second space in time with the other participants. This continued on until I, being last had imprinted myself in the last clay mold. As soon as I stepped away from the wall the clay filled openings began to gently break apart and fall into the opposing room, leaving only the open Octagon windows.

The ceremony complete, we silently exited the place of memories. Unaffected emotionally as we were all now ancient and had done this so many times before.

As we began our walk home (my) dream began to fade and ended. The information I needed to absorb was complete. I am honored to have been shown this passage, its purpose, system and success through the ages.

The humble nature of the chosen young me and the privilege of receiving such a gift and responsibility was a thing generally unspoken. We were chosen without notice of others. Our new knowledge was not necessarily shared with the masses. This passing of memory was done to keep alive the history of our civilization. Obviously the boys returned as men (ancient men). But with the expansion also came the ability to calm the overwhelming nature and output of the wisdom. Moving and living amongst their people with the existence of what they held, basically unknown to the others. If things needed assistance the men could draw on their ancient wisdom to help the community through whatever problems arose. It was their job to take care of their people. They were looked upon as quiet elders, but tried not to draw attention to themselves. It was not secrecy with control or malice at its base. It was a simple way to ensure the history remain exactly intact.

Our understanding was, that of the original 7 men, the last living man in the proceeding group made sure the next generation was chosen and taken to the place for the passing of memory to help secure their continued civilizations legacy.

The astonishing impact involved in this quiet process was born of logic and their knowledge that souls carry their entire history intact and available for any of us to draw from. I'm not sure how it worked. I currently don't know the significance of the 7 windows. Maybe it took 7 to complete the upload of information. Also in the room there was a total of 21 windows, 14 of which were not used. I think we immersed our hands and face because our hands transfer so much energy. Our hands heal and create, we project power from our hands. Was it the place, some mystical component in the clay? Joining the clay and each other, coupled with the belief that such a thing is possible. This triad enabling them to touch their point of origin.

I wonder, if this was a memory of the future, when I do submerge my hands and face into the clay, if the distant recollection of me, now, in this life will present itself, and be added to the memory line. Will I live again in the mind of the young man I am in the future? On the reverse side, I was shown the memory of this past or future life and experience. So, the young stranger lives with me now and has been added to my line. Either way, past or future, I remember, the experience is mine, and I have been infused with the responsibility to share it with you.

In a similar way we, here, in this place, are also able to draw upon eternity. It's ours. Our memory (past or future) to see and use if we choose to. It's as simple as opening yourself to the tidal wave of understanding. Believe what comes to you. The more you believe the more you will be given.

Dedicated to my Granddaughter, Harlo Monroe, who we now believe is an Indigo. To my two tiny dogs, Bell, my best friend and angel on Earth, and Bee, Bell's lively assistant. My Father, Richard Madeira, who passed years ago, but has stayed to watch over his family.

Lisa Hardwick the Publisher of Visionary Insight Press, for giving me the opportunity to share my information. Without this wonderful & accepting person I may have lived my life without being able to complete my purpose for coming here. I want to thank my mother, Lilas Hardin, for her support, my son, Jason Vaughan, and daughter, Kendal Vaughan, for always being available to discuss these complex matters. To my granddaughter, Harlo Monroe, as her existence alone motivates me to share my knowledge.

Thank you, Lisa Hardwick, Publisher and Katina Gillespie, Managing Project Director, for editing my work and making it presentable.

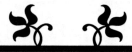

SHARON GAMBRILL

SHARON GAMBRILL, also fondly known as 'Shazza' is a Sydney based comedian, actor, writer, Laughter Yoga Teacher, certified and licensed Louse Hay Heal Your Life® Workshop Teacher and Personal Coach. During a year of medical and holistic treatment following a mastectomy in 2011, Sharon decided it was time to 'go within' to examine the mind/ body health connection and come to terms with a worried childhood being her mother's parent, her mother's subsequent suicide in 2001, absent father abandonment issues, and her lifelong struggle with obesity. What a year it turned out to be! It was a transformational time with healing occurring on a deep emotional level by studying the philosophies of Louise Hay and using her bestselling book, *You Can Heal Your Life* as a guide. Other healthy practises used were laughter, deep breathing exercises, nutrition, EFT/Tapping, Reiki, walking, meditation, music, and visualisation. While at times an excruciating process and at other times smooth flowing, Sharon persevered reading numerous books on health and emotional healing which led her to the Laughter Yoga, Reiki, EFT/Tapping and Heal Your Life® certification trainings, being the modalities she found to be of the most benefit. Sharon has written several children's story books and is currently working with an illustrator to bring them to life. Sharon always writes from the heart and is warm, open, honest, funny, and inspiring, Sharon continues to uplift everyone around her and is now on a personal mission to encourage others to accept themselves fully, release the past, feel empowered, and create a life that is bright, healthy, and filled with laughter!

For workshops, personal coaching sessions or speaking events:
Web: www.sharongambrill.com
Email: info@sharongambrill.com
Or connect with Sharon on Facebook, Twitter, Instagram or Meetup.

 Lessons Learnt!

April 1 2011, April Fools' Day, I had my breast chopped off. This may be a shocking way to start my chapter but don't worry there's a happy ending and I'm here to tell you about it! The story begins with an aching breast and the shocking discovery of a tiny little hard granule inside of a soft lump and I thought, *this doesn't feel right.* The feeling of fear and terror then became an out of body experience with a rush of biopsies, scans and calm, but concerned looking doctors. It's like they're getting you prepared for something not very nice and you can't help but think, *uh oh this is serious.* That feeling then graduated from an out of body experience when nineteen days later I found myself in hospital with an efficient male nurse inserting a pain relief suppository gel in my anus because I kept vomiting from the morphine. That's the time it went from an out of body experience to a completely in body experience and I came back to earth with an almighty definitive thud. As you see the drainage tubes carrying blood and scary looking fluid coming out of your flat left chest, you ironically really know you're alive. Both the surgeon and my wise friend, Louise, who is a spiritual healer and naturopath, told me I didn't need to have a mastectomy, just to have the little lump removed. At the time my first thought was, *just take the whole thing off, there's no way I'm having any of those terrible drugs.* Fear and panic influenced my decision, which is fair enough. Now for some women it is medically recommended, but it wasn't for me. As it turns out the operations went well, nothing had spread, and I have adjusted so am thankful for that, but who really wants two complicated operations instead of one simpler one, plus three painful breast tissue expander procedures, and a year of discomfort getting used to an implant? Someone who had to learn the hard way, and someone who didn't take the time to go within to find out what was really going on at a deeper metaphysical level. I would do that now because I read an amazing book called *You Can Heal Your Life* by Louise Hay about the Law of Attraction and the parallel between thought and the manifestation of an illness. But we're not up to that bit yet so I'll just keep going.

It really does go back to my relationship with my mother. She was a kind, loving, sensitive woman who was into things like crystals and channelling, and wine and pills. She succumbed to depression, prescription pill addiction, bouts of alcoholism and occasional suicide attempts while I was growing up, mainly due to her abusive childhood. One day I arrived home from school and found my mother unconscious. I've got to say it took it out of me. I didn't know what to do. I just sat on the floor by her motionless feet crying and waiting for my big brothers to come home from high school. It's very quiet when it's just you and your mother and she's unconscious. I heard the wind blowing faintly out the back and that was about it. There's a feeling of powerlessness, and a fluttery lack of security which imbeds itself into your psyche as you grow up. I went from being the child to the parent, but not just that, a worried parent. And all the time. I over mothered and over protected my mother out of fear of losing her. At the same time, I was the chubby class clown who did very well at school in a way I think to protect her reputation. I was two people growing up.

Then sixteen years ago, she overdosed in a hotel room in Mosman, a suburb of Sydney. One of my older brothers rang to say he'd had a visit by police. I recall his voice was barely audible, just a whisper. I could hear the shock in its quietness. Even though it wasn't surprising from past attempts, the finality and sense of loss was palpable. I felt like I was in quicksand about to sink into a deep, unbreathable hole. I couldn't eat or sleep for six weeks.

Now the story isn't funny at this point, but stick with me there's a big uplifting finish! So, I feel that, along with other health factors, is the reason this lump grew in my breast. Not in my ear, or bowel, or anywhere else. It makes perfect sense to me now. Louise Hay suggests problems with breasts can represent over mothering, over protection plus deep resentment if a hard lump is involved. I over mothered my mother and was resentful as I did it. As I grew up that resentment came with me everywhere and was amplified by feelings of loss and disappointment I had for my father who lived interstate and had many women in his life. In fact, resentment was a big part of me mingled with grief and guilt for ten years after the overdose right up until I found that hard lump. Then something inside me said, *it's time to change*. So what I learnt is you can't save someone else. You can support them, guide them, but you can't save them. That's up to them. My mother wanted to go and I know she is gracefully floating around up there as pure energy so I am happy for her now, and although at times I admit I can still feel some guilt, overall I at am at peace with it.

During the past six years, big improvements have been put into place. I'm not so moody and angry anymore. I relax, breathe deeply, exercise, meditate, have energy healings, studied Reiki and EFT/Tapping, and eat organic vegetables. In fact, I love them now! Who knew you could get so excited over leafy greens? I've thrown out my deodorant and I suggest you do too. It's full of chemicals that leak into your glands. I now use a crystal rock stick. It doesn't really work so learn to embrace your BO, I have!

It's so important to let go of the past and laugh as much as you can. Whatever makes you laugh do it. Laughter Yoga is great because you laugh for no reason doing fun child-like laughter exercises with deep breathing in between. Plus, as an added bonus you'll look completely silly. It's liberating! Scientists have proven our brain doesn't know the difference between real and pretend laughter and releases endorphins either way which are excellent for our health and immune system. I believe in it so much I have become a certified Laughter Yoga Teacher. So, laugh now, just a chuckle, wherever you are reading this whether it's on a bus, at work, or even in your bathtub! Go ahead, *hahaha*! Doesn't that feel better?

The person who gave me *You Can Heal Your Life,* the book that profoundly changed me, was my mother, in 1986, when she met Louise Hay in Sydney. She must have known I would need it one day and it only took me 25 years to actually read it. Now I'm a certified and licensed Heal Your Life® Workshop Teacher and Coach. Affirmations are statements which reprogram our subconscious mind and create new neural pathways in the brain. When we change our thinking and reduce our stress levels, the science of epigenetics shows it improves our cellular health. So to quote an affirmation from the wonderful Louise Hay, "*I am joyous and happy and free*" I hope you are too!

I dedicate this chapter with thanks to my beautiful and sensitive mother, Lesley. My mother was the person who gave me a personally signed copy of You Can Heal Your Life after she met Louise Hay in Sydney in 1986. I largely ignored the book for 25 years until 2011 when it became my lifeline. What a gift!

I would like to acknowledge and thank my friend, Louise Calleja, from On Healing Wings, Sydney, for picking me up off the floor (literally!) giving me an emergency healing, and firmly pointing me in the right direction after my diagnosis. Also to Anni Casey, from Anni's Healing Garden, Sydney, who has worked with me through many issues (too many to mention!) These two women have been mentors and to them go my love and thanks.

TRISH BOWIE

TRISH BOWIE searched for a miracle after serious loss, illness and years of pain. She found her miracle at the age of 39 when she was introduced to Reiki Energy Healing and Louise Hay's wonderful book *Heal Your Body*. In 1996 she became a Usui Reiki Master—then continued with Reiki training and obtained her Karuna, Shamballa, Jikiden, and Divine Compassion Masters. She is a Registered Massage Therapist, Certified Hypnotherapist and a Certified and Licensed *Heal Your Life*® Teacher. Trish is owner of The Complete Wellness Centre and Day Spa, and The Western Canada Reiki Training Centre, offering workshops for teens and adults in Usui , Karuna and Shamballa Reiki, *Heal Your Life*®, Stress Management, Money Awareness, Divine Compassion, Energy Effects, Meditation and Spa Training. She feels very honored to have had the opportunity to learn from so many great leaders and Masters. Trish is humbled and grateful for the ability to facilitate people to heal.

reikitraining@gmail.com
www.thecompletewellnesscentre.com

🌺 Moving Beyond the Unknown

After growing up and living in the city throughout my childhood years, and then moving to the country, I quickly discovered what it was like to have lots of people around me. Meanwhile, I still felt so alone and terrified, like a caged animal pacing up and down with no escape in sight.

I fell in love and was married at the age of nineteen. A year later I had my first child. A son. Eight months after he was born my husband wanted to leave the city I grew up in to move closer to his family in Northern Alberta Canada. It was his dream to go back home within five years of having our son. Imagine how I felt when he came home a few months later instead and said, *"We are moving"*.

Parts of me were excited and a part of me was really scared to take on this new adventure. Moving to the bush, four long hours away from home, away from my family, the city lights and my security! It was so completely different from what I was accustomed to. We had everything we could ever want in the city and I loved it there. I simply had to hop on a bus if I wanted to go anywhere and we always had enough money to do what we wanted.

I loved fashion, theater, and the endless attractions the city could offer me... and my family. I loved my family! Now here we were packing up all our belongings and moving to the bush. No buses, no restaurants, no fashion, no running water, no money. My husband quit his job so he could go help his Dad, who had been injured by a horse that rolled on top of him. There I was saying goodbye to my beautiful city—wide-eyed and ready to do whatever it was I needed to do to learn survival. It seemed exciting because we were going to rent a house on some land after living in an apartment in the city. I felt so free.

Life in the Bush

The house was a good size and I did my best to make it look nice with the furnishings we'd brought from the city. The living room felt very cozy and inviting with my red shag carpet and red lamps. It had a bay window, from which I hung lace curtains, and they looked wonderful! The couple who rented it to us really loved what I had done. In a short time though I started to feel the negative effects of our decision... we had no running water, which meant we had to catch rain or use melted snow, and heat the water to do the dishes. Then there were the dirty diapers that had to be washed by hand! Going outside to the outhouse in the middle of winter was not fun either!

There were a few other things that were extremely difficult for me to deal with... like that little hole in the kitchen wall, which looked like the door to a mouse house on TV. Well it became my reality because mice did indeed scurry in and out of there. I had nightmares that they were crawling all over me in bed at night, which they very well may have been. Then there was the other issue... the one about the owner having a key and coming in the back entrance of the house where there was a table with chairs to have his lunch—unannounced. I found out the hard way. One day I ran to the fridge, which was right next to that room, to get the baby a bottle... without a stitch on and there he was! I was so embarrassed. I just wanted to go home.

Since we had no money I couldn't easily pick up the phone and telephone my family. It was so expensive to call long distance back in the late 1970's—and we were on a party line where at least three homes shared the same line, so you never said anything that you didn't want people to know because sure as heck someone would be listening. I was starting to feel the stress and was pregnant with my perfectly-planned second child. That fun, exciting place wasn't so much fun anymore. The strain of having no money was weighing heavily on us. We lived on $3,200 that year and when we didn't eat at the in-laws, we ate at home where it was eggs, rice, peas and canned corned beef. I was pretty skinny and my nutrition wasn't the best, so I lost my second baby and I was devastated. I truly wanted that baby. I cried for days... feeling confined and no longer free.

I had to get out of there. I ran outside to get away, up and down the driveway like a caged animal with nowhere to go, no vehicle, no money, no phoning home... It was at that moment that I began learning how to suppress my pain, how to pretend to be happy, how to be the Super Mom and Wife, and how to please everyone but myself. I went willingly to the north, so now I had to live with it.

Just When the Clouds Seem to Lift

A year later I was pretty excited when my husband gave me the good news that his aunt was going to give us money for a down payment on one of the old forestry station houses that had running water! I was so excited! I swore I would never have another dirty dish. My husband and his brother decided they would start a land survey business together. Everything seemed great, since I was pregnant once again and I could actually wash diapers in a washing machine this time.

The house was a three-bedroom home on 4 acres and we had a water dugout which was our drinking supply. We bought three hundred and twenty acres of homestead land, as well as one hundred and sixty acres of farmed land across the road from our house that belonged to my father-in-law. My husband taught me how to disc the field after the baby was born. When it was dark at night and while sitting on that big tractor, I felt so independent, so in control. I was really starting to enjoy the country life as my husband continued to teach me the love of the land.

Then came that horrible day in June. My husband decided to get out his dad's boat and bluestone the dugout. Bluestone (copper sulfate) was used to kill the algae in the water. He and our four-year-old son set out to get the job done. It was a beautiful, peaceful day. The sun was shining and warming every part of my body as I sat in the yard playing with my 14-month-old daughter. My husband and son were in the boat rowing around the dugout with the bag of bluestone hanging from the boat, dissolving into the water and doing its job.

"Mom!" shouted my son from the boat. *"Can I please have some juice?"* I had my husband bring him to the bank of the dugout and I took him into the house for juice. We continued to enjoy the warmth as we sat and chatted about his ride in the boat.

I suddenly heard a funny sound coming from the area of the dugout — a grunting noise and lots of splashing. I ran over towards the dugout only to find my husband frantic in the water with the boat flipped over. He swam over to the boat while I searched around for a rope to throw out to him. The first thing I saw was a garden hose. I grabbed it and ran over to the bank. For some reason, he wasn't hanging on to the boat. I was later informed it had hit him in the head and stunned him! He was in the middle of the dugout with his back turned to me and bobbing up and down. I quickly took off some of my clothes and jumped in to try to save him. When I got to where he was, he was inexplicably gone. Family and friends came right away and jumped in looking for him. The R.C.M.P. (Royal Canadian Mounted Police) were contacted. A diver came in and one hour later his body was recovered.

I was in a state of shock. There I was in the bush with a four-year-old and a fourteen-month-old. No Last Will from my husband, no money for the first three months, no driver's license, thirty miles to the closest town — all at the young age of twenty-four.

I knew one thing. I had to grow up fast. The man I was dependent upon was gone. I had two children that I needed to parent and I had to keep a smile on my face to ease their anxiety and pain. As I continued to suppress my grief, my body started to fight back. First, I had back surgery, then my gall bladder came out, then the next year it was my appendix, then I started showing signs of fibromyalgia, then asthma.

Miracles Happen

I met my present husband a few months after my husband drowned. He was new to the community, single and very nice. After a while he won me over and it was not difficult for me to fall in love again. Five years later we married and had a son together.

I recognized that I wanted to be somebody, to make a difference in the world because of the pain I had personally experienced. I started utilizing one of the artistic modalities I had found at a nearby college where I studied native cultural arts. I had always admired their ability to take something natural and make something beautiful with it.

I very successfully launched a business selling Canadian aboriginal fish scale art to members of government for dignitary gifts and hooked up with a company that marketed native art worldwide. Around the same time, I joined a cosmetic home-based business to help women feel better about themselves.

The thing I loved most about the company was their conventions. It was there that I started to hear positive people speaking and teaching. The more I heard the more I felt my own sadness and pain — and I knew I wanted to be positive like they were. I was feeling so physically drained though, and in such constant pain, that I frankly couldn't figure out how to get there.

It seemed like there were an unusual amount of tragedies happening within a few miles of where we lived. I felt such a heavy weight on my shoulders and I realized it was time for us to leave. To my surprise, my husband agreed. We packed up the family and moved to Central Alberta, conveniently one hour away from my family in the city. I was delighted.

Unfortunately, I continued to get ill and experience more debilitating pain. It seemed like I was becoming allergic to everything in life. It got so bad that each night before I went to bed, I would tell my husband specifically what was wrong with me, because I truly believed that I wasn't going to wake up in the morning and I wanted him to know what to tell the examining doctor after I died.

Eventually, I ended up in the hospital because I could not even lift a cup of coffee. The doctor was concerned that I had Guillain-Barre Syndrome. When acute, this condition can be life threatening and can affect the breathing muscles, so they were checking my respirations every 15 minutes.

An Awakening

That night I felt as I laid there, so afraid and wondering what was happening to my body, I felt an enormous stream of warmth go through the top of my head, down my body and out my toes. The word "stress" came into my mind and I perceived that was exactly what was causing my symptoms. The next morning I informed the doctor and he told me that I needed to change my life or I could end up in a wheelchair.

As time went on, I returned to the hospital a few more times with various illnesses. I knew I had to do something different. I was released from hospital after being on intravenous fluid therapy.

I phoned a friend to come and give me a massage. She came over and said it's not a massage that you need, what you need is Reiki. She explained that Reiki worked on the physical, emotional, mental and spiritual body. I had refused it before. This time I was ready. I was so ill that I was willing to try anything. I was truly amazed! That one treatment had given me enough energy to get up and make a huge meal for my family.

I quickly understood that I had to learn how to do this ancient healing art so I that I could help others the way I had been helped! I took the training and ultimately, I was laying my hands on anyone who was willing to try this therapy. I couldn't get enough of it, so I went on to take my Masters in Reiki.

I treated myself daily and discovered I no longer needed to have a second back surgery. I also had no fibromyalgia symptoms. I went off my two asthma inhalers, as well. Around that time, I heard of a wonderful little book called *Heal Your Body* by Louise L. Hay. It taught about finding your illness, understanding the probable cause, and then developing a positive affirmation to heal it.

Everyday I would go for a walk and say *"I'm stronger and stronger every day. I'm healthier and healthier in every way!"* Subsequently I felt amazing, like I was floating on a cloud. I noticed that I had a lot of control over my thoughts, and whenever I thought positively, it made a huge difference in the way my body felt.

Manifesting My Destiny

I made sure to give myself a Reiki treatment every morning. Later, I started to meditate and continued saying my affirmations daily. I was so excited that I was healing myself. Now it was time for me to touch lives.

Twenty years ago, I started teaching Reiki, as well as meditation. Sixteen years ago, I opened a storefront that offered a Wellness Centre and Day Spa, as well as a training centre. It was an 800-sq. ft. building and we presented a variety of wellness and spa services. It was nice, but I comprehended that I wanted something bigger — so we could offer even more. There was a quaint place twice the size on the next block. One day as I was walking by, I muttered to myself… *I wish you would move out so I could move in.*

The next day to my surprise the renters had moved out at midnight! It was then I realized that I could manifest precisely how busy I wanted things to be, how many gift certificates I wanted to sell at Christmas, even when I wanted things to change within the business. I became aware that my thoughts were powerful and they could make a definitive difference in my life. I continued to manifest my dreams and realities there for another twelve years. I loved the storefront, although it was not allowing me to live my dream to its fullest potential.

It has been quite exciting to touch so many lives and meet a myriad of wonderful souls along the way. In 2012 I decided I wanted to do even more and touch more lives. I recognized it was time for me to move my wellness centre and training centre to the country. It was peaceful there and I grasped that it was exactly what I and my clients needed.

I knew that in order to teach large groups of people how to heal and to be able to have time to write, I would need to close the storefront. It has been over three years. All that I focus on manifesting continues to become a reality. No matter what comes at me in my day-to-day life, I see it now as a gift. A gift to take me deeper into my spirituality, to explore who I am and how I can change my perception of that moment. A gift that shows me how to continue to create miracles in my life.

I am so grateful for every lesson, every ounce of pain and illness, as well as for my losses, for they have taught me to be strong, courageous and forgiving.

To my husband who has so willingly supported me on my journey, my children who teach me to love daily, my grandchildren for their precious wisdom, to my beautiful siblings for their unconditional love and to my friends, clients and students. God Bless you all!

I want to thank Louise L. Hay for her brilliance, and my other teachers and masters, too numerous to mention. Bruce Lipton for the encouragement to never give up on writing, my sister in-law Kim who saw the spark in me before I did! To my dearest friend, Marg who kept me nourished, while I wrote and to God and my angels for continuing to support me.

JENNIFER WADSWORTH

JENNIFER WADSWORTH is an award-winning medical journalist, author, and alchemist. Following a successful career in broadcasting and healthcare marketing, Spirit had her switch gears to become a certified aromatherapist, yoga instructor and Reiki Master. Jennifer is passionate about helping others achieve mind-body balance and tap into their intuition as a daily compass for realizing a divinely orchestrated and exquisite life.

An entrepreneur and inventor, the native Atlantan owns Wadsworth Communications and Naturoil Skin Solutions, a boutique skincare company specializing in hand-made organic health and beauty products. A long-time student of eastern and western philosophy, Jennifer dedicates her life to helping heal the human spirit.

info@naturoilskin.com
www.naturoilskin.com

How To Have It All: 4 Step to Manifest Anything!

You exist as a thought of your soul. I am a thought inside of your soul. And so are the words on this page. *This book found you because you wanted it to.* See how powerful you are?

Right now, you are calling things into being with your thoughts and ideas even if you are not aware you are doing so. Imagine how your life will change once you understand how to harness and direct the power of your thought?

The Power of Thought

Your thoughts are vastly powerful. In fact, the moment you begin to conceive of something, it begins to conceive of you. Where your thoughts go, energy flows and matter grows manifesting both your greatest dreams and fears. Even if a large part of you doubts the truth of this, some part of you—no matter how small—wants to believe, because it senses the secrets of creation are wrapped inside of this idea about your ideas.

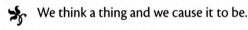 We think a thing and we cause it to be.

~OSCAR WILDE

Your proximity to your goals and ideal life are directly proportionate to your ability to harness the power of your own thoughts and beliefs about what you can *or cannot have*. As a former journalist, who has interviewed hundreds of people from all walks of life, I have learned that success isn't about being born into wealth or advantage. It is more about thinking and believing *you can be anything and have anything you desire.* Success is as simple (and as hard) as training your brain to believe you can have it ALL.

Having It ALL

For me, having it ALL means that I am the author of an Authentic Loving Life (ALL)! This acronym reminds me to stay true to my divine purpose and guides my intentions and actions. Your intentions could be entirely different, but the approach still works. Your life can be whatever you script. Maybe you want to be the CEO of a Fortune 500 company or you want to be a stay-at-home mom or live on an island and be an organic farmer! Whatever it is you want to have or be, it all begins with disciplining your mind and your thought system to BELIEVE you can have what you want.

Your life proceeds out of your intentions for it.

~WAYNE DYER

For example, one of the millionaire businessmen I interviewed told me he scripted his life and thought it into being one thought at a time. At age 24, he began to tape record positive messages about his future that affirmed, "I am the top-ranked commercial real estate agent in Georgia. I have met the love of my life and we live in a house on a lake with our three children."

Every night, he would place the tape recorder by his bedside and listen to the life he was consciously trying to create. Soon his career began to grow, and when he moved into his dream house a decade later, he was delighted to discover the box of his original cassette tapes he had recorded. When he re-listened to the tapes, almost 100% of what he had said had come true. He had just hit a million dollars in sales and moved into a lake house with his wife and three children. He had manifested it ALL!

How did this work? And how can you manifest like this millionaire?

 The word is a force you cannot see — but you can see the manifestation of its force, the expression of the word, which is your own life.

~DON MIGUEL RUIZ

Understanding how our thoughts and ideas transfer out of the mental plane and onto the physical plane isn't magic, but it is a kind of alchemy. It's a science and craft you must master if you want to live in your full power. It's the creative alchemical algorithm of life. It's the truth of who and what you are, and it's how you are going to get where you're going faster than the speed of light.

The Speed of Thought

The knowledge that there are certain Universal Laws that are working for your highest and greatest good *even as you read this book* is the key to unlocking your ability to manifest what you desire. In the next few pages, you are going to learn how to apply the laws of manifestation and attraction to rocket into your best life using the speed of your thought.

 There are no coincidences or luck in life — there are only universal laws working to bring us what we have asked for through our energetic thought.

~JAMES REDFIELD

I invite you to begin to see your thoughts as energy equations that will manifest what you desire. Where your attention goes, energy flows. Indeed your thoughts are magnetic energy forms that draw in and attract like energies. As you nurture the intentions for your life with consistent positive thoughts, you will gain the creative power and momentum to make quantum leaps in your life. It's a type of mental alchemy that will open the door to your inner Merlin. And it is fueled by the speed and clarity of your thought.

We can trace our interest and experimentation with the creative forces of alchemy back as far as 3500 B.C.—to its origins in Hellenistic Egypt and subsequent climax during the European Renaissance. For four millennia, philosophers and craftsmen alike have attempted to apply alchemical knowledge and principles to transmute base metals into precious gold. Now, you are going to use these same kinds of alchemical principles to transform and transmute your life into something golden.

The Creation Equation

Applying the following Manifestation Formula, you will to learn how to activate the atoms of creation on the mental plane so you can have it ALL. And the good news is, crafting an incredible life requires five elements that are already naturally occurring within you.

 The universe is the periodical manifestation
of this unknown Absolute Essence.

~HELENA BLAVATSKY

Mastering the Five Essential Elements of Manifestation

Element 1 is DESIRE.

To manifest, you must first have a desire and then FOCUS on it with pure intention. Your thoughts must be clear to ascend from the mental plane into the manifestation plane. And your focus must be for **the long term**. The more passionate you are about your desire, the better. Just as you would want only the purest ingredients—the freshest meat, organic vegetables and herbs to create a fine dinner—you will need to have only the purest of thoughts to manifest your divine desires on the physical/earthly plane. Your intentions must be pure. And your thoughts unclouded by doubt, fear, greed, pride, jealousy, unworthiness or any emotion other than the pure joy at the "becoming" of your desire.

And how will you attain this purity of thought? *By thinking from your heart*— and not from your head. Some self-inquiry will be required. You will need to examine and monitor your motivations and thoughts to identify the source. Don't waste your energy fueling negative thoughts. They will hinder the flow of your creativity and weigh down your ability to fly. If doubts and negative thoughts appear, shift and lift them into the positive. As you do so, you will remove the blocks to God's power (and your higher power) channeling through you, and *you will begin to manifest with some amount of precision and timeliness.*

Element 2 is STUDY.

Study and learn about the subject of your desire. Drink up every bit of knowledge you can. Would it enhance your ability to achieve this goal or desire, if you had a certification or degree in the subject? Seek to surround yourself with others who have similar desires and likes. Join a professional, social or support group that is focused on this topic. When it comes to manifestation, you will find that group energies are more powerful than individual. In other words, your ability to manifest can be multiplied by like-minded folks who believe in and hold the same vision for your life. Proximity is power, and their presence will quicken your pace and progress.

Element 3 is ACTION.

Take thoughtful and concrete daily or weekly action towards your goal. For me, becoming a full-time writer started with committing to write at least four times a week. Ideally, I like to meditate first and then write. This is how I have created a pattern or habit of activity and energy investment that moves me towards my goal weekly, if not daily.

What habit or pattern can you commit to that will create forward motion towards your desire? Can you see how this activity "activates" the alchemy of your thoughts? Purposeful activity is an essential element that strengthens the creation equation and advances you towards your goal. You can't just think it, your actions have to help you "be" it.

Element 4 is GRATITUDE.

As you begin to see evidence of your manifestation capabilities (and you will) express your gratitude! The beauty and true gift of the law of manifestation is that the more you begin to trust and show gratitude for it, the more it will reveal itself to you. As your awareness increases, so will your power to manifest. If it's not obvious to you what you are manifesting, try keeping a daily journal and see what emerges in the way of synchronicities and concrete "wins" as you advance toward your ideal life.

Element 5 is PATIENCE.

Lastly, as you experiment in your manifestation "laboratory," I encourage you to be patient. Don't put a time stamp on when you must manifest your desire.

 Surrender is the act of being patient and trusting that the universe has heard your intention and is setting about attracting into your life the people, places and events that will create that intention.

~CAROL ADRIENNE

What you desire could happen quickly, but if it doesn't. *Don't give up. Don't stop believing. It will come.* It could take 24 hours or 24 months or even ten years. Just be persistent in the purity of your intention and deposit some energy—in the form of concrete action or visualization—towards your goal as often as you can. Keep putting coal in the fire. Keep your passion burning.

Genesis Point

You have the absolute power to create an exquisite life, a**nd my desire for you is that you will claim that power**. Use the Manifestation Formula and your faith in yourself to harness the power of your thought and create any life you wish.

Rest in the assurance that your thoughts and words are the genesis of your unique world. You and only you have dominion over that world. It is shaped by your desire and devotion. You are the master and maker of your kingdom. **And you can have it ALL.**

Dedicated to my children, Addison and Gabriel.

Special acknowledgment goes to my neighbor, friend and soul-sister, Amy Pazahanick. What a joy it is to have worked on this compilation book together. Lastly, I thank A Course in Miracles for reminding me that I have but one purpose here. I have only to be the presence of love.

MERRILL K. STANTON

MERRILL K. STANTON is a teacher of transformational change. A Licensed Heal Your Life® Coach/Workshop facilitator, hypnotherapist, author, and speaker with a private practice in San Diego, California. She sees clients in person or on Skype and conducts workshops throughout the world. She enjoys travelling and spending time with her daughters Hilary, Justine and son-in-law Rob in Los Angeles, California.

Merrill is also an Integrative Holistic Counselor. As a cancer survivor, she teaches the role of raw foods, green juices and cleanses to bring the body back to optimum health.

Stanton_Merrill@yahoo.com

❧ Miracles Are All Around Us

Let me say from the beginning I expect miracles every day. I believe they are all around us, and the signs and gifts of these miracles, are waiting for our discovery. Miracles come from a world we cannot see, yet they are part of the dance and fabric of our existence in this Universe. I do not doubt this as *miracles and love* are powerful energies that manifest and attract the life experiences we desire. I certainly don't claim to understand it fully but they seem to be intrinsically woven together. This knowing comes from a place within that I call my inner truth. It is what my soul tells me and I continue to trust more and more in the wisdom that comes from within. We all have powerful opportunities to experience miracles daily. I open the door to experiencing miracles with intentions and affirmations. I use them with regards to my health, finding love, creating financial security, meeting like-minded people, when I am travelling or just whatever comes to mind.

I Am Healed!

When I was diagnosed with late stage colon cancer in 2011, I was deeply concerned I may not live to see my daughters get older or even see them with their own future families. I kept thinking," I am too young to die". It was a shocking diagnosis! Within twenty-four hours, thankfully, I began connecting with stronger feelings and thoughts, "No, this is not the end for me. I will outlive this diagnosis! I can learn from this experience, help myself and others". My new *intention* became that I will be able to rise above the diagnosis, be healed and learn from it. I *trusted* these feelings and would not give in to fear. I began to use affirmations to find the right doctors and the right information to have my health restored perfectly. My surgeon and his staff did a magnificent job. The Naturopathic Doctor gave me wonderful supplements and suggested I research Optimum Health Institute in San Diego (OHI). This is a premier holistic detox program designed to look at food as medicine, while examining the role of toxic emotions, positive beliefs, forgiveness, gratitude and our own spiritual gifts as healing forces. In addition, they include classes in breathing techniques, meditation, yoga and all in a beautiful setting with like-minded people. A simple *intention* to listen and learn is powerful. At OHI, health issues are not regarded as health challenges. Instead, they are considered *opportunities to learn and grow*. That is a very positive thought and fits in perfectly with my own mindset as a Louise Hay teacher to transform our fears into love and healing. I could take my own cancer recovery now to a higher level of awareness. It transformed my own anxieties into a joyful experience of miracles and healing. I spent almost four months at OHI and I felt better than I could ever remember in my life. I stayed focused on the present moment while making new friendships. I was learning healthy lifestyle habits while letting go of daily stresses. We were encouraged to share with others what we were learning about ourselves instead of sharing stories about problems or illness. It was a time to go within, face fears, past hurts, release and forgive. It was a time to find new ways to show up for yourself and your relationships on the outside. This new perspective was freeing and exactly what my heart, body and immune system needed to return to perfect health. I came home to do blood tests and scans and continue to be cancer free. It has been more than six years. Hooray!

The Toolbox

I am a seeker of knowledge and love learning new things and experimenting with new thoughts. I am a born cheerleader! I am also a monk and very introspective. It is a way my soul allows me to give to the world around me and receive more of what life is all about; a sense of purpose, laughter, joy, friendship, family, love, gratitude and sharing. It's not complicated to activate and open the miracle doors in life. However, a few tools will make it easier. I remember when I first read Shakti Gawain's book called *Creative Visualization* in the 1980's, I tried every exercise she had in it and found I did have more self-confidence and faith in situations that had previously scared me. I learned that with *intention, visualization and affirmations* my world was affected in powerful ways beyond what I imagined. My favorite quote from her book is "This or something better, now manifests for me in totally satisfying and harmonious ways, for the highest good of all concerned." That thought coupled with a visualization of how I wanted things to turn out lifted me so much higher than my fears. It prepared me for such things as court hearings, depositions, public speaking and sharing honest feelings with others. It is something I have memorized. *My intention* is to communicate easily and effortlessly, to be appreciated for what I need to communicate, and to have it be a reciprocal experience. It works every time and yet when I forget to set this intention the experiences are never quite as good or magical. Could we have a relationship with guardian angels, a Universe, Higher Power or God beyond our physical realm? I believe so, and it is activated with intentions, affirmations and requests.

I Have Prosperity!

My first sign and miracle was when I was a single mother with two young children. My ex-husband didn't send me any child support. It was very difficult, under the circumstances, to pay for the rent, clothe and feed my family at the time. It was even harder to put together a resume for employment when I had been a young stay-at-home mother who had left college before getting my degree. I was overwhelmed with fury and rage whenever I needed to pay a bill, walk into a store, or get gas for my car, etc. this fury was always staring me in the face. How was I to handle an impossible situation? It engaged every aspect of my being. What helped me was looking at this same situation with new tools. I applied what I learned from Shakti Gawain's book and I also read passages in the Bible to help me cope. I decided then to get in touch with a wisdom within, to listen for a still small voice, and to open more fully to God's plans and the Universe that supports us all. I believed and trusted that all would work out.

Eventually, I responded to an employment Ad that didn't require a strong resume. The Ad led me to a hotel in Bridgeport, CT. When I arrived, the room was filled with a few hundred people all waiting patiently to hear how this business offer could open a door to new wealth and income. I was seated in the back of the room when an unlikely heavy set woman with a foreign accent appeared on the stage. She was carrying a *lighted* object with a vinyl cover over it. We heard her presentation and at the end, in a very loud voice she says "Wow!" taking the cover off with a great gesture. It was a lighted *sign* of a large parrot with the words PET STORE on top. Needless, to say, we were all in shock that this was the surprise! The opportunity to sell lighted signs for commission somehow didn't grab the imaginations of people including myself, in that room. She then said, "please remain if you would like to learn more about this opportunity." The room began to filter out quickly. There were so many people in the aisles heading for the door that I remained a bit longer in my seat. It was then I heard deep within, "Stay and listen more!" I literally felt glued to my seat. My "sign" with a sense of humor! I decided to stay along with five other people who were just as desperate to make income as myself. I made a commitment and sold outdoor lighted signs successfully. I also learned how to make cold calls, give presentations, close sales and gain needed self-confidence and higher self-esteem. I now had a stronger resume which led to my next opportunity. This new position came with a salary and a commission. The president of the company heard my story of the lighted signs. That clinched it for him. He said that normally he would not make an offer without experience in his field but if I could sell those lighted signs I will be successful in his company! I literally started with a sign which became my sign for a miracle unfolding.

Everything around us and within us is a powerful reflection of relationship. It's a powerful thought when applied to life's experiences. Miracles are everywhere. Don't give up and look for them!

Dedicated to all those people seeking miracles in their life.

A special thanks to the many authors I've learned from, teachers and mentors along the way, especially Louise Hay, Shakti Gawain, Florence Scovel Shinn, Patricia Crane, PhD, Rick Nichols and Jack Chisum, PhD from Arizona State University. And thanks to all my family, friends and classmates from The Wheatley School who supported me with their prayers and words of encouragement on my cancer journey and healing. Thank you to my guides, angels and ascended Masters who are helping me from the world beyond. Namaste.

APRIL L. DODD, M.A.

APRIL L. DODD, M.A. is an accomplished purpose alchemist, life coach, inspirational speaker, Senior Executive Coach, certified Leadership Circle Profile Practitioner, award-winning actress, author, and humbled mom of two spirited children who offer daily awareness's that there is no perfection, only loving possibilities. With a master's in spiritual psychology, numerous certifications and spiritual studies, and over fifteen years of individual work with spiritual teachers, nothing has ever awakened April's heart, mind, and soul more than the love lessons from her children.

April keeps her head above water in Chicago, IL, with her husband and two children, learning new levels of parenting with the addition of a Labrador puppy.

www.aprildodd.com

❦ Spiritual Leaders

Once upon a time, I thought I was spiritual. Then I became a parent. My spiritual teacher warned me of this. He said, "If you want to be enlightened, wait until after you have children." I guess he was thinking that raising children is a full-time job, and being reverent is also a full-time job. I might sink in the ocean of overwhelm if I tried both at the same time. But then there was this whole "before enlightenment chop wood, carry water, after enlightenment chop wood, carry water" thing, which foretells that enlightenment does not relieve one of the details of daily life ... or parenting, in my case. It means that there are no holidays for sacred practice or parenting. It means that we marry them together and participate as a divine being having and using our parenting experience for the highest good of all concerned.

Parenting, then, IS spiritual practice. Applied spirituality, in fact. And I feel most grateful that the highest good I have enjoyed is to have my children watch me do my devotional exercises so that they too can chop wood, carry water. It hasn't always been easy, but then sacred habits and parenting never promised to be. Turns out that who I am as a spiritual parent is defined by the practices I was willing to struggle for and model. I've meditated while having my children attached to my breast, or next to the crib with one hand inside it for comfort. I've gotten out of my bed at 2 a.m. to do yoga poses. I've listened to tantrums while inwardly chanting mantras of awakening. I've employed true forgiveness while stirring beans on the stovetop.

But spiritual practice as a parent isn't all about fitting our techniques into our world while meeting the demands of our children. It's about buying the time to do the things that create new possibilities for ourselves that leaves a legacy and creates a treasure for our children to find useful and meaningful in their world. Our way of being, then, is what they will remember, and the only way to *be* is memorable. I made it my personal rule to model what brings forward my deepest connection to Spirit, and what I'd want to support my children in their awakening in the love that they are in higher consciousness.

Thus, "By my presence be known" became my mantra. No matter what was unearthing in our family, no matter what button was being pushed, no matter how off-course one of us drifted (we all anchored ourselves in tantrums at times), I openly consulted my favorite spiritual practices to call myself forward into— and hang out as long as I could in— the awareness that I am divinely supported, guided, and sustained by Spirit. From *this* place, I could begin knowing newly that everything I do from here had the ripple effects I would want. Amazingly, my children's curiosity, along with their pain at wallowing in tantrums, brought them to me wanting to know how I was creating the calm, loving, and creative space inside me that allowed me, *at times,* to be the eye of the hurricane.

The first practice learned was on the floor. One of the most precious times I have spent with my son, Hamilton, was simply being quiet together. It began when he was four years-old, and after crawling into to our bed at 3 a.m. the night before, he awoke at seven o'clock in the morning to see me sitting in the middle of my bedroom floor—wrapped in a cozy soft blanket, legs crossed, eyes closed, facing the sunrise. I heard him rustle, and prayed he'd go back to sleep so I could have more time to anchor the beauty of my mystical reality rising within me, before bringing it forward to meet the needs of the reality of being a mom. His cries had interrupted my meditation many times during his short life, and I worked very hard to hold my interior focus as long as I could before succumbing to mommy focus.

As Hamilton slipped out of the sheets, I heard his little feet land and squish the shag of the carpet on their way closer to me. "Mommy?" he whispered, a centimeter from my ear. I wouldn't answer. He took his fingers to my eyes to try to pry them open. I tightened them. "Mommy? You dere?" I restrained from laughing, and pushed my inside attention to my breath. He tapped my shoulder. I sat perfectly still. Inside I was doing everything I could to use this as an opportunity to stay focused on Spirit as my source, not distraction as my reaction. After all, as a mom I wanted this steadiness to be the source that fed every action I took with myself and my children, since my number one job as a spiritual parent was to manage my own emotions, no matter what distraction came my way. I felt his nose touch my cheek, followed by a gentle kiss, before he lifted my blanket and crawled quietly into my lap, waiting for me to "return." Although he couldn't see what was going on inside me, Hamilton got the happy, smiling, calm and loving hug that came out the other side when I came "home" to him.

Many morning sits and hugs later, I completed my meditation before he awoke, leaving my blankets on the floor while I went to the restroom. My son came in and upon seeing my empty blankets, filled them with his own little crossed legs and closed eyes, facing the sunset on his own. I felt my eyes lift, a smile spread across my face as I backed away and let him have his moment.

Later that morning, my son asked me what I did when I sat under my blankets. For him and his particular age and mindset, I shared that although I often change up my routine to keep myself from getting stuck or attached to any one way, I always keep it new by practicing one key thing each time: I focus on (if not stalk) the pulse of newness I am aware of inside of me. I could say this to him because throughout his toddlerhood we'd say hello, good morning, or goodnight to the trees, doll friends, and to the energy of life pulsing all around us. I could ask him, "Have you said hi to Life Itself today?" and he seemed to understand this at his level. This became useful at the time of sharing my meditation focus, and created a curiosity from which he could now enter into his own system, however he decided that would look, whenever he decided to get to know the life force inside his own being.

There are plenty of avenues out there offering techniques to teach our kids to meditate, some with story, some with music or mantras, and I encourage everyone to find one that fits their family's values and devotional approach. For me, what I felt was most important was teaching that meditation wasn't about blissing out or checking out, but about participating with the pulse of aliveness that beats within everyone of us. I understand the importance that subtle things inside must get played out on the outside in order to get attention. If we place our attention inside, we can begin to walk in the awareness of the loving and tenderness of the Life that resides inside of us, always. It is this Life that we bring with us wherever we go and whatever block of wood we must chop along our way.

But each child comes into the world with a different sacred curriculum, and will appreciate the spiritual practices that resonate most with their soul's yearning. My eight-year-old daughter, Grace, resonated most with the creative side of connecting with possibilities. After losing so much of what she loved through our move from Austin to Chicago when she was seven, and a year's worth of handling a new school, new home, new culture and neighborhood, as well as the heart-wrenching loss of her favorite and only grandma, she accepted my offer to join me in doing an honoring ceremony.

In this ceremony, Grace helped me light candles while setting an intention that its light would break through any darkness that either of us were holding about ourselves, others, or Life Itself in regards to our new environment. This sacred step brought forward feelings of grief for her, and the awareness that she was afraid to cry about her beloved grandma for fear that it meant letting her go. I realized then that she believed that if she cried, it acknowledged that grandma was truly gone, and that was far too great a grief for this granddaughter to feel. Instead Grace believed she could hold on to her grandmother if she never put herself through the sadness of her leaving. My heart ached watching her wet eyes well-up in the candlelight, yet the ancient sacredness of being a mother watching her daughter grieve her grandmother gave me the gift of holding a space of generations of tenderness for my own daughter's process.

After a moment of hugs, we took small slips of paper and wrote on them what we loved about Grandma, what she loved about us, and what fears we'd like to let go of. We then offered them into the fireplace, along with a heartfelt prayer asking that they be transformed into something new, or we lifted them up to be held in Grandma's heart forever, for the highest good of all concerned. This process, held in the sacredness of our intention, allowed us to shine the light on the darkness as we acted as a stabilizing force holding in the quiet loving space that defined who we are as mother and daughter, and as divine beings having a human experience.

The final honoring in our ceremony used the new energy lifted into our hearts by the fire transformation to create what's called an Ideal Scene. It's like a manifestation map, a way of acknowledging what we want to create in our lives, while honoring what is seeking to emerge through us, if we would only give it loving attention. I'd been using this heartfelt visual tool for fifteen years to manifest my heart's desire and my most important and long-held dreams.

Grace was happy to see I'd brought her favorite scented markers and clean white paper to create a heart in the middle of the page big enough to write "I am" in the center of it.

Extending out from the heart she wrote "spokes" of intention statements, stated in the positive present tense. I was amazed to see her take to it so easily, writing, "I am easily being in my loving with my brother" and "I am a great big sister" as her most sincere intentions to raise the level of relationship she was working to create with Hamilton, her only brother.

As a close to our ceremony, we blew out each candle with a prayer of thanks and appreciation to the Guidance that supported us through the unfolding of our process. We then found a window-lit sacred place next to our favorite Buddha (who happens to leave notes for the kids every now and then) on the stairway landing to hang our Ideal Scenes where we could see them every day. To keep the energy alive, Grace made a small basket with pens and sticky notes next to our scenes so we could each write daily action steps aligned with manifesting our "spoke of choice" for that day.

Over the coming months, you could find us on the stairway next to a mosaic of sticky notes enjoying many heartfelt chats about Grandma's love and how our action steps were coming along in manifesting our Ideal Scenes. This unique configuration that is my daughter was becoming the evidence that Spirit found Its celebration through her, and I was a blessed parent to be a memorable witness along the way.

There is no either/or to being a spiritual parent. Our own hallowed path will give us children as easily as it will give us a shaved head and a cave in which to meditate. What Spirit cares most about is what you do with it. I think the key for me has been to surrender to the present circumstances and realize that I'm always being guided ... sometimes that means sitting in silence and sometimes it means cooking beans. I try to chop wood and carry water with reverence and remembering that I am the drop *not* the ocean.

To Grace, you are the brightest light in my cloudy days. To Hamilton, you are the magic in the mundane. You are both miracle workers, and a true gift from Heaven.

Moms out there, you've got this. I deeply love and acknowledge you for your journey through parenthood, self-care, and soul care. Keep it up. Generations of moms have your back, and so does the Universe.

VALENTINA GALANTE

VALENTINA GALANTE is Certified Heal Your Life® Workshop Leader, Life Coach, and Founder of KickAss Joy. She is dedicated to using her inner peace, compassion, and insight to inspire and guide people to experience their own inner peace and kick-ass joy in a world where everyone loves themselves and each other unconditionally.

She and her two daughters live in Bradenton, Florida, where they enjoy going to the beach, wearing their mermaid tails, and discovering new ways to have FUN!

athomeValentina@aol.com
www.kickassjoy.com

❧ The Art of Noise

❧ Sound: "the sensation produced by stimulation of the organs of hearing by vibrations transmitted through the air or other medium."

Aaaaahhhhh, my children's laughter, a babbling brook, birds chirping to greet the day, a beautiful melody… these are just some of my favorite sounds. As a person blessed with a high sensitivity to what I hear, I've always noticed the sounds around me, and have paid close attention to how they make me feel. Sound is vibration, like everything else in the Universe, so it naturally follows that it would have a great influence on our well-being. When we perceive it as pleasant, it affects us in positive ways, and when it becomes excessive, or discordant, it becomes noise and can affect us negatively.

I remember a time, years ago, when I was an International Flight Attendant with a major airline. I had a home-based business, was stuck in an unhappy marriage, was experiencing other family issues, had two wonderful very energetic daughters to take care of and was not managing my stress very well. I became hypersensitive to all sounds, including the ones I used to love, was anxious all the time, and was completely overwhelmed. I eventually developed health issues so severe that my life came to a screeching halt. I was scared, and didn't know if I'd ever have a normal life again. I knew I had to make some changes.

During that time, I was introduced to a book by Louise L. Hay called *You Can Heal Your Life*. This book changed my life! I learned, among other things, that I was co-creating my reality with my thoughts, words and focus. I learned that thoughts, like sound, have a vibration, and they become "noise" in our head when they are negative, excessive, or obsessive. They can contribute greatly to our stress levels. I learned that specific thoughts could affect specific areas of the body. For instance, people who have lower back issues often have worries about the future and about money. Louise's book includes a huge list of physical ailments, their probable causes, and the suggested new thought patterns to help heal that area of the body.

I became fascinated with learning more about the mind/body connection and even started seeing a biofeedback therapist. My therapist hooked me up to monitors that measured my skin temperature, muscle tension, and brainwave activity. I was able to see on the monitors how my thoughts affected my body, and that when I changed my thought patterns, it had a very positive, or healing effect on me. It was strong proof for me that if I changed my thoughts, and that if I quieted the negative mind chatter, I could change my life.

My transformation was quite dramatic once I learned this information! I was eventually able to completely turn my life around. My body now feels wonderful, I love my life, and am finally able to feel real joy in a way in which I never had before. I became so passionate about helping those in emotional pain turn their lives around as well, that I became a Certified Heal Your Life® workshop leader and life coach in the philosophy of Louise Hay. What follows are just a few of the many tools I used to quiet both the inner noise and external noise in my life that helped me heal, and that I now use to help others to access their own inner peace and happiness too.

Pay Attention to Your Thoughts

 Be the silent watcher of your thoughts and behavior. You are beneath the thinker. You are the stillness beneath the mental noise. You are the love and joy beneath the pain.

~ECKHART TOLLE

This was a *big* one for me. The Law of Attraction states that what we focus on expands. One reason I had been so stressed-out was because for many years I kept focusing on what *wasn't* working in my life. I was continually focused on my frustration about it. It just seemed to be automatic. I would obsess about things that had occurred, would talk about it often and would worry about things that might happen in the future, without realizing that doing so caused me more stress and that it attracted more negative experiences to me. I was in a contracted, fear-based energy or vibration. When I finally learned to pay attention to those thoughts and learned how to turn them around, everything changed.

Whenever I caught myself worrying or complaining during those early days, I would say "STOP, Valentina! What are you thinking about?" This exercise was *extremely* helpful in allowing me to realize exactly where I needed to make changes in my thinking. I then would focus instead on what I wanted to *create* in my life, what I was grateful for, and on using positive affirmations. To this day, if I'm feeling stressed I ask that same question, and then consciously turn my thinking around. I now say many positive affirmations daily, which helps keep me in that positive space. I now feel like I'm in the flow of life, and good things are happening every day. It feels great!

Our *perception* about events has a tremendous impact on our inner peace and happiness, as well. My mentor, Marci Shimoff, author, featured teacher in the movie *The Secret*, and happiness expert, encourages us to look at the "gifts and the lessons" in every situation. Although doing so is not always easy, it *can* be incredibly rewarding. *Every* time I do this when it comes to a difficult situation in my life, or when I think about something that has happened in my past, I learn from it, gain valuable insight, and feel more peaceful. It quiets that negative mind chatter. Marci Shimoff has also taught me to ask, "If this were happening for a bigger purpose, for my soul's growth, what would that be?" We can learn from every situation, and when we are able to slow down and look at the bigger picture, it can bring great clarity, understanding, and calm. We may not always have control over what happens in life, but we always have control over how we look at it.

Self-Love

 Loving yourself is the most important thing you can do, because when you love yourself, you are not going to hurt yourself or anyone else. It's the prescription for world peace.

~LOUISE L. HAY

Sometimes we are our own worst critics. I know I was. Through reading *You Can Heal Your Life* by Louise L. Hay, I learned the importance of loving myself. It was a *huge* game-changer for me. I started to pay attention to some of the ways in which I would criticize myself, and gradually stopped saying anything negative about myself, even jokingly. When I learned how to quiet my inner critic, it was incredibly healing.

When I was going through my divorce, I would look at myself in the mirror, and say nice, kind, loving things to myself... out loud! It's what helped me get through that emotionally-challenging time. Whenever I felt down, I would just talk to myself and praise myself for what I was doing right, for being strong, for being loving to my two daughters, and for persevering. My kids probably thought I was "coo-coo", but that's okay. For those of you with teenagers, you know that's kind of par for the course anyway, right? When we love ourselves, we also set a great example for our children. So many kids—especially adolescents—feel insecure, and don't feel "good enough" compared to others. When we can send them out into the world knowing their worth, they will also reach for all the good the Universe has to offer.

If it sounds strange to talk to yourself in the mirror, just imagine what you might say to your best friend in that situation, or to your 5-year-old self. Then look at yourself in the mirror and say one positive thing. That's a good start. Start by doing it every morning and you'll see that it becomes easier and easier.

Ultimately, we're the only person we're guaranteed to be with from the first day of our lives, until the last day. Doesn't it make sense, then, to create the most harmonious, positive, and loving relationship with ourselves? Doesn't it make sense, then, to be our own best friend? When we treat ourselves with love, we go into the world in a more peaceful way. When we love ourselves, we won't put up with being in dysfunctional relationships, we don't stay in jobs where we're not appreciated, and we don't mistreat our bodies. Instead, we reach for quality in our lives because we feel deserving of all the good the Universe has for us, not in an arrogant way, but in a grateful way. It keeps us in an expanded energy which brings more happiness and joy into our lives.

Get rid of the drama!

 There comes a time in your life, when you walk away from all the drama and people who create it. You surround yourself with people who make you laugh. Forget the bad, and focus on the good. Love the people who treat you right, pray for the ones who don't.

~JOSE N. HARRIS

Drama in our relationships causes both inner and outer noise that affects us in many ways. In her book, *Happy for No Reason*, Marci Shimoff shares that "our relationships have a biochemical effect on our bodies. When we make healthy connections with people, our brains flood our cells with happiness chemicals, and when we have unhealthy social interactions, harmful chemicals are released." She also cites a study by Daniel Goleman, author of *Emotional Intelligence*, and *Social Intelligence*, that shows that "emotions spread from one person to another much like a cold, and that while it can be good to 'catch' an uplifting feeling, it can be damaging to take on others' feelings of anger, jealousy, anxiety, or hate."

So, if we want to feel good, it is extremely important to examine our relationships. Sometimes our best teachers are those with whom we have the most difficulty, and we can experience the most inner growth from interacting with those people. However, if we know that we can be positively or negatively affected by the relationships we have with others, we have to be very careful to limit the time we spend with toxic, chronically-negative people who always complain, who are always unhappy, who are always creating drama, and who are what I call "energy vampires". All of that drama can be extremely distracting, and is a waste of our time and energy. Stepping back from or letting go of a relationship that is unhealthy or toxic can be one of the healthiest moves to make. We can't change the people around us, but we *can* change the people we choose to be around.

It's up to each of us to heal ourselves. No one else can do it for us, and we cannot do it for someone else. We only have control over ourselves, and it's important for us not to create drama, too. Our job is to stay on our side of the street and do our own inner work. What someone else does is completely up to them. We can let them go while wishing them love and healing and, when we let those unhealthy relationships go, it creates a space, or opens a door for the Universe to bring an even better-suited person to us. As I went through this letting go process myself, I felt lonely at first, but once I had created that space, I found that I started meeting wonderful new people. I'm now blessed to have loving and healthy friendships with people I can truly trust, and I'm finally able to relax in the knowing that I no longer have to be on guard for any drama.

Meditation

 The best time to take a five-minute break to sit still, be quiet, and listen to your breathing is when you think you have the least time for it. The busier you are and the more overwhelmed you feel, the more you need the clarity and decluttering of meditation.

~PH.D., GARY R. MCCLAIN

For those of you who don't meditate, you may be saying "oh my gosh, here we go again with that meditation message!" I can relate! I resisted, and resisted, and resisted meditating... for years! My first experience with it was when I flew to Raleigh, North Carolina to attend Oprah's *Live Your Best Life* tour. Oprah and Cheryl Richardson spent the whole day sharing great insights into how to live a meaningful and enjoyable life. At one point Oprah encouraged those of us in the audience to close our eyes, take some deep breaths, silently ask "what am I here to learn?" then be quiet for 15 minutes or so. There I sat, in perfect silence and as I found myself relaxing, I heard a voice say "To Love". It wasn't a real voice, it came from somewhere inside, and I remember feeling surprised and a little indignant at that answer. "To Love?" I remember thinking, "I know how to love, what the heck are you talking about?" Immediately, I heard that voice again... and it said, "Yourself." Well, that shut me up. Bingo. It's exactly what I knew I still had to work on at that time of my life. I felt humbled and in awe of how powerful that answer was. I know that answer was the Truth with a capital T.

That experience peaked my curiosity about meditation. I incorporated it more and more often, and even learned Transcendental Meditation, which is done twice a day for 20 minutes each time. I had never felt such a feeling of energized calm. I know that sounds contradictory, but I felt a deep calm inside, coupled with an increase in natural, calm energy. Meditation accomplishes two goals for me. It allows me to quiet both the inner and outer noise in my life. I credit meditation for my increased intuition, mental clarity, and for helping me feel the guidance from God, the angels, my guides, and my higher self.

Do I meditate twice a day, every day? No. When I do, however, I feel SO much better! I've learned not to beat myself up when I skip a few meditations. As a single mom of two busy teenagers, I do my best! Meditation for me is like a mini vacation, twice a day. It's an opportunity to listen to my soul and is a way to feel deep, inner peace. I would highly, highly recommend it. Even if all you can do is sit still, turn off the phone, close your eyes and breathe for five minutes, it will be beneficial. I promise!

Silence the external noise

> If you listen closely enough to the silence, you
> may just hear something incredible: You.

~JEFF FOSTER

Have you noticed that we seem to be moving at a faster pace than ever, and that we're exposed to more noise and information than ever? In Shawn Achor's book *Before Happiness: the 5 Hidden Keys to Achieving Success, Spreading Happiness, and Sustaining Positive Changes* he cites a report that shows that per capita time spent consuming information in American households increased by 60% between 1980 and 2008. Wow! As humans, part of our natural instinct is to pay attention to sounds and stimuli around us—it's part of our survival instinct. Our minds are constantly trying to differentiate between important information and unimportant information. However, our brains can only pay attention to a certain amount of information at one time.

When we go on brain overload, it takes a toll on our health and well-being, and keeps us from leading our best lives. Shawn Achor also shares in *Before Happiness* that, according to research in positive psychology and neuroscience, by consciously decreasing the flood of information our brains receive by just five percent, we can improve our chances of boosting the positive signals that our brains receive which will point us to better decisions, improved health, and greater achievement.

So how can we do that? Since everyone is different, my suggestion is to pick a day, and set the intention to pay very close attention to how you feel throughout that day. Notice what sounds and stimuli are pleasant for you, and which ones bother you. It's what I did during that extremely stressful time in my life. I then made a plan. For me, it meant limiting my time watching television, muting the commercials when I did watch television, avoiding violent or noisy television shows, and discontinuing the habit of watching the same news stories over and over. I stopped obsessively checking my e-mail and limited it to only looking at it several times a day. I turned the ringer off on my phone when I needed to focus on a task. I avoided noisy places when I could, and would avoid busy traffic whenever possible. I made many more changes, and as I did, I began to feel much calmer. That, along with the inner work I was doing enabled me to feel better and better every day.

So, although that period of time of overwhelm was very difficult me, the gift it provided was that it gave me the awareness that we all create our own reality through the Law of Attraction. The lessons I learned were that I needed to pay attention to my thoughts, practice self-love, eliminate drama and dysfunction in my life, and quiet my mind and outside noise so I could hear the beautiful messages my soul and God give me every day.

I'm so grateful that I can experience the richness that life has to offer, and to feel true happiness! As a life coach, I now delight in guiding others to experience their own healing so they, too, can be more aware and lead happier, more vibrant lives filled with kick-ass joy!

To all of my soul sisters on this life journey with me. Thank you for inspiring me to reach for my highest self by your example. I am in awe of you.

Dedicated to my daughters, Tatiana and Isabella. You are both so beautiful, inside and out. I am constantly amazed by your inner wisdom and ability to clearly see the truth. Thank you for blessing me with the honor of being your mother. May you always know your worth, have inner peace, and live the life of your dreams. I love you.

LOWELL OWEN GILLESPIE

LOWELL OWEN GILLESPIE has lived most of his life on the same central Illinois farm while working at a local university and serving our country for 20 years in the Illinois National Guard. He has served as a youth director, Sunday School teacher, Sunday School Superintendent, Music Booster President, Lay Leader, Steven Minister, Hospice Helper, 4-H Leader, FFA Councilman and Master Gardener. He and his wife and best friend, Judy, raised four wonderful kids together. He loves to share the Gospel with others and loves writing poetry.

logillespie@eiu.edu

🕊 FAITH, HOPE, and LOVE

I am the father of the organizer of this book and would like to tell you how she developed into the beautiful woman and seasoned counselor she is today. During my many heart problems I have had throughout the years, Katina was sometimes the only one who could say the right words to get me back on my journey to better mental and physical health.

I named this chapter "FAITH, HOPE, and LOVE" for good reason. These entities are described in the Bible (1 Corinthians 13:13) as realities that will last forever. Katina's middle name is FAITH and her sister Kimberly's middle name is HOPE. Katina experienced God's LOVE from her family as she grew up with two brothers and one sister on the family farm. Her oldest brother's name is Michael (Angel in charge of the Lord's army and the one who escorts people from life to death). Her other brother's name is Matthew (a disciple of Jesus) who we consider our ambassador to China.

Katina began her counseling training at the age of eleven when her sixteen-year-old sister would come home late at night and wake her up to tell her everything that happened during the night out and the emotions she was having at this time of her life. As a result of these late-night sister to sister talks, Katina became a very good listener.

She developed a very good work ethic while working on the family farm, raising goats, planting potatoes in the garden, mowing the yard and driving the baler tractor in the hay field. At about the same time her early counseling sessions were taking place she was also taking care of her herd of goats. One year on April 1, she came into the house after feeding her goats to tell us one of her nanny goats had just given birth to twins. We did not believe her since it was April Fool's Day. She said, *"Really, there are two baby goats out in the pen. Come on out and see for yourself."* Sure enough, there were two kids standing on wobbly legs getting their first taste of their momma's milk. Since one of them was a male, she stated *"I'm going to take this goat to the Coles County 4-H Show next year, win Grand Champion Market Goat, then take it to the slaughter house so we can eat him."* Everything happened just like she said it would. Katina learned early on that following through with her goals was very beneficial and rewarding.

When she became old enough to drive, she and some of her friends gathered in front of their favorite restaurant on Route 16 across from Morton Park. A young man drove up on his brand-new motorcycle and ask if anyone wanted to take a ride. She and a friend squabbled over who would take the first ride with him on his shiny pride and joy. Katina won the squabble, but before she jumped on the back of the of the motorcycle, her friend held out her newly purchased leather jacket for her to wear. She slid her arms into the soft suede sleeves of the borrowed jacket, hopped on the seat behind the young man just before they sped off on the first ride of the hoped to be many rides of the evening. Zipping down Fourth Street past the Wesley United Methodist Church they rounded the curve that lead out of town and charged off toward Lincoln Log Cabin. Turning around before reaching their destination, they rocketed back toward town. As they maneuvered around the Fourth Street curve at the edge town, the bike skidded on some loose gravel hurling both of them off the new bike. The leather jacket was lacerated as Katina slid across the asphalt and her head bounced on the hard surface as she was flung into the ditch. The young man was not hurt. A classmate of hers and her boyfriend drove upon the scene shortly after it happened. He went for help while her classmate held her head up out of the water filled ditch until the paramedics arrived. This happened before there were cell phones.

We rushed to the hospital emergency room as soon as we heard the news, arriving shortly after they brought her in. All her friends were crowded in the waiting room praying for her. I ran back and forth from her room to the waiting room informing them of her condition. She suffered a severe head injury from hitting the hard asphalt but not a scratch was found on the rest of her body. The leather jacket saved her from scarring her body and might have even saved her life. The doctors decided to transfer her up to another hospital 50 miles away, where they were better equipped to treat head injuries.

When she arrived at the hospital, they placed an ice pad over her to reduce her body temperature to prevent her brain from swelling. They also put her in a coma so she would not move. Her brain had bounced around in her head when it hit the pavement. They kept her in a coma for a week. We would take turns sitting with her, telling her how much we loved her. Matthew read books to her during his time with her. As she was coming out of the coma she started saying random numbers which no one could figure out why. We finally looked up to where she was pointing on the wall and saw numbers scrolling across a screen.

Brother Michael (the guardian angel) came home from his Naval ship off the coast of California to be with her during her recovery. Since he was used to being up during the nighttime hours, he took the graveyard shift to keep an eye on her. One night she decided she had to go to the bathroom, so she slipped out of bed without setting off the bed alarms nor waking up her brother. When Mike noticed she was gone, he panicked: he had shirked his duty. Relief came to him when she came out of the bathroom and hopped back into bed.

From the very beginning of this tragic ordeal, my wife and I had an unexplainable heavenly peace come over us. We both knew that whatever happened to Katina was okay, even if she did not survive. We knew that God was in control. This comforting peace was reinforced as friends and family came to pray for us and to just be with us.

The young man who was driving the motorcycle was very perplexed. He came to the hospitals several times to see how she was doing and told us over and over how sorry he was about the accident. My wife and I had every reason to be angry at him, but we were not. We did everything we could to comfort him and assure him we forgave him completely. He just could not understand why we were not upset with him. God's ways are higher than man's ways.

Katina was in rehab for several weeks after her accident learning how to walk and talk again. My wife and I made the fifty-mile trip up to be with her every day. Sister Kim stopped in to give her HOPE. Matthew went up and read to her as much as he could between his college classes.

The father of the friend who lent the jacket organized a fundraiser night to raise money for our extra expenses we entailed during Katina's recovery from her accident. A large number of people attended the event. Her Mother went to the event to thank everybody for their love and concern.

When she finally came home for good, she had missed out on so much school that we had to get a tutor for her so she could complete her junior year of high school. When she went back to school in the fall, the kids were astonished to see her walking and talking again. However, the school administrators would not let her back on the varsity cheerleading squad because they did not want to be liable for any further injuries she might receive while performing her cheerleading routines. This hurt her almost as much as the accident. After she graduated from high school she got accepted at the local university and immediately tried out and made the Freshmen Cheerleading Team. The Gillespie family is tough. The lasting difficulties of her accident were her loss of smell and taste, frequent headaches, confusion and depression. FAITH, HOPE, and LOVE brought us all through Katina's nightmare.

The next summer between the university classes, she signed up for the Miss Coles County Fair pageant. Although she had a gait in her walk, she gracefully walked up and down the stage and delivered a beautiful but slurred speech about how she overcame the struggles she encountered while recuperating from her accident. This speech boosted her desire to help people overcome their difficulties no matter what has happened to them.

While serving on the student senate at the university, her desire to motivate people to change their lifestyles became evident when she spearheaded the recycling program. This program had been tried two other times but fizzled out both times it was attempted. With determination, she never gave up when she took on the challenge. She contacted the university president, vice-president, physical plant manager, student senate, a local metal recycling company, and others to start the recycling program that has now lasted over 25 years. I helped her place the first recycling containers inside buildings where they would be more assessable to the students and office personnel.

Wanting to serve the university in a more influential way Katina decided to run for president of the student senate. Some of the students that were opposing her threatened her life and made it so stressful for her that she dropped out of school. Shortly after removing herself from the stress, she decided she would finish her education out of state where a specific psychology professor taught. She wanted to leave immediately. I told her she was not leaving without having a place to stay. She made some calls and had a place to stay that very same day.

We helped her pack what she could into her old beat up mini station wagon and off she went on her 350-mile drive. Knowing that she would need a job to support herself she stopped at a well-known chain restaurant close to where she would be living. As she opened the door to the restaurant she was greeted by a young waiter who ask if he could help her. When she informed him she was looking for employment he said he would take her to the manager. On the way, he asked, *"What is your name?"*

"Katina Gillespie"

"Where are you from?"

"Charleston, Illinois"

"Do you know Lowell Gillespie?"

"He is my dad."

"While going to National Guard meetings with your dad, I attended the church services he was presiding over each month. If it weren't for your dad, I would not be a Christian today."

Distraught by the circumstances life threw at her, Katina had her FAITH and HOPE renewed when she found God's LOVE had gone before her to prepare the way. A small world and a big God.

In 1998, on Friday before her mother's birthday, she got a call from her big sister telling her that their dad was going to have open heart surgery early on the following Monday, but the doctors told him he might not last over the weekend. Still not functioning very well herself, she drove the seven and one-half hour trek to give HOPE and LOVE to her dad. After the successful triple bypass surgery, Katina drove all the way back to Memphis to continue her employment at the chain restaurant.

After working at the restaurant for a year, Katina enrolled in classes at the University on a full ride medical scholarship due to her head injury. She also started working as a lab manager for the Psychology professor she moved to study under.

During one of her visits home she got involved with a man that she eventually married. His drinking habits and mental abuse turned out to be too much for Katina, so for her own safety, she got out of that troubled marriage. She inherited all the debt they had accumulated which she eventually paid off by working long hard hours in the restaurant business. Before their divorce and after Katina graduated from the university, they moved to Florida so he could go to culinary school. Since Katina wrote all his papers for him, she learned everything about managing restaurants.

Putting this knowledge to good use, she worked her way up through hostess, waitress, bartender and manager of restaurants in Florida and Maryland. She worked twelve to fifteen hours a day (sometimes three weeks in a row without a day off) which stressed her out so much it was too much for her already weakened condition. The whole left side of her body started going numb. Since she could not push the clutch down in her little manual shift sports car, we traded her car with ours to take some of the stress of driving from her. Realizing the restaurant business was draining her mentally and physically, she changed from managing restaurants to managing hotels where she used her skills as a manager in a less stressful atmosphere.

Working her way up in the hotel management industry, she was awarded manager of the year, winning a trip to the Bahamas. Soon afterwards she landed a training and development position where she trained hundreds of employees how to do their jobs effectively. Then, having some different viewpoints with the hotel work environment, she left. Looking for some less stressful work she started working as an office manager for a local service and supply company. Katina was a big asset to them since she loved working with spread sheets and organization.

This employment stint also came to an end when she met the man of her dreams. I had been praying that God would send a man into her life that would take care of her. She was looking for a relationship that would last. When they came up to Illinois for a special visit, I shared my prayer with him. He quickly told me, *"Here I am. I will take care of her if she will let me."* When he asked me for her hand in marriage, I gave both of them my blessing. I have never seen her so happy.

She wanted to be married down by the creek here on the home farm when they came back up to Illinois for our 50th wedding anniversary. As time for the big anniversary and the wedding drew near, they realized they could not afford flying everyone they wanted to be here for their wedding from Florida and other places. I personally think they probably spent too much on our anniversary.

Katina spearheaded plans for the anniversary with her siblings. Watching the four of them having fun while preparing for the event was one of the biggest blessings of the whole celebration.

After the anniversary, they hurried home to continue making plans for their wedding. The two of them got married on the same day they planned in a beautiful garden close to their home with a few of their close friends attending. They gave up their original plans of having their wedding by the creek on our farm so they could spend their time and resources planning our 50th wedding anniversary. John 15:13 in The New Living Bible says, *"There is no greater love than to lay down one's life for one's friends."*

The lessons I have learned watching Katina travel through her life are these:

- Where a person is raised makes a difference
- How one is raised makes a difference
- Troubling times are a part of life
- Do what to takes to overcome times of trouble
- Learn from these troubled times
- Use experiences to improve life
- Enjoy life each and every day
- Have FAITH in yourself
- Always HOPE that good days are ahead of you.
- LOVE others more than you love yourself.
- Know God is with you wherever you go.

Meeting people from all walks of life throughout her lifetime and in her unique types of employment experiences has prepared Katina for the counseling position she is presently in today. She can relate to the physical and mental hardships people are going through enabling her to help everyone who asks her how to cope with their struggles. Her FAITH instills HOPE in people so they can learn how to LOVE again.

I want to dedicate this story to Katina. Thank you for being who you are and using your life experiences to help other people. Love You.

AUBREY RHODEN

AUBREY RHODEN is a wife, mother, internationally published author, photographer, and artist. I'm a native of Colorado, but find most of my inspiration from the South, where I lived & attended the University of Tampa. I come from a long line of storytellers, grew up camping in the Colorado mountains, and even lived in a bus for a few years. I write to create something that can be passed on from generation to generation. I write for my children, for my friends and family, and for anyone who needs a little reminder that this so-called "life" we are living is ever-changing. With my stories, I have only one hope: that just a sliver of something I have said will leave an imprint on another's heart forever.

You can purchase my books directly from me and receive an autographed copy at www.arhoden.com or find them on Amazon and Barnes and Noble.

❦ The Letter

She was always prepared. One night a few years ago, I found her up late in her office, crying. When I went to comfort her, she said she had just finished two letters, one to the children and one to me.

"Letters? What for?" I asked.

"Just in case."

"In case of what?"

"Just in case something ever happens to me. You won't have to explain life without me to the children, you can just read."

I stood up from the bathroom floor, realizing I had locked myself in last night and cried myself to sleep. I looked into the mirror. I was always a strong man, never one to really show my emotions, but as I looked at myself, more tears began to pour down my face. I knew a part of me had died with her last night. "Daddy, are you ok?" a tiny voice called for me from the hall.

I quickly washed my face and began trying to pull myself together. "I'll be out in a second, buddy."

Hunched over the bathroom counter, I peered through a stream of tears. From the corner of my eye, I saw the unopened letters laying on the floor, next to the full glass of scotch I couldn't bring myself to take a sip of last night. I heard another little knock on the door. It was our other son, the youngest, "Daddy, where's Mommy? I can't find her anywhere." I tried to bend down, falling over just a little; I was sick with emotion. I grabbed the letters, folding mine into the back pocket of my jeans while I held the other addressed to the boys.

I opened the door and two little boys were standing there in their jammies, both looking up at me with their beautiful, but worried blue eyes. Just then the doorbell rang. I knew who it was…family. Before I could make it downstairs, people started piling in. Everyone was crying. Again, our youngest turned to me and asked "Daddy, what's wrong? Where's Mommy?" I could see that the boys were both obviously scared now. I started to panic again, but remembered what she'd said: "You won't have to explain life without me to the children, you can just read." I took the boys' hands and brought them into my oldest son's room. After I'd sat them on the floor, with my hands shaking, I began opening the sealed envelope as I slowly slid down the wall with total exhaustion, settling between them.

"Something happened to Mommy last night, boys. She wants me to read you this letter, to help you understand. Would that be ok?" I whispered to them. They nodded and I cleared my throat, knowing I was about to deliver my wife's final words to our children.

I began, trying desperately to hold myself together.

My Sweethearts,

If Daddy is reading this letter to you, you must be wondering where I am, and what's going on. Please do not be afraid, my boys, because I am always going to be watching over you. Just like the wind that caresses your cheek, and the sun that warms your body, I will be by your side. Life is a gift. Love and live each day as it could be your last, because someday, it will be. I wrote this letter with hopes that you would never have to read it, but unfortunately no one can ever know when their time is up. Yesterday, I was called back home, for reasons unknown. Death is part of life, but there is one thing you should expect: The sun will rise tomorrow and then it will set, only to rise once again. A lot of things will be different, but love will surround you like a blanket until you feel safe again. We are a family and Daddy will always be there to remind you of my love and answer any questions you may have about life, love, or who I was as a person. I am lucky enough to be able to watch over you like an angel, now I will always be by your side. Wipe your tears of sadness away and know that time will heal your hearts. You will survive this pain and I have written this letter to you so that you can re-read it anytime you need to feel my love and guidance. Use these words as a compass to steer you toward your destiny. This is the first day of the next chapter in your life. Be brave, my sweet boys. You are superheroes. Every superhero rises from something terrible and becomes even greater than he ever thought was possible. Give Daddy a hug and kiss because I am right here watching him read this. Have I told you lately how much I love you? I hope you feel my love, because that feeling is something that will never be able to be taken from you. It's a part of your soul now, that's why love is the greatest gift you can possibly give.

My voice cracked as I fought to keep from falling apart. Trying to control my emotions, I watched the color in our children's faces drain, they were in shock—we all were. What was I supposed to say? What am I supposed to do? No one can prepare you for this. The kids crawled into my lap and I explained to them about the car accident, that she didn't suffer or feel any pain. She was with the angels now—*our angel.*

"If Mommy is gone, will we still be a family?" our youngest asked, fighting his tears.

"I will be your Daddy forever, and Mommy will always be with us. We are a family. Change is just a part of our lives now. If anything, our love for everything will be stronger."

We cried together. I squeezed both children tightly to my chest as they buried their sobbing faces into me. After what seemed like hours locked in embrace with these two heartbroken boys, I cleared my throat and pushed to regain some composure.

By the time I felt I could read on, both children had fallen asleep on the floor, leaning into me. I squinted and wiped away the tears, picked the letter back up and continued to read quietly to myself.

I have loved you all like there was no tomorrow, then one day, there wasn't. I want you to plant an oak tree in my memory, and put a bench underneath its branches so that you can lie there and watch them sway. Spread my ashes to the wind, then turn your back and walk away. For I am everywhere now, not bound by my body, or buried six-feet under. My blood runs through your veins and my soul is forever imprinted on your heart. Your children's children will have a piece of my legacy, as well as yours. It is now your job to set forth ripples that will change the course of the lives around you. Always go with kindness, truth, integrity, and passion. Never give up on yourself or give in to the obstacles that are strategically placed throughout your life to help you grow. As your mother, all I can do is set a solid foundation for you to build individually upon, I only wish I'd had more time. Never forget that everything starts small, brick-by-brick, but over time those tiny blocks can become something remarkable with perseverance and determination. Tell yourself, "I love you," daily. Do this for me, because I am saying it, even if you can't hear me. Remind yourself that you were the greatest things that ever happened to me. Challenge each other to always strive to find your authentic selves. Always be there for each other, you two will be the only ones who can truly understand how the other is feeling. Never lose that connection, or let anyone or anything come between you.

Life

*In life, you will learn that you can't have anything you want simply because you want it. Things don't just "appear", so you will have to set up a plan to map out your success. I believe that anything you want, you can achieve, if you take the time to follow the recipe and put in the effort. Do well in school because it will instill a perseverance that will ease struggles later in life. Never give up on your dreams. Don't grow up too fast. The best part of childhood is figuring out who you are, what you like, what you don't, and how to treat others, without having to concern yourselves with the daily worries of adulthood. Knowing that when a storm hits, you are strong enough to survive it and rebuild. Learning how to love, and to be loved in return. What it means to not only be a friend, but a **good** friend. Knowing how to process your feelings, when to act and how to react. Understanding that time gives you the ability to process your feelings. As a child, you don't know that the cold, bitter winter will soon pass and the flowers will bloom once again. Be brave, my boys, give yourself time to trust in the process of life. All I could ever ask is that each day you are someone that you can be proud of, that you're filled with integrity and honor, love and respect. That you're the kind of man that will clean under a fridge, not because anyone will see it, but because you know it needs to get done. That you treat the people you meet with truth and kindness. Find comfort in knowing that the only person who can decide your future and protect your destiny, is you. You will always have control over your actions and the direction in which you want to take your life. Don't make your journey too complex. Think things through when you need to make a decision, but learn to trust your intuition, too. Every decision you will make in life will have a ripple effect, some good, and some bad, some you'll never see coming. With your choices, ask yourself, "Is this really worth the risk?" One of the hardest things to remember in life is that you don't have to be accepted by everyone. Ultimate happiness is achieved only when you are completely accepted by yourself.*

Always remember that someone's opinion of you does not have to become your reality. Become your own best friend. Do this with integrity. Never do something behind closed doors that you don't want someone to find out about. Be open, honest, fearless, strong, and reliable.

If you live with this philosophy, you can live freely. Your spirit can flow naturally and you won't be exhausted trying to swim against the current. Remember that no matter how hard you may try, not everyone is going to like you. That's ok, because their opinion of you is not going to affect those who do like you. Learn how to not take other peoples' opinions of you too personally. You can do this by knowing that you are doing everything you can to become the best version of yourself. If others don't accept you, or agree with you, or even like you, remind yourself that there will be someone who will cross your path and see the world as you do. Don't compromise who you are in an effort to become what someone else thinks you should be.

*Keep your vices in check. You're going to experiment with so many different indulgences in life. Intimacy, money, fame, substances, people ... Too much of **anything** can be a bad thing. The pursuit of any vice that changes the foundation of who you are is something to walk away from before it's too late. Life can be overwhelming sometimes, so don't ever be afraid to take a moment to walk alone. Never feel bad or guilty for giving your undivided attention to yourself. When you are alone, you can take time to remind yourself of who you are and who you want to become. Your goal is to become uniquely authentic and that independence will not only make you more likeable, but more interesting, both to those around you and, more importantly, yourself. Remember that when you stand alone, this doesn't mean you are without strength, it means that you are strong enough to handle things for yourself. You are stronger than you could ever imagine, if I were there, I would constantly remind you of that. You'll surprise yourself a few times along the way. Strength doesn't come from what you can do, it comes from overcoming the things you thought were impossible. I'll be watching and smiling from above.*

Your attitude will need your constant attention. When terrible things happen to people, their positive attitude is the easiest and fastest thing to lose grip on. I've always said a positive attitude gives you power over your circumstances, instead of your circumstances having power over you. These are the cards you've been dealt. Now you have to find a way to win the game, even if it means losing a few hands in process.

I always found it hard to not let my mind steal the present moments, but I can say that when I succeeded in quieting my thoughts, I realized that those were the moments I found myself reminiscing on later in life. Those were the moments that made me better and, more importantly, gave me the energy to help those around me.

Be brave. Go after what you want, or you will never have it. If you want something, earn it so you won't be afraid to ask for it from those that make the decisions. Find comfort in knowing that the only person who can decide your future and protect your destiny, is you. Fight for your success, you deserve it.

Relationships

*When it comes time for a relationship, take the time to learn your partner's love language. People usually feel loved if it is expressed in one of these five ways: **Words of Affirmation**: expressing how you feel about someone may be the only way they'll feel that you truly love them. **Quality Time**: someone may need your full-undivided attention, so put the phone down, and everything else on hold and simply **be** together. **Receiving Gifts**: not necessary materialism,* *but typically this person thrives on love, thoughtfulness and the effort you put behind the gift.* **Acts of Service***: this can simply mean helping out around the house, many people feel actions speak louder than words and when someone does something for them to make their life easier, they feel loved and appreciated. Finally, there's* **Physical Touch***: these people love hugs, pats on the back, holding hands and thoughtful caresses. Most people have a combination of the five. It's important to understand yours and figure out theirs so that you can shower them with all the love that they require, in a language they can understand. Once you know what they need, then ask yourself if you can learn to "speak" their languages. Always strive to transcend the "language barriers" and try to speak directly to one's soul. Remember that dark times never last. Pain of some kind is usually a constant linger, but suffering is a choice. Anything worthwhile is worth a good fight.*

When you do finally fall in love, remember that true love is meant to be cultivated over time, so don't rush things. Give the connection time to blossom. Don't overstimulate your mind with too many options. In order for you to invest in someone completely, you can't continue to shop the market. Don't cheat! Cheating is never acceptable. Dating is all about finding what you like and what you don't like. But when you commit to getting to know someone, do it with integrity. Close the door to other distractions. When you present yourself with too many choices, you could start taking people for granted. Simply because you have access to something, doesn't mean you should do it. I've found myself up late at night wondering what the world will be like when you are old enough to date. I hear people talk about dating apps and easy hook-ups. Don't allow technology to cheapen or bypass the experience of truly getting to know another soul. Life is about the journey, the long walks and hours spent talking to someone about thoughts and ambitions are irreplaceable parts of the path.

When you decide it's time to invest your time and energy into getting to know another person, it's important to get a general ideal of what you need. How do you want them to act? What do you need from them? How should they treat you? What type of relationship are you looking for? Take a few moments—hopefully longer—to figure that out. Take a good look at what you want, what you're willing to give up to achieve it, and what you're willing to give to another in exchange.

Don't be afraid to date, but don't mistake physical intimacy for love. Love is not easy. With love, you don't seek for something greater, you cherish what you have. With love, you will go to sleep feeling fulfilled. You won't destroy the people you love. Never replace one relationship with another, as one relationship ends, it is important to take time to find yourself again. Each experience and relationship will change the way you look at life, so embrace that new perspective. Make sure your foundation is in check and you have taken the time to weave that experience seamlessly into the tapestry of your life. Don't end something you care about until you have done everything you could to make it work. This way you will never find yourself going back for seconds. Remember, you've read that book, and you know how it ends.

Please wait to get married until you're at least in your thirties. It takes time, heartache, and personal triumphs to truly prepare for that commitment, so don't feel that you need to dive in to lock down a relationship. If it needs to be locked down with a ring, it isn't the right time. I want you to promise me that you will invest in your own happiness before you try to make someone else happy. So many people fail to know who they are individually before they get married. I have found that it's only in your thirties that you finally realize that knowing who you are is a constant journey, you are never meant to be "found", but to continue to develop over time. In one's thirties, you are free from that relentless quest and your spirit begins to settle down, you are finally old enough to quiet down your own soul just enough to hear another's dream. When you truly love someone, you can put your own selfishness aside and fully invest in that commitment without compromising who you've worked so hard to become. By then, you should know what you like, what you don't, what you're willing to sacrifice for another's happiness, and what you're not. By then you should be able to choose a partner who not only enthralls you, but also inspires you to become the man you've always dreamed of. When choosing someone to spend the rest of your life with, ask yourself a few questions: Do they have an unwavering moral compass that points to the same north as your own? People don't always have to do everything perfectly, but someone who knowingly does the wrong thing is not someone you should trust your life with. Are you attracted to the person? Do they move you not only physically, but emotionally as well? It's important that you understand a relationship should begin with an undeniable spark. It should continue with not only physical passion, but emotional desire as well. Treat each other with kindness. Do you like who they are as a person? Above all, you must be friends. Laughter will carry you from one memory to the next. Trust is everything. Without trust, you will have nothing. I'm going to say that again, without trust you have nothing. Don't ever give someone a reason not to trust you. You can spend a lifetime earning it and you can lose it in the blink of an eye. Your word is everything. Never use it to manipulate or deceive someone else. Never do anything to another person you wouldn't want done to yourself. Karma is always there to hold you accountable. If you know in your heart that your love has dwindled, spare her the heartache of dragging things out. Be a man, tell her the truth, and leave knowing that you were honest with yourself and her.

Having a partner is making a daily choice to be a part of that someone you can grow old with, not something to exchange for what you think might be better down the road. A relationship is like a house. It's built on a solid foundation, but when a light bulb goes out, you don't burn the house down, you simply fix the light.

Daddy once told me that he never thought he would get married. When I asked him how he knew he wanted to marry me, he said, "For the first time, when I looked at my life ten, twenty years down the road, I couldn't picture it without you. There is no me without you."

The World's Influence

You will be growing up in an amazing time. Technology will continue advancing and soon the world as I have known it will be irrelevant. I caution you, my sweet boys, not to be fooled. You are growing up in a world of filters, half-truths, and biased information. It's more important than ever that you realize that the truth is often very hard to see, most of the people you will meet are lost somewhere, buried under the false preconception that they are "fine". With all my heart, I urge you not to believe everything you hear. Or everything you see on social media.

Everyone is dealing with heartache. No matter how perfect someone's life may seem, remember that most photographs are staged. The bitter truth is often revealed under several layers of sugar, so dig it up. Own your truth, don't hide it, or bury it. Be proud of who you are because of the decisions you make, day-in and day-out. People will have more respect for someone with integrity than someone who tells them what they want to hear all the time. Don't be afraid to fail. When you fall, you will learn to appreciate what it feels like to rise. It increases the depth of your character and your ability to empathize. Constantly work on a plan to build your dreams, because if you don't, someone else will hire you to build theirs.

There are a few things that I want you to remember as you navigate through the choppy waters of your teens. Don't ever forget that your self-worth cannot be calculated by likes and shares. Take everyone's "profile" with a grain of salt, remember they are creating the best possible representation of themselves, showcasing their most magnificent moments in their life and hiding the most painful. You need to know how dangerous it can be comparing yourself to someone else. Having said that, be careful what you say, because once you say it, it can never be unheard. Don't air your dirty laundry on social media. Keep a balance between your life and the world. Respect your own privacy as much as you should others'. Emotions are like farts, they can stink the entire room and a few moments later, you can't smell a thing. Trust that in time you may not feel the same way.

Sex

Yeah, I said it… I'm sure you have plenty of questions, never be afraid to ask your daddy. Remember he was a young boy once, too. If I were there, I would listen with a compassionate heart about your questions, curiosities, insecurities, lusts, guilt, shame or emotions. I would blush and probably stumble over my words. I don't know a mom who looked forward to having this conversation with her children about sex, but some things need to be said and you're far too young now to have this conversation. So, when you are ready to hear your mom's "Birds-and-the-Bees" speech, you can read the next paragraph.

*There will come a day when your interest in sex and voyeuristic behavior to satisfy your sexual urges will occupy the majority of your time. I want you to know that you're not alone and that you are completely normal. Having said that, we need to discuss the subject of pornography—it's not **if** you will see it, it's **when** you will see it. I hope that you wait as long as you can to give yourself time to understand women for who they really are and what they really need. Love, sex, and adult relationships are not accurately portrayed in any sort of entertainment media, so don't follow that as an example or you will never be satisfied and always chasing that fantasy. Be careful not to train your mind to see your partner as an object to be used, rather than a person to be loved. You are physically and emotionally wired for intimacy. If you watch these portrayals too often or start too young, the images stimulate the brain in the same ways that drugs do. Be careful what you see, the scenes will linger in your memory. If you're not vigilant, you can find yourself losing your perspective and grip on reality. Under no circumstance is it alright for you to disrespect a woman and her boundaries to achieve pleasure. Do not let society downplay the significant harm done by objectifying women as they do in pornography.*

Sex is meant to bond a man and a woman together. So, when you lust for pornography, you are bonding yourself to those images, not the actual person. Remember that they are actresses and actors playing out a part. Never lose sight of the fact that they are actual human beings, that woman you see is someone's daughter. Don't allow your humanity to be set aside for a moment of pleasure. Please don't get someone pregnant until you are married and ready for that commitment. Children are the greatest gifts in the world, but they deserve to be raised by committed adults. Don't be a fool, wrap your tool.

In The End

I'm sorry to be the one to tell you this, but life is hard. There is no easy way to reach a goal. Life is not about how many times you get hit, it's about how many times you can get hit and keep moving forward. There are things in life, like death, that we don't want to happen, but we have to accept. Things we don't want to know, but we must learn. Giving up is not in our blood, it is not an option.

*There's a famous proverb that I love: "He who says he can and he who says he can't are both usually right." You are here in this lifetime for a reason. No matter what you think happens when you die, the absolute truth is that no one **really** knows. You have to find your faith. Find something that makes sense to you and hold onto it. Until that time, just tell yourself to "live this life as if each day is your last, live as if it matters."*

Never lose the fire that lights your soul, or give someone else your power. Every moment is new, every day is different. As your mother, I have tried to teach you everything I could in the time I had with you, except how to live without me. This is your time to show me how great you are. There are people in your life that you don't feel you can live without, but you will have to let go and push onward. Be brave my boys. I love you.

Love, Mommy

I carefully folded the letter and placed my hands on my children's backs. Our oldest awoke and looked up at me, tears immediately began welling in his eyes as reality came crashing back to him. He said nothing, but his expression conveyed two simple words, "Help me." I pulled him close and we both mourned the loss of our queen.

The Letter. We never know when our last day will come. As a mother and a wife, the uncontrollable scenarios life presents daily are the most terrifying truths I must wrap my mind around. What if? If I am gone tomorrow, did I teach my children well? Did they know how much I loved them? The Letter is written to my children, Dylan and Casey, with hopes that it never has to be read to them. The Letter is written to anyone who has ever lost someone they love, I hope these words provide you nothing but comfort in knowing you are never alone. It is dedicated to my husband, Connor, for being the most amazing father to our children. You inspire me to be great every day. Together you and I are the foundation for future generations. Thank you for teaching me, inspiring me, and being there for me, day-in and day-out. More importantly, thank you for showing me what love is supposed to feel like. I love you.

MIMI TRAN

MIMI TRAN is a day spa business owner, author, life coach, workshop leader, and motivational speaker.

She resides in East Brunswick, New Jersey, where she enjoys and shares her miraculous journey with two amazing teen-daughters, her mother, family, friends, and her soul-mate. She loves to write and travel to different places for leisure, as well as to give motivational speeches, workshops, and to life coach. Mimi's passion is to serve and inspire others to create their reality that is even better than a dream, and/or enhance it in any way possible. She embraces her remarkable life experience and uses this enthusiasm to fuel her passion every day. She believes life is a celebration and every day is a new birthday.

Mimitran26@yahoo.com

Be the Best of You

When people ask me if I have any children, I always answer with pride that I have two amazing daughters. Then people ask, "*how old are they?*" I say, "*fourteen and seventeen.*" I always get this response right after they hear the ages, "*WOW! Two teenagers huh, you must have your handful.*" Then I reply, "*Yes! I do, I have my handful filled with wonderful moments, fun, love, and I can't get enough of them.*" I am not just saying this because they are my children. Well, maybe a little bit. I am truly blessed with the opportunities to give birth to two amazing kids, and it is my privilege to be able to guide them and show them how to live. A few years back, when my oldest daughter turned thirteen, she believed that she was going through puberty and that means, she explained, "this is the time kids are growing away from their parents, and starting the rebellious stage. So, all kissing, hugging, and being affectionate in public is totally embarrassing now mom!" I responded, "*WOW! I remembered being ten, eleven, twelve, thirteen, fourteen, and on and on. I always yearned for all of the above. I just want to remind you that I didn't turn forty-two overnight, you know what I mean? However, I didn't remember that I was allowed to be rebellious or misbehave in any way to any adults, not just family. I couldn't get enough love from my mother because she was always busy working and was never around. So, kissing, hugging, and caring was out of the question.*" I added, "*by the way, do you realize how lucky you are to experience the wonder of TLC?*" She said, "*but mom, that's how kids are acting here, we don't like to be close to the parents!*" I said, "*really! Well, I don't believe that, and of course, I am not buying that, and I am going to prove to you that it was merely an excuse for teenagers to do whatever they wish. You are your own individual and you don't have to act like everyone else just because, and best of all, you are my daughter and I raise you to be the best of you, not just be like everyone else.*" She said, "*that is how it is now mom.*" I said, "*again, I don't buy that at all and we shall see!*"

Shortly after that conversation, my girls and I took our usual day trip to New York City. We usually take an hour or so train ride into the City. We would go for a nice lunch, see a matinee Broadway play, enjoy a nice dinner and head back home. As usual, we headed for the ticket booth in Times Square and decided together which play we all would like to see. If we can't decide which play to see, then we would vote. Whichever play got two votes would win, since there was only three of us. They picked a play that I didn't care for, but there were two votes for the play, so they won and I had to join the crowd, as I agreed with the deal. The name of the play was "The Perfect Crime." It was not only off-Broadway, it was a drama and not a musical, no dancing and only five cast members. There were only one floor theater and one scene on the stage. The play has been playing for over twenty years and was also one of the longest-running plays in New York City. As soon as we walked into the theater, we knew it was very different than what we were used to and expected. Only twenty percent of the seats were filled up. We got good seats since there was not too many people sitting behind us. Throughout the play, my kids acted like they were my parents. They kept asking me, "*mom, do you enjoy the play?*" I said, "*yes!*" *And they asked, "do you like the play?*" I said, "*yea…*" The whole time, they were acting like they really enjoyed the play and understood what was going on with the play, but I can see they were acting and I knew if I was the one who picked the play, I would hear them saying, "*mom, this is boring and we have no idea what's going on.*" They finally asked me, "*mom, do you want to leave?*" I said, "*nah, let's just try to enjoy this since we already paid for it.*" It ended a bit sooner than regular musical plays. We made it through the play without any one of us saying "*let's get outta here!*"

It was still early, about 4:00pm, so we were wandering around Times Square. We walked the same way we have been walking all day. My youngest daughter held my hand and my oldest daughter was holding my youngest daughter's hand on the same side. My oldest daughter continued her declaration about puberty, so she would not let me touch her hand. As we walked through the crowded city, I had to constantly look over to make sure that she was still with us. At some point, my youngest daughter felt bad that her sister didn't want to hold my other hand. She told me, "mama, don't worry, I got your other hand too," as she reached over to try to hold my other hand thinking she would keep my other hand busy as well. She thought I would just want to hold their hands while we walked, and not realize the safety walking in the crowded city with young kids. It was obvious that they were disappointed about the choice of play they made, including me, but afraid to say anything. I, on the other hand, thinking out loud, said, "what just happened? Pinch me please! I wish we can stay here late and see a really amazing musical play tonight, but…" My oldest daughter heard me from the other side and broke out of her silence. She rushed from her sister's side to get in front of my face, and stopped me from walking any farther. She held my face and kissed my forehead, my cheeks, my chin, and she said, "mom, that would be amazing if we could stay here tonight and see the musical play, and you can pick anything you want to see, mom, please please please, can we please do that?" I just smiled and let her do her thing with my face. She kept kissing my face all over again and again trying to convince me to stay. I finally said, "OK, ok." She then hugged me so tight and said, "this turned out to be the best day ever!" I replied, "indeed, because you just proved to me that the puberty thingy was just a total excuse as I said, so thank you love, you just made it my best day ever as well!" She smiled in agreement with me. We went to the ticket booth and picked the "Newsie" musical play. The play was amazing and was exactly what we came to the city for. Since that day, there was no more puberty excuses and everything went back to normal and then some. And the normal is we hug, kiss, and hold hands, and tell each other, "I love you!" every chance we have and just be us. Even now, they are fourteen and seventeen. We always kiss, hug and show love everywhere we feel like, no matter where we are. It's very interesting how we easily adopt the idea which we believe of being like someone else or acting like someone else for a certain reason early on in our childhood. And if there is no interruption or redirect, that pattern or behavior will become the way of our being, as we grow into our adulthood. At times, we may wonder who we are and try to be us. We may often do the things that we don't like or want to do, and try to be something or someone that we're not. The reality is, no one can be you. I feel that in order to be true to ourselves, we must be the best of ourselves. I feel such a privilege to have the opportunity to show my children, from early on, that the best they can be, is be the best of themselves because everyone else is taken.

Dedicated to Jessica and Celina. This universe has only one sun and one moon. I am blessed with two of each. You both are truly my sunshine in the morning and my moonlight at night. You are light and always shine bright.

Thanks to Lisa Hardwick for another wonderful opportunity to share my story. Thanks to my children for their inspiration, love, growing and non-stop support. And last but not least, thanks to the love of my life/soul-mate/best friend. Your endless love and support make me believe I can fly.

KALPANA PAREKH

KALPANA PAREKH, MSW, LCSW is a psychotherapist, personal and executive coach, speaker, author, workshop facilitator and singer whose life purpose is bringing light and inspiration into the world. She is the Founder and Owner of Wellness Around The World, LLC, an international practice whose mission is to inspire people and empower them with the tools they need to live flourishing lives. Author of *Hold On To The Paperclip*, a chapter in *The Empowerment Manual* (Visionary Insight Press, 2015), Kalpana earned her MSW from Columbia University in New York City, has a Certificate in Applied Positive Psychology, a Certificate in Music Therapy from India, is a certified yoga teacher, a licensed Heal Your Life® teacher, a Flourishing Skills group facilitator, and has studied reiki and pranic healing. She helps individuals and audiences of many sizes to thrive and live in alignment with their higher purpose. Knowledgeable, warm and inspirational, she is a highly sought-after speaker and trainer in the U.S.A. and India. She creates and conducts workshops on a wide variety of topics such as emotional well-being, therapeutic writing, stress management, leadership, emotional intelligence, and the healing power of music, for people from all walks of life.

Music, travel, healing, writing and snorkeling are among Kalpana's many passions. A talented vocalist, she sings Indian spiritual, classical and old Bollywood music as well as American pop music, and has released three of her own CDs. Passionate about documenting and preserving helpful traditions, she has traveled extensively and brings to her practice an appreciation for and tools from wellness traditions around the world. She recently spent six months in India assisting her music Guru (who was diagnosed with cancer) and his family by researching complementary cancer treatments, and advocating to his allopathic doctors, to improve the quality of his life. She provided support to her Guru until his very last breath. Kalpana founded "Letters From the Heart", a *Facebook*-based project (see "Letters From The Heart" Facebook Community page) that encourages people to write letters of hope and inspiration on a regular basis to those who are in need. She can be found journaling on any evening, capturing all that is good and beautiful about the world.

Website:
www.wellnessaroundworld.com
E-mail:
wellness1027@gmail.com

☙ Light The Way!

S ome of the most memorable moments of my life were centered on light. I cannot forget the sight of candles floating down the Ganges River at night, nocturnal lantern kites peacefully gliding through the sky during India's Kite Festival, the beauty of moonlight dancing on the ocean waves, sunlight peering through the window, rows of lanterns in Japanese temples, a candle maker's candle in his window at night, brilliant stars in the dark sky of the Rajasthan desert, the urge to chase the sunset at the Jersey Shore and being passed on a lantern of knowledge on my alma mater's symbolic Lantern Night.

During my childhood, as the sun set and darkness began to descend, my grandmother would strike a matchbox, light a candle in our altar, and give us the gift of light. Bright, warm, inspiring, and hopeful, this sacred flame became the center of focus, converting darkness into light, and melting away the worries of the day. The next morning, my grandmother would face east and eagerly await the rising of the sun. As it slowly came up, her palms were drawn together in a prayer position, and she bowed to the sun, greeting it with *Namaste*, the salutation that means '*I bow to the Light within you, which is also within me*'. Light is a symbol of the soul and every virtue under the sun.

Mother Teresa once said: "There are many in the world who are dying for a piece of bread, but there are many more dying for a little love." Though much of the world is starving for food, it is also starving for light. Our world is filled with negative news and emotions like anger, hatred, prejudice and fear. Psychologists now know that our brains are wired for negativity. We are more likely to recall negative experiences than positive or neutral ones, and negative experiences have a stronger influence on us. To counteract this, the world is in need of higher levels of consciousness, and the cultivation of more positive emotions like **L**ove, **I**nspiration, **G**ratitude, **H**ope and **T**ruth.

If each of us lights our own candle and that of even one other person, we could light up the whole world. 'Lighting our candle' means taking responsibility for our vibrational footprint and maintaining a level of consciousness that uplifts us, and those around us. Be it negative or positive, our energy is contagious. When we walk into a room, does our energy provide light? Do we contribute optimism, upliftment and inspiration, or do we contribute to more darkness? In his book, <u>Power Versus Force</u>, Dr. David Hawkins outlines a scale (0 to 1000), on which every level of consciousness, from shame to enlightenment has been calibrated, based on the concept of applied kinesiology. While supremely enlightened ones like Christ, Buddha and Krishna calibrate at the 1,000 level, most of society calibrates at the level 200. Hawkins asserts that one individual who lives and vibrates to the higher calibrating energies of optimism and a willingness to be nonjudgmental of others will counterbalance the negativity of 90,000 individuals somewhere on the planet.

Lighting My Candle

We do not need to curse the darkness and try to rid ourselves of negativity. Rather, we can focus on 'lighting our candle' by cultivating positive emotions. I commit myself to daily practices that help me plug into higher consciousness: 1) Every morning, I light a sacred candle in my altar and commit to bringing the virtues it symbolizes to every situation of my day. During low moments of the day, I close my eyes and visualize this anchoring light. I imagine every cell of my body as well as my mind and soul being filled with this healing light, and then extend this to the entire planet. 2) I spend a few minutes in silence to still my mind, focusing on light, a mantra or a deity of my choice. 3) I pay respect to my spiritual teachers and connect with their consciousness by recalling their lessons or reading a passage from one of their inspirational books. Invariably, I am led to read what it is I most need. 4) Throughout the day, I am mindful of the thoughts I think, replacing any negative thoughts that arise with more optimistic, balanced thoughts. 5) I recall and savor positive life experiences that brought me joy, warmth, or inspiration to uplift my emotional state, and utilize these experiences to help me uphold a positive space when others around me may be negative. 6) Listening to inspirational talks during mundane tasks and surrounding myself with uplifting quotations also 'light my candle'. 7) Singing from my heart takes me out of my mind, and into a state of flow. During music practice, I am in the present moment, using both sides of my brain, accessing insight and intuition in a way not available through cognition, and connecting with my soul. 8) Journaling allows me a place to release, explore, get centered and watch amazing insights emerge. With a backdrop of silence and non-judgment, I often feel I'm sitting in a sacred place of worship.

These daily practices lead me to feeling centered, inspired and strong. On particularly difficult days, when I'm dealing with a challenging person, intractable thoughts of my own, or crises, I tap into a world beyond my thoughts, and surrender. I turn my vessel upside down, empty out all the darkness, and place it right side up, allowing the light of the Divine to enter. I empty out fear, and allow in faith; I empty out aversion, and allow in love; I empty out resistance, and allow in graceful acceptance. When I make room within myself, the light has place to enter.

Sharing The Light

There are infinite ways to shine our inner light in the world. We each have to choose our own. My personal mission is creating sacred spaces and inspiring experiences that uplift the energy in any situation I find myself. A dinner party I recently hosted was infused with meaningful conversation after I gave each person a thought-provoking question to ask of another guest. Instead of superficial small talk, the evening was filled with warmth and heart-to-heart connection. After my family experienced a difficult year of loss and tragedy, I initiated a tradition I call *Moments of Joy* at our dinner table. No matter how the day has gone, each person shares one moment of joy experienced that day. After a few weeks of practice, everyone started bringing stories to the table full of meaning, depth, reflection and even humor. There are always moments of light in our day; we just have to seek them out and savor them.

Music can raise the energetic vibration of an atmosphere. When I lived in India, a group of senior citizens who met once a week would ask me to sing a powerful spiritual song which translated means: "No matter what country you are in/or what situation you are in/ always remember the Divine". Singing from the depths of my soul, I could feel my heart energy directly touching theirs. People would be crying, heads shaking, bodies swaying and hands clapping, asking for an encore because their hearts were on fire. When we sing, or take any action with our whole heart, we bring our inner light into the world.

When my music Guru, a world-class vocalist, was diagnosed with advanced stage esophageal cancer and lost his voice, his entire family and I were devastated. It was heart-breaking to watch our multi-talented maestro and poet robbed of the ability to speak or sing anymore, but he communicated what was in his heart through his eyes and facial expressions, and he could still listen. I helped him spend his last days enjoying music, singing to him, and playing his favorite Western classical songs. Filling the room with the uplifting vibration of music that his father once played when he was a child led him to spontaneously sit up in bed while he was lying down in his physically weakest state, raise his arms up with every ounce of effort he had in him, and start to conduct. His face lit up and he was in Heaven.

One spiritual teacher taught me to send blessings of light to those who may be sending me negative energy. A former employer often spewed negativity toward me, and when I started internally sending him light and blessings, I felt protected. This connected so well to my grandmother's lesson that when darkness descends, we have only to turn on the light. By sending blessings of light, I did not descend into the same negative state. During these times, we must plug ourselves into higher vibrations by remembering our spiritual teachers, positive affirmations, visualizing light or holding a physical anchor charged with spiritual energy. Loving-kindness meditation helps to generate a feeling of warmth for oneself and others, and research shows that it has biological, emotional and social benefits.

As a psychotherapist, coach, and speaker, my professional practice is dedicated to empowering people with the tools they need to experience emotional and spiritual well-being and inspiring them to flourish. While I draw on a variety of schools of thought and healing modalities, I see my most important job as creating a sacred space in which every client feels safe, unconditionally accepted and able to fully express themselves. This is an environment of light — acceptance, warmth, compassion, hope, and knowledge. Research shows that the greatest healing factor in psychotherapy is not any particular modality, but a positive therapeutic *relationship*. It is within this environment of light that magic happens. In sharing my own light with clients, the light within themselves is often kindled. Aside from our relationship, I maintain a warm and serene office space. Facing every client that comes in is a perfectly positioned quotation by Robert Alden: "There is not enough darkness to put out the light of even one small candle."

I had the privilege of watching Phil's[1] life transform before my eyes. Phil had never been to a psychotherapist before, but his family had strongly encouraged him to seek help.

---

1 The name of this client has been changed for his protection and confidentiality.

After his fiancée broke off their relationship, he was depressed, crying often, unmotivated, thousands of dollars in debt, suffering from a severe loss of self-confidence, miserable at a dead-end job, about 30 pounds' overweight, and nicotine-dependent. Phil felt rejected, dejected and overwhelmed, and though he was gifted with a towering height of more than six feet, one would not know it. After creating a strong rapport, and an environment in which he felt accepted and not judged for having built up credit card debt and hiding it, he started to open up more. He was ready to talk about things he had kept in the dark and expose them to the therapeutic light of non-judgment and compassion. There were many tools I shared with him that initiated progress, however, one of the most healing exercises for him was writing an unsent letter to his fiancée. Poured into that letter was all the negativity that had accumulated towards her and the situation. Being able to write the letter helped him make room for the light — more constructive thinking patterns, optimistic thoughts of hope, confidence and belief, and a newfound self-compassion. One never knows what tool will create a spark, and light the inner candle. Phil was fired up! While progress in the beginning was slow, after three months of work together, things just started falling into place. With new confidence, he started going on more interviews, applying himself more at work, standing at his full stature, courageously asking women out on dates, and eventually started a new relationship, lost 25 pounds, and quit smoking. Every week, I would witness a change, and over time, I witnessed a transformation. Phil became a force to reckon with! After we felt that our work was done, he kept in touch about his progress. One year after treatment was completed, Phil, who never once talked about spirituality during our sessions, told me that he could not wait to share with me a spiritual experience he had. In this magical follow-up session, I saw that he had maintained all the gains he made. He said that our work together gave him the tools he needed to lift himself up whenever he had down days. A greater confidence in his ability to transcend dark moments made him more fearless. I believe this new foundation of emotional health and arsenal of tools helped to raise his vibrational level to the point where he was ready to receive and experience the spiritual.

I have had the honor of witnessing transformation in the lives of countless people during our work together: a suicidal client who later began to have spiritual experiences that confirmed she was in tune with the meaning of her life; a top-ranking federal officer (who after the 9/11 tragedy had to remain stoic with his staff of 500 and his wife of 30 years) be able to release his innermost feelings and find a place to be himself; and a personal trainer who reconnected with her purpose of exercising as a way to take care of the "temple of [her] soul".

Workshops are a sacred opportunity for kindling hearts and minds. During a writing workshop, I conducted for college women who appeared to be eager but shy, I reluctantly shared a personal journal entry with the class, and was amazed to see the students start to clap and give me a standing ovation. My personal struggle and the insights that subsequently emerged resonated with them. I mustered the courage to share my light, and it sparked something within them. One young woman wrote to me a year later stating she had continued to journal, and it was bringing her closer to the "golden nuggets" waiting to be discovered within herself.

In 2015, I launched a *Facebook*-based project called "Letters from the Heart", encouraging people to write notes, letters or e-mails on a regular basis to people who may be in need. My best friend in college, who was struggling with a terminal illness, used to slip encouraging notes under my dorm room door that uplift me even today. Filmmaking is another passion that lights me up, as I strive to document and preserve ideas, practices and ways of life that could help enhance the spiritual and emotional well-being of the planet. "What do you think brings happiness?" is the first question I asked of an accomplished artist. Bringing light to this important question in the midst of his harried schedule caused him to sit back, take a deep breath and smile. What he had to say was very inspirational, but just having the opportunity to reflect on this and say it, seemed to bring light back into his life.

Light The Way!

Dear Reader, let us be grateful for darkness for it leads us to seeking the light. Every one of us was born a leader in our own right. What resources, talents, gifts, and skills will you bring into the world to shine your light?

In loving memory
of my beloved
Kaki, Jayantibhai and Gulbhai
You shined your lights bright
You showed me the way
You continue to guide me every single day
As my true Gurus, you showed me my Inner Light
With you by my side, my life will forever burn bright

I'm deeply grateful to my grandparents, Kaka and Kaki, for introducing me to the spiritual path and the tools I would need for a happy and healthy life; to Gulbhai for his selfless example and teaching me the preciousness of every breath; to Jayantibhai for teaching me how to make friends with darkness; to my parents and my 'extended' parents for their unconditional love and support in following my dreams; to the Mir Family for opening their hearts and home to me during a period of loss and tragedy; and to the darkness in my life, for it has shown me the value of light. To all my loved ones who left us this past year: your love and the lessons from your lives can never keep us apart; you are forever in my heart.

AMY PAZAHANICK

AMY PAZAHANICK is a professional athlete, author, motivational speaker, serial entrepreneur, and life coach. As the Founder and CEO of Agape Ventures, Amy has built her business and life around the core principle of unconditional love or "agape." She is dedicated to empowering others to create their own authentic "playbooks" for achieving peak potential.

Amy lives in Roswell, Georgia where she operates Agape Tennis Academy. Her articles and books on mental self-mastery, and sports and business performance have been featured in the *Huffington Post* and dozens of other magazines across the nation.

When she's not coaching on the courts or captivating audiences with her "game changing" success strategies, Amy enjoys cuddling up with her two cats to read, play golf, listen to Frank Sinatra music, and travel to exotic corners of the world to experience new cultures and cuisine.

www.amypazahanick.com
amy@agape-ventures.com
www.agape-ventures.com

The Courageous Heart

I am sitting alone on the floor of a completely empty bedroom, in a completely empty apartment. I have just broken with my boyfriend, rented a new apartment, and left my secure and comfortable job to start my own tennis academy. Everything about my life right now is uncertain and empty, literally and figuratively! I dwell on these feelings of emptiness and uncertainty but only for a moment because there is an accompanying feeling of liberation and excitement at the thought of what could be. This is a new beginning. My life is at a crux. I am in the position to write my life anyway I choose, just like the first page of a new book with many chapters ahead. I created this blank canvas and I intend to paint a beautiful picture. "Where do I begin?" "How do I begin?" I ask myself.

I decide the best place to begin is to write down the core values I want my tennis business to embody. One by one, I write down different words that are absolute musts to me. Excellence is the first word that comes to mind. I firmly believe in doing my best and giving my full effort in all that I undertake. Teamwork is the next word I write down. Teamwork is paramount to success. My staff and students must work together. I write a few more words on the paper; attitude, honesty, and responsibility. I scan the paper to see the five words I wrote. As I gaze down at the words, it hits me like a ton of bricks! "Holy S@%$!" The five words put in order, using the first letter of each word spell out heart: **H**onesty, **E**xcellence, **A**ttitude, **R**esponsibility, and **T**eamwork. I can't believe my eyes! Moments earlier, I was uncertain whether I had made the right decision to follow my heart and start this new venture. I take this "coincidence" as a direct sign that I am on the right track. A couple weeks prior to this moment, I decided to call my business, Agape Academy. I chose Agape because the word means unconditional love in Greek. Agape also fit well with my newly established core values. It is my desire that each and every student who participates in Agape Academy feels unconditional love and support. This was a defining moment in the founding of Agape Academy because it gave me a feeling of certainty that I was meant to do this work.

Live with Heart

Allow me to give you a brief of history on my tennis coaching career, which began seven years prior to the moment I describe above. I began working full time at a tennis club where I was brought on as the assistant tennis professional directly after graduating college and playing collegiate tennis. I was ecstatic to have my first full time job. Once I began working, I immediately made goals for myself. My long-term vision was to have my own tennis academy by the age of twenty-six. When I received my very first set of business cards, I turned one of them over and on the opposite side of the card I wrote, "I am thrilled to have my own tennis academy at the age of twenty-six." I would make it a point to see the card every time I opened my wallet. Often, I would fixate on the card and read it multiple times to create a feeling within me that it had already happened. I was also lucky enough to I have a mentor who taught me the ins and outs of running a tennis business. I was like a sponge, collecting, retaining, and soaking up everything I could learn. Four years have passed since I accepted that first coaching position. Now the time had come to put all I had learned into action. Not to mention, I was narrowing in on age twenty-six.

Fast forward to the beginnings of Agape Academy. I took the first steps. I left my job at the previously mentioned tennis club, and have started to breathe life into my new tennis academy, Agape. I am now clear on the company's core values and on the long-term vision I intend to create. Even though I just had an unbelievable moment of synchronicity with H.E.A.R.T, more reality is about to sink in. I have one hurdle after the next.

I still have no permanent facility. I am constantly talking to different contacts including neighborhoods, parks, and private and public tennis clubs to find somewhere I can call home. Nothing is working. I figure anywhere is better than nowhere, so I start teaching at two tennis courts in a nearby neighborhood. The homeowner's association is extremely restrictive over the hours and times that I can use the courts to teach. In addition, these courts have a lock box to enter that only works half of the time. Here I am, a new "CEO", scaling a twenty-foot fence just to teach tennis lessons! Talk about unprofessional! As I am trying to court (no pun intended) new clients, I have to say, "hold on a minute, while I scale this fence so we can start our lesson. Go ahead, throw your water bottle over, I'll catch it." This isn't good!

Not only that, this facility has only a couple of restroom stalls. The number of stalls is not the problem; the problem is they looked like they haven't been cleaned in years! So, guess, who has to clean them? That's right, me, the high-powered CEO of Agape Academy. The homeowner's association agreed that if I clean the restrooms and help maintain the property, I can use the courts to run some tennis camps and classes. Of course, I agree. Here I am, having left a good job, in a good community, so I could be cleaning toilets!? I am disgusted and unhappy when my dear friend, Ben, who really is a high-powered CEO of one of the largest manufacturing companies in the United States, stops me. He is kind enough and smart enough to have the foresight to tell me, "Amy, I want you to remember this exact moment. Notice where you are right now and what you are doing. Take this moment in fully. This will be a really funny part of your story in the future. You'll get to tell people that you had to clean toilets, climb fences, and all kinds of crazy things, just to get your business off the ground. This is part of the journey. You're going to make it. You're going to have a successful tennis academy and a beautiful facility you can call home. You will reflect on this moment in the years to come and you will appreciate the journey of how far you have come."

That moment stopped me dead in my tracks. Ben changed my perspective and he was right. No matter how hard things got, or how much money I saw slowly disappearing from my bank accounts, there was always something in me that kept believing, that kept seeing the vision for what was possible. I was not about to give up the fight for finding a home for my business that easily. I would grind it out. I would do the work. I would put in the time, the sweat, the blood, and the tears because after all this is what having heart exemplifies. The act of showing courage, grit, or resilience in body, mind, and spirit. The journey is what makes the ultimate victory ever so sweet! And once again I was encouraged, at one of my lowest points.

Trust Your Heart

It is now closing in on my twenty-sixth birthday and I am still not in a facility I can call home. I start to gain more momentum with existing and new students for Agape Academy. The logo, branding, and marketing is coming together. The structure of the company and all the legal documents are underway, but we still don't have a home. After scaling the twenty-foot fence and plunging enough toilets, I was able to move into a better situation with four tennis courts, but still nowhere close to my bigger vision for the business. The four courts were located in what I call "the desert". They were miserable to play on. They have no shade, no water, and after a while you start seeing pink elephants walking across the courts. It is a desert! I am certain I saw the only cactus in Georgia start growing next to court one. Fortunately, the courts were in a decent location in the community and I began to grow a large client base. Maybe they liked the challenging circumstances!? You have to pee, do you? That will be a half mile jog to a port-a-potty for you. This facility naturally provided lots of great mental and physical toughness training techniques!

It is now the summer season and I am running camps and classes in the "desert" with success. There are still a lot of additional hurdles, but the biggest of all is that summer would soon be coming to a close and the tennis courts had no lighting. How can I run a successful tennis operation when I can only teach half of the day? The answer is, I can't. I am doing everything I can to stay positive and to be resourceful. I am constantly looking for solutions and trying to figure out how to make my circumstances work! Finally, I decide to make a pact with myself that I will do my absolute best for each person who I coach. I know that if I do that, I will be successful. I know that success tends to have a "snowball" effect. The snowball picks up more and more snow as it starts rolling. The key is to just get the "snowball" rolling. I figure if each one of my happy students tells one other person and then that person tells someone, and so on and so forth, soon enough I'll have a pretty big snowball—and I do! However, I have nowhere to put it! I am faithful and positive during this time. A lot of people in the community start telling me about a nearby club that might have an opening. This is a nice facility with seven tennis courts. I figure I might have to change my business model to go to that club, so I am hesitant at first.

I meet with the manager of this nearby club in mid-July. I have previously been rejected two times by him. I go into this meeting with the manager with nothing to lose. Okay, that was easy because I didn't have anything to lose! It was only a couple days later, July 19th, I got a call from the general manager. Agape Academy has a home! I got the call two days before I turned twenty-seven years old. My dream was the have my own tennis academy by the time I was twenty-six, I made it by two days!

It is now several years later and Agape Academy has had hundreds of tennis teams and has done programming for thousands of students. Agape has been thriving with great success reaching more and more people in the community each year. Today is a very far cry from when I was cleaning toilets just to get a chance to teach a tennis lesson! There have been plenty of new challenges since the beginnings of Agape Academy, but because of the challenges at the outset, I know I can face anything that comes my way. As I reflect on how far Agape Academy has come since its inception, I am also thrilled by how far Agape has yet to go. I'll save all of that for the next chapter!

Wisdom from the Heart

These experiences have taught me many significant things that I know can help you too. There is no better feeling than following your heart and chasing down your dreams. The sense of fulfillment and satisfaction of going after your dreams, whether you fail or succeed is worth every ounce of pain, sacrifice, and struggle. It was Theodore Roosevelt, who said,

"It is not the critic who counts; not the man who points out how the strong man stumbles, or where the doer of deeds could have done them better. The credit belongs to the man who is actually in the arena, whose face is marred by dust and sweat and blood; who strives valiantly; who errs, who comes short again and again, because there is no effort without error and shortcoming; but who does actually strive to do the deeds; who knows great enthusiasms, the great devotions; who spends himself in a worthy cause; who at the best knows in the end the triumph of high achievement, and who at the worst, if he fails, at least fails while daring greatly, so that his place shall never be with those cold and timid souls who neither know victory nor defeat."

To create a beautiful life, life will require of you:

<u>Resilience</u>: Know that making your dream a reality is going to be hard work and that you will fall down many times before finally succeeding. *What reasons do you have that when you fall down, they will propel you to get back up again?*

<u>Faith</u>: You must believe that the world is setting you up for your ultimate victory if you will just hold the vision and never stop believing in your dreams. *How many hurdles are you willing to get past for your dream?*

<u>Courage</u>: Not everyone will believe in you. Be your own ultimate cheerleader.

<u>Resourcefulness</u>: You must constantly be looking for ways to win. You've got to get creative. If you keep looking, keep trying, keep adjusting, you will find a way. *What new options or strategies can you think of that might get you back in the game?*

Vision: You've got to be able to see the big picture of what you are doing. **_Where is this all leading you? What is the final outcome that you want? Why?_**

Focus: You get to choose what you will focus on. Keep the negative thoughts and people away!

What can you choose to focus on today that makes you feel inspired, grateful, or encouraged? Look for the good and you will find it. Look for the bad, and you will find that too.

Heart: Most importantly, you must have heart! Having heart as we refer to it at Agape Academy, is courage, passion, faith, resourcefulness, vision, and focus combined. Heart is giving full effort even if there is a good chance of failure. Heart is being fearless in the face of challenges and hard times. Ultimately, it takes heart to follow your heart. It takes heart to live with heart. Most of all it takes, heart to follow the wisdom that comes from the heart!

Dedicated to every person who has ever chased or decides to chase a dream in their heart.

I am deeply grateful to all of the teachers and coaches who have gone before me and shown me the way. Your words, books, personal stories, and vulnerability have given me the strength and courage to fearlessly chase down my own dreams. To every child who has ever, who is, or will ever be a part of Agape Tennis Academy. Each one of you is my why. To every person who has been in my life, whether short or long term, you have all led me to exactly where I need to be and taught me exactly what I needed to learn.

Thank you, thank you, thank you.

NICOLE STEVENSON

NICOLE STEVENSON is an advocate for a life well lived. She believes that we are all destined to live our lives by design and not default. She is passionate about helping others do just that. She spends most of her time empowering and teaching others how to break out of the confines of traditional employment and health. Inspired to lead people to embrace the infinite possibilities this life offers us, she enjoys igniting the fire in the souls of all those she meets. Nicole lives in Calgary, Alberta with her husband and her most favourite person on earth…her daughter, Shelby. She is admittedly a workaholic but says, "How could I not be when I have the best job in the world…lifting people up!"

❧ Dear Abby

Spiritual Leader. Do me a favour and just repeat those words out loud a couple times and tell me they don't sound like something that should be said with a British accent. Am I right? Maybe it's just me. All jokes aside, I feel like those two words come with some seriously strong responsibility. If you're a leader, especially a spiritual one, it would suggest people are following you, listening to your advice and creating their lives based on the examples you set. Let's be honest here...I feel like those are some big shoes to fill! While there are several meanings behind the title Spiritual Leader, the term brings to my mind a person who possesses the ability to guide others through the problems and trials of life.

When I look in the mirror, I don't see someone who fills those shoes for myself never mind others. I've never stood in front of a mirror, looked deep into my own eyes and said, "You, Nicole, are a Spiritual Leader!" Maybe I should but I can tell you as I stand in this moment, it's not even crossed my mind in the slightest. I'm well aware that I've made some really shitty decisions throughout my life and I'd be a liar if I told you I won't make a few more along the way. Knowing that, how in the hell would I be in any position to guide or lead others? I, like you, am a work in progress, learning and stumbling along this journey called life, picking myself up and figuring it out as I go.

That being said, I do have a big heart and I care about people deeply and have always felt compelled to help them in any way I can. So much so, that I'm guilty of sacrificing myself for the benefit of others more often than I'd like to admit. Yep, I've allowed myself to be a door mat far too many times and for far too many people but that's a whole other chapter, or therapy session...I'll let you decide...moving on.

Regardless of whether or not I viewed myself as a leader, I found myself in this position repeatedly throughout my life. That is as true today as it was 20 years ago. Whether a leader in my circle of friends, in the corporate ladder I was previously eager to climb or my newly cherished journey as an entrepreneur and advocate for a life well lived, I consistently find myself in a position to guide and lead others. In fact, as I write this, its undeniably obvious that all those instances were a culmination of lessons that have prepared me for this position. I feel compelled on a soul level to assist people in this way, to see them achieve their deepest desires, find greater meaning in their relationships and for some odd-to-me reason, people seem to seek me out for this purpose. So, if by no other rhyme or reason, but default alone, I guess I am a Spiritual Leader. Excuse me while I own that for a moment. I AM a Spiritual Leader.

Before we go much further, I should probably tell you that I've always wanted a Dear Abby column. Ok, stop laughing, I'm serious! If you asked me to stand up and give a training, teaching others how to approach or handle a specific dilemma or challenge, my brain would begin to whirl with a million different ideas. I'd struggle to provide you with a clear, concise presentation and although I'll rise to the challenge and deliver something that contains value...my best work is done as if we were two BFF's chatting on the phone. You ask me a question, and I, with my ninja-like skills would immediately dig into my most authentic place and succinctly provide you with some award-winning advice that would light up that inner light bulb in your head, leave you feeling inspired, and ready to tackle the obstacle. You're sitting there thinking...ok, that's nice but what does that have to do with a Dear Abby Column? Well, I like to think that I have the ability to see things from all perspectives. Like a bird's eye view, from above, able to see the entire situation from all angles. I have no opinion or judgment on either varying position; nor am I attached to the outcome so I'm able to give objective insights and provide clarity. But if I'm to be honest, I get to the place within me that can reach those deeper insights in a question and answer format...hence, my desire for a Dear Abby column. I can't even begin to understand why but it's how I roll and how I get my greatest insights. It's in the moment of being asked the question that my mind, my heart and my soul are able to respond without the time to over analyze. Perhaps it's being in the place of an observer, the space of detachment, or perhaps it's that I'm so innately determined to ensure all parties in a situation are heard and understood. Regardless of the reasons behind it, it's one of the many things that makes me who I am. It's one of the main reasons I'm able to support and lead others.

I'll stop for a moment here and let you know now, I won't be sharing with you any Fail Proof 7 Step Plan on how to help people while maintaining perfectly identified boundaries that honour you and those you choose to bless. Why? Mainly because I haven't completely figured it out yet. As I mentioned before, I'm just like you...a work in progress. More importantly, I don't think anyone can really tell you how to do that! It's just one of those things that you will have to explore and define for yourself. No one will ever see your life or the situations you face in life from your eyes, from your heart, from your soul. What I do believe someone could do for you is empower and inspire you to see circumstances from a place of authenticity...your authenticity. I believe people can help you see the bigger picture, seek understanding, open honest conversation that will guide you to finding solutions that honour all involved. That to me is the epitome of a Spiritual Leader and yes, I'll admit, I totally just said that with my trusty British accent.

Being a Spiritual Leader for others is going to require you to be able to not just talk the talk but walk the walk. It means you are going to have to learn how to do this in your own life before you go out and start sticking your nose in the business of those around you. Just a side note, unsolicited advice is never received well...wait for others to seek you out and approach you.

Let's start off with how you can become your own Spiritual Leader and see what that looks like first. Being a Spiritual Leader means you're able to view all perceptions of your current situation, how you showed up in that moment, how you could have showed up and how you want to show up in the future. The key here is that the clarity and discernment is coming from that bird's eye view we spoke about earlier. No agenda, no attachment to the outcome, just perspective. You see when you can put yourself in this position you're able to find a place of understanding. To see why people, do what they do, what motivated them to behave in a particular way and ultimately the source of the situation at hand. If you seek to understand first, your response and how you choose to play your part in that circumstance will radically change. You will grow from the person who is always defensive and critical, seeking only to have the other person agree that you're right and they're wrong, to the person who can see objectively how you played a part in the obstacle and seek resolution through connection. When you are able to do that, keeping your own personal ego at bay, this is being a responsible leader...this is how you become a Spiritual Leader for yourself and eventually others.

Let me just clarify something here, being a spiritual leader doesn't mean you've been elevated in the spiritual hierarchy to the position of people the likes of Ghandi or Mother Theresa. So, before you put on the monk's robe, pledge to a life of sacrifice and register yourselves at the closest monastery, keep in mind that average, ordinary people exude spiritual leadership all the time. You don't have to be that type of leader to affect change in someone else's life. If you aren't already aware, you lead people and you influence people every single day, whether you know it or not. With that kind of influence comes responsibility. I'm certainly not suggesting you go out, start a Dear Abby blog, and start handing out advice all willy nilly. As I mentioned, there is a profound responsibility in offering advice and spiritual support. There are a few things you need to ensure you yourself are able to keep in check prior to effectively blessing others with your insights. Be mindful that the advice you give, the suggestions you make, will impact those individuals lives... for better or worse. You are responsible for the actions you encourage them to take and so you must remove yourself from the situation, set your ego aside and be fully present for that person without so much as a pinch of judgement. If you can't handle that kind of responsibility...then you should consider not giving advice. I'm serous...you play a role in how people make decisions for their life and if that spontaneously erupts into a cataclysmic disaster in their life...guess what, you are equally at fault. Remember, what I said about big shoes to fill? Do the work in your own life first, be vulnerable, try, fail, try again but perfect the results before sharing them with anyone else.

True spiritual leadership requires you to operate from a place of servant leadership. The highest possible outcome or end for that particular person needs to be the primary focus for those you are in service to. If you are to become a Spiritual Leader and to be seen as someone trust worthy enough to guide others you must possess humility and compassion. Be careful to not place yourself in a position that emanates a perception that you are better than they are. Thinking too highly of yourself, as a Spiritual Leader, prevents you from genuinely caring for others. In fact, humility is the attitude that puts others ahead of you, that considers others more important than yourself. Again, healthy boundaries are necessary and helping others at your expense is neither healthy for you nor them. It took me many years and many lessons to learn this and to be completely honest...I'm still learning. You are but a beacon of light helping to guide them through the storm and back to calmer waters. People want to follow leaders who serve alongside them and set the example for them, helping them to see the obstacles in front of them and how to navigate around them.

Although being a Spiritual Leader comes with its fair share of responsibility it is truly a heartwarming and life altering experience. I cannot even begin to articulate to you the sheer joy I gain from helping and guiding others, knowing that the triumphs of their lives were in some small part a reflection of advice and guidance I may have offered them. The knowing that their perception of another may have shifted, a relationship may have been repaired or rekindled because of something I did or said lifts my spirit to levels that the English language cannot express. If I may, I'd like to take this opportunity to ask a favour of you. If you have someone in your life that provides this kind of leadership and support, please, tell them. Communicate to them the impact they make in your life, share with them your successes not just your challenges. Share the stories of how their presence in your life, when you needed it most, made all the difference. It's just as impactful for them to know they've made a difference in your life as it is for them to help facilitate that process. Lift them up so they may continue to be inspired to be that system of support for others. Not only will you validate their purpose and provide them with an inexpressible gift but you elevate yourself to a higher vibration as well. You, in essence, turn the tables from receiving to giving back. In doing so, it all comes full circle and you then become the Spiritual Leader in their lives.

I dedicate this chapter to Lisa Hardwick. Looking back over the last 6 years it's become obvious that you have this uncanny ability to offer the opportunity to write in the most synchronistic times in my life. It's as if you intuitively know, with each chapter I write for each different book project, comes my next level of growth. Each invitation to co-author has led me to greater and greater heights bringing more peace, more passion and more happiness into my life. I thank you, from the deepest depths of my soul, for allowing me to embrace these shifts. While I sincerely hope those, who read my chapter walk away feeling like they gained something from it...I know in my heart that it is I who will benefit more profoundly from the experience. Without your encouragement and the platform, you've created all of this would not be possible. I cannot begin to express the gratitude and love I have for you for bringing this blessing into my life and to the lives of so many others. May the Universe bless you beyond measure my friend.

JERI TOURAND

JERI TOURAND, B Ed. is the Founder of "Living From Heart Center." Jeri is a self-love and forgiveness coach, mother of three, published author, inspirational speaker, radio show host, Zen Trilotherapist and energy healer. Her mission is to assist people in awakening and opening their hearts, inspiring them to live life to the fullest, and courageously express their highest potential and truest nature.

Jeri facilitates Heart to Heart circles, workshops and retreats including Zen Trilotherapy retreats and Unconditional Love retreats to help people awaken and lead us to the tipping point of a more united world that is healed, connected and driven by Love.

Jeri believes that the only problem in the world today is that people don't love themselves. Having healed herself of several health challenges, emotional trauma and adversity, Jeri now coaches individuals and groups to identify and heal the inner conflict between their mind and emotions, awakening their souls to lead them to a place of inner peace, happiness and true freedom. She strives to be *the world's greatest lover*; being and sharing unconditional LOVE with others, awakening deep truth and remembrance within, of the Divine LOVE that we are.

Jeri is a lover of the adventure of life, embracing the exploration, expansion, and expression of our authentic, empowered and joyful selves in order to experience Heaven on Earth! Her motto is that *life is beautiful and meant to be fun!*

For workshops, personal coaching sessions or speaking engagements,
please contact Jeri Tourand at:
Website: www.livingfromheartcenter.com
Email: livingfromheartcenter@gmail.com
or connect with Jeri at Living from Heart Center on Facebook and Meetup

Life is Beautiful Because *I AM*

As you awaken to your divine nature, you'll begin to appreciate beauty in everything you see, touch, and experience.

~DR. WAYNE DYER

One by one, I asked each participant at my workshop, "Why is life so beautiful?" The answers were astounding. Almost everyone was able to let go of the mind chatter from their critical heads and connect with the gratitude in their hearts to express a heartfelt and often deep and profound answer. Then something amazing swept through the room; audible relief, palpable love, quieted minds and open hearts.

This shows us the power of a question! Our hearts will be excited to know that asking questions about what we wish to experience directs our monkey minds to work *for us* rather than against us as the saboteurs of our heart's longing, instilling doubt and fear that our dreams are unsafe and too risky. In addition to keeping us safe, our heads are designed to look for answers. All good teachers know this. Unfortunately, many of us are still asking the "wrong" questions, things like "Why can't I do this? or, "What is wrong with me?" come to mind. Better choices might be, "Why is this so easy for me?" or "Why are the perfect answers and opportunities coming to me so quickly and easily?" And of course, "Why is life so beautiful?" and "How can life get better than this?" are the most perfect catch-alls!

Life is beautiful is a mantra that has been transforming my life for over five years, since it was given to me as homework by one of my primary spiritual teachers, Zen Buddhist Master, Nissim Amon. It has become deeply engrained in my very being. It has awakened parts of me I did not know existed. I walk it, talk it, sleep it, breath it, sing it and wrap myself in its warm embrace.

Mantras are a powerful way to shift your life. Much like an affirmation, they set an intention going forward and are a powerful declaration to the Universe that you are ready, willing and committed to making a change or a vibrational shift to align with the energy of these statements. This is not an easy task as most people are still deeply committed to their pain and suffering. Suffering is familiar and dare I say, even comfortable. How many of us have identified ourselves through the filter of our guilt and shame? The shame filled stories of our past are never far behind us and we know this because our self-sabotaging behavior patterns remain and the guilt continues to surface. "Guilty people should be punished," says our conditioning, and so we continue to punish ourselves, sabotaging opportunities, playing small, putting ourselves last, attracting and staying in abusive relationships, procrastinating, resisting our light, withholding our love and doubting ourselves. We say things like, "if you really knew me, you wouldn't love me." This is how I know when someone is still inaccurately seeing themselves through that filter of shame. We've forgotten who we are and we've buried our purpose in a pile of shame and suffering.

I want each of you to know that there is a way to connect with your purpose and to live authentically; courageously expressing yourself and sharing your gifts with the world. When you remember who you are and begin to see through the eyes of your heart, life becomes beautiful and you will feel the support life offers you when you live your truth in full alignment with who you are. When you believe that life is beautiful, it becomes safe to express yourself authentically and take those courageous steps toward your dreams.

"Beauty is in the eye of the beholder" is an old proverb credited to Margaret Wolfe Hungerford in 1978. The literal meaning is that perception is subjective. I love this phrase as it points out that it truly is a choice to see the beauty of life. Through the soft eyes of an open heart, we can finally begin to see the truth of who we are, beyond the physical, meeting our own soul and other souls, heart to heart. We will begin to know that who we are has nothing to do with what has happened to us, nor what shameful acts we've carried out. When we know who we are, we cannot help but love ourselves. We are that which we seek. Our essence is love, and thus it would be most accurate to say that the most kindhearted, compassionate and loving thing we've ever done or experienced is actually the closest to the truth of who we are. The magic is that when we know ourselves and love ourselves, our eyes are open, and we begin to see everyone through those very same eyes of LOVE. When we see ourselves through the filter of love and beauty, beauty abounds. As we awaken to our own beautiful divinity, our very presence begins to awaken others that come into contact with us.

"*Once the truth of life's timeless beauty has been discovered it flows through you to awaken the consciousness of all who come your way,*" says Matt Kahn in his book, *Whatever Arises Love That.*

Life is beautiful simply means that you have finally come to the recognition and revelation that you, being life itself, are beautiful. Indeed, nothing is outside of you. To know yourself is to know love and to awaken to the beauty in everyone and everything.

How much do you *believe* that life is beautiful? I would like to share with you some powerful steps you can take to move you closer to this awakening and realization that life truly is beautiful. Just think how your life would be different, and what it would mean for you and your family to really believe this!

1. *The first step is to forgive.* That which you have not yet forgiven will prove to be your nemesis and your very best friend, never failing to show you your work; the very thing that blocks you from seeing, experiencing, and finally truly knowing,

beyond a shadow of a doubt, that life is beautiful. Put your hand over your heart, look deeply into your eyes in the mirror and forgive yourself, for every time you ever believed you were not loved or lovable, not good enough or that something was wrong with you. The mantra I use for this is another that I have running fairly constantly in the background of my life. It is the Ho'oponopono prayer: *I'm sorry. Please forgive me. Thank you. I love you.*

2. *The second step is to tell yourself the truth.* The truth is that you are loved and lovable just as you are, that you have always been good enough and that there is nothing wrong with you. You are not broken, nor do you need fixing. You have everything you need. You are beautiful and filled with divine wisdom. With these words, and other words you've longed to hear, spoken to your own heart (also known as your 'inner child') from your own mouth, you can begin to feel safe to open your heart and reconnect with the truth of who you are, thereby deepening every relationship and particularly healing the one between your own head and heart.

3. *The third step is to tell others the truth.* The best way to do this is through giving them a genuine compliment. You'll be very good at it since you'll have been practicing on yourself. Your soul recognizes another soul and does not see the stories that our ego would find it necessary to judge and that keep us withholding our love. This is the pain of life. Since we *are LOVE*, withholding love and carrying resentments that stop us from expressing our love is the greatest pain of all, preventing self-expression, and disconnecting us, not only from others but from the core essence of who we are. According to Matt Kahn, the spiritual purpose of a compliment "acts as a selfless blessing of appreciation that reminds others how much they are valued."

4. *The fourth step is to give yourself the directive, "Who am I?"* In every cell of your body ... *FEEL...WHO...YOU...ARE.* You can begin this inquiry by taking a deep breath and on the exhale, release who you are not. Create the space for that feeling of who you ARE to overcome you, YOU, meaning your mind and *who you think you are.* This is how you connect to the "I am" presence and this truly is a secret to living a happy, fulfilling, purpose driven, and love filled life! The energy of the *I am* is that of infinite love, pure potential and divine inspiration. Allow this directive, combined with the breath of life to open you, releasing your grip on all that you are not and replacing it with all that beautiful *life force love energy* that heals and awakens your spirit, so that you can have an experience of who you are.

5. *The fifth and final step is to simply practice seeing yourself and others through the soft eyes of your heart.* With perfect intention and each loving breath, soften and bring every person you meet into your heart to feel the healing power that your love offers. Bring the trees, the animals, even the rocks; bring everything into your heart. This will help it expand and open to the truth and connect to the *all that*

is; true oneness. As you make this a daily practice, something miraculous will open for you, a window of clarity where beauty can and will come flooding in and leave you filled with love and gratitude. This is a simple, yet profound practice of softening and opening in full presence. When I am driving and stopped at a light or in a traffic jam, I get excited about the opportunity to just look around and bless everyone and everything, every car, person and even the traffic lights with my loving gaze and with a deep feeling of appreciation; I breathe it all into my heart. Sometimes a mantra or blessing will come to me as well. "*Divine love flows through me to all things,*" is one of my favorites, or, "*May you be safe, happy, healthy and live with ease.*"

I would like to share a beautiful story that one of my friends, Carmen Braga (co-founder of *Healing Hearts Centre*) gave me permission to share, about her awakening experience to the beauty of life:

> "About 5 years ago, I was coming back from a long walk. It was a beautiful sunny, summer morning and all of a sudden something happened…it was like the trees around me lit up and became brighter!! It actually stopped me in my tracks and its beauty encapsulated me and held me there for a few moments. I was absolutely stunned by what I was seeing!! It was like the nature that was around me suddenly woke up but the truth was, it was me who had woken up.
> I remember thinking to myself…*my God!! How have I lived my whole life and not even noticed these beautiful trees!!* Suddenly I felt a bond, a love for all nature in that moment and that moment has never ended as I still feel that way today."

Carmen went on to describe her heart centered KNOWING that this experience was simply nature matching the vibrational frequency of the peace that she was feeling as she was walking that day. How she felt on the inside was being reflected for her on the outside.

This work is so important that our very survival may depend upon it, individually and collectively. Many are saying that our survival depends upon the awakening of humanity to the love that we are, one heart at a time. May your heart feel safe to open and may your love and self-forgiveness release the judgments that lie in the way.

The day of enlightenment is the day we treat ourselves like we are someone we love. We begin to see for the first time, with the soft and loving eyes of our hearts, like an innocent and curious child, seeing beyond the physical to the truth. We see the beauty in everyone and everything. Each time we look through these eyes of love, it opens us even more to the flow of life. We appreciate all the beauty that surrounds us, and we realize that this beauty *is us*. It was in us all along. It must be, for beauty is in the eye of the beholder!

Dedicated to my three beautiful daughters, Mackenzie, Rylee and Morgan. May you know, beyond a shadow of a doubt, that life is beautiful...because you are. I love you unconditionally, always and all ways!

Thank you to my beautiful partner, Cal Beaudoin who has been a role model of unconditional love, an inspiration and one of my greatest teachers of personal mastery. Thank you to my Heart to Heart group for your continued support and for challenging me to be my best! Thank you to all my teachers, especially Zen Master, Nissim Amon, the late Brian Klemmer and authors Matt Kahn, Wayne Dyer, and Robert Holden. I also wish to thank my amazing family. I know it has not always been easy for you and that my life has been somewhat unconventional. Your love and acceptance means so much. I love you.

SUMYA ANANI

SUMYA ANANI is a life-long learner and can usually be found in a class or workshop. She loves being with family and friends, traveling, reading, and playing ball with her German shepherd.

Sumya owns Learning2Fly, an aerial fitness and children's discovery center in Kansas City. She offers regular classes and birthday and bachelorette parties to participants of all ages. Her youth camps and K-12 field trips, 'A Chakra Circus of Health,' are loved by parents, educators, and kids.

A former four-time world champion boxer, Sumya loves helping others develop their inner athlete and discover their full potential in every area of life. She is a successful coach, yoga instructor, and teaches aerial arts including aerial yoga, weight training, and boxing classes.

Sumya appears regularly on local television programs discussing health topics and is available to teach transformational workshops in private studio and corporate settings.

www.Sumya.com
www.iAMLearning2Fly.com
Sumya@iAMLearning2Fly.com
Connect with her on Facebook at Sumya Anani or Learning2Fly.

A Chakra Circus

YOUR SEVEN WONDERS OF HEALTH

We are in an age of transition, and it can be a time of fear, uncertainty, stress and anxiety. But these times can also be times of birth, of discovering, of pushing through blocks, of growth, of becoming who we are truly meant to be, and of victorious outcomes. To borrow Oprah's saying, 'What I Know For Sure," is each of us is responsible for creating art in our lives.

We are all artists. The chakra system is the perfect medium for us to awaken the artist within. An artist is more than someone who holds a paintbrush, sculpts clay, or draws animals and people. Our lives are the highest form of art we can create. It's time for each of us to own and express our creative genius.

As a yoga teacher and success coach, I love using the seven chakras to help others understand and navigate their personal and professional paths. I facilitate weekend workshops for groups and integrate intentional movement, meditation, journaling, small group discussions, and art. The format is focused around the "Seven Habits of Health" I have developed, with each habit aligning with one of the seven chakras. I've used these habits successfully in programs for kids at my studio in Kansas City. These habits, when applied in our lives daily and responsibly, can and will transform our world.

It is my hope you will get your creative juices flowing from the following writing exercises. Get a pen and take time to sit with your thoughts about each area of your life. Ready? Set? Let's get clear about 2017.

1st Chakra — Nutrition

Your body is your home. Keeping your body healthy is the number one priority because without health, you won't be able to enjoy anything or be of real service to others. Health is wealth.

How are you feeding and nourishing your body? We have to take our health into our own hands. You have complete control over what you put in your mouth and yes, you can change nutritional habits. Acquiring better nutritional habits is something we all need to continue to refine. Your body is a self-healing organism but if you fill it with refined sugar and colas, adverse health effects will be a reality.

Take sugar for example. Most people eat way too much sugar. It's hidden in many foods and there are now more than 60 names for sugar. See the movie 'Fed Up' for a startling expose about the sugar industry.

When working with new clients as a personal trainer, we usually start with a sugar detox. Sugar is addictive. But if you change the biochemistry of your body, you will crave different foods. You really don't have to feel like a slave to food habits. What other new habits around food are you ready to look at this year?

2nd Chakra — Exercise

Once you're properly fueled, then it's time to look at your movement habits. Are you getting enough exercise? Exercise is powerful in circulating healthy neurotransmitters and endorphins, like dopamine and serotonin, that make us feel good.

As a former world champion boxer, I sought out many forms of exercise to get in tip top shape. We are lucky today that there are infinite ways to find joy in moving. Varying your workout reduces both injury and boredom. Focus on activities that minimize impact on joints and focus on these critical aspects of health: strength, flexibility, and endurance.

Step out of your comfort zone and take a class that requires a partner like dance. Get a friend and sign up for classes together. Keep each other honest. But learn to rely only upon yourself. Over the years I've had workout partners come and go. Ultimately, you are your own workout partner. Exercise will help you reduce or eliminate stress, anxiety, and depression. Bless your body with the habit of daily doses of movement.

3rd Chakra — Learning & Self-Confidence

Learning new things adds to the quality of our lives, improves self-worth, and keeps our brains engaged. Harness your curiosity in positive ways and sign up for a new class or workshop. The happiest people are always learning.

Pick one new activity you've always wanted to try each year and give yourself the whole year to explore it. If it turns out it bores you to no end, then pick another one. Are piano lessons calling your name? What about crocheting or cooking lessons?

Community colleges are a great resource. The local libraries have books on CD that make great companions for long work commutes or trips. Explore something new in your city, learn about its history, or take a daytrip to a neighboring community.

Boredom is never an option if you're open to learning and asking questions. What new activity or skill would you like to learn this year? Be curious. Be brave. Expand your horizons. You'll empower yourself along the way.

4th Chakra — Environment

Many are concerned about their perception of Trump's attitude toward the environment. We need to inspire him to implement the correct policies. Recently, a mom posted her young daughter's comment to someone who said she did not care about the environment.

"If you don't care about the environment, then move to Mars." This makes sense. If we don't protect the environment, then life will not survive on earth.

What environmental commitments can you make? Can you call your Senators and Representatives to voice concerns about preservation of the natural world? Tell them to invest in solar and wind energy. Be an active voice. It's your right. Whether you believe in global warming or not, the fact is fossil fuels are limited. Native Americans understood their actions affected seven generations. What kind of world will we leave for our great great great grandchildren?

Join an environmental group. Learn alternative ways to have a positive influence on the climate. Do you take advantage of area recycling programs? Can you turn the lights out and be more mindful of water consumption? Clean air and water is essential for everyone. Preserving our oceans and forests is everyone's responsibility.

5th Chakra — Family & Community

We are social animals. Our health depends on deep, loving relationships. People who are socially connected are happier and healthier. Loneliness can be eliminated through personal interactions with others.

Limiting use of social media is one suggestion for people who feel lonely, sad, or depressed. Spend more time on face to face interactions. Create a new family ritual. Take turns making surprise date nights with your partner. Go on 'field trips' with your friends. Join a book club.

Think of all the communities you are involved with. You have your family, work, church, and gym communities. These places give you opportunities to deepen bonds with others. We need others, and they need us too.

Volunteering for something you are passionate about is a great way to meet people and give back to your community. Volunteer to walk dogs at a local animal shelter. Maybe you can adopt a pet. Pets are part of the family too and make an impact on our health in positive ways too. Many programs take pets to nursing homes or children's homes.

How can you reach out to others? Write down a few ways to make new friends and build community connections.

6th Chakra — Global Appreciation

We are global citizens now. We learn much about ourselves and our own culture when we learn about other cultures.

Have you wanted to speak a new language? Join a club. Most colleges have international clubs. What international destinations are on your bucket list? How long have you wanted to go to the Fiji Islands, Australia, or Italy? You can go there virtually, through reading, as well as physically. Start your research in the library. How can you begin to save money for these once in a lifetime trips?

You don't have to go out of the country for a taste of the world. Many local museums host international exhibits. Looking for a great multi-cultural gift? Check out Ten Thousand Villages or other organizations that sell fair trade goods.

7th Chakra — Spirituality

What spiritual qualities would you like to embody more in thought, word, and action? Patience, acceptance, and love are a few ecumenical qualities we can all aspire to living. Begin with your own inner dialogue. Do you lovingly talk to yourself? Are you critical of your body? Take time to reflect and write down new affirmations to improve the quality of your thinking.

I call it 'weight training for the mind.' When you lift dumbbells, every repetition makes a difference. The mind benefits in the same way. Every time you think a positive, loving thought you are using the 'Law of Attraction' to draw good things to yourself. Think, read, write, and speak affirmations often. Thoughts become words, and words become actions.

Seven Chakras, Seven Wonders of Health

The seven chakras are a roadmap for our journey as artists. Every day, every year is an opportunity to grow, expand, thrive, and create the masterpiece of art that our lives form. You are holding the paintbrush and you are choosing the color scheme. Together, let's make life become art.

I hope you enjoy your discovery and creation of your own work of art. These seven habits can transform your life and the world around us. We must awaken them for ourselves, and for the benefit of all humanity. Let's make 2017 our best year yet with theses seven wonders of health.

Dedicated To: Mom, Phyllis and Dad, Sufian. Thank you for the gift of life.
  Son Matthew. You can do anything you set your mind to.
  My known and unknown ancestors who paved the way for me to be who I am today.
  I walk with each of you every day.

I want to acknowledge: Istvan Javorek, my strength and conditioning coach, who helped me get strong and prepared me for a career in professional boxing. You have taught me so much.
  Barry Becker, my boxing trainer, the best trainer in the world. I won four world championships and more, because of you. You are the champion of my world. Thanks for being 'in my corner.'
  Thank you for E=mc2.

BERYL HUANG

BERYL HUANG is a leading Attitudinal Psychologist who, every year, helps thousands of people across the globe through her private and group sessions, speaking about Motivation and Self-Improvement. She has conducted numerous sold-out seminars and workshops. Beryl is also a regular guest on Television and written about in the Press in both North America and Asia.

She is also currently serving as Chairman and CEO of an International Entertainment Group located in Los Angeles, California.

Beryl enjoys fast cars, trying out new food and cuisine, travelling around the world and exploring life in general.

⚘ The Art of the Broken Heart

Sometimes you have to die a little on the inside in order to be reborn and rise again as the strongest, wisest version of yourself.

Seven years ago, when my father passed away, I thought my boyfriend would lend me his shoulder, support me in my time of need and be my rock. Do for me, as I had done for him. I entrusted him the responsibly of handling all my business and financial assets whilst I dealt with my grief. Not long after I lost my beloved father, when I began to come out of the haze that was my grief, I came to realize I had lost everything in America. And by saying everything, I mean everything that I had worked so incredibly hard for in the past twenty years. My homes, my money, my sport cars and my valuable belongings all were gone. Not only had he stolen my hard-earned fortune but he also had stolen my life with him, cheating on me countless times including with one of my girlfriends.

Devastated and deeply heartbroken, I was forced to close my business, file bankruptcy and leave America because I had no way of surviving with what little to no money was left to my name. The day I packed to leave the United States is a day I shall never forget. Seeing that all I had left was a pile of name brand fancy clothes, bags and shoes—and that none of this was remotely important—useless symbols of success and wealth, I broke down into a sea of tears. I was overcome with emotion. Dead broke and the only things I had left were these silly expensive yet useless items.

So, I decided to donate them—all of them—to various charities before I left America. They and the memories they brought were not welcome on my difficult road ahead. My broken-hearted journey started after I returned to Taiwan and lived there with my mother.

My mother was still living with the sadness caused by my father's departure. To not add to her stress and in an attempt to be strong for her, I did not share any of what had happened to me in America. I only told her that I was coming home to take care of her, to take a little break from work and eventually I would return to America afterwards. To this day, I know deep down in my heart that it was a most difficult but necessary lie.

During the daytime, I would fake a smile and make jokes to cheer my mother up. Yet every night when she went to bed, I would lock myself in my bedroom, cover by blanket and bite the pillow trying not to cry out loud. Countless nights I fell asleep only after having spent all my energy holding back my tears. And every morning, the first thought that would come to my mind when I woke up was "oh no…why? why am I still alive?"

We lived in a high-rise building and I cannot remember how many times I looked out the balcony and had the terrible thought of "what if"? And to be honest with you, if it were not because of the fact that I worried about my mother, I might not be sharing this story with you today.

My thoughts were constantly fighting within myself to not fall into hatred, to revenge, to self-pity and self-destruction. Every single day I prayed to God to please help me and to not let me become a bitter, heartless person. It was an unbelievable hardship—the inner war between the angel and the demon fighting inside me every day.

My first savior came in the most unlikely of times, in the most unlikely of forms. This happened during a night when a class 4—typhoon was passing thru Taiwan with its pounding rains, deafening thunders and a piercing wall of wind. The noise was so intense that you could scream at top of your lungs and not be heard. I saw this as an opportunity and took my chance. Opening the balcony door, I cried out into the storm with all my might. The rain, the cold, the wind and the flashing thunder in the sky washed away the tears on my face as they became one with the elements and I don't know how long I cried or how much I screamed but I knew for a fact, even though my whole body was soaked to the bone, somehow, something had happened in my heart. It felt like the heavy weight in my chest that had caused me such difficulty to simply breathe had been lifted—had gone away. I felt lighter. Not really knowing why I did it, I opened my arms facing the rainy sky and, with the wind still blowing thru me, I said: "Thank you God!"

The very next day, as I removed all the window covers that have been keeping me in darkness, I allowed the after-storm sun to shine brightly into my room. It gave me the strength to greet my mother with the first genuine smile since my return to Taiwan. Was it the end of pain? Was life going to be always awesome from this point forward? Had the storm washed all my troubles away?

No, things were still hard. Trying to stay positive every day is an almost impossible task when you can't see the light at the end of the tunnel or even the path under your own feet. The worries about tomorrow, the worries about the future were trying every moment to creep into my mind attempting to paralyze me, to bring me back down to a place of depression where I could be hateful. I struggled and I struggled and I even dreamt about revenge. The hate had begun to take over my soul—until my second savior appeared.

During a phone call with a very dear friend of mine, I told him: "I am so angry. It is unfair that my Ex-Boyfriend now owns everything that was once mine. He is living a happy life, my life, while I am hurting and completely broke. I want revenge, I want him to go to jail!" I told my friend I could easily make a phone call to the American Authorities and bring him that way to justice because I had found out that he had forged some financial documents to take control over my Holdings and had lied to the Government as well as an Insurance Company for profit. With the urge and the desire of wanting to destroy that man, I could feel the fires of hatred coming out of my body.

To this very day, I thank my friend on the other side of that phone call from the bottom of my heart. I thank him for not telling me: "sure, why not, go ahead and do it!" instead he said: "No Beryl, please don't. You will never find peace in your heart that way and, even worse, you will become like him." Yes, he was so right. After I hung up the phone, I looked at the mirror and told myself: "Beryl, this is not you."

Before starting the healing process, the first thing I needed to do was to let go. Not letting go had always been holding me back—allowing me no freedom to move forward. I wrote an email to my Ex-Boyfriend and stated that even though what he had done to me was wrong, I had chosen to forgive him. Forgiving him did not mean that what he had done was right or that his acts would be forgotten. By forgiving him, I then would be able to forgive myself for what I had allowed to happen and therefore manage to stop blaming myself. Then and only then would I be able to stop poisoning my own soul and body with hatred. After I pushed the "send" button, the heaviness that had been crawling all over my chest had suddenly...disappeared.

From that day forward, I began to practice living in the moment of NOW. Whenever I would start worrying about tomorrow or the future, I would immediately ask myself to focus on "What can I do now? What can I do today?" to redirect my mind to concentrate on things within my control. I needed to focus on being thankful that I still had a roof over my head, food on the table and that my family was well. I started living my life one day at a time.

By applying this philosophy, I can say that, in less than two years, I managed to finish and publish a Chinese book that went on to become one of the bestselling books in Taiwan in 2014, selling out quickly. I also returned to America, reopened my practice and soon became a regular guest on Chinese Television news and talk shows. And then, by chance, I accidentally found my way into the Entertainment business working in the Hollywood Film Industry.

Seven years after my father passed away, after the double betrayal from my Ex-Boyfriend and the healing journey across the ocean, I am now a therapist during the weekend and a Chairman and CEO during the week, leading an international entertainment company which has been involved in $100 million budget feature films last year and continues to get stronger and moving forward. If anyone had told me all this would have happened seven years ago, I probably would have felt it was cruel to play such a heartless joke on me.

Now, I want you to know am not here bragging about my success as there is still a long way to go. I only sincerely share these true events in own my life, hoping to help those who suffer from a broken heart or a broken spirit right now. All of us have experienced heartbreaks. They can be quite tragic, and though they may not end your life, they can influence some people's lives with a feeling of despair.

When people ask me for advice on how to move on, I share this: *LIFE DOESN'T END WITH JUST ONE HEARTACHE. THIS TOO SHALL PASS.* Certainly, it will pass, those sad moments will end. Nothing is forever. Once you were happy and now you are not. One day, you will find yourself "fully recovered." And if you are finding it hard to move on, simply *TRY*. When you feel like you cannot, ask yourself: *"But what if I could?" and then TRY* again. Nobody can help you except yourself -not even your friends or the people around you.

And if you are experiencing a time right now where you are broken hearted, I have something to share with you:

Take this time for yourself—You need to figure out what is best for you during this time. Spend time thinking about what it is you want for yourself. You probably spent a lot of energy on your previous relationship. Now you can take this energy and focus it on you and your own happiness.

Believe things happen for a reason—I know this can be a hard phrase to hear when you are in the midst of depression but it is the truth when it comes to relationships. And sometimes, the only thing you can hold on to during these low times is that mentality of "it will all make sense one day."

Stay busy—A busy body makes for a busy mind. And a busy mind helps you when all you are doing is replaying the breakup over and over in your head. Staying busy with work or other activities is important to counter those moments of over-analysis. Sure, it is crucial to not "bury your emotions" but there is some truth in keeping your mind occupied.

Remember: It's okay to be sad as long as you need to be—There is no timeframe for a grieving process. Every person grieves differently and that is okay. Don't beat yourself up for still thinking of your Ex-Boyfriend/girlfriend or crying over him or her. Let it take as long as it needs for you. You're the only person who knows when you are ready to move forward.

Look at the negatives—For once in your life it's important to be a negative Nancy. When all you're doing is daydreaming about those happy memories this can be soul-crushing. This is where you need to make a list of the negatives in that relationship. Look at it every morning to remind yourself why it needed to end.

You will come out of this a stronger person—As difficult as it is to believe, working through that pain truly will build up those emotional muscles.

Go cold turkey—Think of your Ex-Boyfriend/Ex-Girlfriend as a bad habit. Sometimes your best option is going cold-turkey. Depending on the breakup, the only thing that will help you is having zero contact with him or her. No one said going cold turkey isn't painful but, much like ripping off a Band-Aid, it hurts like hell but the pain doesn't last that long.

It's a breakup because it's broken—When some time has elapsed after a breakup, we have a tendency to go back and forth trying to understand the reasons why. When someone reminds you: "It's a breakup because it's broken," it can hurt but it can also help. This reality can move your grieving process along faster because you start to accept that this relationship wasn't working out.

Get creative—Now is the perfect time to get your creative juices flowing. Some of the best works of art have been created by broken-hearted souls. Have you heard Adele's music before? This is the moment where you can get out your feelings, creatively. Who knows what you are about to create.

It's a blessing in disguise—Sometimes the most painful events in our lives are the best things to happen to us. It's hard to see it in the moment but, as times passes, you will see the blessing of it all.

Every day will get a little better and better—When we are feeling hopeless we need to know that better days are ahead of us. In the beginning, a breakup can feel shocking and devastating. Thankfully, with every passing moment, you are one step closer to a better day. Always believe that if you can handle day number one, you can handle the rest of your life.

Make a playlist—Let Kelly Clarkson and Beyoncé help soothe your broken heart. There's nothing better than singing at the top of your lungs to help you through this period of time.

Get up and move—Get those endorphins going. You could use them right about now. For some, getting out of bed is like being asked to run a marathon. Take it slow and steady. Any small step is a step in the right direction.

Surrounding yourself with positive people—You could use some positivity in your world right now. Call up those friends of yours who are going to make you feel good about yourself. Invite your family members over who will make you smile. A little ray of sunshine can make a world of difference.

When one door close, another one opens—Sometimes doors shut on us, even if we didn't close them ourselves. You feel like you're stuck in a dark and scary room. But as time passes, you will find another door to open. And, when you open it, you'll find a bigger and brighter room than you could have ever imagined.

Delete, delete, delete—Hit that delete button. Goodbye phone number. Goodbye text messages. Goodbye following his or her social media accounts. Now, don't you feel "cleaner"?

Channel your anger—There is a fine line between love and hate. Sometimes after a breakup you are angry. Feel that anger and channel it. Running and screaming are some healthy ways to release anger and this is a crucial part of the healing process.

Dating detox—If you are one of those people who go from relationship to relationship, you might want to consider a "dating detox". You can choose however long the detox needs to be. Standing on your own and learning how to be alone and single is crucial. Through this process, you will learn to love yourself instead of finding love through another person.

Therapy—Having your own space to talk about the breakup is vital. Going to therapy can help immensely and could give you that outside unbiased listener you so need.

Write—Journal. You need to get your thoughts out there. One way to do this is with pen and paper. It doesn't have to be a masterpiece—it just has to make you feel better.

Healthy distractions—When the pain is unbearable, it's vital to have momentary distractions. Whether it's a trashy reality television or playing Angry Birds or Candy Crush on your phone for hours—do it! A little distraction goes a long way.

Let your friends know what will help you—You'll get by with the help from your friends. But your friends need to know when they are needed. Call them up when you're down. Let them know you're going to need their support at that moment.

Treat yourself—If there was ever a time to treat yourself, that time is now. Take a bubble bath and drink champagne. Wine and dine yourself. Buy yourself that outfit you've been eyeing for months. You could use a little pick-me-up.

Pet therapy—A pet can be a woman's best friend after a breakup. Your dog doesn't care how much you're crying or that your mascara is running down your cheeks. Hold on to your pet for comfort. Those furry kisses will make you feel positively better.

During this time of pain and self-doubt, everything and everyone can turn into a stabbing reminder of what we have lost. We may either do too much or too little eating, sleeping, going out, crying; we may smoke, drink or engage in other bad habits in the hope that we will be able to forget. We may rush into a replacement relationship. We may even consider giving the Ex-Boyfriend/Ex-Girlfriend another chance, in the hope that, maybe, it was just a terrible mistake, a misunderstanding or just one of those things. More often than not, we know this is a desperate act of refusing to accept the truth.

Spiritually (if you're into that type of thinking), you need to practice whatever it is. Go to church, light a candle, slip into meditation or offer up a prayer. Go sit in the forest. Whatever floats your boat and makes you feel you're connected with more. Feed your soul. As Lao Tzu said: "To a mind that is still, the Universe surrenders."

Most of all, time needs to pass. I promise you, from the bottom of my broken-and-mended-so-many-times heart, things eventually get better. WAY better. Like, unimaginably better. Stick it out, do your time, then be free. Give time some time.

"Living well is the best revenge." That is and has been MY quote all these years. The truth is you don't even have to show anyone you're living well—that's the beauty of it—you just do it—all on your own.

To my mother and father who, through their love and courage, gave me the strength to find my life's calling. Thank you. To Jason who has been there for me through the dark times. Thanks for your love and support. To my dear friends, Andy and Bruno, who believe in me and challenge me. Thank you for your friendship and love. And to all the readers who upon finishing this book will set forth on a new and better life's journey. Thank you for doing your part and making our world a better, more joyful place.

DAJON FERRELL

DAJON FERRELL is an Army Veteran who served for 13 years. After experiencing her own struggles with Post Traumatic Stress Disorder, due to military sexual trauma, she worked toward healing and found a path of choosing meditation over medication. Seeing a need for holistic healing modalities in the Veteran community, Dajon created a non-profit that provides veterans with mindfulness training to help restore and empower them so that they can create a healthy and purposeful life. Dajon's coaching empowers people who are struggling to step out of the busy and complacent daily grind so that they can excavate and cultivate the wholeness and value that has always been within. Dajon has taught for the Department of Veteran Affairs, while also speaking at conferences for entrepreneurs and veterans. Her voice has also been featured on the Huffington Post.

For workshops, coaching or speaking opportunities, please contact Dajon at:
dajon@dajonsmiles.com
www.dajonsmiles.com
Or connect with her on Facebook, Instagram or The Huffington Post.

Clarity in the Creative Chaos

"**S**o, no shit, there I was…"

Most military stories start with this phrase. It's part of an expansive dictionary of military jargon that has been programmed into me. The military also helped instill me with integrity, strong work ethic and respect while helping fulfill my heart's mission to serve at my highest capacity. It was easy to put on a uniform, show up, do your job and still feel this great sense of purpose. After all, you are an American hero that's part of the 1% who took the oath to 'support and defend the Constitution of the United States against all enemies, foreign and domestic.'

Then the day comes where it's time to hang up the uniform. This experience is parallel to becoming an empty nester, retiring or any life change that completely shifts the reality of who you are in the world. No longer defined by the previous labels, I was now a civilian and my inner compass became completely overwhelmed by the creative chaos and monkey mind.

Complete freedom to schedule your time the way you want? Outstanding! Having the opportunity to follow your dreams and create a career around your passion? Sign me up! But wait…how do you know what your purpose is?

While sifting through the creative chaos, life happened. Anxiety and depression created a fog over my existence. The numbing of emotions for 13 years caught up with me. Nightmares from the military sexual assault turned me into a walking zombie during the day. My nights filled with panic and frustration. Why was all this happening now? I'm a free woman. No more contracts holding me back. No more being told that I need to smile more or that I should just suck it up and soldier on!

Little did I know that this dark path would lead me to the light within me. The Divine purpose that had been etched into my heart, even before I found my passion for service. I started doing the healing work that was long overdue. And not the way that the Veteran Affairs therapists were telling me to do it. I found alternative healing modalities like cranial sacral therapy, reiki, Yoga Nidra, meditation and kundalini yoga. I started to see how much anger was pent up in me. I was always reaching for acceptance from others, as I could not see my inherent value.

Childhood abuse and abandonment stories began to resurface. Damn! This turned my creative chaos into a bit of a shit storm! I found myself in debt, facing foreclosure and planning to live out of my car, which had every service light flashing on the dashboard. My 6-year-old son would stay with his father and new step mom while I 'got back on my feet.' I went from being a newly freed woman to one caged by the filter of darkness that surrounded her heart. I cried out to God, "There has to be more than this. I don't want to be here anymore. Please help me see the light!"

One day, I received the news of a veteran friend taking his life. This sparked an anger in me that illuminated the light within that darkened heart. I knew that I needed to speak up. There were so many others who were also feeling the same. You see, this human thing doesn't come with a manual. For empaths, such as myself, the emotions that come with being a human can be overwhelming. This is our gift though. I had a great teacher by the name of Sunny Dawn Johnston who helped me find the value in my experiences. Through this, I learned that our souls have infinite wisdom and all the answers are provided in Divine timing. Seek and ye shall find. Be open and it will be provided.

I stepped into my power by being vulnerable and sharing my thoughts. As I opened up and talked about my frustrations with being 'too sensitive' or feeling all the feels, people connected with my story. They had their own experiences, but through sparking a dialogue and sharing, we navigated through their stories and found the value in those experiences. My purpose began shining through the shit storm.

This crazy idea came to host a woman veteran retreat. Wait! Who was I to host a retreat? I had no certifications or licenses. I did it anyway. I set the intention to create a safe space for these women to share openly and to be empowered through connecting with other veterans. On my way to the retreat, I was in a car accident. My car was towed with all the food and supplies for the weekend. Was this a sign? What the heck!

An angel friend saw my post on Facebook about the accident and offered to pick me up and load their car with the supplies. It was a 3.5-hour drive up to northern Minnesota. I had a volunteer show up and help get the ladies settled. I arrived to a welcoming and kind group of woman who teamed up and helped me unload the car. The angel friend ended up staying the night as it was too late to drive home. The next day, that same friend ended up helping with the retreat and offering coaching services, which attendees greatly benefitted from.

What's the point of this story? Everything came together in a Divine way that I couldn't have even created myself. We shared, we laughed, we cried. The retreat was a success…but not from my worry, control or ability to plan the perfect event. I showed up anyway!

The next year, the retreat was completely paid for through a fundraiser. I was able to pay the volunteers this time. The food was provided through an amazing veteran non-profit. I was fully supported to do this work, without a certificate or license and with my crazy monkey brain. Where I lacked, Spirit stepped up and provided.

Equipped with the knowledge that the Universe had my back, I became a manifesting ninja. This knowledge had to be shared and I was now free of worrying how I would be supported to share it. No more questioning who would care to read my blog. No more self-about asking who I was to try and be a published author. We are all channels for God's Divine messages. This information is available to all of us and there is more than enough abundance to support us showing up in the world to share our gifts.

So here I was, feeling on top of the world and bursting at the seams to be of service and help empower others live a purposeful life. There were a few life details still blocking my freedom. Remember that foreclosure and the care with all the flashing service lights? Well, the bank made a mistake, which resulted in me receiving a 7-figure check that allowed me to move into a beautiful lake home with a healing center attached. My car? It turns out there was a lawsuit against the manufacturer and they bought it back from me for three times it's actual value. The car had 150,000 miles on it and I owed more than it was worth, but I was now able to make a profit off it and pay cash for my next vehicle.

Miracles, my friends, are available to those who are willing to receive. Is life all rainbows and unicorns now? Heck no! I'm still a human that forgets what a flipping miraculous creation I am. I still self-sabotage and I'm in my first healthy, romantic relationship as a 34-year-old. I cry myself to sleep and feel all the feels. The difference is that I've found my tribe. I have the knowing that I am never alone. The creative chaos swirls possibilities and opportunities around my monkey brain, instead of excuses and roadblocks.

Imagine that you signed up for those challenging experiences in life before you even came into your beautiful human body. See these experiences as opportunities to expand on your human knowledge database. Your choice to show up and share your gifts makes a profound impact and difference in this world. Period. It's not a matter of how to show up or when. You show up any way possible and NOW! This world needs your gifts. We are stepping into a new chapter of human evolution that requires us to be comfortable with the uncomfortable. To find stability within ourselves, as this ever-changing circus flips and tosses us about. That stability could cause illusions that we are separate and divided. This is merely an illusion.

Time? An illusion. You have the time needed to fulfill your Divine purpose. You have perfect time each day to make things happen, even if that includes two salt baths, a nap and reading a book. Listen to your body. Nurture it, for this is your vehicle down here. It allows you to be a channel for Source. What a magical gift you are!

 Create your day or your day will create you.

~SUNNY DAWN JOHNSTON

I dedicate this chapter to all the unicorn ninjas out there. May you find your light and shine it so bright that you never forget the miraculous creation that you are. May you share that light with others, illuminating the collective consciousness, raising the vibration like a cosmic alchemist!

I would like to acknowledge and thank my soul mama, Sunny Dawn Johnston. Thank you for seeing the light within me. Thank you for mirroring the unconditional love I thought I was lacking. You truly showed me my value and helped me remember how to manifest unicorns so that I could help others do the same. Your selflessness and ability to teach in with such grace and honesty is something I'll always aim to embody myself. Thank you, dear sister. I love you!

ANGELA SERNA

ANGELA SERNA is an Author, Professional Life Coach, Workshop Leader, Seminar Facilitator & Yoga Instructor. She inspires people to live happier, healthier, and more successful lives through life coaching, workshops, and Yoga. This work is her passion. She helps individuals create change in their life by uncovering the mindset that limits success in their relationships, career, health and prosperity. She helps individuals create the change in their life that their soul desires. Using simple yet powerful techniques, she guides them toward a realization of their own power, inner wisdom and strengths. She also teaches stress management in the workplace, Power of Positive Thinking in the workplace and has a true passion for the Conscious Parenting workshops that she leads. She volunteers her time in helping those with addictions. Her favorite part about life is being a mom to her amazing son Javier.

She has co-authored the book "Awaken" and "Whispers of the Heart".

Finding Peace in a World of Chaos

Trusting the universe, knowing the Universe has your back when it appears that nothing is working in your favor. My journey from the corporate world of chaos to the universe forcing me out of my corporate job, at the time little did I know the universe was offering me a few years of being able to practice my inner work, grow emotionally and spiritually while raising my son.

Several years later I am now back to the chaos of working full time and in almost the exact same position that I held when I left. I recently went from teaching five yoga classes a week, giving workshops periodically on weekends, volunteering twice a week and spending plenty of time with my son, I am now back to the corporate world and working more than a normal 40 hour work week, I have adjusted well and I fully contribute it to all that I have practiced over the last several years. Something I have learned alone the way is being on a spiritual path does not prevent you from facing times of darkness but it teaches you how to use the darkness as a tool to grow.

This corporate world, the world that most call it "the real world." Everyone says "Welcome to the real world". I'm still trying to understand why it's called the real world when it appears very superficial, superficial conversation, superficial behaviors. Being back to work has been a true test of being able to stay peaceful when you are in the midst of chaos. I found myself observing the conversations, observing people's egos, people having the need to be right, the need to do it better than everyone else, the need for approval, the need to fit in, people being addicted to stress, drama, fears, insecurities and being unconscious. In the beginning I thought where is the mindfulness? Where is the peace, the calm, the consciousness? It was nowhere in sight and the more I observed, my thoughts were, ok that may not be the world that most live in but, my intention was to stay centered and peaceful during this journey.

So how do you survive in this world of constant chaos while trying to remain calm, sane, peaceful and centered?

I realize more now than ever that everyone is looking for a life of fulfillment. Instead of looking within, we are looking for something outside of us to fill a void, the perfect job, perfect partner, perfect body, perfect house, or more money to make life complete, and some of us are chasing enlightenment to make our lives more fulfilling. For a few years, I was that person chasing enlightenment to find my way to happiness. One thing I did obtain was knowledge, at least if we are chasing enlightenment we are probably learning something about ourselves alone the way, but don't be attached to thinking one more book is going to get you there. It's not all in what you read, but what you practice on a daily basis. If you are thinking any of the above are going to bring you happiness, you are far too concerned about the destination and not enjoying the journey and that is keeping you from being present in the moment. Being able to stay in the present moment contributes greatly to our happiness. Keep in mind enlightenment is a destructive process, it's not always about being happier it's more about seeing through the illusion of what you once thought was truth. It's crumbling away of the untruth, changing the beliefs that you were taught from others and finding your own truth.

As much as we have all read happiness comes from within. Stop and think about what that really means to you. Are those just nice, feel good words that you read but you still want the perfect job or the perfect body or the perfect partner, or you need to read just one more book on self-development/motivation/inspiration to bring you happiness? Please don't get me wrong I'm all about the self-development/motivational/inspirational books as these are the very books that contributed to changing my life! But at what point do we realize that reading just one more book will not be what fulfills us, it will definitely bring knowledge and offer tools to live a better life but only if we are willing to change or willing to commit to putting those tools and techniques into practice consistently on a daily basis to bring fulfillment. Everyone wants change but no one wants to make changes in their everyday routine.

> The standard of success in life isn't the things, it isn't the money or the stuff. It is absolutely the amount of joy you feel.
>
> ~ABRAHAM HICKS

The first few weeks that I was back to work I realized that I had put myself in somewhat of a bubble over the last few years as most of the people I surrounded myself with were those who attended my classes and workshops as they were all looking for change, wanting to improve their life in some way or they were also teaching others how to improve their life, which made for great conversation over coffee or lunch. Now I'm surrounded by those who think differently than I do, handle most situations a little different, certainly have very different conversations, and their focus and view on life are different. The first few weeks was an adjustment, and I wanted nothing more than to just go back to my bubble as I watched people intentionally create drama and stress not only in their world but in their co-workers world, it almost seemed like everyone was in a competition to see who could throw the other person under the bus the quickest, the gossiping and criticizing was a little more than I thought I could take. Everyone was looking for something outside of themselves to make them happy, most think that a job title will do it for them because that gives them a label of who they are.

At what point in our life do we realize it's all in our everyday practice of mindfulness, gratitude, compassion, being conscious of our thoughts, being conscious of our perspective of others by not judging, criticizing or complaining. Doing random acts of kindness for others.

Happiness is found in embracing all of it, the good, the bad and the undesirable. Accepting what is, letting go of expectations of how it should be, Looking at every obstacle and challenge in our life as an opportunity to grow. How do we begin to do this? Change begins when we start doing things different than we did it yesterday. You will never get different results by doing what you have always done. We start by being still, listening, meditating, spending time in nature, practicing yoga, spending time with only yourself, and learn how to enjoy being alone without feeling lonely. We all have busy schedules so I recommend that you take ten minutes in the mornings to spend in silence, notice your thoughts, notice the patterns with your thoughts, and release them as you bring your attention and focus to your breath, connecting to your breath will bring calmness. While you are in the shower or driving in your car use that time to be grateful for all the good in your life, be grateful for the things that we often take for granted, for example your breath, all of your internal organs that function properly and your body's natural way of healing. Be mindful of your negative thought patterns and put forth effort to flip those to focus on the positive in your life, if you want more love in your life give love freely, love without conditions. If you want more success, celebrate others success. If you want more respect in your life be more respectful to others. If you want happiness in your life practice random acts of kindness and bring happiness to others. Be what it is that you want more of in your life. If you want peace in your life spend time in meditation or in nature and every moment you get breathe that peace into every cell of your body. Also, being mindful of the people that you spend your time around, my thoughts are use the MISS formula, if they do not Motivate you, Inspire you, Support you, or Strengthen who you are, they need to go MISSing from your life. You become the average of the top five people that you spend your time around so choose carefully. Who do you want to be? Find people who have those qualities, learn from them.

 The thoughts that we choose to think are the tools
we use to paint the canvas of our lives.

~LOUISE HAY

I fully believe and trust that I am exactly where I need to be, I look at my current situation as an opportunity to just reach more people with my work as a life coach, since I manage most of the people I work with I have found some really great opportunities to bring my coaching work into the "real world" on a daily basis and I am ever grateful for having this opportunity. I have encouraged them just as I encourage those who are reading this to set personal goals, write them down, it sets the energy into motion to achieving them, finding balance in your life, being mindful that most of what people do to you has absolutely nothing to do with you and everything to do with what is going on within themselves. Be mindful of the words that follow "I am", make all of your I am statements positive. I am happy, I am healthy, I am peaceful, I am calm, I am powerful, I am beautiful, I am successful, I am grateful, I am amazing, I am energetic, I am loving, I am compassionate, I am confident. When you find yourself stressing always look for something to be grateful for, a mind that is in a state of gratitude is no longer stressing. Stress is only the thoughts that we create around a situation, the beauty of the mind is that we have the option to create a happier thought or a more peaceful thought. Start your day in a state of gratitude or with positive affirmations choose any of the above, changing your self-talk is one of the most important things that you can do for yourself. Show compassion to others as we do not know the battles that they are fighting within themselves. Trusting that the Universe has your back and is working for your higher good, accepting what is as if you chose it. Practicing mindfulness will allow you to see the wounded inner child in others as this gives you great compassion for their behavior.

> ❧ There is a force in the universe, which if we permit it, will flow through us and produce miraculous results.
>
> ~GHANDI

I highly recommend that you spend time in meditation and practice yoga the benefits are endless. Some people are overwhelmed by the thoughts of yoga, you don't have to do a perfect asana or even a full class you can do some simple forward folds in the morning to start your day. It's great for blood circulation and anytime that you are practicing any form of yoga it brings body awareness. The following instruction will help you to get the most out of forward folds.

Stand up nice and tall really lengthening up the spine reaching up through the crown of the head, reaching your arms overhead, bend at the hips, with a nice long spine as you move into a complete forward fold allowing your arms to fall down by your side and towards the floor.

Make sure that you bend at the hips not at the belly. Take about five full deep breaths. As you breathe, feel your body relax into the stretch allow your shoulders to be heavy, allow your arms to just relax and hang, feel the stretch in the hamstrings, feel the stretch of the lower back, feel your shoulders releasing and letting go, relax your neck muscles, allow the crown of the head to drop towards the floor. Feel the breath moving through your body, feel the tension releasing from your body and know that your blood is circulating and anytime we do a forward fold we allow the blood to flow to the brain it's like brain food, it's also great for the lower back. On your way back up slowly come up as you soften your knees and bring your arms out to the sides and all the way up overhead, coming up with a nice tall spine and gently reach the fingertips towards the sky, and lengthen the torso with just a gentle backbend take a full deep breath, come back to center release the arms down beside you and now feel what's going on in your body by connecting to the breath.

Yoga is not about touching your toes, it's
what you learn on the way down.

I am grateful for all of my teachers and my resources that have been available to me and has taught me so much about life. I completely contribute where I am in life to them. Gratitude to a special friend Angie Stewart who has been of great support through the years, grateful that the universe brought you into my life.

Bibliography/References

A Course in Miracles: Combined Volume. Second ed. Mill Valley, CA: Foundation for Inner Peace, 1996.

Abramson, Lisa. "Six Amazing Benefits of Loving Kindness Meditation Backed by Science". *Lifehack*. Web. 4 Jan. 2017.

Achor, Shawn; Before Happiness, Crown Business, 2013

Aron, Dr. Elain, *The Highly Sensitive Person*, 1996, Broadway Books a division of Random House Inc., New York, NY

Browne T. *Spiritual Seas: Diving into Life, 12 Strategies for Riding the Waves of Life*, Transcendent Publishing, 2016

Byrne, Rhonda; *The Secret*, Beyond Words Publishing, November 28, 2006

Chapman, Gary D., *The Five Love Languages: How to Express a Heartfelt Commitment to Your Mate*. Chicago, Northfield Pub, 1995 Print

Discourses from a ten-day course in Vipassana meditation as taught by S.N.Goenka

Dr. Seuss (Theodor Seuss Geisel); *Oh, the Places You'll Go!* (1990)

Eadie, Betty; *Embraced by the Light*, Bantam, September 1, 1994

Farrar, J. (1980). Magic [Olivia Newton-John]. On *Xanadu* [CD]. California: MCA Records.

Goleman, Daniel; *Emotional Intelligence*, Bantam Books, September 27, 2005

Goleman, Daniel; *Social Intelligence*, Bantam Books, 2007

Hanson, Richard, Ph.d. (2013). *Hardwiring Happiness: The New Brain Science of Contentment, Calm and Confidence*. New York, New York: Harmony Books

Hardwick, L. (2016). *Manifesting Modern Miracles*. Charleston, IL: Visionary Insight Press.

Hawkins, David R., M.D., Ph.d. (1995). *Power Versus Force: The Hidden Determinants of Human Behavior*. Carlsbad, California: Hay House, Inc.

Hay, Louise, L; *The Power is Within You*, Hay House, 1991

Hay Louise, L; Official Website. http://www.hayhouse.com and http://www.louisehay.com/about/

Hay Louise, L.; *You Can Heal Your Life*. Hay House Inc, 1984

Hay, L. & Holden, R. (2015). *Life Loves You*. Carlsbad, CA: Hay House, Inc.

Heal Your Life Training. http://www.healyourlifetraining.com/teacher-training/

Hicks, Abraham; *Ask and it is Given*, Hay House; October 1, 2004

Hicks E. *Law of Attraction*. www.abraham-hicks.com

Hoff, Benjamin, *Cottleston Pie* from the Tao of Pooh by Benjamin Hoff, 1982; text and illustrations from Winnie the Pooh and the House at Pooh Corner, CR 1926, 1928 by E.P. Dutton, copyright 1953, 1956 by A.A. Milne. Used by permission of Dutton, a division of Penguin group USA Inc.

Hogg Ashwell, Jenny. *Love's Curriculum: Messages of Enlightenment—The High Council*. Bloomington, IN: Balboa Pr, 2015.

Holmes, E. (1938). *The Science of Mind: A Philosophy, A Faith, A Way of Life*. New York, NY:

Jeremy P. Tarcher/Penguin Katie B. *The Work*. the work.com

Kahn, Matt, Whatever Arises Love That: A Love Revolution that Begins with You. Boulder, CO: Sounds True, 2016

Katie B. The Work. the work.com

Makennah Walker, *As I Am—Empowering Portraiture*

Oxford Dictionary https://en.oxforddictionaries.com/definition/faith

Rabellino, Daniela and Ardito, Rita B. "Therapeutic Alliance and Outcome of Psychotherapy: Historical Excursus, Measurements, and Prospects for Research". *Frontiers in Psychology*. 2. 270 (Published on-line 18 Oct. 2011). *NCBI*. Web. 8 Jan. 2017.

Shimoff, Marci; *Happy for No Reason*, Free Press, 2008

Weiss, Brian; *Many Lives, Many Masters*, Simon & Schuster, 1988

Williamson, Marianne; *A Return to Love: Reflections on the Principals of A Course in Miracles*.

Zukav, Gary, *The Seat of the Soul*, 1989, Simon & Shuster Paperback, New York, NY

CPSIA information can be obtained
at www.ICGtesting.com
Printed in the USA
FSOW01n0921270317
32217FS